THE QUEST FOR
CHRISTIAN ETHICS

AN INQUIRY INTO
ETHICS AND CHRISTIAN ETHICS

THE QUEST FOR CHRISTIAN ETHICS

AN INQUIRY INTO ETHICS AND CHRISTIAN ETHICS

IAN C. M. FAIRWEATHER

and

JAMES I. H. McDONALD

THE HANDSEL PRESS

1984

First published 1984
by The Handsel Press Limited,
33 Montgomery Street, Edinburgh EH7 5JX.

ISBN 0 905312 27 9

British Library Cataloguing in Publication Data

Fairweather, I.C.M.
The quest for Christian ethics.
I. Title   II. McDonald, James I.H.
241   BJ1251

ISBN   0-905312-27-9

Printed by The Universities Press (Belfast) Ltd., Northern Ireland.

CONTENTS

PREFACE

It would have been impossible to attempt such a book as we have written had it not been for the labours of many who have preceded us in the field. The index goes some way towards indicating the extent of our indebtedness, but we are conscious that we have learned from a wider range of sources than we can identify here. To all who have in any way informed and challenged our thinking we are indeed grateful.

It is a pleasure to acknowledge the particular help given to us by certain friends and colleagues. Professor Duncan Forrester, Dr Alastair V. Campbell and Dr Robin Gill, all of the Department of Christian Ethics and Practical Theology in the University of Edinburgh, read the whole manuscript and made many detailed and valuable criticisms. Dr Andrew Ross, also of Edinburgh University, read part of chapter nine in draft form and we appreciate the encouragement he gave.

We acknowledge the help and forbearance of our wives, especially Mrs Jenny McDonald who has typed several complete drafts of the book and prepared much of the final manuscript for the publishers; also the assistance of Mrs Elspeth Leishman, who typed several chapters in their final form.

Our thanks are due to our publishers, The Handsel Press, Edinburgh, especially Mr Douglas Grant, to Mrs Avery Brooke, and to Dr Charles S. McCoy of the Pacific School of Religion, whose encouraging and critical comments motivated us to make the final revision.

IAN C. M. FAIRWEATHER
JAMES I. H. McDONALD

January, 1984

INTRODUCTION

Either: Abortion is wrong; contraception is an unjustifiable interference with nature.

Or: The population explosion must and therefore ought to be controlled for the welfare of mankind.

Either: Nuclear power—no thanks. Remember Harrisburg.

Or: The development of nuclear power is right because it is essential to the well-being of many nations, not least the poor of the Third World.

Either: To secure peace with justice, one may have to turn to force of arms as a last resort and as a moral duty.

Or: How can one rescue dignity and humanity by the gun?[1]

Either: 'Let every person be subject to the governing authorities . . . One must be subject, not only to avoid God's wrath but also for the sake of conscience . . . Pay all of them their dues . . .'[2]

Or: 'Because earthly princes forfeit all their power when they revolt against God . . . we should resist them rather than obey'.[3]

Each of the above presents us with a moral issue or dilemma. Life is full of them. For this reason, important questions arise about the nature of morality. How far, and in what way, can we settle moral issues? Do we settle them by counting heads (e.g., by what society approves) or by appealing to our own individual tastes, feelings or inclinations? Or do we settle them by giving reasons other than these?

To consider ways of settling moral issues is more than a mere academic exercise. It is to develop a greater degree of moral awareness. It is to assert our autonomy as rational beings over against the mind-benders and propagandists who condition our responses rather than treat us with integrity, and against the power syndrome which requires from its subjects compliance rather than independent and creative thinking. Hence, we are concerned in this book not to find 'the right answers' which we can then impose on others: that would defeat our whole purpose. Our concern is to ask what reasons are appropriate for settling the moral issues in question.

---

[1] Peter Matheson, *Profile of Love*, 1979, p. 152.
[2] Romans 13:1, 5, 7.
[3] J. Calvin, *Lecture XIII;* quoted by Beyers Naudé: see *The Trial of Beyers Naudé: Christian Witness and the Rule of Law*, 1975, p. 162.

Morality is concerned with action and behaviour, character and dispositions, life-style and patterns of living, states of affairs and human goals, and
when these are right or wrong, good or bad, virtuous or vicious. Moral
issues arise when, for example, individuals, groups and nations have to
make choices about particular actions, but these choices may reflect the sort
of person one is (character and dispositions, virtuous or vicious), or the
nature of the group that makes the choice. *Ethics* is a reflective enquiry into
morality and moral issues: in particular, it is concerned with reflecting on
what reasons justify particular forms of action and behaviour, and with
examining the basic concepts used in morality, such as rightness, duty and
obligation, natural law and goodness, virtue and vice. As these questions do
not go away when we turn from ethics to Christian ethics, we consider that
they must be faced in our work on Christian ethics.

Since moral issues are so pervasive in human activity, and a similar
claim is often made for religion, do morality and religion overlap and
interrelate, or are they to be treated as independent? Various views have
been held about their precise relation, and we examine some of them and
draw appropriate conclusions. This question of the relation between morality and religion requires discussion in any book about ethics but it is of
particular relevance to a book about Christian ethics, and we shall also
discuss it specifically in relation to the Christian faith. That connection
must be consonant with our view of the relation between religion and
morality, but Christian faith may well provide its own perspective on it.
Viewed through a wide-angled lens, morality, ethics and Christian ethics
cover a vast area, and therefore books in this field can be vastly different.
What is particular about this book, apart from what we have already
mentioned?

In writing a text-book for students in Universities and Colleges, studying Christian ethics at a variety of levels and in various perspectives, we
have adopted a number of objectives, principally the following:

(1) *To display the problematic character of Christian ethics.* This we propose
to do by looking both at the ethical material in the New Testament and by
showing some of the different shapes and models in past Christian ethics. It
is important to note at the outset that Christian ethics has never received
definitive shape, not even in the New Testament. Nor can it, for any shape
or model must be relevant to the culture in which and for which it is
formulated; and, like the forms in which the gospel itself is presented, such
shapes may well be culturally determined.

(2) *To use basic source material to form an understanding of Christian behaviour
and moral decision-making.* The major source is the Bible, especially the New
Testament, but classical and modern positions in Christian ethics are also
important. In particular, we must try to answer the question, pressed upon
us in recent times by Frankena, whether Christian ethics is a form of one of
the traditional ethical positions or whether it is a different sort of ethical
theory altogether.

(3) *To look carefully at challenges, past and present, made to any religious ethics,
and Christian ethics in particular.* Some of these challenges are as ancient as

Plato. Some are more recent: for example, David Hume's assault on the 'naturalistic fallacy'. These and other problems have been pushed to the fore today because the nature of society itself has undergone a remarkable degree of change. Societies which once called themselves Christian now recognise that they are secularised and pluralist, as well as enshrining Christian elements. Other societies are multi-religious, and Christians may form a small minority group in them. In such cases, ethical reflection—the examination of the relation between the Christian's behaviour and his faith—becomes more of a priority than ever. No less a problem is the relation between secular morality and Christian ethics, and between the Christian moral tradition and that of other religious faiths. A practical concern is the question of the basis on which Christians can cooperate with non-Christians (atheists, agnostics, humanists, adherents of other faiths) in building community in the local area and working for freedom, justice and peace. Moreover, science and technology are continually raising new issues, and these often have major implications for morality and ethics. Thus a variety of challenges presses upon Christian ethics today, and cannot be ignored in a book of this kind.

(4) *To attempt to learn from past shapes and models of Christian ethics.* Since Christianity has almost two thousand years' history and holds that God is at work in history, learning from the past is a proper part of Christian ethics today. We can learn both from the strengths and weaknesses of past positions, examine their view of the relation between Christianity and culture, and discern criteria for the construction of any viable model for Christian ethics.

(5) *To propose a model of Christian ethics for today.* In doing so, we recognise that it must be culturally appropriate and properly grounded biblically and theologically.

We decided that it made sense to start with Frankena's question, set out above in our second objective. In the first three chapters, therefore, we look in turn at three main types of theory of the moral norm: (1) deontological, (2) teleological, and (3) motive, theories. In the first section of each chapter, we expound the theory in its various forms. In the second section, we look at the biblical material and ask whether it is consonant with the theory just expounded. As a result, we hope to answer the question, Does it approximate more to one type of theory than another, or is it totally different from all of them? By the end of chapter 3, we hope to have brought out some important features of Christian ethics, and to have discovered in the process how problematic Christian ethics is.

Part One

MORAL DECISION-MAKING

1

IS THE ACT ITSELF THE MEASURE?

A. DEONTOLOGICAL THEORIES

Actions possess a decisiveness, a finality which makes them particularly significant in the field of human experience and conflict. They speak louder than words—or so the proverb assures us, although the ancient Greeks and Hebrews were well aware that a word once released could operate with all the potency of an action. Society makes laws to control and restrain actions; and when the New Testament uses the symbolism of the last judgement it focuses upon acts of commission and omission.

Moral decision-making involves choices about actions and plans of action. But what, apart from the facts of the situation, are we to take into consideration in making our decisions? It is frequently held that while some actions are intrinsically right others are intrinsically wrong, and that any appeal to the goals they may achieve or the consequences that may follow from them is irrelevant to the question of their rightness or wrongness. 'Come hell or highwater, this is what I'm going to do because it's right'. 'Do the right thing, and forget the consequences!' Remarks such as these sum up in a popular way the kind of ethical position discussed in this chapter. If the Duke of Wellington could advocate the policy, 'Publish and be damned!',[1] are we to take as our moral maxim, 'Act and damn the consequences!'?

Ethical theories of this type are termed 'deontological'.[2] They hold that actions are right or wrong *in virtue of some quality or characteristic of the action itself*, and not in virtue of the good consequences the action produces or is thought likely or intended to produce. In some deontological theories, however, emphasis is also placed on the behaviour of the agent in acting, and so not merely the outward act but its motives and intentions also come into the picture.

---

[1] Arthur Wellesley, 1st Duke of Wellington (1769–1852), who defeated Napoleon at the Battle of Waterloo, 1815, later a British Prime Minister, is supposed to have written these words across a blackmailing letter from a publisher and sent it back to him.

[2] The noun is 'deontology', the adjective 'deontological'. Their derivation is the Greek *dei* (stem, *deont-*), meaning 'it is right', 'it is necessary'. By contrast, theories which are concerned with the goal (*telos*) of moral action are termed teleological: see chapter 2.

There are several versions of deontology, which we now proceed to discuss.

1. *Rule-deontology or rules-ethics*

Ethics is concerned not only with actions of individual people as they affect other individuals but also with group action, where the group in question may be, for example, family, community, trade union, institution or state. Any adequate position in ethics and Christian ethics must therefore come to terms with social morality. Since there can be no social morality without rules, ethical positions that ascribe importance to rules merit careful attention. One such position is rule-deontology.

This position holds that the rule is the norm or measure of right and wrong. Right action is an instance of a (moral) rule, law, maxim or principle. These terms can vary enormously in meaning, but in this context they all belong to rule-deontology, for the rules or principles are held to be valid independently of whether or not they promote the good. In other words, the moral standard is held to be non-teleological, covering any structured ethical material whatsoever *except* a teleological standard such as 'seeking the greatest good of the greatest number' or 'promoting the welfare of mankind'. Rule-deontology holds that the standard of right and wrong consists of one or more rules, and these rules may be either fairly concrete ones, such as 'Always keep your promises', 'Always tell the truth', 'Do no murder', 'Avoid adultery', and 'Always pay your debts', or rather abstract ones such as 'Treat like cases alike, and different cases differently' or Kant's third form of the Categorical Imperative, 'Act in such a way that you always treat humanity, whether in your own person or in the person of any other, never simply as a means, but always at the same time as an end', for which the term 'principle' is more appropriate than 'rule'.

Since there is a world of difference, as we shall see, between such concrete rules and abstract principles, rule-deontology is too broad a classification to be useful in the discussion of ethical theories or of Christian ethics. We, therefore, propose to speak of a narrow and a wide rule-deontology, the former to cover an ethics of concrete rules, and the second to cover an ethics of principles.[3]

(1) *Narrow rule-deontology.* This is a popular ethical theory as well as a philosophical one, and most of its adherents have never given it sophisticated formulation. In fact, despite the prevalence of deontological views in Judaism and Christianity, it was not until Kant that rule-deontology received any philosophical attention—and Kant belongs to wide, rather

---

[3] This terminology and the corresponding terminology for other ethical theories was first recommended to writers on Christian ethics by the American philosopher, W. K. Frankena. By the use of it throughout our work, we take seriously his challenge to them to be careful in definition, clear in statement and rigorous in argument: cf. his 'Love and Principle in Christian Ethics' in Alvin Plantinga (ed.), *Faith and Philosophy*, 1964 (an essay which Paul Ramsey summarises in chapter V of his *Deeds and Rules in Christian Ethics*, 1965) and Frankena, *Ethics*, (2), 1973.

than narrow, rule-deontology.[4] The one notable exception who may be claimed for narrow rule-deontology is the twentieth century philosopher, W. D. Ross.

The most naive form of this narrow view is that right action is action in accordance with a moral rule or rules which specify the class of actions that are right or wrong and the outward behaviour demanded: e.g., 'Keep your promises', 'Work for a living, and don't scrounge from others' and 'Direct abortion is wrong'. In other words, all actions that belong to a certain class or classes are right, and all actions that belong to the contrary classes are wrong; or those actions that belong to class or classes x,y and z are intrinsically right, while those that belong to class or classes not-x, not-y and not-z are intrinsically wrong.

An immediate difficulty is how the rule or class is to be defined: 'Always tell the truth' obviously needs modification of the 'always', for not all situations call for us to tell the truth; for example, when we are alone, or attending someone who is too ill to talk. This difficulty, however, may be surmounted by adopting Dorothy Emmet's definition of a moral rule: 'a moral rule is a directive for right conduct to the effect that an act of a given kind x ought to be done *on an occasion to which it is applicable*'.[5] Part of moral learning consists in learning the occasions on which any moral rule is applicable.

This kind of theory has appealed strongly to many religious people through the ages, for they have believed that they ought to do the will of God, that what is right is what is commanded by God or what he wills, and that what God commands or wills is not good intentions or a vague good will to all men, but actions of certain kinds. Thus in rabbinic Judaism, the Mishnah and the even more extensive Talmud go to great lengths to classify actions as right or wrong, permitted or not permitted, in terms of a divinely given law. Similarly, in Islam, law is regarded as essentially divine (the *shari'ah*), not secular, and as such is basically unalterable. The Muslim has to obey Allah in every detail of his life, and the whole of life is therefore covered by the divine *shari'ah*. In the manner of rule-deontology, all human actions are subsumed, according to a widely accepted classification, under

---

[4] Perhaps the two chief factors that inhibited sophisticated formulation were first that Greek ethics (both Plato and Aristotle) had been teleological i.e., non-deontological, and secondly that it was only with the emergence of utilitarianism in the seventeenth but particularly the eighteenth century that any great need was felt to give it philosophical formulation: utilitarianism conceived itself as an attack on deontology with the latter's view of the intrinsic rightness and wrongness of actions belonging to certain classes (e.g., adultery, stealing). Some British moralists before Kant (1714–1803) or contemporary with him, but working independently, *viz.*, Samuel Clarke (1675–1729), Richard Price (1723–1791) and Thomas Reid (1710–1796), have been held by W. K. Frankena (*Ethics*, 2nd. ed. 1973, p. 17) to be rule-deontologists in some form. This case can be most convincingly substantiated in relation to Clarke, but, in so far as the claim is true, they *assumed* some form of rule-deontology—none of them afforded it systematic formulation.

[5] *Rules, Roles and Relations*, 1966, p. 56 (our italics).

five categories.[6] The same view is found in several Christian traditions. According to one Roman Catholic writer, E. Welty,[7] the evil is objectively given in certain classes of actions—including fornication, adultery, homosexual acts, contraception, abortion, euthanasia, sterilisation, suicide, cheating and calumny, divorce and remarriage, and artificial insemination—though some Roman Catholic writers nowadays are questioning this whole tradition. Paradoxically, John Calvin, despite his adherence to the doctrine of justification by grace through faith, held that God's will comes to a man as a requirement for obedience to the divine law. Rule-deontology in this form is found in Puritanism, e.g., in Richard Baxter and Jeremy Taylor; indeed, in Puritanism, theatre-going, card-playing and Sabbath-breaking come to mind as characteristically wrong acts. Today, the conservative evangelical position embraces this kind of theory. Among the sects, the view predominates: Jehovah's Witnesses, for example, follow rules-ethics in this narrow sense when they hold that blood-transfusion is always wrong; and Mormons prohibit the taking of tea, coffee or similar drugs.

But not all these have embraced rule-deontology in the rather naive form in which we have so far expounded it. For example, the Jewish tradition held that at least some of the acts commanded or prohibited by the rule (e.g., murder) are not merely *outward* acts, but acts with a specific motive or intention. Murder is not simply the outward act of killing but killing with the intention to kill. When the rabbis expounded the Law of Moses, they were quite clear that they were placing emphasis on the inward life of intention, motive and disposition. This is true not only of the tenth commandment, 'Do not covet', but of most of the others as well.[8] For example, it is not the mere act of making an image that is condemned, but the treating of it as an idol, an image to be worshipped—and worship is a matter of the inner life, not of mere outward actions.[9] Again, 'Bearing false witness against your neighbour' is never a cold-blooded act, but has the

[6] These are: (i) as commanded by Allah; (ii) as recommended by Allah, and one who so acts may expect to be rewarded, but one who does not will not be punished, in the next world; (iii) as left legally and so morally indifferent by Allah, and it is only with regard to this category that there is in theory any scope for human legislation; (iv) as reprehended by Allah, and one who so acts may expect to be punished, but one who refrains will not be rewarded, in the next world; and (v) as prohibited by Allah. Cf. the place of *dharma* and *karma* (action) in the brahmanical Hindu tradition and the attempt to classify actions as in accordance or not with *dharma* in the law Book of Manu.

[7] *A Handbook of Christian Social Ethics*, 1960, pp. 155f. For an account of other views held in Roman Catholicism, see pp. 153–55 below; cf. also p. 233 below, footnote 18.

[8] The popular notion that the Ten Commandments are for the most part concerned with outward acts only is altogether false.

[9] Although the Jewish tradition and, even more, the Islamic tradition tend to avoid making images at all in order to respect the commandment against idolatry, images are in fact found in both traditions (e.g., in the Temple of Solomon and in the art of Persia).

inevitable accompaniment of malice.[10] Thus in a rather less naive formulation, narrow rule-deontology centres on the behaviour of the agent in acting, rather than merely on outward actions, and is distinguished from teleology by its lack of appeal to the consequences, actual, likely or foreseeable, of the action.

This leads us to distinguish between legalism and most forms of rule-deontology, for the two need not be synonymous. Legalism holds that the necessary and sufficient condition of morality is action in accordance with law, usually conceived in terms of rules and regulations. To hold that action in accordance with law is a necessary but not a sufficient condition of moral action is not legalistic: as, for example, if a place is allowed for some other factor, such as motive, intention or disposition. Some forms of rule-deontology, as we have noted above, can keep a place for some factor of moral significance other than mere outward obedience to the rule, and so are not legalistic. An example may serve to clarify what is meant by legalism. Imagine the situation in which parents and children are held hostage in their own home by armed and desperate criminals seeking escape from the police. The criminals threaten violence against the children if the parents give any indication that anything is untoward. When neighbours observe a change in the daily routine and make enquiries, the parents are compelled to lie in order to save their children. If anyone says the parents ought not to have told lies even to save their children, that is legalism.[11]

A near relation of legalism is rationalisation. When people become legalistic and are out to defend the rule simply because it is the rule and for no other reason, they are apt to 'discover' all sorts of other reasons to support action in accordance with the rule. Of course, such reasons have 'nothing to do with the case'; they are simply the result of that unconscious process that we call rationalisation, which may include elements of self-deception and wishful thinking. People may deceive themselves into believing that the reasons they offer for their behaviour are the real ones. Like legalism, rationalisation is not a characteristic of rule-deontology as such but a danger into which some of its unwary advocates may fall.

There are, however, several major difficulties in a narrow rule-deontology. It will have been noticed that its advocates do not agree as to which concrete rules are to be the measure of right and wrong, and this suggests the question of how rules can be known. In religious ethics, the usual answer has been a divine-command theory, while in general ethics the favourite theory has been intuitionism.[12] But these answers only thrust the

---

[10] So also with swearing falsely ('taking the Name in vain'), while intention or disposition can hardly be separated from honouring parents or the sabbath, or even from adultery and stealing. In the case of the latter, the simple outward act is appropriating an object: stealing implies a particular intention or motivation (kleptomania is a special case).

[11] For an example of legalism in Church administration, see B. Häring, *Morality is for Persons*, 1971, p. 122f.

[12] The divine-command theory is discussed later in this section, while intuitionism is described under act-deontology.

difficulty one stage further back: *viz.*, how does God appear to command such different behaviour at different times for different peoples, and how do people come to intuit such different classes of actions as right or wrong?

A second difficulty concerns how one is to decide what to do when two rules conflict.[13] Ought one to keep one's promise, even when it will lead to murder? Should I tell the boss the truth, even if it means losing my job and causing distress and hardship to my wife and family? This difficulty would be met if rules could be arranged in a rank-order so that there was no conflict between rules but rather an overriding of lower-order rules by higher-order ones, and an overriding of all the others by the highest-order rule. But no rule deontologist has put concrete rules into a hierarchy, and Ross said that it was impossible.

A third difficulty is that rules do not allow for exceptions. That one should not keep pets that cause nuisance or alarm to one's neighbours may seem a sensible moral rule for people to impose on themselves; but a local authority rule forbidding the keeping of pets in high flats may mean that an old lady living alone is denied her cat, her only companion. One way of trying to offset this difficulty is to incorporate all the exceptions in the rules—i.e., to state more precisely in the rule itself, or in supplements to it, the circumstances in which it is to apply. This involves trying to build into the rule itself all the conditions and exceptions—all the 'ifs and buts'—so that it becomes absolute: i.e., it applies in all situations, including those that may have arisen since the rule was formulated in its original version (e.g., in the case of legal rules and Church or canon law). Again, even the clearest rules need some interpretation. What precisely constitutes murder, fraud, or work on the sabbath? For this reason, legal and other rules have often to be reframed or interpreted by law-courts, tribunals and the like; and when rules are badly framed, lawyers have a field day. Moral rules, in so far as they are rules and not principles, share this characteristic with legal rules. This process of interpreting and updating rules so that they apply in all cases and of stating the specific conditions in which they are to apply is known as casuistry.[14] To make rules both absolute and specific is an extensive and continuing process, whatever the age or culture—whether in rabbinic Judaism or in the Catholic tradition of Christianity: in both these traditions, the application of the rules to new situations has led to the multiplication of rules.[15]

[13] On the narrow rule-deontology we are at present discussing, the standard of right and wrong is concrete rules, not abstract principles: so on this view there cannot strictly be a conflict between a rule and a principle.

[14] The term is used in a technical and neutral sense that does not raise the question of whether the process is approved or not. Before we are too quick to condemn casuistry, it should be remembered that most of the positive law of any modern state constitutes a casuistical system and is applied by an extensive and continuing process of casuistry.

[15] Another way of dealing with the difficulty of exceptions is to say that a rule has only exceptions when it has to be overriden by another rule. But this brings us back to the difficulty we have already noted, *viz.*, of placing the rules in rank-order.

The philosopher, W. D. Ross, overcame the problems of the conflict of duties and exceptions to the rules by distinguishing (a) various and often conflicting *prima facie* or *conditional* duties, or obligations which tend to be my duty, and (b) my *actual* or *absolute* duty to do one particular act in particular circumstances. What is actually right or obligatory or my duty is what one actually ought to do in a particular situation where there are no rules which do not admit of exceptions. When more than one of the *prima facie* duties is incumbent on me, I have to study the situation as fully as I can, until I form the considered opinion that in the circumstances one of them is more incumbent or stringent than any other: this latter *prima facie* duty then becomes my *actual* duty in the circumstances. Ross gave the following examples of *prima facie* duties: fidelity, such as keeping our actual or implicit promises;[16] reparation for wrong done; gratitude[17] where we return services received; justice; beneficence; self-improvement and not injuring others. Ross held that no general rules can be given for the estimation of the comparative stringency of these *prima facie* obligations:[18] the whole act and its circumstances had to be taken into account before one's actual duty could be recognised, and no feature of the act could be dismissed as having no bearing on its rightness or wrongness.

Ross's solution was characteristically deontological in that he rejected the teleological view that all 'conflicts of duties' should be resolved by asking, 'By which action will most good be produced?'. This teleological principle seemed to Ross to imply that the only morally significant relation in which my neighbour stands to me is that of being a possible beneficiary by my action. Rather my neighbour also stands to me in relation of promisee to promiser, of creditor to debtor, of wife to husband, of child to parent, of friend to friend, of fellowcountryman to fellowcountryman, and the like; and each of these relations is the foundation of a *prima facie* duty, which is more or less incumbent on me according to the circumstances of the case.

We are, Ross held, in no doubt about our *prima facie* duties, for these are

[16] For example, 'the implicit undertaking not to tell lies which seems to be implied in the act of entering into conversation (at any rate by civilized men) . . .' *The Right and the Good*, 1930, p. 21. Ross's other important work was *The Foundations of Ethics*, 1939.

[17] Ross admitted that fidelity and gratitude strictly mean certain states of motivation, but there were no convenient words in English to express what he meant. He claimed that considerations of motive do not affect the rightness of actions, though they do the moral goodness of the agent. Thus he used the term 'fidelity' for the *actual* fulfilment of promises and implicit promises, *irrespective of motive*. So too he took gratitude for the returning of services, irrespective of motive. Further, the use of terms such as fidelity, gratitude and justice must not mislead us into thinking that his *prima facie* duties are abstract principles: in fact, they refer to concrete actions. His duties of imperfect obligation, however, seem to belong to a different class (see fn. 18 below).

[18] He did, however, incline to the view that a great deal of stringency belonged to duties of 'perfect obligation'—duties of keeping promises, repairing wrongs done, returning the equivalent of services received—as against duties of 'imperfect obligation' such as that of relieving distress.

self-evident to those who have reached a sufficient mental maturity and have given sufficient attention to the matter. But our judgements about our actual duty in concrete situations have none of the certainty that attaches to our recognition of our *prima facie* duties. An act may have two characteristics: first, it may be an instance of breaking a promise, in virtue of which it is *prima facie* wrong; secondly, it may be an instance of relieving distress, in virtue of which it is *prima facie* right. In such a case, we are not certain whether we ought or ought not to do it; and when 'we come in the long run, after consideration, to think one duty more pressing than the other, . . . we do not feel certain that it is so'.[19]

Ross's theory avoids the worst excesses of a narrow rule-deontology. While we shall argue later that rules do have a place in morality, to justify them in the manner of a naive and narrow rule-deontology is to imply that certain actions are always right or wrong because they belong to a class; it is also to deny the element of situationism involved in moral decision-making. Ross does not fall into either of these errors, and denies strongly that for example a promise is to be kept in all circumstances. Further the need constantly to revise regulations in a rule-form (whether it is the highway code or rules for shipping in the Channel) should be a sufficient warning to those who would invest any kind of rule with an absolute (i.e., context-invariant) authority.[20]

(2) *Wide rule-deontology.* One way of overcoming the difficulties of a narrow rule-deontology is to posit principles of which the more concrete rules are merely expressions and applications, and to make these principles the standard or measure of right and wrong. Principles are much more elastic than rules. Rules are intended to specify the behaviour being commended or prohibited, e.g., 'Do no murder', 'Honour contracts freely entered into', 'pay your debts'. Indeed, if rules are not lucid in their specification, then they are useless as rules, since they will then require interpretation and that in turn will involve principles of interpretation. Principles, however, are more general, less concrete than rules. They 'allow for exceptions' or, more strictly, with principles there are no exceptions. For example, the principle of beneficence does not inform us what actions in any particular situation will express beneficence, and it would be compatible with in one case giving hand-outs to someone in need and with helping another to stand on his own feet by refusing continual hand-outs. In the attempt to be both absolute (i.e., to apply in all circumstances) and specific (i.e., to name the circumstances in which they are to apply), rules often seem too inflexible to be guides in moral decision-making, especially to people who have reached some degree of autonomous awareness. They may have no scruple with the absoluteness of a principle (e.g., 'Never harm your neighbour' or 'Don't inflict cruel treatment on the innocent'), but their conscience is offended by rules. Are promises *always* to be kept, even in circumstances likely to lead to murder?

There is another advantage of principles over rules: they often express

[19] *Op. cit.*, p. 31.
[20] This is not to deny any place to rules: they are relevant both to moral education and social morality. For our justification of rules in social morality, see p. 46.

the intention of the rules better than the rules themselves. Many people think that there is no difference between 'Don't tell lies' and the principle of veracity. But any school teacher knows better. She is trying to find out something (e.g., 'Who broke the window?' or 'Where has Johnny gone?'): to all her questions, the pupils answer truthfully. But there is something being held back which none of her questions evoke, for she fails to get on the right track. The pupils are obeying the rule, 'Don't tell lies', but they may not be observing the principle of veracity.[21] On a wide rule-deontology, rules can be regarded as attempts, often inadequate ones, to express in a convenient rule-form what the principle intends. Further, moral rules sometimes conflict with a moral principle, and on such a wide deontology the principle can be treated as overriding. Should I keep the rule 'Always tell the truth' when a critically ill patient asks the nature of his illness and when I know that such knowledge is likely to shorten his life and destroy any faint chance of even temporary recovery? Does the rule not here conflict with the principle of beneficence or consideration for his welfare?

So far we have distinguished rules and principles, and have brought out the advantages of principles over rules. But can we say anything else in favour of a wide rule-deontology? What principle or principles can serve as the standard of right and wrong? There are in fact only four candidates for this role in an ethics of principles: (1) justice or equity; (2) prudence or rational egoism, *viz.*, 'We ought to seek our own welfare'; (3) utility, *viz.*, 'We ought to seek the greatest balance of good over evil' (whether for oneself or others); (4) beneficence, *viz.*, 'We ought to do good and prevent doing harm'. Of these, the principle of utility clearly depends on the more basic principle of beneficence; for we could have no duty to seek the greatest balance of good over evil, if we had not a logically prior obligation to do good and prevent doing harm.[22] Further, prudence and beneficence are teleological principles which can have no place in a deontological theory, unless we desire (as we may for other reasons) to embrace a *mixed* deontological/teleological theory. As far as pure deontology, then, is concerned, we are left with only one principle—that of justice.

What can be said on behalf of justice or equity as at least one of the standards of right and wrong? It is clear that rules (conventional, legal and moral) are highly vulnerable to the criticisms of cultural relativism. How do we know that these rules are not just the ones of our century, society or

---

[21] Nor is the rule 'Always tell the truth' an adequate expression of the principle of veracity, for the rule is quite compatible with always remaining silent on the ground that the agent may incriminate himself or others or both. To accept the principle of veracity is to commit oneself to the truth and not to let it go by default, but is compatible with *sometimes* remaining silent in trivial instances (e.g., 'Do you like my new hat?') where nothing but hurt to the other would be achieved. But, of course, this is not pure deontology, for the teleological principle of beneficence is being permitted to override veracity.

[22] Indeed, the principle of utility is a compromise, for there are many situations where the choice is not between an action which will bring about good, and another which will bring about evil, but between actions where the promotion of good *and* bad will ensue, so that all we can (and 'ought implies can') seek in these cases is to achieve the greatest balance of good over evil.

culture? But the same question may be asked of principles. Justice certainly spans the centuries, for Plato and Aristotle had much to say about it, and so had the Hebrew prophets from Amos in the eighth century B.C. onwards. But can we be sure that this is not a principle begotten of our Western culture which has received the inheritance of Athens and Jerusalem? If we hold that there are a number of such sets of rules and principles acceptable according to different cultures, then we are cultural relativists. The question before us is in what sense that is to be taken. If we say that it is an *empirical fact* that people's moral principles and convictions are found to vary in different societies and cultures (descriptive relativism), that fact does not mean that there are no norms, standards or criteria by which right and wrong may be tested (normative relativism).[23] A number of moves may be open to us.

The question becomes, can we avoid normative relativism in the case of justice, or what move can we make to avoid passing from descriptive to normative relativism? A wide rule deontology may hold that, while regulative rules, as expressions and applications of principles, give guidance for specific kinds of acts (and may be regarded as descriptively relative), there are certain principles of morality which lay down what *constitutes* a moral judgement. If this is accepted, then can we regard justice as one of these principles constitutive of morality?

Various formulations of the principle of equity or justice seem to have a remarkable degree of substance of intention in common, despite important variations which occur in them. For example, Rashdall's Axiom of Equity is 'I ought to regard the good of one man as of equal intrinsic value with the like good of any one else'. This clearly rules out discrimination on account of race, colour, sex, accent, wealth or poverty etc. Rashdall's formulation may be compared with the principle of justice as formulated by Henry Sidgwick:

> 'It cannot be right for A to treat B in a manner in which it would be
> wrong for B to treat A, merely on the ground that they are two different
> individuals, and without there being any difference between the natures
> or circumstances of the two which can be stated as a reasonable ground
> for difference of treatment'.

This also clearly rules out treating people differently unless there is a reasonable ground for difference of treatment. For example, a teacher may believe that she ought to treat all her pupils in the same way and have neither favourites nor whipping-boys, but that a backward child should receive special attention. Sidgwick's principle is the test of universalisability which is often contracted to 'Treat like cases alike and different cases differently'. This is developed in moral thinking into the 'Golden Rule', interpreted[24] as 'Treat other people according to the principles on which

[23] Cf. D. M. Emmet, *op. cit.*, pp. 92f.

[24] The Golden Rule as stated in the Gospels ('As you wish that men would do to you, do so to them': Luke 6:31; cf. Matt. 7:12) refers to altruistic actions: otherwise, it would mean (e.g.) that I should give to others the same presents as I wish they should give me.

you would wish to be treated yourself'.[25] Such a principle, however precisely formulated,[26] is likely to be appealed to in any culture in criticism of regulative rules or *mores* by and on behalf of the exploited. The principle of universalisability, though in itself a logical one saying only that rules should be applied consistently,[27] is thus, as D. M. Emmet says, 'capable of leading on by an internal logic, to a universalising of obligations because discriminatory treatment has to be justified'.[28] It is, in fact, found in *many* cultures and centuries: when we recall Nazism and dictatorships of the extreme right and left, we cannot say 'all'. R. M. Hare has argued that what he calls 'Golden-Rule' arguments of the type 'Imagine if you were treated cruelly like that' only work when an appeal can be made to people's interests, but when ideals such as the Nazi ideal of blood and soil intervene, they cease to persuade, for the Nazi would reply, 'If I were a Jew, I would deserve to be treated like that'.[29] There is some evidence then, that this principle bridges cultures, and when it does not, some factors can usually be found to account for the aberration.

Research into moral development supplies further evidence relevant to our case. The sequence in stages of moral development may be universal in all cultures,[30] suggesting that the higher stages correspond to some fundamental constitution in man.[31] Further, they involve an internalisation of rules and a universalising of obligations, comprising a principle of justice or the Golden Rule as above interpreted, where the principle of reciprocity in relationships has been grasped to the highest degree. Justice does then seem to be one of the principles constitutive of morality.

[25] Emmet, *op. cit.*, p. 105.

[26] Our argument does not depend on the adequacy of any of the above formulations, but only that each is pointing to a principle of justice. For example, it is arguable that Sidgwick's formulation is defective in that it fails to bring out what constitutes 'a reasonable ground for difference of treatment'.

[27] Cf. R. M. Hare, *The Language of Morals*, 1952, and *Freedom and Reason*, 1963.

[28] *Loc. cit.*

[29] *Freedom and Reason*, pp. 104–11; cf. Hare's essay 'Ethical theory and Utilitarianism', in A. Sen and B. Williams (edd.), *Utilitarianism and Beyond*, 1982, p. 29f., where he claims to have found a formulation which enables him to 'deal in an agreeably clear way with the problem of the fanatic, who has given me so much trouble in the past'.

[30] Most of the research whether in terms of cognitive development theory or social learning theory has been based on the observation of children brought up within Western culture, but (e.g.) R. W. Wilson has done research on Chinese children from Taiwan, Hong Kong, Chinatown New York City, and black and white children from New Jersey: see *Journal of Moral Education*, Vol. 5, No. 3; and Vol. 7, No. 2. Despite the important qualifications he desires to make, he seems to accept the basic point that there may be a universality of sequence in stages of moral development, but suggests that 'certain aspects of the learning environment' may 'inhibit the full development of the conditions that are necessary for mature moral behaviour'. Perhaps more research will reveal the same to be true of certain aspects of the learning environment of some Western children.

[31] That some people never reach this 'final' or adult or mature stage, or that external influences in some environments may inhibit development towards it does not in itself invalidate this hypothesis.

No discussion of wide rule-deontology would be complete without reference to Kant's exposition of it. Kant overcame some of the difficulties of a narrow rule-deontology by holding that it was not sufficient that an action to be right should be an instance of a certain class—in his case, the class of actions that conformed to law. There was an additional requirement, *viz.*, that an action had to be done from the right motive, i.e., because it was one's duty.[32] Further, he tried to avoid (probably not wholly successfully) the difficulties of conflict between rules or even principles by adopting a monistic type of wide rule-deontology: i.e., he posited *one* basic principle, *viz.*, the categorical imperative which he formulated in three ways:

> *first*, 'I ought never to act except in such a way that I can will that my maxim should become a universal law';[33]
>
> *second*, 'Act as if the maxim of your action were to become through your will a universal law of nature';[34]
>
> *third*, 'Act in such a way that you always treat humanity, whether in your own person or in the person of any other, never simply as a means, but always at the same time as an end'.[35]

Kant is here stating a principle, very similar in its first two formulations, to those of Rashdall and Sidgwick. It has often been remarked that the third owes much to the Christian tradition, and is the Kantian version of 'love your neighbour as yourself'. By maxim, Kant meant, for example, 'I shall keep my promise, because it is right to do so' and one could will that all others should keep their promises, i.e., could will that one's maxim was acted on by everyone. We cannot recite here the voluminous discussion regarding the correct interpretation of Kant's principle. Hare has suggested that

> 'If Kant is interpreted as meaning that a man who says that he ought to act in a certain way, but says "Let others not act in this same way", is guilty of an implicit contradiction, then the Kantian principle is a way of stating a consequence of the logical thesis of universalisability'.[36]

Hare, however, holds that there is more to morality than this. Kant's principle may be a *necessary* criterion for determining what more concrete maxims or rules should guide behaviour that claims to be moral and not immoral, but it is not a *sufficient* one. For example, one can imagine a prosperous man willing that the maxim 'Never help anyone' should be universally acted upon—presumably because he believes that he will never need help. And we have seen how a Nazi could adopt the principle of universalisability without it affecting his views on the consignment of Jews to the gas-chambers.

   3. *The divine-command theory of ethics*. Another version of a monistic

---

[32] See chapter three on motive.

[33] *Groundwork of the Metaphysic of Morals*, chapter 1 (as translated in H. J. Paton, *The Moral Law*, 1969, p. 67).

[34] *Op. cit.*, chapter 2 (p. 84 authors' translation).

[35] *Op. cit.*, chapter 2 (p. 91).

[36] *Op. cit.*, p. 34.

rule-deontology is the divine-command theory of ethics. This holds that the measure of right and wrong, good and bad, is the command or law of God. Frankena[37] equates this theory with theological voluntarism, which makes the will of God the moral standard: but to hold that the will of God is the moral standard does not entail holding that the divine will always comes to us in the form of a command. The form of the theory in which we are interested is the view (a) that the divine will always comes in the form of a command, and (b) that an action is right or wrong, *if and only if and because* God commands or forbids it.

Many people at the popular and relatively unreflective level (believers and non-believers alike) suspect or take for granted that a religious-based ethics is tied to such a divine-command theory. But many Christian thinkers have rejected it in this form, including Thomas Aquinas. We shall argue in chapter 3 that the divine-command theory is inappropriate to a Christian understanding of the God-man relation.

But many who use 'command' language in Christian ethics do not intend to hold this form of the theory. For example, they may use 'command' in a metaphorical sense and may hold that, although God's command is the standard, he always commands what is good, and that therefore an action is right or wrong, not *simply* because God commands or forbids it but because he commands what is good and forbids what is evil. We shall give further attention to the theory at later points.[38]

Islam is often taken as the example *par excellence* of a divine-command theory of ethics. According to the strictest school of Muslim orthodoxy, human beings have no moral discernment except what is given in divine revelation; and further, good is good and evil is evil solely because God has commanded the one and forbidden the other. But other Muslims, including the Shi'is and many Hanafi jurists, hold that human beings frequently discern for themselves the difference between good and evil, though in such cases divine revelation *confirms* such human knowledge, and in the others it is required to make clear what human beings could not otherwise discern. Muslims with these less extreme views think that God commands the good because it is good and forbids the evil because it is evil. Thus they deny the divine-command theory as we have defined it.[39]

2. *Act-deontology or act-ethics*

On this view, no classes of actions are always right in themselves or wrong in themselves. The act that is right to do is always *this* action in this particular situation, and there are no rules which are applicable in different situations. The technical phrase is that no rules are context-invariant:

'... the basic judgements of obligation are all purely particular ones like "In this situation I should do so and so", and ... general ones like "We

---

[37] *Ethics*, 2nd ed., 1973.

[38] See pp. 82ff., 90f., 103f.

[39] Cf. p. 103f. below; cf. also J. N. D. Anderson, *Islamic Law in the Modern World*, 1959, p. 9f., and *Law Reform in the Muslim World*, 1976, p. 3f.

ought always to keep our promises" are unavailable, useless, or at best derivative from particular judgements'.[40]

There are two versions of this view—an intuitionist and an existentialist one.

(1) *Intuitionism*. Intuitionism in the widest sense may be taken as the view that we have an immediate awareness of moral values. It is the theory that traces our moral judgements to a unique form of perception or apprehension, *viz.*, intuition, of which no rational account can be given. Such apprehension or knowledge is *sui generis* and cannot therefore be analysed into other factors. Sometimes this intuitive awareness has been held to be analogous to sense-perception—sometimes to the sense of beauty or of taste (as in the sense of 'good taste')—and has therefore been given the name 'the moral sense'. Sometimes intuition has been held to be analogous to the apprehension of the self-evidence of axioms in mathematics. Moral sense theories, however, have long since fallen into disuse, and in any case the embracing of different geometries, each with its own axioms, has compelled the abandonment of this kind of analogy. But there have been ethical thinkers who have held that when we make moral judgements about particular acts, we do so not by deduction from moral rules but by direct insight.[41]

There have been many forms of intuitionism, and there is more than one way of classifying them. We are concerned here mainly with that form of intuitionism, sometimes called 'individual intuitionism',[42] which holds that somehow we have an immediate form of non-rational awareness, in each *particular* situation, of what is the right thing to do, without appeal to any rules, and also without looking at the consequences 'to see what will promote the greatest balance of good over evil for oneself or the world'.[43] Individual intuitionism is therefore the view that it is purely *particular* moral judgements that are intuited, as distinct from 'general intuitionism' according to which we have intuitions of certain *kinds* or *classes* of action that are right (or intuitions of moral rules), and from 'universal intuitionism' according to which we have intuitions of moral principles (e.g., benevolence and equity).

If we hold the view known as non-naturalism, i.e., that moral evaluations (such as 'X is right') are not identical with empirical facts (such as 'The majority of people approve of X'), then perhaps intuition may be used to answer the question, 'On what are these moral evaluations based? How do we discover what things are good or bad, what acts are right or wrong?' We know these things, it will be said, because we can see them with an inner faculty: we know them by intuition. 'Of course, many people commit errors in intuition because they do not truly allow their inner faculty to speak: they rationalise, they hear what they want to hear . . . their moral

---

[40] W. K. Frankena, *op. cit.*, p. 16.
[41] C. D. Broad, W. D. Ross, H. A. Prichard and E. F. Carritt have all held some form of intuitionism.
[42] This is the terminology of H. J. Paton in *The Good Will*, 1927.
[43] Frankena, *op. cit.*, p. 16.

vision is blurred or distorted by all sorts of personal factors which get in the way of a true vision'.[44] There will, therefore, be a place for moral training to ensure people are not blinded by habit or tradition and so on, for moral truths are there to be discerned and the trained and impartial eye can see them.

But, in the case of individual intuitionism, what is to be done when there is disagreement—when one person claims to intuit that he should help the wounded man, and another claims to intuit that he should do the work for which he is paid and therefore hurry to get to work? What is to be done, if one claims to intuit that he should return good for evil and another claims that he should return evil for evil? If a third party claims that one of them is mistaken, how is that person to know which one? Let us say that one of them is morally blind. But then suppose that both are sincere, intelligent, informed about the facts of the situation, and striving to remove their distorting spectacles, such as rationalisation, what other people have told them about moral matters and all other personal factors. How then are we to decide which was the right intuition?

The intuitionist may reply that the problem of disagreement on moral matters is not confined to intuitionists, and may even admit that not all moral evaluations are known by intuition. All he needs for his argument, he may say, is *one* intuition. Which one, then, is it to be? It has to be an intuition of a moral value, not merely of what to do in a specific situation. Perhaps the likeliest candidate for such a single intuition is 'Happiness is good', and 'right' will then be defined as what is productive of maximum happiness, or a greater balance of happiness over unhappiness. In that case, you do not have to intuit the particular acts that are right, for you find that out empirically by discovering what leads to most happiness. You intuit only that happiness is good. But even this single-intuition view is vulnerable, for not everyone agrees that 'right' means the same as 'productive of maximum happiness': Kant, for example, did not.[45]

But if the introduction of even *one* intuition brings in problems of validation, how shall we validate thousands of intuitions? That is what individual intuitionism demands, for it holds that we intuit *in each particular situation* what is the right thing to do. For if there is disagreement about values, norms and principles (such as 'Happiness is good'), there appears to be much more disagreement about what particular action is in accordance with the value, norm or principle. But, of course, the individual intuitionist makes no appeal to rules, principles, consequences or whatever, and we come back to the question, 'How do we decide which is the right intuition in this particular situation?' The individual intuitionist appears to have removed all means of deciding the question.

(2) *Existentialism.* There are serious difficulties in the way of giving an over-all brief account of existentialism, for it does not so much constitute a school with one set of clearly defined doctrines, as a mood or even a

[44] John Hospers, *Human Conduct*, 2nd impression 1970, p. 539.
[45] For Kant, see p. 73f. below.

life-style. One can see at most only a family resemblance between the existentialist views held by Kierkegaard, Heidegger, Marcel, Sartre and Jaspers. Again, no completely successful account can be given of existentialist ethics,[46] for the simple reason that there aren't any—not in the sense, of course, that existentialists do not behave morally, but in the sense that they do not engage in the reflection on moral issues that is characteristic of the philosopher. Indeed they are inclined to despise reflection that is a substitute for 'getting involved' in action.

For our purposes, it is sufficient to call attention to the common ground existing between 'individual intuitionism' and existentialism (in probably every form). For both, each moral decision must be made in the situation, without reference to any rules, systems of rules or principles. While existentialists do not use the term 'intuition', they hold the view that each man must decide for himself what to do. No man can choose for another. These choices 'must be described as what each *individual* plans as he looks out at the world from his own personal angle . . . Systems of rules are of their nature impersonal. To live according to such a system is to fail to face the facts of individual freedom and responsibility'.[47] Accordingly,

'. . . reliance, at whatever level of discourse, upon general rules or principles is taken by Existentialism to be a denial of freedom. The only general law of ethics must be to avoid general laws'.[48]

'Where there are rules, there is no morality; where there is morality, no rules' has been proposed as the characteristically existentialist slogan in ethics.[49]

Some criticism of existentialist ethics seems inept, because it proceeds on premises that existentialists do not accept. For example, one line of criticism goes like this. Reasons can always be given for a moral judgement, but reasons cannot be given if moral judgements are purely particular (as the existentialists claim), for reasons cannot apply in a particular case only. But it is then open to existentialists to reply that they simply reject the giving of reasons for moral judgements. Hence such a line of argument will seem to the existentialist a mere begging of the question. But there are several philosophical positions that one has logically to accept, once one has granted the premisses. In such case, the only line of criticism is to refuse to accept the premisses, and this will not constitute a begging of the question. It is unfair to dismiss all forms of existentialist ethics out of hand, if only because they differ so much from each other. We cannot discuss all of them, but we shall look later at one form of Christian existentialist ethics, that of Bultmann.[50]

From the above discussion of act-deontology, it should be clear that all

---

[46] Cf. M. Warnock, *Existentialist Ethics*, 1967.
[47] M. Warnock, *op. cit.*, p. 54.
[48] *Ibid.*, p. 56.
[49] Cf. A. Manser in *Symposium on Existentialism* (with A. Kolnai), Aristotelian Society Supplementary Volume XXXVII, 1963, quoted by R. L. Cunningham in the Introduction to his edited work *Situationism and the New Morality*, 1970, p. 16f.
[50] See chapter 9.

versions of it which are expressions of pure act-deontology and are not modified by giving some place to rules, are subject to the major criticism that they are applicable only to the relations between individuals and not the area of social morality,[51] where the reference to rules seems to be necessary for moral decision making.

3. The problem of situation ethics

There is no reason except convention why act-deontology or act-ethics in both its intuitionist and existentialist versions should not be called situation ethics or situationism, for both hold that moral judgements can be made only in each particular moral situation. Indeed, existentialism has been a strong influence on most situationists. The situation ethics of Joseph Fletcher, however, differ markedly from act-deontology in several important respects.

Fletcher claims that situation ethics is a methodological thesis—about how to do ethics. It is an approach to ethics which does not enter into the question of the content of morality. Its methodology could be adopted by atheists, humanists, theists, vitalists and many others—people who would have widely differing answers to the question of the content of morality and how they would specify the moral standard, i.e., they would differ as to what was the ultimate principle of moral valuation.

But Fletcher does specify his moral standard, *viz.*, love (*agape*). His approach is that in deliberating on what is right or wrong, good or bad in the moral sense, in any situation (and whatever other terms such as 'ought' or 'duty' one cares to use), there are only TWO considerations, *viz.*, our moral principle or principles (e.g., pleasure, happiness, beneficence, life, love or *agape*), and the situation itself. For Fletcher, love is the only principle that has absolute and intrinsic worth. Unlike rules and other principles, it alone is context-invariant. In all situations love is to be promoted and *nothing else without qualification.*[52]

Fletcher does not tell us by what process we recognise *agape* alone as intrinsically good.[53] It is clear, however, that while he regards situationism

---

[51] On social ethics, see pp. 31–35, and also chapters 2, 9 and 10 below.

[52] Fletcher holds that there are only three approaches to ethics: (i) the legalistic; (ii) the antinomian, the opposite extreme; and (iii) the situational: cf. his *Situation Ethics*, 1966, p. 17 (henceforth cited as *S.E.*). He sees situationism as mid-way between these two extremes. Legalism is 'bound by its principles, the other has none': cf. H. Cox (ed.), *The Situation Ethics Debate*, 1968, p. 251. With legalism he rejects rule-deontology and any theory of ethics which treats its principles as rules which have no exceptions whatever the situation. But he is also anxious to distinguish his position from antinomianism, which does not use any principles when a decision is taken in the situation. Situation ethics, Fletcher argues, does have principles (or at least one principle) but is not bound by them. 'If you refuse to give intrinsic validity to moral principles', he writes plaintively, 'you are assumed to have none'.

[53] Nor is it clear why Fletcher does not allow that first order principles (e.g., beneficence, justice) are intrinsically good: they are not to be confused with rules or classes of action like abortion or blood-transfusion. Cf. C. A. Campbell, *In Defence of Free Will*, 1967, essay 'Moral and Non-Moral Values', reprinted in (edd.) W. Sellars and J. Hospers, *Readings in Ethical Theory*, 1970, pp. 169–87.

as a way of approach to ethics, he adopts it as a way of doing *Christian* ethics. Yet while he takes the situation very seriously, it is possible to argue that he is not so aware of the full context in which he is operating: for example, he seems to obscure the necessary distinction between general ethics and Christian ethics, which has a context of its own and a theological one at that. However, in making a moral decision one has to look carefully at the situation and ask how love may be promoted in it. Love does not tell us independently of the situation what actions are right or wrong, good or bad: love does not give us this information either in advance of the situation or automatically or mystically in it. Love does not instinctively home on its object (as John Robinson holds):[54] knowledge of the facts surrounding the situation, including technical 'know-how' and sometimes scientific knowledge, are required. Charges of sentimentalism in the making of moral decisions or of making it 'too easy' are unfair to Fletcher. He is clear that the Christian has no private line to God; he has no inside knowledge of God's will and so cannot short-cut the necessity to decide in the situation. '. . . *I simply do not know and cannot know what God is doing . . . What is special about him*' (sc. the Christian) 'is his faith, not his knowledge'.[55] The Christian must look at the situation with great care before he can see what is God's will for him in it, and even then he may not be sure. For all that, he will not contract out because 'the whole thing's too difficult' but he will choose and act—and act in faith in the living God.

If this position seems close to act-deontology, Fletcher is quick to point to two important differences. First, he stresses the teleological aspect of right action, i.e., the promotion of an end or goal, *viz.*, *agape*.[56] Secondly, he regards act-ethics as antinomian, i.e., as ethical extemporism which makes up its principles *ad hoc* for each situation. It is an ethics without any principles.

But if Fletcher rejects act-ethics because it has no principles, he rejects rules-ethics because it is bound to its principles. He prefers to call his position 'modified rule-agapism'[57] or in another place 'modified or summary rule-utilitarianism'. In this he has adopted the terminology of Frankena, later taken over by Paul Ramsey in his *Deeds and Rules in Christian Ethics*. Ramsey defines 'pure rule-agapism' as the view that maintains that

'we are always to tell what we are to do in particular situations by referring to a set of rules, and that what rules are to prevail and be followed is to be determined by seeing what rules (not what acts) best or most fully embody love'.[58]

'Modified rule-agapism' for Paul Ramsey may take various forms, depend-

---

[54] Cf. J. A. T. Robinson, *Honest to God*, 1963, p. 115.

[55] *S.E.*, p. 254 (Fletcher's italics); here he differentiates his position from that of Paul Lehmann, who links the notion of context closely to the *koinonia* (community, fellowship) of the Church—an emphasis that does not appear in Fletcher.

[56] This is discussed in the next chapter.

[57] Cf. J. C. Bennett *et al.*, *Storm over Ethics*, 1967, p. 157; and *Situationism and the New Morality*, p. 279.

[58] P. Ramsey; *Deeds and Rules in Christian Ethics*, 1965, p. 95.

ing on what precise modification is made to the basic position: e.g., pure rule-agapism may be taken to apply to a great extent to public morality or social ethics, where the case for regulation of behaviour by legal enactment, i.e., for rules, seems irrefutable, while some modification *in the direction* of act-agapism (i.e., act-ethics with the one principle of *agape*) may be desired for private morality. All that Fletcher makes clear as far as his own position is concerned is that rules are helpful in moral decision-making as convenient summaries of past ethical practice for dealing with these sorts of situations, but these rules may be bypassed if love is better served thereby.[59] What is significant is that Fletcher in these later and perhaps more careful statements of his position does not outrightly reject all place for rules in the moral life. But the rules are not to be absolutised, and must always observe *agape;* and where love cannot be promoted in a situation by the application of a rule, then that rule must be set aside.

B. IS NEW TESTAMENT MORAL TEACHING DEONTOLOGICAL?

It is a common presumption that the New Testament or Jesus himself provides, if not a ready-made rules-ethics, at least the fundamental principles or imperatives for such a system of Christian ethics. In other words, the assumption is that Christian ethics is deontological and finds it authoritative basis in the New Testament. Such a view has been severely challenged,[60] and it raises issues of great importance both for the study of Christian ethics and for New Testament studies. We pose the question here: is New Testament moral teaching essentially deontological? Or, to put it in an even more open way: is N.T. moral teaching *consonant with* rule-deontology?

It will, of course, be appreciated that the N.T. writers do not carry on the kind of discussion on moral matters which we call philosophical. Rather, their moral teaching flows from their faith and experience and forms an organic unity with the Gospel message itself. But answers to the questions we have raised may be given in their writings, although they do not think in these terms. We have first to understand the N.T. writings in relation to the authors' intentions and milieux, and then see whether what they say is consonant or not with rules-ethics (in any of its forms), or with act-ethics or some form of situation ethics. Sometimes, for example, we find them transcending all forms of rule-deontology, although they do not use that kind of language.

The N.T. writers belong to a particular cultural and historical setting that has a distinctive world-view and one that is very different from that of *any* modern interpreter. By their time (and it is reflected in the N.T.), rabbinic Judaism was well on the way to acquiring the elaboration and

---

[59] *Situationism and the New Morality, loc. cit.*
[60] Cf. J. T. Sanders, *Ethics in the New Testament*, 1975.

sophistication that are so evident in the Mishnah and, as we have noted above, it provides an excellent example of rule-deontology.[61] It would be surprising if Christian moral teaching were not influenced by similar procedures, but it is even more important, as we shall see, to understand that the heart of the Christian moral position is not to be located here. Other factors were having a profound influence upon the Jewish milieu at this period. In particular, there was a veritable rash of apocalyptic and otherworldly sects and movements, whose orientation was towards some impending, cataclysmic event that would overturn the existing order of things and effect a cosmic transformation. Among the sectarians were various baptist movements, of which the Qumran community is now the most celebrated. John the Baptist belongs to a similar ethos; his message is one of repentance and preparation before the great and terrible Day of the Lord. Both Jesus and the early Christians were profoundly involved in eschatological concern of a comparable kind. Such an emphasis on eschatology has repercussions for the understanding of morality, and it is one strong reason, as we shall see, against subsuming the kind of moral teaching found in the New Testament under either rule- or act-deontology. The issue is important enough to justify a closer examination.

1. *Eschatology and ethics in the New Testament*

If one's outlook is dominated by eschatological expectation (e.g., that the end of the world or the existing order is at hand), then one's understanding of moral obligation or responsibility to the existing order is radically affected. One may be inclined to take historical existence (i.e., existence in this world) less seriously; what matters is otherworldly concern. Hence, detachment from this world becomes a priority. This can take a gnostic direction: one's life is geared to the knowledge (*gnosis*) of salvation that one has been granted; the world is a prison from which to escape. Or it can turn in the direction of rigorous asceticism, as in the monasticism of Qumran or Jewish-Christian scrupulosity to observe the divine Law with total devotion; or it may adopt other forms of pietism. It could conceivably take an antinomian direction: one is freed from *all* that binds one to the existing order of things and therefore one has no moral responsibility in terms of worldly duties or values. Yet while such tendencies manifest themselves in the early Church, they do not characterise it. The Thessalonians who have given up work in view of the impending End are told in no uncertain terms to go back to their jobs and get on with the business of earning their living (2 Thess. 3:7–10). The antinomians at Corinth are given a lesson on how to make responsible moral decisions—Paul's teaching here coming near to a more fully formulated Christian ethics-in-the-situation (1 Cor. 8 *passim*,

---

[61] The Mishnah (second cent. A.D.) was written down after the disasters of A.D. 70 and A.D. 132. While Judaism had to adapt to the loss of land and Temple, the conservatism of rabbinic Judaism ensured that the Mishnah reproduced the general tenor of the rabbinic teaching of the preceding centuries. In the N.T., however, Jesus' controversies with the Pharisees have probably acquired something of the tone of later Christian arguments with rabbinic Judaism.

10:23–11:1). The Colossians are told not to submit to the pressures of the over-scrupulous legalists (Col. 2:8–23). In the New Testament, therefore, there is evidence that Paul and others like him[62] are exercising a careful control of eschatological expectations and their implications for Christian faith and life. Paul's teaching on moral issues *is*, of course, directly influenced by eschatology—witness his attitude to marriage (1 Cor. 7:26, 29–35); but the treatment he accords to eschatology is markedly different from that of the sectarians. The Christians' attitude to it—and consequently their conception of the relation of eschatology to moral conduct—is complex as well as varied.

The reason for this is not far to seek. Christian eschatology was not concerned simply with an impending event—whether the Day of the Lord, the Parousia or some other related concept. The coming event had cast its shadow before it in the Christ event. God had *already* intervened decisively in history in the Christ who had lived, died and risen. 'God has made him both Lord and Christ, this Jesus whom you crucified' (Acts 2:36). Hence, Christian expectation of the future was understood more and more in terms of the Christ who had already come, in whom the End or Completion was already manifested in the midst of history. Yet the course of history and the world continued . . . for the moment. Christian moral teaching, therefore, had a focus in the Christ event that had already occurred (and in the religious tradition of Israel and the Old Testament which it presupposed), as well as in the future. Paul, for example, refers in several places to a tradition of teaching that was believed to originate with 'the Lord'.[63] Above all, the event of Christ provided certain motifs that were definitive for Christian living: the motif of the incarnation prompts one to humility and service (Phil. 2:5ff.); the 'grace of our Lord Jesus Christ' to generosity (2 Cor. 8:9ff.); the sufferings of Christ to patient endurance (1 Peter 2:21ff.); the death and resurrection of Christ to moral transformation (Rom. 6:4). Thus, the imitation or example of Christ (cf. 1 Cor. 11:1; John 13:15)—even the imitation of God (Eph. 5:1)—supplies a christocentric, or even a theocentric, motive for moral endeavour. Christian morality is therefore inextricably linked to the framework of belief in which it is set.

The debate about eschatology in New Testament scholarship has not been free of confusion. The term itself has been used in a variety of ways,[64] and in the New Testament itself each writer may be said to have his own eschatology. There has also been a tendency to isolate this doctrine from others even though all doctrines cohere in the attempt to express the

---

[62] There is room to doubt whether all or part of the Thessalonian correspondence, together with Colossians and/or Ephesians, come directly from Paul (as distinct from Pauline circles). There is no need for us to take up such issues of criticism here.

[63] Cf. 1 Thess. 4:15; 1 Cor. 9:14, 9:4, 7:10f. (cf. 7:1–16), 11:23–26.

[64] Cf. J. Carmignac, 'Les dangers de l'eschatologie', *New Testament Studies* 17, 1970–71, pp. 365–390; I. H. Marshall, 'Slippery Words I. Eschatology', *Expository Times* 89, 9, 1978, pp. 264–69.

meaning of the Gospel. The consequences for Christian morality and ethics can be illustrated from two differing interpretations of eschatology.

Perhaps the most celebrated and influential view of eschatology was that put forward by both J. Weiss and A. Schweitzer and known as consistent or thorough-going eschatology.[65] According to this interpretation, Jesus was obsessed by the imminence of the end of the world; his ministry and teaching were entirely governed by it; and he died in the attempt to force God to make the End a reality. Instead, he himself was broken; but in his death he broke the power of this eschatologically conditioned world view (or so Schweitzer argued) and set man free to live morally and autonomously. Although this position was exegetically weak and this resolution of the problem of eschatology is simply the application of Hegelian presuppositions, consistent eschatology has continued to be influential in German scholarship in particular.[66] On this view, the teaching of Jesus is *interim ethics*, designed to guide his followers in the brief interlude before the End comes. Because of the eschatological crisis, all worldly duties and responsibilities are set aside, and one is free (as never before) to turn the other cheek, go the second mile, love one's enemy and suspend all other considerations while one acts as the good Samaritan. With the failure of Jesus' hopes (so the argument goes), *interim ethics* lost all relevance, and the Church had to adjust to a quite different situation: it had to rethink its eschatology and with it its ethics. The Church in fact opted in the main for rule-deontology. Schweitzer himself adopted humanistic principles such as reverence for life.

On the other hand, C. H. Dodd, in his realised eschatology,[67] and a number of other scholars, with proleptic eschatology[68] or 'eschatology in the process of realization',[69] emphasised that it was in Jesus himself that the 'last things' (the *eschata* as the final goal of all God's work) received definitive or proleptic expression. In their view, therefore, Christian ethics *is* rooted in the teaching of Jesus, for the life and work of Jesus have a permanent or continuing relevance for Christians in the sense that he does not belong to a radically different age (eschatologically speaking) from ourselves. Hence, Dodd inclined to the command theory of Christian ethics: we are commanded by Jesus to love our neighbour as ourselves, and the Christian takes his orders from his Lord; while J. Jeremias was intent on recovering the *ipsissima verba* of Jesus as definitive instruction for all his followers. Against the background of this whole discussion—whether Jesus' teaching was time-conditioned (Schweitzer) or has permanent value (Dodd)—the words of Ronald Preston are highly relevant:

'The more thoroughly the New Testament is studied the more the

[65] J. Weiss, *Jesus' Proclamation of the Kingdom of God*, Eng. tr., 1971 (German, 1892); A. Schweitzer, *The Quest of the Historical Jesus*, Eng. tr., 1910, (3) 1954 (*Von Reimarus zu Wrede*, 1906).
[66] Cf. J. T. Sanders, *op. cit.*, pp. 7–29.
[67] Cf. *The Parables of the Kingdom*, 1935, rev. ed. 1961, p. 81.
[68] Cf. R. H. Fuller, *The Mission and Achievement of Jesus*, 1954, p. 48.
[69] Cf. J. Jeremias, *The Parables of Jesus*, Eng. tr., 1954, rev. ed. 1963, p. 230.

eschatological freedom of Jesus stands out, rooted in his situation as a Jew in first-century Palestine and in the history of his people, but transcending it by the very fact that he did not deal with the relativities of particular ethical decisions'.[70]

Without entering the fray for or against Schweitzer, Dodd or anyone else, we are content to underline the fact that the New Testament itself, our primary source, locates the groundwork of Christian morality not in the words of Christ in isolation but in the organic unity of his life, teaching, death and resurrection, as expressed in the resurrection faith of his followers. For this reason, it would be difficult to justify either the *ipsissima verba* of Jesus or a theme such as 'the moral teaching of Jesus' as the starting-point of a study of ethics in the New Testament.[71] Christians confess the crucified and risen Jesus as Messiah and Lord. They see him as 'eschatological event'—the decisive event in which God has disclosed his final purpose for his creation and thus an anticipation of the End itself. Christian ethics expounds the consequences of this Christ event for Christian morality. No N.T. writer, of course, takes it upon himself to write to this specification! Instead, in a variety of ways and with differing emphases, the N.T. writers illustrate or indicate how Christian commitment gains expression in Christian living, even if the perspective in which the latter is viewed is frequently determined by eschatological considerations. As the following sample of N.T. writings will show, the continuing interpretation of eschatology by Christians serves to open up and express important perspectives in Christian morality.

2. *Deontology and the New Testament writers*

It seems appropriate to begin our sampling of the N.T. writers with Matthew, in whose Gospel the connection between eschatology and Christian morality is evident, not least in the Beatitudes and in a number of solemn utterances in the prophetic tradition.[72] At the same time, the 'great commandment' emerges as the basic principle by which the Law is to be interpreted,[73] although it is clearly not the only one. Matthew, in fact, gives definitive expression to the Jewish-Christian understanding of how the Law is to be observed in the light of the Messiah's work.

'Think not that I have come to abolish the Law and the Prophets; I have come not to abolish them but to fulfil them. For truly, I say to you, till heaven and earth pass away, not an iota, not a dot, will pass from the Law until all is accomplished' (Matt. 5:17f.).

[70] *Explorations in Theology*, 9, pp. 62ff.

[71] As is done in R. Schnackenburg, *The Moral Teaching of the New Testament*, 1965. See on this point, J. L. Houlden, *Ethics and the New Testament*, 1973, p. 4f.

[72] For example, Matt. 6: 14f. (cf. 5:19), 16:27 (cf. 18:23–35): see J. T. Sanders, *op. cit.*, p. 42f. and the basic work of E. Käsemann, 'Sentences of Holy Law in the New Testament', in *New Testament Questions of Today*, Eng. tr., 1969, pp. 66–81. Käsemann's article is open to question in some respects, but that need not concern us in this context.

[73] Cf. G. Barth, 'Matthew's Understanding of the Law' in G. Bornkamm, G. Barth and H. J. Held, *Tradition and Interpretation in Matthew*, Eng. tr., 1963, pp. 75–105; J. T. Sanders, *op. cit.*, p. 41f.

Far from abolishing God's requirements as revealed at Sinai, the Messiah's work brings them to full expression—reveals the full dimensions of their meaning and implications.[74] In no sense is the demand of the Law diminished. On the contrary, the demand is even more radically interpreted (5:20). The implication is that the scribes have trivialised 'righteousness' by interpreting the Law so that its full meaning is reduced and restricted to a narrow rule-deontology, a set of regulations which it is possible and obligatory for men to keep. But the Messiah's 'I say to you . . .' eradicates all human equivocation and dissimulation and throws into bold relief the proper application of God's demand to both outward action and inward disposition—in fact, as we might put it, to the entire person in its rational, conative and appetitive functioning. Thus the limitation inherent in the principle of proportionate retaliation (5:38) is radicalised. Whereas Deut. 19:21 commands 'Your eye shall not pity; it shall be life for life, eye for eye . . .' Jesus teaches that in the end what is required is the non-violent response to the oppressor, the waiving of all one's rights, including that of justifiable retaliation—in short, in modern terms, the absorbing of the aggression directed to oneself, thereby creating peace. Again, the command to love one's neighbour is interpreted with similar openness to the other party, even if the latter could be regarded as one's enemy. Love, not hate, is God's requirement. All of this teaching can be described as a counsel of perfection—and that is precisely how Matthew sums it up (5:48). Elsewhere in the Gospel there are similar indications. The advice given to the rich young ruler is governed by the clause 'if you would be perfect' (16:21).[75]

[74] This involves what K. Stendahl calls 'the sharpening of the Law, its restoration in its ultimate radicality . . . a Messianic intensification, producing the true righteousness which belongs to the Kingdom': *Peake*, 1962, p. 776. W. D. Davies argues that the *substance* of the New Law, the New Sinai, the New Moses, is present, although Matthew avoids these terms: *Sermon on the Mount*, 1966, p. 32. For a more recent discussion, cf. R. Mohrlang, *Matthew and Paul*, 1983.

[75] Our use of the term 'counsel of perfection' is not to be construed as an acceptance of the medieval doctrine explicitly rejected by Luther but which Roman Catholic teaching has inherited. This doctrine is based on a distinction which goes back to St. Ambrose, c. 340–397 and which itself may be acceptable, between precepts and counsels of perfection, but we reject the understanding of it in medieval moral theology which went somewhat as follows. The *precepts* or commandments of God, as setting forth the minimum requirements of the Christian life, are binding on all, and obedience to them is necessary for salvation, while the *counsels of perfection* or 'evangelical counsels', issued by Christ in the N.T., set an ideal standard binding only on a few, and are, in Tertullian's words, 'advised rather than commanded'. Cf. J. O. Urmson, 'Saints and Heroes' in Joel Feinberg (ed.), *Moral Concepts*, 1969: Urmson, without accepting this doctrine and writing as a philosopher, gives hard-headed reasons in favour of the basic distinction between actions which we *all* have a duty to do and those actions which may present themselves as duties to *some* and certainly have moral worth but are far in excess of anything that any moral rules could plausibly require; cf. P. F. Strawson, 'Social Morality and Individual Ideal', first published in *Philosophy*, 1961 and reprinted in Ian T. Ramsey (ed.), *Christian Ethics and Contemporary Philosophy*, 1966. Similarly, J. Houston, 'Precepts and Counsels'

The language of perfection or completion (*teleios:* complete) indicates something of a transvaluation or radical reinterpretation of eschatology as well as ethics. While traditional eschatological motifs, such as watching for the End and preparing for the Day of Judgement, are not absent from Matthew's Gospel, the temporal concept that underlies or is presupposed by moral teaching of this kind is replaced in the Sermon by what we may call a qualitative description of the eschatological goal in terms of perfection/completion, the perfect love that characterises the Father. But this is incompatible with a narrow deontology of rules, for the Sermon does not specify precisely the behaviour commanded or forbidden, nor does it even frame rules that people can readily (or with some effort) observe;[76] nor does a wide deontology of principles characterise and express the radical meaning of Jesus' teaching[77] which

'... presents an absolute ethic concerned to register the immediate impact of the divine demand, uninfluenced by the contingencies of experience or the crippling realities of circumstances'.[78]

It is therefore more properly described as illustrative of what it means to make a total response in one's living to God as King—as pointing to the unconditional standard of life within the Kingdom.[79] And if we enquire of Matthew how mere mortals can relate to such a standard, then doubtless he would have agreed that no one by his own efforts can attain it; he would have spoken of repentance in the Hebrew sense of a turning to God, of the gift of

---

(*footnote 75 continued*)
in Richard W. A. McKinney, *Creation, Christ and Culture, Studies in Honour of T. F. Torrance*, writing as a theologian, adduces arguments in favour of the basic distinction but refuses to accept the medieval doctrine that the counsels are only for a few Christians and can be ignored by the majority: he wonders whether the distinction is not simply between injunctions which are binding on all and those which are not *each* binding on *everyone*, and he offers suggestions how the counsels may be understood as relevant to the lives of the majority of Christians. While these suggestions are useful, it must be emphasised that in the New Testament *all* are called to perfection.

[76] Cf. J. Houston, *op. cit.*, p. 186: '... much ... of the Sermon on the Mount does not consist of precise rules for behaviour, such that we would almost always know what is and what is not a breach of them'.

[77] Some scholars have advocated that the concrete terminology of the Sermon (e.g., turn the other cheek, do not sound a trumpet) should be translated into general principles and given a wider range of application although 'care must be taken lest the general principles prove to be considerably less radical than the illustration given by Jesus': H. K. McArthur, *Understanding the Sermon on the Mount*, 1961, p. 112; cf. p. 111. But does the concrete injunction or illustration from life not provide a better safeguard against the dilution of radicalism than the general principle, which has loop-holes almost inbuilt? Is this not a better teaching technique than the framing of principles? The ethical commonplaces that we might finish up with when we transplant such principles back into specific injunctions could not long stand beside the sharp edge of these sayings.

[78] W. D. Davies, *op. cit.*, p. 107. We take Davies to mean by 'absolute' in this context 'unqualified' or 'unconditional'.

(*footnote 79 on page 28*)

God that comes to those who seek it; and of the yoke of the Messiah who gives rest from the oppressiveness of misconceived religious and moral obligation. In the Messiah's name, the apostles go out to make disciples of all nations, that they may learn of him ...

There can be no suggestion that the Sermon supplies a basis for social or even individual morality which the Church can demand of the world. The use of the term 'brother' (5:22f.) and the emphasis on cultic action and mutual forgiveness suggest that we have here something like the community rule of a messianic disciples-group that presents at least some resemblances to Qumran. Its eschatology is the key to understanding and interpreting the interplay of religion and ethics that stands at the heart of its constitution. Thus, the call to perfection is not only accommodated but made central in a way utterly foreign to rule-deontology as described above.

Of the other two synoptists, Mark presents Christian discipleship in the perspective of the kingdom of God. 'For Mark, the answer to the question, "What is my duty with regard to X?" is "God is sovereign—live under his rule" '.[80] Mark also places emphasis on 'eschatological virtues' such as watchfulness, perseverance and reliance on God's Spirit, as well as on the imitation of Christ, especially in his self-sacrifice (cf. Mark 5:34). Luke is obviously still wrestling with the problem of eschatology and the continuity of history after the decisive events of salvation have been accomplished. Familiar eschatological motifs like 'watching' and 'waiting' persist, but the time perspective has lengthened and the world mission of the Church becomes itself part of the eschatological scene. The divine action prompts a corresponding response: generosity, compassion, concern for the needy ... The discussion of the 'great commandment' (Luke 10:27f.) leads on to the parable of the Good Samaritan, in which the demand of God is seen to transcend the boundaries of the Law (which can even obstruct moral duty, as in the case of the priest and Levite) and to define 'neighbour' as anyone in need, irrespective of race or creed. Does this, we may ask, suggest a command-theory of ethics? Apart from the fact that there is something paradoxical, to say the least, about a *command* to *love*, in any literal sense of these words,[81] the parable does not tie in neatly with rule-deontology in either of its forms, even if *love* as *principle* is inherently more attractive than a narrow rules-ethics in this context. There is no hint in the text that Luke (still less, Jesus) is simply commending the principle of love. The parable confronts the hearers with the real nature of moral obligation in terms of the relationship in which they stood, or claimed to stand, with God.[82]

---

[79] Cf. J. Houston, *loc. cit.*: '(Hence) counsels should be regarded as inspiring, prompting, lines of action and even types of life style, rather than as rules ... Perhaps, therefore, we should regard the counsels as one body of teaching by which all Christians should allow themselves to be prompted, by opening themselves again and again to its suggestions'.

[80] J. L. Houlden, *op. cit.*, p. 44.

[81] See chapter 3, where this issue is discussed.

[82] As the 'great commandment' inevitably does, for the command to love God is equally, or even more, paradoxical than the command to love one's neighbour.

An earlier Christian writer than Luke, namely Paul the apostle, had already won through to what is, in principle, theological ethics, though not expounded as a system. His view involves the rejection of rule-deontology as an adequate understanding of Christian morality, as can be seen in his discussion of salvation. It is true that he does not attack the concept of the Law (Torah) of God, which is for man's good. 'The law is holy, and the commandment is holy and just and good' (Rom. 7:12). He urges the Galatians (6:2) to fulfil the Law of Christ—i.e., the messianic Law. He thus recognises the place of obligation in Christian ethics: his position is not antinomian.[83] Yet, 'if a law had been given which had power to bestow life, then indeed righteousness would have come from keeping the law' (Gal. 3:21, N.E.B.). Man being what he is, this is not the case. At a stroke, Paul demolishes any form of legalism—indeed, any form of rules-ethics, broad or narrow—as an adequate means of understanding Christian living. A rules-ethics can prescribe what man must do to be righteous (Gal. 3:21; Rom. 10:5) and what man must not do (Gal. 3:20). Its great weakness is that, while it may convince a man that he is sinful and even restrain him to some extent, it cannot adequately motivate him or give him the power to do what is right (cf. Rom. 7:7–24). Indeed, it may be counter-productive in that it may stimulate desire for what is forbidden (cf. Rom. 7:7f.). Again, it may deceive man into believing that he can attain to goodness by his own efforts and so bring him to spiritual death rather than life (cf. Rom. 8:2; 2 Cor. 3:6ff.). As Paul sees it, the very attempt to make oneself 'righteous' through obedience to rules is an act of human presumption and therefore sinful and futile. Rule-deontology stops far short of coming to terms with the extent of man's predicament, or with the degree of alienation and moral powerless-ness which are characteristic of it (Rom. 7:14ff.; cf. Col. 1:21). The answer to such problems comes at a far deeper level than any rules-ethics can encompass (cf. Rom. 8:1–4) and is bound up with the operation of God's grace in Christ apprehended through faith (Rom. 3:28; 5:1).

(footnote 82 continued)
The paradox is resolved by taking seriously the setting of the commandment in the context of the Shema (cf. Deut. 6:4ff.), where we see that this is not a command in any literal sense but properly belongs to the covenantal realm of discourse in which love to God is a response to the divine love. In a similar way, love to one's neighbour (Lev. 19:17) is part of the so-called holiness code, which begins 'You shall be holy, for I the Lord your God am holy . . .' (Lev. 19:2): in other words, a relational understanding of morality is presupposed rather than a divine command theory as such.

[83] Paul's opponents suggested that his position was indeed antinomian. Among modern scholars, J. Knox has argued that 'Paul's doctrine of justification has in itself the seeds of antinomianism and Paul's critics, or perhaps heretical follow-ers, were not being merely perverse in saying so': *The Ethic of Jesus in the Teaching of the Church*, 1962, p. 76; cf. *Chapters in a Life of Paul*, 1954, pp. 153ff. Knox's criticism of Paul turns on a misunderstanding of his basic model of Christian ethics. For a reply to Knox, cf. C. F. D. Moule, 'Obligation in the Ethic of Paul' in *Christian History and Interpretation: Studies Presented to John Knox*, (edd. W. R. Farmer, C. F. D. Moule and R. R. Niebuhr), 1967, pp. 389–406.

'It is not that grace abolished law, but that dependence on grace, instead of the attitude of legalism, is the only way to fulfil God's law. There is obligation, but it is to grace, not law'.[84]

But while for Paul the definitive expression of the *eschaton* has already taken place in the death and resurrection of the Messiah, the act of God's grace, eschatology has also for him a present and future significance. His calling, his apostleship to the Gentiles and the work of the churches are eschatological—part of God's final work. The experience of the Spirit is a foretaste now of the salvation that is to come and has, as its highest expression, a deeply moral kind of life—the 'fruits of the Spirit'. When interpreting the Spirit, Paul speaks to his churches with the authority given him by the Spirit (1 Cor. 7:40); and it is not surprising to find him using prophetic-type formulae.[85] As for the future, the End is conceived in christological terms and thus suggests a goal towards which one strives as well as the completion of God's work of redemption for which one longs.[86] Yet there are indications in Paul of 'distancing'—as when he is wrestling with the problem of the salvation of the Jews (Rom. 9:11), and when he is dealing with exaggerated eschatological expectation at Thessalonica. Here, his concern is to use traditional eschatological symbols to give a longer perspective on the End-time and to insist that the Christians there should apply themselves to responsible living in the present.

In the Johannine literature, the eschatological perspective is no less operative, however subordinate it may seem at first sight. It is this literature which gives unforgettable expression to the Incarnation (John 1:14ff.), to the divine initiative of saving love (3:16), to responsive love (1 John 4:19), to eternal life and the Christ who has overcome the world. Here are themes or motifs of profound moral and ethical significance, which however is not developed to a great extent by the writers themselves. While in the Johannine literature there is 'the world' which God so loved, there is also the world in its alienation from God to which the writers have an antipathy. This antipathy combined with their sense of living in the last hour, turns them in upon themselves. As a modern writer puts it, 'Love seems almost like a huddling together for warmth and safety in the face of the world'.[87] Christ's 'commandment' is 'that you love one another as I have loved you' (John 15:12). Yet Johannine eschatology should not blind us to the value placed on community nor to the responsive element in this formula. Christ's love for them is both stimulus and model. Elsewhere, his 'commandments' (otherwise unspecified)[88] carry the same implications.

Finally, the epistle of James, which is probably best regarded as the product of Jewish Christianity, derives its ethical understanding primarily from the Law (Torah) interpreted from the standpoint of Christian belief in Jesus as Messiah: a belief which gives definitive expression to the Law in its

---

[84] C. F. D. Moule, *art. cit.*, p. 394.
[85] For example, 1 Cor. 3:17, 5:3ff., 14:38, 16:22.
[86] Cf. Phil. 2:9f., 3:12ff.; 1 Cor. 15:24–28; cf. Eph. 1:20–23.
[87] J. L. Houlden, *op. cit.*, p. 39.
[88] Cf. John 14:15, 21; 15:10.

fulness. Hence, the Christian's concern is with the Law in its perfect completion (*teleion:* 1:25), 'the Law of liberty', 'the royal Law' which sets the Christian, with scripture as guide, to love neighbour as self (2:8). Thus James strives to transcend both legalism and a narrow rule-deontology: the perfection of God's Law liberates man so that he can genuinely love his neighbour and follow out in his living that unity of faith and action which submission to God (4:7) as King entails. An eschatological perspective is still apparent: 'Be patient, brethren, until the coming of the Lord . . .' (5:7). Meanwhile, the emphasis on compassionate action which characterised Hebrew religion (cf. 'doing justly' and 'loving mercy') persists in the complete messianic version of the Law. 'Religion that is pure and undefiled before God is this: to visit orphans and widows in their affliction, and to keep oneself unstained from the world' (1:27).

So far, we have concentrated upon possible examples of rule-deontology in the New Testament. Is there any evidence of act-deontology in it? One might cite the prominence of prophets and prophetism in the early Church. Their ethical extemporism is reflected also in a variety of sectarian movements through the ages, from the Gnostics and the Montanists to the Anabaptists, certain charismatics and groups such as the Mormons today (in certain respects).[89] It is to be noted, however, that, while the early Christians wanted to respect the integrity of the true prophet, they recognised that prophetic claims had to be scrutinised (cf. 1 John 4:1).[90] As well as contributing to the edification of the community (cf. 1 Cor. 14), the prophet had to submit to the discipline of apostolic authority and conform to the Christian prophetic tradition. Above all, the quality of his life had to be consonant with the profession he made: a criterion which assumes a norm of Christian behaviour independent of individual prophetic intuitions. Act-deontology, therefore, can hardly be taken as a basic model of Christian ethics on the strength of the New Testament evidence.[91]

3. *Deontology and social teaching in the New Testament*

Social morality is a sphere that lends itself to rules-ethics. Man in society requires laws to govern his conduct; local communities require by-laws to regulate and protect local life and interests; clubs and groups have their regulations and constitutions, frequently in written and official form, and all members must respect them. Such laws, rules and regulations operate in

[89] For example in the weight put upon 'revelations'.

[90] Rom. 12:3; 1 John 4:2f., 20; Didache 11:3–12; Hermas *Mand.* 11:8; cf. D. Hill, 'On the Evidence for the Creative Role of Christian Prophets', New *Testament Studies* 20, 1973–74, pp. 262–70; J. D. G. Dunn, 'Prophetic "I"-Sayings and the Jesus Tradition: The Importance of Testing Prophetic Utterances within Early Christianity', *N.T.S.* 24, 1978, pp. 175–98.

[91] One is tempted to see it in the parable of the last judgement (Matt. 25:31–46); in the story of the rich young ruler (Mark 10:17–22); and in the parable of the two sons (Matt. 21:28–31); and in the anointing at Bethany, where the woman is said to have done a 'beautiful' thing (*kalos*): Mark 14:6. But it is doubtful if any of these are true examples of act-deontology. In each case an alternative classification or explanation is more likely.

accordance with, and share the characteristics of, rule-deontology, as described at the beginning of this chapter.

The early Christians formed communities—eschatological communities, the 'saints' called out of the world for service to their Lord. Their position is paradoxical, for they still live *in* the world. What kind of responsibility do they have for it? What is to be their response when it forces itself upon them—through work, the political system, mixed marriages and the like? The 'desert island' position is impossible to maintain consistently. As we have seen in relation to work and earning a living, Paul positively discouraged the Thessalonians from the attempt.

Sometimes, as in the Sermon on the Mount, community ethics takes the form of an eschatological 'ethics of perfection'. Elsewhere, while retaining the eschatological reference, community teaching is much more specific to particular problems. In the case of marriage, for instance, there is a tradition stemming from Jesus as to its indissolubility (cf. 1 Cor. 7:10f.; Mark 10:6–9; Matt. 19:5f.). This central principle, based on a Creation motif, is then qualified in the tradition by concessions to human weakness; in other words, a kind of casuistry is applied to it. This expands the tradition in a number of directions. Mark's version seems to be set in a Graeco-Roman milieu where the initiative in divorce can be taken by the woman. Matthew's account is typical of Christian scribalism in a Jewish milieu and connects with the debate between Rabbi Hillel and Rabbi Shammai (Matthew inclining to the latter on this issue). Paul, writing at an earlier stage in the formation of the tradition, uses a gnomic instructional form (1 Cor. 7:10f.; 11a is probably added comment) to summarise the general principle, and thereafter proceeds on a concessionary basis to deal with situations at Corinth which call for a severe modification of it—even in the eschatological crisis in which they are all involved (7:26). Presumably, this kind of casuistry is a process that could go on indefinitely as new situations arise. After the apostles, it would almost inevitably be attached to Church law; community ethics opens the door to rule-deontology. The great danger is that the whole of Christian ethics will be modelled in this way—as happened in the Catholic tradition, to the great impoverishment of the Christian ethical tradition.

The relation of the Christian to the State is an unavoidable subject for Christian social ethics. The Gospel tradition, 'render to Caesar what is Caesar's and to God what is God's', suggests a dual responsibility, though not a simple division of obligation. Viewed in the eschatological perspective which Jesus employed, God's demand is total—nothing is exempt from his sovereignty. Life in the world, however, carries its own obligations, so Caesar also has a demand that must be met. Romans 13 represents this position. All authority is from God (13:1); the ruler is 'God's servant for your good' (13:4); the Christian must therefore not resist the civil power but submit to it (13:1f., 5ff.). This 'ethic of submission', together with the concern to 'do what is good' (13:3), is the expression of love to one's neighbour, which sums up all the commandments (13:9f.). Similarly, in 1 Peter 2:13–17, the Christians are to be subject to the temporal authorities but nevertheless remain 'free men' and servants of God. Thus, not only the eschatology but the motivation of such civil obedience (whether love or service) transcends the kind of ethics which rule-deontology, in its narrow form at least, represents. Even in these conventional expressions of civil duty, the Christian's concurrence in civil matters is seen as springing from a higher loyalty. Would he therefore act in the same way if the demand made by the civil power were inconsistent with or opposed to that which was good and orderly—even more, if it were unloving and destructive of Christian freedom? The question is not raised explicitly here, but we know what the Christian answer was when persecution broke out. Why then is such a submissive line taken here? The answer is again situational. It represented conventional moral teaching; it related to life in a totalitarian empire; and it expressed the Christian's responsibility for supporting all forces working for order, for the 'good' or 'right' in society. It had a certain usefulness in indicating the general nature of the Christian's attitude to civil and political issues, including the payment of taxes, revenue, respect and honour (Rom. 13:7). And if such duties appeared unjust, compromising or demeaning, then the Christian was left to reflect on the transiency of the world, the nearness of the End (Rom. 13:11ff.), and the example of Christ's patience in suffering (1 Pet. 2:21ff.).

In relation to family life and the life of the household (including slaves), the pattern of conventional morality is again followed, though in a christianized form.[92] But can you legislate for family life and inter-personal relationships? Is it likely that any New Testament writer thought you could? Can you make rules about how a husband shall treat his wife? Rules may identify certain boundaries: e.g., how far a father may chastise his child. Clearly, this is not the main concern of the passages under review here. Rather, though the language of 'rules' is used—largely for the purposes of exhortation and perhaps also for basic moral education—much of this language of command is not in the form of rules in the strict sense. Thus 'Honour your father and mother', 'Do not provoke your children to anger', 'Husbands, love your wives' and 'treat your slaves justly and fairly' are none of them strictly rules, for they do not specify the behaviour that is being commended or prohibited. 'Guidelines' would be a better term than 'rules', though some of them are principles. Besides, the notion of Christian community undergirds this whole pattern of relationships and duties. Families and households were 'in Christ', extensions and expressions of the eschatological community (the community of the saints or the saved). The result of this was that Christianity, despite its eschatological orientation, served to reinforce the importance and quality of primary groupings in

---

[92] The *Haustafeln*, or 'household codes', include Rom. 13:1–7; Eph. 5:21f.; 6:1–9; Col. 3:18–4:1; 1 Pet. 2:13–25; 3:1–7; 1 Tim. 2:1f.; 5:1–16; 6:1f.; Tit. 2:4–10; also Didache 4:9ff.; Barnabas 19:7. While they follow prescriptive models in both Jewish and Graeco-Roman culture, these codes are 'christified' by such concepts as 'in Christ', 'pleasing the Lord' and 'for the Lord's sake'; cf. especially Eph. 5:21–33.

society.[93] This kind of teaching recognised that the structures of society were important and that Christians must come to terms with them.[94]

But in the end it is the limitations and inadequacies of this kind of social teaching which loom larger than its virtues. The personal realm of discourse, which alone can support a proper presentation of family and relational matters, is submerged in the general mass of exhortation and paraenesis. Where is the radical questioning of worldly values appropriate to those who 'turned the world upside down'? Where, amid all the exhortations to slaves to obey their masters, is there a hint that any one of them might be accepted 'no longer as a slave but a beloved brother'? Already one can almost hear Jerome lament that slaves are lazy and you can't get enough work out of them! Already one can envisage the 'German Christians',[95] and many others in different times and situations, quietly acquiescing in the separation of religion and politics when some vital issue was at stake—and claiming biblical warrant for doing so!

It was perhaps inevitable that, as time went on, the Church turned more and more to the procedures of rule-deontology. How else could they make concrete their sense of obligation to their neighbour and to their understanding of the Christian life in face of the ethical assumptions of the Jewish and Greek worlds, not to speak of the necessity to safeguard the faithful against the perils of antinomianism and paganism? Then there was the growing institutionalism of the Church itself and its developing authoritarian structures and canon law. At any rate, cultural factors played an important part in the progressive over-emphasis on rules, and by the second century the process was well advanced. The *Didache* has been described as 'practically devoid of any reference to grace received, or continuing experience of God',[96] while *Barnabas'* rules-ethics 'would have satisfied the most devout rabbi'.[97] In other words, later New Testament ethics, like the ethics of *Didache* and *Barnabas*, are increasingly time-conditioned.

Indeed, the misgivings we have expressed about this whole process underline an important feature of social ethics, *viz.*, its historical relativity.

---

[93] On primary groups see C. S. Cooley, *Social Organization*, 1909, p. 23; W. J. M. Sprott, *Human Groups*, 1958, pp. 15, 21.

[94] Cf. J. E. Crouch, *The Origin and Intention of the Colossian Haustafeln*, 1972.

[95] The term 'German Christians' is used to refer to those Church members in Germany who from 1933 to 1945 directly or indirectly supported Hitler's 'blood and soil' philosophy and his anti-Jewish policies and laws. It was coined to distinguish them from the members of the German Confessing Church who had formed their own Church because they were opposed to the Nazi philosophy, policies and laws.

[96] K. E. Kirk, *The Vision of God*, 1931, p. 135. Jean-Paul Audet took the Didache to be as early as A.D. 50–70: cf. *La Didaché: instruction des apôtres*, 1958. Most scholars, however, would opt for a more conservative date, about the end of the first century or early second.

[97] J. B. Lightfoot, *The Apostolic Fathers* I, vol. II, 1890, p. 503. Jewish models also influence the apostolic decree in Acts 15: cf. B. Gerhardsson, *Memory and Manuscript*, Eng. tr., 1961, pp. 245–61. But the historicity of the council at Jerusalem is problematic.

As G. Winter has put it succinctly,

'. . . social ethics is historically relative, dealing with issues which are appropriate to a time and situation, concerned with universal imperatives but as they bear on particular issues. This fact about social ethics makes the simple application of historical examples to contemporary problems relatively meaningless, even when those examples are drawn from holy texts'.[98]

It may be that the most we can expect in this area are general guidelines, or 'middle axioms' as J. C. Bennett has called them.[99] These are useful for moral education because they give a more concrete expression to the kind of direction which individuals and communities might take (e.g., 'deference but not subservience to the State, racial equity, sexual responsibility and economic justice').[100]

But it must be an equal priority to penetrate beyond this middle area to the creative heart of the gospel. Here neither rule nor principle will serve the purpose completely. Rather, we are brought into relation with God in covenant with his people: with his purpose in creation and redemption, and with the ground of our own being. We are brought into touch with the personal dynamic of the Gospel, which has to be translated, with the aid of the Spirit, into a living Christian way. Anything less is a reduction of the realm of meaning adumbrated, if not fully developed, in the New Testament itself.

Conclusions

It is possible to draw some conclusions even from this very brief review of some of the New Testament evidence.

(a) Obligation is not conveyed by means of a consistent or thoroughgoing deontology (whether rules-ethics or act-ethics). The sense of obligation is indeed high, and it seemed natural to New Testament writers to express it in the language of command. After all, one of their basic images for God is that of King. But this command is integral to the relationship in which they stood to God and Christ. It is part of the Master-disciple relationship, of the Father-child relationship. Viewed two-dimensionally, as it were, it presents the face of paradox. The command is to love; the disciples are told, 'You are my friends if you do whatever I command you'; Paul, who knows that salvation cannot be effected by law, obeys the 'law' of Christ. But careful attention must be paid to the *meaning* of this language of command, to the *context* in which it is used (e.g., the divine-human

---

[98] G. Winter (ed.), *Social Ethics*, 1968, p. 8.

[99] Cf. *Christian Ethics and Social Policy*, 1946; also 'Principles and the Context', in *Storm over Ethics*, 1967. The term 'middle axioms' first appeared in *The Church and its Function in Society*, W. A. Visser't Hooft and J. H. Oldham (edd.), 1937. The term was taken up by William Temple in his introduction to the Report of the Malvern Conference (*Malvern, 1941*, p. vii) and in the Church of Scotland Report 'The Interpretation of God's Will in our Time' (sometimes called the Baillie Commission).

[100] W. D. Davies, *art. cit.*, p. 47.

relationship), and to the *question of the over-all model* for Christian ethics which the N.T. prompts.[101]

(b) The over-all model for Christian ethics must not be simplified by a process of reduction. For example, it is tempting to take love (*agape*) as a principle, and the one central principle of Christian ethics at that, from which everything else derives. Some of Paul's statements may seem to encourage such treatment. But when placed in the context of Paul's whole procedure (or that of any other writer), the inadequacies are at once apparent. The problem of motivation is taken very seriously in the New Testament: that would require to be built in to the love-principle, as would the divine-human relationship, the concept of response and a whole variety of theological and soteriological motifs which are inextricably connected with Christian morality.

(c) Eschatology need not be regarded as a major stumbling-block, as if it consigned New Testament morality to the ancient history museum along with the 'three-decker universe'. Eschatology is constantly open to reinterpretation in the N.T. itself, and its relation to morality is also many-sided. It therefore can be reinterpreted by Christians today, and there is no justification for jettisoning eschatology like so much lumber (cf. Schweitzer's 'semi-Hegelian *tour de force*')[102] and reducing Christian ethics to 'respect for life' or some kind of humanistic principle (cf. H. Braun).[103] Eschatology is one of the motifs mentioned above that is integral to a fully developed model of Christian ethics.

(d) There can be no question of neglecting the importance of the situation. Human beings are in constant dialogue with the situation in which they find themselves, including their historical milieux. This fact, of course, underlines the weakness of rule-deontology: cultural factors have played a part in the shaping of supposedly absolute rules through the ages.[104] Indeed, such factors constitute one of the grounds of our claim that each new generation has to embark on its own quest for Christian ethics.[105] Nevertheless, as far as an adequate formulation of Christian ethics is concerned, Fletcher's position would appear to represent a serious oversimplification and reduction.

(e) Though we have not made much explicit reference to the Church context, all that we have said implies that Christian morality is related to the religious community. But what about our multi-faith society? Does Christian morality bear any relation to moralities based on other faiths?

---

[101] This whole question is discussed in later chapters, especially ch. 10.

[102] Cf. G. Lundström, *The Kingdom of God in the Teaching of Jesus*, Eng. tr., 1963, p. 76.

[103] H. Braun, 'The Problem of a New Testament Theology' in *Journal for Theology and Church* 1, 1965, pp. 169–83; also in T. J. J. Altizer (ed.), *Toward a New Christianity: Readings in the Death of God Theology*, 1967, pp. 201–15.

[104] Cf. Church rules on pacifism, abortion, contraception, divorce, gambling, abstention from alcohol. Some of these issues are discussed from the sociological point of view in R. Gill, *Theology and Social Structure*, 1978.

[105] See in particular ch. 10, where the quest for Christian ethics today is worked out in terms of contemporary technological society.

This is a question which cannot be ignored in our discussion.[106] And does it bear any relation to non-religious morality? There are some indications in the New Testament of such a relation: namely, the fact that moral teaching patterns are taken over by Christian teachers,[107] Paul's adumbration of natural law in Romans (e.g., 2:14f.), and appeals to the divine purpose in the created order (e.g., marriage). It will be important to map this relationship, to encourage dialogue with non-Christians and to find points of contact.[108]

(f) If anything is clear from our discussion, it is that Christian ethics involves a multiplicity of ethical procedures which serve in different ways and situations to express the Gospel in action. Among these procedures are, of course, rules and principles which have a contribution to make, e.g., to moral education and social ethics, if not in a wider sphere. But other procedures also have a place. We have noted in passing teleological ethics—the ethics of goal and consequences. How does this operate, and how far is it relevant to Christian ethics? It is now time to explore this dimension. We turn to it in the next chapter.

---

[106] Cf. our discussion of natural law in ch. 7 and of the new quest for Christian ethics in ch. 10.

[107] Cf. J. I. H. McDonald, *Kerygma and Didache*, 1980, pp. 69–100.

[108] See in particular ch. 7 below.

2

ARE CONSEQUENCES THE MEASURE?

A. TELEOLOGICAL THEORIES

'That action is best, which procures the greatest happiness for the greatest numbers'—Francis Hutcheson (1694–1746).[1]

Everyone is familiar enough in everyday life with the notion that actions have consequences and that such consequences can be serious or trivial. If grandmother or some other aged relative comes to reside, the effect on the family's way of life may be slight or immense, depending on how she fits in. If children play with their new lab kit in the garden hut, there may be a successful experiment or an explosion.

We are also familiar in everyday life with the fact that people judge actions, and apportion praise or blame, according to their consequences. Political policies are judged in terms of the likely or foreseeable consequences of their implementation. Will they contribute to cutting the rate of inflation or unemployment, or will they worsen the situation? Will they increase or lessen international tension? The progress of industry is determined by its ability to 'get results' in terms of production, exports, profits and so on. If an accident occurs—say, a serious fire, the collapse of a bridge or an explosion in a factory—an enquiry is set up to determine responsibility. Was someone's negligent action (of commission or omission) responsible in whole or in part, i.e., did someone fail to reckon properly with the likely consequences of his action, or might the accident be described, in the peculiar parlance of the insurance companies, as 'an act of God'? Again, when there is a disagreement about a course of action, someone may say 'Only time will tell which of us is right'. In this case, the actual consequences are taken as the criterion, although the dispute revolves round the difficulty of determining in advance precisely what these will be.

Here then is a fascinating, though problematic, set of ways in which moral decisions can be made. Everyday language is full of phrases such as 'Stop and think', 'Consider the consequences' 'What if everyone did that?'—which suggest that the criterion by which we test the rightness or wrongness of an action is whether it will promote or is likely to promote good or bad consequences. Such ethical theories—they are many and varied—may be conveniently termed teleological: i.e., they are concerned

---

[1] *Inquiry: Treatise II*, 'Concerning Moral Good and Evil'.

with the *telos*, the goal or consequences of action. Can they provide a viable alternative to rule-deontology, the limitations of which were noted in the previous chapter?

One major difference may be noted at the outset. In teleological theories, the good is treated as the primary concept in ethics, while the right is subordinated to it and defined as what is conducive to good. Rules, precepts and even secondary principles have to be justified, if at all, by reference to an end or ground outside themselves, to a first principle (i.e., the good that they promote or are likely to promote: e.g., the promotion of human happiness in the long run, the diminution of human suffering, or the production of human excellence in the widest sense). There is no such thing as intrinsic rightness or wrongness applied to actions: actions are right only in so far as they promote or are likely to promote the good. But there is such a thing as intrinsic goodness. Indeed, theories of this type differ over what they regard as intrinsically good—whether pleasure, happiness, welfare or excellence. But whatever they claim as good, that intrinsic good ought to be promoted. Our duty is always to act so as to promote the greatest possible intrinsic good.[2] The best known form of teleological ethics is utilitarianism, some discussion of which is now called for.

Utilitarianism is not only the most famous but perhaps the most important version of teleological ethics. It was largely the product of the eighteenth century[3] when it was the implicit assumption of thinkers and writers in various fields in Britain, France and Germany.

Utilitarians believed that they had found a new way of deciding moral questions, for they had eliminated the notion of intrinsic rightness and wrongness, and had substituted something quite new. They believed that they were attacking Christian ethics, as in their minds the notion of intrinsic rightness was integrally tied up with a Christian ethical position. For them, Christian ethics was identified with the view that right actions

[2] It is fairly common usage to say that hedonists have held that the good is pleasure, and that eudaemonists have claimed that it is happiness. The term 'utilitarian' is sometimes applied to those who hold that what is intrinsically good is 'the greatest good of the greatest number'. But there is no consensus as to the use of these three terms. The last is sometimes applied in a more narrow sense to those who hold that the greatest good is the greatest happiness (sometimes called 'hedonistic utilitarianism'): whereas 'ideal utilitarianism' is said to be the view that the good consists, not in happiness, but in certain 'ideal' goods which possess intrinsic value, such as knowledge, beauty, affectionate personal relations (e.g., G. E. Moore).

[3] Its precursor was John Locke (1631–1704). Sidgwick, himself a utilitarian, assumed that it began with Lord Shaftesbury (1671–1713) and Francis Hutcheson (1694–1746). The major 18th century figures are David Hume (1711–1776), Adam Smith (1723–1790) and Jeremy Bentham (1748–1832). To these must be added, of course, J. S. Mill (1806–1873) and Henry Sidgwick (1838–1900). Utilitarianism has had a notable revival in the period after the Second World War; cf. S. E. Toulmin, *An Examination of the Place of Reason in Ethics*, 1950, and J. J. C. Smart, 'An Outline of a System of Utilitarian Ethics', 1961 (a monograph), reprinted in a revised version in J. J. C. Smart and Bernard Williams, *Utilitarianism For and Against*, 1973. Other literature will be referred to later in the chapter.

were to be derived by a process of deductive or *a priori* reasoning[4] from the
Law of God, the law of Nature or the laws of God's kingdom. They
therefore attacked the notion that certain actions were wrong, simply
because they belonged to a specified class: e.g., fornication or adultery, as in
the Catholic tradition (followed in this regard largely by Lutheranism and
Calvinism),[5] or Sabbath-breaking, theatre-going and card-playing, as in
Puritanism.

John Locke, the precursor of the great utilitarians such as Bentham and
Mill, applied no *a priori* criterion, but the test of experience. Does a given
Act of Parliament promote the general happiness? Is it useful or beneficial
to people? Shall we see how it works in practice? We can detect the
influence of the scientific revolution on ethics. Science had shown a new
way of ethical thinking—in terms of consequences. If you go too near the
fire, the result is bad (you get burnt)—this is a scientific fact. Similarly,
adultery was condemned not as an intrinsically wrong act but in terms of
the eighteenth century principle of prudence: adultery tended to have
unhappy consequences—e.g., the wrath of a husband (or wife), or the pox.
But whether in science or in ethics, explanation was not in terms of
anything mysterious like God or an evil spirit. As there was no demon in
the fire, so no classes of actions were indelibly imprinted as right by the
Almighty or as wrong by the devil. Cards were not the devil's pictures, nor
sex Satan's playground.

Instead of a deductive or *a priori* criterion, an inductive test was being
applied, and thus there had begun the modern demand for inductive
evidence. Today in law-courts and in education, in the treatment of the
prisoner or in social work, what is asked for is evidence in the form of
statistics, reports, Royal Commissions, and surveys of every kind. Utilitarianism was a critique of any moral beliefs which were based merely on an
appeal to some traditional authority (e.g., Scripture or the Church) and not
on evidence. Likewise, it was a critique of *Christian* moral beliefs insofar as
they were justified simply on the ground of obedience to the will of God, or
by an appeal to the providential character of government.[6]

Of course, Locke was no atheist. His conception of utility had a divine
ground, for God had made an inseparable connection between virtue and
public happiness, so that what is for the public welfare is God's will. For
Locke, moral beliefs were still expressive of the claims and presence of the
Transcendent. But this type of theory was increasingly championed without
that divine ground for utility, and utilitarianism became a theory in its own
right. Ethics was asserting its independence of theology, as science had
begun to do when Laplace made his famous reply to Napoleon, 'I have no
need for that hypothesis'.

---

[4] *a priori:* 'Independent of all experience', applied to ideas that are claimed to have
no basis at all in experience.
[5] Cf. pp. 179f. for the legalistic strain in Lutheranism and Calvinism.
[6] E.g., 'the powers that be are ordained of God', Romans 13:1; cf. 1 Peter 2:13–14
and Titus 3:1.

Utilitarianism, then, parted company from any ethical theory that held that some actions were intrinsically wrong because they belonged to a specified class. Likewise, it criticised the moral beliefs of Christians insofar as they held that some actions were right in themselves or justified for their own sake (a form of rule-deontology). Retirement from the world and self-sacrifice were condemned unless they could be shown to promote the general happiness. David Hume anticipated the utilitarianism of Bentham and J. S. Mill in his famous attack on the monastic virtues.[7] Personal merit consisted, not in the mere possession of certain qualities, but in having those qualities that are *useful* or *agreeable* either to the person himself or to others.

'Celibacy, fasting, penance, mortification, self-denial, humility, silence, solitude, and the whole train of monkish virtues; for what reason are they everywhere rejected by men of sense, but because they serve to no manner of purpose; neither advance a man's fortune in the world, nor render him a more valuable member of society; neither qualify him for the entertainment of company, nor increase his power of self-enjoyment? . . . A gloomy, hair-brained enthusiast, after his death, may have a place in the calendar; but will scarcely ever be admitted, when alive, into intimacy and society, except by those who are as delirious and dismal as himself'.[8]

This rejection of 'the whole train of monkish virtues' is, according to Hume, the view of natural, unprejudiced reason. In the 18th century, many had little sense of divine transcendence and of the 'infinite qualitative difference between God and man', characteristic of a Kierkegaard or a Barth. Hume was every whit a child of his age when he regarded morality as simply a matter of commonsense and reason. Later, men were to realise that wars were not stopped by such appeals, and that peace was not achieved simply by approving a reasonable plan.

At any rate, utilitarianism is the opposite of an ethics of 'virtue for virtue's sake' or 'duty for duty's sake'. For utilitarianism, duty and virtue had to be justified at the bar of utility, i.e., 'usefulness' for an end, such as the general happiness.[9] On the other hand, there is no reason why an 'ideal utilitarianism' should not regard some or all of the monastic virtues—e.g., self-denial, humility, and heroism—as among the 'intrinsic goods' to be promoted by our actions, just as Moore was later to regard the contemplation of beauty as among the intrinsic goods to be cultivated. But no one in the eighteenth century ever thought of that possibility.

---

[7] Hume also anticipated Bentham and Mill by his constant and explicit use of the term 'utility': e.g., in *Treatise of Human Nature* 1740, Book 3 and in *An Enquiry concerning the Principles of Morals*, 1751. Hume did not pursue an *ethical* enquiry (and so cannot be strictly regarded as a utilitarian); he sought to explain how moral beliefs come to be held and function, not how they are to be justified.

[8] *An Enquiry concerning the Principles of Morals*, Section IX, Part I 219. (Second Edition of Selby-Bigge, p. 270).

[9] Bentham coined the phrase 'the greatest happiness of the greatest number', though others before him had had the same idea.

On this type of theory, what kind of consequences are to be considered in judging the rightness or wrongness of an action?

the actual consequences, or

the consequences that are likely to ensue or are reasonably to be expected, or

the intended consequences?

Are we to judge by the actual results? G. E. Moore was probably confused on this issue, but some things he wrote can be interpreted as meaning precisely that.

'All moral laws, I wish to show, are merely statements that certain kinds of action will have good effects . . . What I wish first to point out is that "right" does and can mean nothing but "cause of a good result", and is thus identical with "useful": whence it follows that the end always will justify the means, and that no action which is not justified by its results can be right'.[10]

However, actual consequences seem to be both an impossible and undesirable criterion. We can never know all the consequences of our actions *before* we act and often we shall never know them. Once we act, our action may have all sorts of unforeseen and unforeseeable effects on others which are quite unknown to us before we act and will remain so. The Greeks were more realistic with their proverb, 'Call no man happy until he is dead'. If actual consequences are to be the criterion, it is only of use at most to 'the subsequent critic of action',[11] though even he cannot know all the consequences. What the agent needs is some measure by which he can judge the rightness or wrongness of an action *before* he acts.[12]

Not only are actual consequences impossible as a criterion, they would

---

[10] G. E. Moore, *Principia Ethica*, p. 146. This quotation appears on the fly-leaf of Fletcher's *Situation Ethics;* the latter, who takes a teleological view of ethics, apparently approves of the view expressed by Moore. Cf. for example *M.R.*, pp. 21ff.

[11] Anthony Quinton, *Utilitarian Ethics*, 1973, p. 49.

[12] It is in this context that we can understand why this kind of ethics has been ambiguously called 'teleological'. Consequentialist theories of the ethical criterion are often distinguished from deontological ones in being called teleological. But in what sense a theory is teleological depends on whether we are looking *forwards* from the *proposed* action, or *backwards* from the *actual* consequences. In the former case, we may be thinking of the agent acting and directing his behaviour towards a *telos*, an aim or goal—i.e., to the consequences he either *intends* or considers *likely to result* from his action. Of course, his aim may be poor, like that of some marksmen: the score may be very different from what he intended or foresaw. Theories of this sort are teleological in the proper sense. In the latter case, we are looking back from the actual consequences to the behaviour that produced it or we may be deferring judgement till we see what the actual consequences are (e.g., 'Let's see how this act of Parliament works in practice before we say whether it was right to pass it in this form'). Either way we want to look back with hindsight before we pronounce on the rightness or wrongness of an action. Our measure here is not the *telos* to which the agent directed his action, but the actual consequences which his behaviour has brought about. If the actual consequences are to be the test, a theory is teleological in a second and different sense from the first: probably Moore's belongs to this second class.

be undesirable anyway, for they have nothing to do with the moral rightness or wrongness of an action.[13] In some contexts, we regard an action as wrong, even when the actual consequences are fortunate and not disastrous. For example, if a new vehicle goes out of control owing to a fault in design, but the resultant accident causes no injury, we do not for that reason congratulate the designers. If it be said that on the contrary we blame them because the result of their behaviour was that the car went out of control, and that the test is still the *actual* consequences, we are not convinced. We consider their conduct disreputable, not because of the actual results, but because they failed to take account of the likely consequences. We say, 'they ought to have known'.[14] This seems to be confirmed when we look at that kind of situation the other way on. In designing and building a bridge, the civil engineers may take every conceivable precaution and take into account all foreseeable factors. They calculate the maximum loads of heavy lorries on the bridge, when driven nose-to-tail the whole length of the bridge. They calculate the maximum wind-stresses, taking into account the winds in that region for as far back as records go, and adding a reasonable margin to the highest known winds for the area. If, after the bridge is built, it collapses owing to some quite unforeseeable factor—e.g., a freak hurricane for that part of the world causing the bursting of a huge dam several miles upstream—the actual results are indeed disastrous. But would we not consider the civil engineers who built the bridge free from blame despite the subsequent loss of life—*because they carefully considered beforehand every foreseeable and reasonably-to-be-expected consequence?* Wouldn't we say that they were just the victims of cruel fate? In deciding their responsibility, we do not look at the *actual* consequences, best or worst, disastrous or fortunate, but at the behaviour of the agent. When he doesn't take precautions, we call him thoughtless and careless, even if the outcome is happy. When he does, we call him (*sic*) 'very responsible', despite any stroke of ill luck there may be in the outcome.

It is, therefore, much more plausible to hold that the criterion is not the

---

[13] C. I. Lewis made a three-fold distinction: an action is *absolutely* right, if it has the best actual consequences; *objectively* right, if it is reasonable to expect that it will have the best consequences; and *subjectively* right, if its agent expects it to have the best consequences: *Values and Imperatives*, 1969, pp. 33–8, as alluded to by Anthony Quinton, *loc. cit.* To expect the best consequences is clearly not a sufficient criterion of rightness, because the agent often says 'I expected something different', even when he has not considered what it is reasonable to expect: subjective rightness is clearly not the central concept in making moral judgements. Actual consequences, on the other hand, as we have remarked, are no help to the agent in making a decision before action. Anthony Quinton (*loc. cit.*) is clearly right in suggesting that the central concept of these three is *objective* rightness.

[14] If it be replied that they could not possibly have known the effects of some new material used, or of some new unit installed in the car, then it would be replied that new materials and components should have been bench-tested, if not to destruction, at least with a considerable degree of greater stress and strain than a new vehicle would receive before its first service. We are back at the consideration of all likely or reasonably-to-be-expected consequences.

actual consequences, but the likely, foreseeable and reasonably-to-be-expected ones. What, however, about the intended consequences?

Intention is a slippery word, and we shall devote attention to it in the next chapter. Here we shall use it only in the sense of the consequences intended by the agent. There is an important difference for morality between accidental and intended consequences. Even the law of the land distinguishes murder, into which is built the notion of intention to kill, and an accidental killing, for which there is a reduced charge of manslaughter. This distinction is ancient and is found in many legal codes.[15]

Accidental consequences, however, have nothing to do with whether an action is right or wrong; but they are often used as an excuse when the consequences are harmful to people, and have not been properly thought out beforehand. Scissors are left on the sofa, and an elderly relative, not as alert as once she was, sits down and receives an injury. The apparatus in the gym is faultily erected or not removed after use. A workman leaves a floorboard up overnight. In these cases, the person responsible may say, 'I didn't mean it; it was only an accident'. At this point we have to judge whether the consequences were in fact accidental. A child receives a dog as a present and takes his part in training and looking after it. If the dog one day runs out of the house and is run over, we would probably say that was a genuine accident and accept the child's reaction that he 'didn't mean (intend) that to happen'. If, on the other hand, the dog had been neglected and untrained, then 'I didn't mean it' would be judged only an excuse for not taking into account what was reasonably to be expected. Intention can rest as often in what we choose to ignore as what we choose to achieve. The Jewish law was quite sure that people were not only responsible for the harm they had done, but were equally responsible for the harm they could have prevented.[16]

To sum up, consequences, if genuinely accidental, have nothing to do with whether behaviour is right or wrong in the moral sense. Intentions, however, seem to be one way of deciding the right and wrong of action. This means that we can hardly be morally praised for the good consequences which we did not intend, nor can be blamed for bad consequences which occur, if they were genuinely accidental, and not the result of carelessness or thoughtlessness.

It is time for us to glance at recent discussion which has classified versions of utilitarianism as follows: Act-Utilitarianism, General Utilitarianism and Rule-Utilitarianism. We shall look at each of these in turn, and make criticisms of each.

1. Act-Utilitarianism

According to this theory, one is to decide what is right or obligatory by

---

[15] Cf. e.g., *Exodus* 21:12–14; Numbers 35:10–11, 16–24; in these passages the distinction between deliberate or intentional killing and accidental killing is clearly drawn, and the penalty varies accordingly.

[16] Cf. Exodus 21:28–29; Deut. 22:8.

trying to see which of the actions open to one will or is likely to produce the greatest balance of good over evil.[17] It is consonant with any view of what is intrinsically good.

Moral rules in the form of generalisations, such as 'Truth-telling is *probably always* for the greatest good' or 'Promise-keeping is *generally* for the greatest good' may be useful as rule-of-thumb guides based on past experience, but they are not to be regarded as rules necessary for social living. The situation is always to be looked at in the light of the general principle, but such rules may sometimes have to be overridden. One is to ask, 'What effect will *my* doing *this* act in *this* situation have on the general balance of good over evil?', not 'What effect will *everyone's* doing this *kind* of act in this *kind* of situation have . . . ?'[18]

This was probably the view of Jeremy Bentham and G. E. Moore,[19] perhaps even of J. S. Mill, though of course this way of classifying utilitarian theories (into 'act', 'general' and 'rule' utilitarianism) had not been invented even in Moore's day. Today its outstanding protagonist is J. J. C. Smart.[20]

We shall mention two objections to act-utilitarianism, though there are others.

First, the theory seems cogent only where the action, being justified in terms of its good consequences, is itself right in terms of some moral principle. For example, a man is proved guilty in court of robbery with violence. It then seems plausible to hold that it is better for such a criminal to be restrained in prison than for the interest of many to be damaged by his going free in society. But is it right to send him to prison because of the good consequences to society of so doing, or because it is *unjust* that convicted criminals should go free? Suppose that the man is innocent of the crime for which he is charged, though the prosecuting counsel and the police are certain that he has committed other crimes of a like nature, though they have not the evidence to convict him of these. Would it be right to falsify the evidence so that he is found guilty of a crime which the prosecution know he did not commit? Would it be right because the interests of society would be protected in this way against a known criminal, though he is innocent of the crime of which he is charged? Such a procedure is surely to be rejected as unjust. It is not necessary to introduce the notion of an intrinsically wrong act, as Fr. McCabe does, in order to

---

[17] As expounded by Frankena in his *Ethics* (2 ed.), p. 35f. Cf. B. A. Brody (ed.), *Moral Rules in Particular Circumstances*, 1970, pp. 5ff.

[18] Frankena, *loc. cit.*

[19] G. E. Moore *Ethics*, p. 232.

[20] Cf. Smart's definition of act-utilitarianism in J. J. C. Smart & Bernard Williams, *Utilitarianism For and Against*, 1973, p. 4. Insofar as they are utilitarian, both act-agapism, according to which *agape* or love is the one intrinsic good, and situationism in its purest form are versions of A.U. Fletcher's version, however, is (as we have seen) ostensibly a considerably modified form of situationism, though the modified place given to rules in A.U. corresponds exactly to the status Fletcher sometimes gives them: see above Chapter One, pp. 19ff.

over-all consequences of the one act. The question is not, 'What will happen if *this act* is performed?' but 'What would happen if *everyone* did the *same*?'

General utilitarianism attempts to meet the moral convictions of ordinary people which seem to be outraged by act-utilitarianism's view of moral rules. For example, the consequences of my breaking my promise on this occasion may be more generally desirable than the results of keeping it, but the plain man is not convinced by act-utilitarianism's conclusion that it is right then to break the promise. He believes he should still keep the moral rule, unless it conflicts with another moral rule or principle. General utilitarianism tries to meet this difficulty by saying, 'Yes, if everyone were to break promises, the results would be generally undesirable'.

Despite this advantage of general utilitarianism over act-utilitarianism, the significance and application of the generalisation principle and its relation to the principle of consequences are matters of dispute. The usual objections concern the inherent difficulty of generalisation: 'everyone' and 'the same' ignore the differences of specific situations which may be crucial to deciding what is right or wrong.[26] For example, the poor man deliberating whether he should steal to feed his starving wife and family can say, 'But not everyone is without enough money to feed his wife and family. The results would not be so bad, if everyone precisely situated like me, in exactly or sufficiently similar circumstances, were to steal'.[27] The doctor contemplating exceeding the speed limit as he drives to an urgent case can similarly urge that his specific situation constitutes a proper exception to 'everyone'. Again, the owner of the orchard is a friend, but lives in another part of the country. We turn up unexpectedly to find him away for the day. If he had been at home, we know that he would have given us some apples, as he has done on previous occasions when we have seen him on our yearly visits. If we take some in his absence, and let him know when he returns, is this action to count as stealing? When is a practice not 'the same'? It is problematic whether the generalisation principle can cope with such differences in situations that threaten the force of 'the same'.

An act, it seems, cannot be divorced from its context. There are various factors, including friendship and family relationships, that come into a consideration of context. Are these merely sentimental irrelevancies, or do relationships of father to child, and friend to friend, for example, impose special duties and modify others?

Let us take the slogan, 'What if no one bothered to vote?' and illustrate two such further factors. Imagine a constituency where in past elections there has been a 70–80 per cent poll of electors. Jones is a Conservative in this predominantly Labour Constituency, where over several elections Labour has received over 70 per cent of the votes cast, and Conservatives have received less than 30 per cent of the votes cast. In these circumstances,

---

[26] The reader who desires to come abreast with this discussion is directed in the first instance to Sellars & Hospers, (edd.) *op. cit.*

[27] Cf. Frankena, *loc cit.*

'What if no one were to . . . ?' loses its force; and Jones's vote is not going to make any difference to the result, nor will his failure to vote! If the general utilitarian replies that we are considering the result of Jones's voting or failing to vote, instead of the consequences of *the general practice* of no one voting, then we shall say that he is missing the point. It is granted that if nobody were to vote, the consequences would be undesirable—i.e., the consequences of the general practice of not voting would be undesirable. But it is argued that *that* proposition does not entail that the results of *anyone's not voting* would be undesirable: the latter has to do, not with a general practice, but with particular actions.

Now for the second factor. If another constituent, Smith, remains at home to vote, he will not be able to travel to a distant town for an interview for a public appointment which, in view of his qualifications and experience, he may well get. Unfortunately Smith did not know of the appointment early enough to arrange a postal vote, and is rather surprised that such interviews should be held on polling day! Do the alleged desirable consequences of voting (e.g., the maintenance of our democratic institutions) really outweigh in this instance the desirable consequences of not-voting (e.g., people should make contributions to the common life according to qualifications, abilities and experience, and the contribution to the general welfare Smith can make in his new job if he gets it)? General utilitarianism does not seem to provide a criterion by which this issue can be settled.

To meet these difficulties, we may be led to a revised version of general utilitarianism, 'What would happen if everyone acted on the maxim or possible rule on which I am proposing to act now, namely, "that in my or sufficiently similar circumstances, everyone should do X"?'[28] But, as we shall see presently, this is one version of rule utilitarianism.[29]

This scrutiny of general utilitarianism suggests an important feature of moral decision-making. When one looks at the *data* of moral decision-making, i.e., at moral issues as they arise in life, the attempt to reduce decision-making to a single formula, whether a generalisation principle or anything else, seems futile and ill-conceived. Is not moral decision-making the result of taking account of a number of disparate factors that cannot neatly be reduced to one? We shall continue to propose this view from a number of angles throughout this book but especially in this and the following chapter.

3. Rule-Utilitarianism

We now come to a form of utilitarianism which, in the sophistication of its formulations at least, is certainly a product of the twentieth century,[30] though some have claimed to find it in past thinkers.[31]

---

[28] This version of G.U. sufficiently resembles Kant's categorical imperative ('Act as if the maxim of your action were to become through your will a universal law of nature') for it to be called a Kantian-type version.

[29] This is why in this country G.U. is commonly held to reduce to R.U. or to be better stated in R.U. terms.

(footnotes 30 and 31 on page 50)

The question that rule-utilitarianism tries to cope with is, 'How can some rules be justified within a utilitarian theory?' Act-utilitarianism cannot do so, and general utilitarianism either seems unsatisfactory or reduces to rule-utilitarianism—these are typical claims of adherents of 'rule-utilitarianism'.

Essential to any form of rule-utilitarianism are two distinct criteria, according to whether we are justifying an act or a moral rule.

First, we are to judge the rightness or wrongness of an *act*, not by its consequences, but by showing that it falls under some moral rule. This moral rule may be taken to be either an *actual rule* (such as, 'Don't tell lies') or a *possible rule* or maxim as in a Kantian-type theory.[32] We use a possible rule when we propose as the rule of our action that 'in our or sufficiently similar circumstances, everyone should act as we are acting now'. In that case, we judge the rightness or wrongness of an act by appealing to the principle of generalisation or universalisation, i.e., that everyone should act according to the rule I am proposing to act on now.

Secondly, we validate a moral *rule* by showing that the recognition of that rule promotes the ultimate end or first-order principle (whatever that is taken to be).[33] Thus actual rules (such as 'Always keep promises', 'Do no murder', 'Tell no lies') are justified when they promote the ultimate end. No rules are absolute, for they require validation in terms other than themselves: indeed, the theory acknowledges that social and legal rules need to be constantly revised and amended, so that they continue to serve

---

[30] In one form or another, its plausibility has been urged by J. D. Mabbott, 'Moral Rules' in *Proc. of the Brit. Academy*, vol. 39, 1953, pp. 97–118; Toulmin, *op. cit.*; R. F. Harrod, 'Utilitarianism Revised' in *Mind*, vol. 45, 1936, pp. 137–56 (who presents a Kantian-type R.U.); and J. O. Urmson, who has defined it in 'The Interpretation of the Moral Philosophy of J. S. Mill' reprinted from *Philosophical Quarterly*, vol. 3, 1953, pp. 33–39 in (ed.) Philippa Foot, *Theories of Ethics*, 1967. J. D. Mabbott has suggested some emendations to Urmson's formulation of R.U. in 'Interpretation of Mill's "Utilitarianism"' reprinted from *Philosophical Quarterly*, vol. 6, 1956, (ed.) P. Foot, *ibid*. Other adherents of R.U. are P. H. Nowell-Smith, *Ethics*, 1954, and John Rawls (who has since abandoned it), 'Two concepts of rules' in *Philosophical Review*, vol. 64, 1955, pp. 3–32, reprinted in (ed.) P. Foot, *ibid*. In his *A Theory of Justice*, 1972, Rawls rejected utilitarianism. R. B. Brandt does not advocate R.U. but believes it is more acceptable than any other type of utilitarianism: cf. his 'Towards a Credible Form of Utilitarianism' reprinted in (ed.) B. A. Brody, *op. cit.* No attempt can be made here to summarise the discussion of R.U., which can be highly technical.

[31] J. O. Urmson has argued that Mill was, on the whole, a R.U., while J. D. Mabbott claims that the gist of R.U. was in Francis Hutcheson.

[32] We have already given an example of a possible rule in our discussion above on general utilitarianism. J. J. C. Smart, an advocate of A.U., holds that there are two such versions of R.U.: cf. Smart and Williams, *op. cit.*, p. 9. It is not, of course, being suggested that Kant was a utilitarian, but that, on one possible interpretation of Kant, his use of maxim (=possible rule) is sufficiently like its use in this version of R.U., and that possible rule or maxim in the Kantian sense can be combined with utilitarianism. On the other hand, Stephen Toulmin's version of R.U. takes rule to be actual rule.

[33] So Urmson in P. Foot (ed.), *op. cit.*, p. 130.

the ultimate end. In the same way, possible rules or maxims can only be validated by appeal to the first order principle.

As we have indicated, the question with which rule-utilitarianism tries to cope is, 'How can some rules be justified?' Much of the discussion of rule-utilitarianism has been directed at a formulation which 'is not open to obvious and catastrophic criticisms'.[34] For example, if rule-utilitarianism tries to validate rules by holding that their fulfilment *generally* leads to the greatest good or the greatest balance of good over evil, this does allow for the exceptional breaking of the rule, but, on the other hand, seems to reduce to act-utilitarianism. Again, if rule-utilitarianism holds that the fulfilment of rules *always* leads to the greatest good etc., this is either factually incorrect or cannot be easily established. The formulation we have adopted[35]—*viz.*, 'we validate a moral rule by showing that *the recognition* of that rule promotes the ultimate end'—avoids these difficulties and permits rule-utilitarianism to cope with the exceptional breaking of a rule.

But there is an important criticism which rule-utilitarianism shares with all other utilitarian theories and with which our formulation fails to cope. If of two actions (act-utilitarianism), rules or practices (rule and general utilitarianism), each produced the same balance of good over evil, but one produced a more equal distribution for a greater number, while the other produced a less equitable distribution for a smaller number, how do you choose between them? Most people would probably hold that the former is more desirable, but if so, they are appealing to a non-utilitarian first principle, *viz.*, a concept of justice.[36] The first-order principle in utilitarian terms is not sufficient.

Finally, even if we accept rule-utilitarianism as a plausible theory for the justification of rules in social morality,[37] is it equally plausible for personal morality? Here it must fall back on act-utilitarianism and is subject to a number of difficulties shared by all teleological forms of ethics, to some of which we now turn.

General criticism of utilitarian theories

First, utilitarianism seems to deny our convictions about the priority of justice. For such reasons, John Rawls rejected utilitarianism in his massive work, *A Theory of Justice*. According to common-sense convictions, 'we give a certain priority, if not absolute weight'[38] to the claims of liberty and natural right.

'Each member of society is thought to have an inviolability founded on

---

[34] R. B. Brandt, *op. cit.*, p. 145.

[35] From Brandt, *op. cit.*, p. 161; there and in the preceding section he argues for the removal of any possible ambiguity in Urmson's formulation, making it clear that a viable form of R.U. must speak of something like '*recognition of* a rule having the best consequences', instead of 'conformity *with* a certain rule having the best consequences'.

[36] Cf. Frankena, *op. cit.*, pp. 41ff.

[37] Cf. D. M. Emmet, *Rules, Roles and Relations*, pp. 84ff.

[38] John Rawls, *op. cit.*, p. 28.

justice or, as some say, on material right, which even the welfare of
every one else cannot override. Justice denies that the loss of freedom for
some is made right by a greater good shared by others'.[39]
His explicit aim is to work out a theory of justice that represents an
alternative to utilitarian thought generally, and so to all its various
versions.[40] Whether or not we accept the theory of justice he carefully works
out in this work, we cannot but be impressed by the reasons which
prompted him to work out a doctrine which 'accepts our convictions about
the priority of justice as on the whole sound' and which is therefore different
from utilitarianism which 'seeks to account for them as a socially useful
illusion'.[41]

The second difficulty of all teleological ethics is a dilemma. Either there
is more than one end or principle, and there is a conflict between such
ends or principles, without any means of resolving it; or there is one end to
which all other ends or principles are subordinate. But in the latter case, if
such an end or principle is to be sufficiently general to hold in all situations,
then it will tend to be too vaguely conceived or stated for the means-to-end
calculation to be plausible. This is the weakness of all candidates for the
role of the good—the general happiness, welfare, beatitude, the glory of
God. If the moral norm is indeed one teleological principle—and it is this
which makes right acts right, etc.—it gives little help to the individual in his
decision-making.[42]

Conclusions

As we have seen, it is generally agreed that the two basic concepts of ethics
are those of the right and the good. Other concepts (e.g., that of the
virtuous, or morally good, person) are treated, rightly or wrongly, as
derivative from these.[43] In teleological theories, the good is defined independently of the right, and then the right is defined as that which maximises
the good. For them all, the good is the basic concept, but they differ in how
the concept of the good is specified. That is, they differ in their normative
theory of value (e.g., hedonism, eudaemonism, etc.). Grouping them
together, as we have done here, enables us to draw attention to the basic
question that must be settled in order to determine whether we shall accept
teleological ethics in any form or not, viz., 'Is right action always that which
maximises the good (however that good is specified)?'

In deontological theories, on the other hand, the two concepts of the

---

[39] Loc. cit. Cf. pp. 3–4.

[40] Ibid., p. 22. Cf. pp. 22–3, 183–92.

[41] Ibid., p. 28.

[42] Cf. the criticism heard when Church leaders make public pronouncements, viz.,
that such statements are too general to give any guidance.

[43] The utilitarian will judge character-traits as desirable if they are likely to produce
right acts: e.g., a person of a benevolent disposition is more likely to perform
deeds that promote the welfare of others, than a person who is indifferent, icily
cold, self-regarding or hateful. The virtues are treated, on such a view, as
desirable instrumentally, not intrinsically. Cf. J. Hospers, Human Conduct, 1970,
p. 220.

right and the good are related in exactly the opposite way. The right is taken to be the primary concept, and the good is related to the right as that which is produced by doing right actions. A deontological theory is characterised in one or both of two ways: either it does not specify the good independently of the right, or it does not interpret the right as maximising the good, or it makes both of these denials.

'It should be noted that deontological theories are defined as non-teleological ones, not as views that characterise the rightness of institutions and acts independently from their consequences. All ethical doctrines worth our attention take consequences into account in judging rightness. One which did not would simply be irrational, crazy'.[44]

How then are we to decide between teleology and deontology? We can now see that the main issue in this chapter is not whether consequences are to be taken into account in judging whether an act is right, but whether consequences in some sense of that term constitute the ethical norm—e.g., whether the end *always* justifies the means, and whether the end constitutes the only or the final court of appeal in matters of rightness and wrongness. If we believe that moral judgements have to be made about means (e.g., actions), independently of ends (i.e., consequences produced, likely to be produced or intended), we shall have to reject teleological ethics, though not refusing to take account of consequences in some contexts.

The issue is between those who believe in some moral principle or principles (e.g., justice) independent of utility and those who believe in the principle of simply maximising the good. If it be alleged that utilitarianism does have a concept of justice, viz., 'everyone is to count as one, and not more than one', the deontologist will reply that this principle can be interpreted as meaning that a minority has no rights against a majority and even that an individual has no rights against the state: in other words, such arithmetical or quantitative concepts of justice are not enough.

Further, when a means is morally condemned, it is condemned, not because it is a means, but because it is wrong. When we condemn an action on moral grounds, the question of whether it is a splendid, foolish, inept or poor means to the chosen end is irrelevant or nearly so: the qualification is required in view of the place given to prudence, but those who choose unwisely a technically 'wrong' means to a good end are not morally condemned as are those who choose an evil means to an end, good or bad. The action is morally condemned in terms, not of the end, but of a moral principle.

Teleology, indeed, is of doubtful ethical significance. People, of course, do set themselves goals of various sorts, some of them understandable, others strange and odd—to get to the top, to be successful in business, to meet a T.V. personality, to climb Everest, to sail single-handed across the Atlantic, to eat more sausages than anyone else at a sitting. But these goals are not in themselves morally good. They are regarded (at least by the people concerned) as desirable or valuable, and at most they are 'good' or

---

[44] John Rawls, *ibid.*, p. 30.

'bad' in the general value-sense, not in the specific sense of the morally good. We have, however, to bear in mind that many states of affairs that are morally bad are regarded by some as ends to be pursued (e.g., the 'final solution' of Hitler to the 'Jewish problem', the removal of the moral agent's freedom to choose by various schemes of conditioning as in Soviet Russia, Franco's Spain, etc.). Even those goals that are generally considered in the liberal West as good—e.g., knowledge or truth, health, material welfare, beauty, quality of life—we do not call *morally* good, though the pursuit of them may be so called. On the other hand, good goals can be treated as ends to be pursued, but it cannot be said that we *ought to* pursue them because they are ends but because they are good (at least in the general value-sense). Thus the ethical significance of teleology is problematic.

There is another point. While it has been convenient in this chapter— e.g., in outlining A.U., G.U. and R.U.—to speak of the right being conducive to good, however the good is specified, such discussion may suggest that 'the good' has an existence of its own, like one of Plato's forms, instead of being a quality we predicate of actual occurrences and states of affairs over a period of time. To call God good is to use an analogue that has its basis in such experience, though Christians may refuse to cash it in totally experiential terms, maintaining that the divine goodness is similar to, but different from, the best of human goodness. At any rate, we must beware lest the use of 'the good' suggests that we have a knowledge of the good without any reference to experience. We cannot pronounce that something is good till we know what it is!

Of what, then, do we predicate 'goodness' in the moral sense? A full answer and our final appraisal of teleology must await the next chapter. But we may raise the curtain a little. Good houses, play-areas, theatres, opera-houses, sports-centres, health-clinics—indeed all states of affairs—are not morally good. If their pursuit is regarded as morally good, is it not because such 'goods' are *for people*, and justifiable in terms of a moral principle such as justice, or a 'quality of life' which refers not to material affluence as such, but to the kind of life that ought to be desired by and for persons? Primarily, we predicate moral goodness of the agent's dispositions, including his motives—e.g., the disposition of doing our duty because it is our duty and not for some ulterior motive; the disposition of treating people sometimes as ends in themselves, as persons in their own right, and not always as mere means to our interests. Of course, we cannot avoid treating people as means, for we do it all the time in quite innocent ways: as you read this book, you are using its authors; at school and university, pupils and students use their teachers: when you are ill, you use the doctor as a means to getting well. Then derivatively, we apply the term 'morally good' to the agent himself, i.e., to his character as possessing these dispositions: he is pronounced a good man because he possesses such a character.

All this suggests that rightness is not in the calculation of means to end (however valuable the ends), for that is a technical matter, but somehow in the behaviour of the agent. Indeed, to look in the direction of likely, foreseeable, reasonably-to-be-expected and intended consequences for a criterion of rightness, rather than in that of actual consequences, is to justify behaviour, to distribute moral praise and blame, not so much in terms of its goals or ends, as in terms of how the agent behaves before and in acting. 'When he doesn't take precautions, we call him thoughtless and careless, even if the outcome is happy. When he does, we call him (sic) "very responsible", despite any stroke of ill-luck there may be in the outcome'.[45] So we wrote earlier in this chapter.

Teleology fails to provide a knock-down formula by which all our moral dilemmas will be solved. W. D. Ross made the complaint against utilitarians that they

> 'took too narrow a view of persons in that they regarded them simply as receptacles into which as much good as possible was to be poured, and did not do justice to the numerous personal relations which hold between men: as debtor to creditor, child to parent, etc'.[46]

Related to this is the criticism that in a serious moral dilemma it is not a question simply of maximising the good but of achieving whatever balance of values can be promoted in the situation. However, this balance may be taken as an example of justice in one of its senses, which can then be considered the end to be achieved.

B. IS NEW TESTAMENT MORAL TEACHING TELEOLOGICAL?

In this section we ask whether the norm for Christian behaviour is solely one of consequences. Shall we go for a form of Christian utilitarianism? Is Christian ethics teleological, i.e., does it treat the good as the primary concept, and rightness as maximising the good? A teleological ethics can be held to be implied in the Shorter Catechism, 'the chief end of man is to glorify God and enjoy him for ever', and in the Lord's Prayer, 'Thy will be done, on earth as in heaven'. Thomas Aquinas's position is an important example of Christian teleological ethics, where human behaviour that is moral is directed towards 'the ultimate end of man' conceived as the beatific vision of God in heaven.[47] Christians, therefore, need not be prejudiced against teleological ethics simply because its various forms champion (as not all do) values to which they cannot comfortably subscribe, such as worldly success, 'it's right because it works in practice' (pragmatism), or even the greater good of society. But does it follow that Christian ethics requires to take a teleological shape? This is the main question with which we are concerned here. We must not expect, however, to find in the Christian scriptures the finer distinctions (e.g., between Act-, General-, and Rule-Utilitarianism), for their writers simply did not

---

[45] Cf. above p. 43.

[46] A. C. Ewing, 'Recent Developments in British Ethical Thought', in C. A. Mace (ed.), *British Philosophy in the Mid-Century: A Cambridge Symposium*, 1957, 1966 (2), p. 73, where Ewing refers to W. D. Ross's complaint.

[47] See chapter 7 below where we discuss Aquinas's ethics.

engage in that kind of ethical analysis. Why, then, you may say, introduce them at all? If we are to favour and therefore construct a Christian form of teleological ethics for today, we shall be faced with the questions, 'How are rules justified, if at all?' and 'Is Christian morality only an individualistic one, or can there be a Christian social ethics, where rules and an earthing of principles in social structures and institutions seem to be a prerequisite?' In that case, we shall have to choose between these forms of utilitarianism, invent a new form of our own, or adopt another theory.

1. *Utilitarianism in the New Testament*

As we have already seen,[48] one of the distinctive features of Fletcher's situation ethics is the teleological shape he gives to it. He holds that what is right or one's duty in a situation is to be decided by doing that action which will produce the greater balance of good over evil in that situation. In other words, we are to look at the consequences that will accrue from our action for human welfare. He quotes Kenneth Kirk, sometime Bishop of Oxford:

> 'Every man must decide for himself according to his own estimate of conditions and consequences; and no one can decide for him or impugn the decisions to which he comes. Perhaps this is the end of the matter after all'.

Then Fletcher adds: 'This is precisely what this book' (*Situation Ethics*) 'is intended to show'.[49]

That good is to be defined or described in terms of human welfare comes out clearly in the following passage:

> 'What, then, is good? Asking this question drives home the basic fact that . . . situationism is a moral strategy or procedural doctrine that has to be seen in tandem or partnership with a substantive companion doctrine—personalism. And 'personalism' here means the ethical view that the highest good, the summum bonum or first-order value, is human welfare and happiness (but not, necessarily, pleasure). Good is, first and foremost, the good of *people*. Christians call it "love", meaning neighbour-concern or *agape* . . . The great commandment orders Christians to love, i.e., to seek the well-being of people—not to love principles'.[50]

The position here advocated is clearly a form of Christian utilitarianism, and we have already seen (in the last chapter) that he calls his position 'modified rule-agapism' or 'modified or summary rule-utilitarianism'.[51] Fletcher quotes William James with approval: 'There is but one unconditional commandment, which is that we should seek incessantly, with fear and trembling, so to vote and to act as to bring about the very largest total universe of good we can see'.[52] The calculation of means to ends, characteristic of utilitarianism, is here brought out.

[48] Cf. above, p. 20, and the whole discussion on pp. 19ff.

[49] *S.E.*, p. 37.

[50] *M.R.*, pp. 33–4. But in the same pages Fletcher seems to get an ethic of consequences and one of motive confused. For a discussion of *agape*, see below pp. 57–60; also chapter 3, pp. 82–6 and chapter 9.

[51] See above, p. 20.

[52] *S.E. Debate*, Essay by Fletcher, 'Reflection and Reply', p. 260.

Indeed, Fletcher makes an outright admission that *agape* is utility or the general well-being in an essay written about the same time as the one just quoted:

'Frankena has complained that theologians avoid the question whether there is any real difference between agapism and utilitarianism. . . Perhaps, then, this is the time and place to confess that up to now I too have avoided the issue. I have avoided it, in effect, by saying that we ought to unite in a coalition the Christian norm of love or *agape* with the utilitarian "procedural principle" of general utility. In this gambit I have taken the procedure to be one of seeking the greatest amount of the "good" possible for the greatest number of neighbours possible, and the standard of the "good" to be *agape* or loving concern for the neighbour—as judged by one's understanding of situations and human needs. But we can now cut through this issue clearly: I am ready to turn the coalition into an organic union. Let's say plainly that *agape* is utility; love is well-being; the Christian who does not individualise or sentimentalise love is a utilitarian'.[53]

He sums it up by agreeing with Frankena that 'where theologians talk about love, philosophers talk about beneficence or general utility'[54] and that 'the difference between the Christian and most utilitarians is only the language used' and their different answers to the question, 'Why be concerned, why care?'[55] (This last difference, however, is not one that Fletcher often develops.)

Fletcher, then, espouses a form of Christian utilitarianism. The Christian decides what is the right thing to do by asking what action best promotes *agape* in this situation. The right thing to do may not be what first occurs to one, e.g., giving money to the poor: the situationist has to think it out carefully, and

'if help to an indigent only pauperises and degrades him, the situationist refuses a handout and finds some other way'.[56]

But the 'good' end is all that matters, whatever be the means.

'Once we realise that only love is intrinsically good, and that no action apart from its foreseeable consequences has any ethical meaning at all—only then will we see that the proper question is, "Does an evil means always nullify a good end?" And the answer . . . must be "No"'.[57]

Fletcher's version of 'ideal utilitarianism' is not the only possible shape of Christian teleological ethics. It is a form of agapism, but some Christians who adopt a version of agapism would reject utilitarianism, though Fletcher accepts both.

[53] (edd.) G. H. Outka and P. Ramsey, *Norm and Context in Christian Ethics*, 1969, in an essay by Fletcher 'What's in a Rule?: A Situationist's View', p. 332.

[54] W. K. Frankena, 'Love and Principle in Christian Ethics', in *Faith and Philosophy*, (ed.) A. Plantinga, 1964, quoted by Fletcher in the essay 'What's in a Rule?: etc.' cited in previous footnote. Cf. Frankena, *Ethics* (2), pp. 56ff.

[55] *Norm and Context, loc. cit.*

[56] *S.E.*, p. 26.

[57] *M.R.*, p. 22–3. Cf. an essay by Fletcher in reply to Fr. McCabe in (ed.) R. L. Cunningham, *Situationism and the New Morality*, p. 82. Some of our criticisms of Fletcher's position were implicit in section A.

Pure agapism is the view that the sole principle for deciding questions of right and wrong, duty and ought, goodness or moral value, is love in the Christian sense, for which there is no term but *agape*, and that all other principles, values, commitments and rules are either simply expressions of *agape* or (if not) are to be discarded: e.g., no other moral principle such as justice is independent of *agape*. It should be noted that agapism is not a mere procedural doctrine, but is a normative theory of ethics. Again, Fletcher's Situation Ethics is only one of various forms that pure agapism can take.

Pure *act-agapism*[58] is the view that in deciding what is right or our duty, we are to get clear about the situation and discover (without the use of principles, values, commitments or rules other than love) what is the loving or most loving *act* we can do in that situation. There is only one basic moral valuation, *viz.*, love, which has to be expressed or promoted in every situation; and in deciding what is right or our duty in a particular situation (indeed, in *any* situation), we are not to take account of other similar situations, or generalisations drawn from them, i.e., the principles of generalisation or universalisation are not to apply. This is 'situational' ethics in its purest form, but the term suggests that in making moral judgements *only* the situation is to be taken into account and that moral principles are irrelevant. But this is simply not true. All forms of pure agapism take both principle and context or situation into account. This misunderstanding has led to a debate as to the rival claims of context and principle, and, as James M. Gustafson pointed out in an essay now rightly famous, this is a misplaced debate in Christian ethics.[59]

Pure *rule-agapism* is the view that, in deciding what we ought to do, we are not to ask, 'What *act* is most loving (or will most promote love) in this situation?' but 'What *rules* best or most fully embody or promote love?' and then follow these rules in particular situations, according to which rule applies. Conflict of rules will mean appealing to the ultimate principle, *viz.*, love, and proceeding in these cases as a pure act-agapist.

Both these positions may be modified in various ways (e.g., modified or summary rule act-agapism, and modified rule-agapism), and both Fletcher's and Paul Ramsey's positions are different modifications, though it is often difficult to see where they differ except in mood and style, the one sounding very radical and progressive, the other rather conservative and 'fuddy-duddy'. But such modifications of pure act-agapism and pure rule-agapism are to be distinguished from another form of agapism, *viz.*, 'mixed agapism'—so-called because it is not a form (as the above are) of pure agapism.

Mixed agapism is the view that love is *one* of the principles or valuations of Christian morality but not the only *basic* one. It will not do simply to say,

---

[58] The terminology here used to distinguish forms of pure agapism was first used by Frankena on the analogy of act-utilitarianism and rule-utilitarianism etc. Cf. Paul Ramsey, *Deeds and Rules in Christian Ethics*, pp. 93ff.

[59] 'Context Versus Principles: A Misplaced Debate in Christian Ethics' *The New Theology* No. 3, edd. M. E. Marty and D. G. Peerman, 1966, pp. 69–102.

'not the only one', for even act-agapism can give a place to other principles, valuations, commitments and rules, provided they are not independent of, but are merely expressions of, love. Mixed agapism is the view, then, that there are basic principles other than love, and that moral judgements have to take account of these as well as love. Frankena cites C. H. Dodd's *Gospel and Law* as an example of this type of theory; and Paul Ramsey wonders if W. D. Davies' work on the Sermon on the Mount does not preclude act-agapism as a viable theory in Christian ethics, but he is uncertain whether it supports pure rule-agapism or mixed agapism.[60] Theories of divine law, as well as 'Christian natural law' and 'orders of creation' (or 'mandates') are examples of mixed agapism, since they hold that 'laws', principles or precepts that are not derived from love are binding on the Christian.

Is agapism necessarily teleological? If agapism is conceived as utilitarian and therefore teleological, then the view is that in our moral decision-making we should seek the good as our end, the good being defined or at least described as love or *agape*. But other views are possible. Paul Ramsey suggests that agapism should be treated as a special form of deontology, where love is not the good to be promoted or brought about *by* the actions we do, but rather is 'what is right, righteous, obligatory to be done among men'[61] *in* the actions themselves: in other words, love is more analogous to rightness than to goodness.

The conflict of ethical interpretation undoubtedly reflects the richness and many sidedness of the concept of *agape itself*. The thirteenth chapter of 1 Corinthians, containing as it does the definitive description of *agape* in the New Testament, clearly suggests that *agape* is, if not the sole, then at least the only completely permanent principle, quality or value (cf. 1 Cor. 13:13), and therefore it is presumably pre-eminent among values. Equally clearly, gospels and epistles alike present *agape* in the context of commandment, even if a commandment of a very special kind.[62] When Paul writes 'make love your aim . . .' (1 Cor. 14:1), he is employing a teleological perspective, which he maintains in his insistence on upbuilding and edifying the congregation: spiritual gifts should be deployed to that end. When he appeals for genuine love (e.g., Rom. 12:9), he would appear to be thinking of *agape* as a powerful motivating force that will build up community, promote good relationships with others, and enable one to bless one's persecutors, to act with forgiveness rather than vengeance, and to overcome evil with good.

If these dimensions by themselves exceed those which make up the more usual or conventional theories of agapism, it must be pointed out that only one side of the N.T. view of *agape* has yet been indicated! *Agape* is not merely a moral principle: indeed to describe it as a principle is inappropriate. It belongs to a living, relational realm of discourse: it has to do with a

---

[60] *Op. cit.*, p. 106.
[61] *Op. cit.*, p. 97.
[62] Cf. Matt. 22:34–39; Mk. 12:28–31; Luke 10:25–28; Rom. 13:9; Gal. 5:14; James 2:8; John 13:34, 15:17; 1 John 2:7–11. The problem of whether love can be commanded (literally) is discussed below, pp. 82–86.

particular kind of response and with the quality that evokes that response. 'We love', writes the author of 1 John, 'because he first loved us' (1 John 4:19). *Agape*, in the particular sense of Christian love, is awakened in man when he encounters and responds to the total self-giving of God in Christ that becomes definitive of *agape*. 'In this is love, not that we loved God but that he loved us and sent his Son to be the expiation of our sins' (1 John 4:10; cf. John 15:13). Leaving aside the language of atonement, we find here the notion of *agape* as having its source in God (1 John 4:7f.), as encountering man in Christ (cf. John 3:16) and as characterising the human response to the divine initiative and approach (1 John 4:11; John 15:14, 17). This response of *agape*, however, constitutes not only a kind of love-mysticism ('God is love, and he who abides in love abides in God, and God abides in him'—1 John 4:16) but simultaneously and necessarily the expression of love in practical ways to one's fellow men. If we love one another, John says, God abides in us (1 John 4:12). Anyone who professes to love God and who hates his brother at the same time, invalidates his profession on that score (4:20). The Lord's command is that he who loves God should love his brother also (4:21).

All this may doubtless be termed poetic, but it is not therefore mere sentimentality. On the contrary, such language expresses a moral claim to translate faith into action. Further, the richness of its relational concepts and the variety of its ethical perspectives contrast sharply with the aridity and limitations of the debate about agapism. If agapism is to have any claim to represent a normative position in Christian ethics, it must both diversify its approach and find a way of expressing the ultimate or metaphysical roots of *agape* portrayed with such simplicity and economy in the New Testament. Otherwise, agapism completely fails to do justice to the connection between Christian faith and conduct.

2. *Teleology in the New Testament*

The main question which commands the interest of Christian ethicists is not what kind of theory agapism is but whether Christian ethics can best be described as teleological. Some New Testament material points in this direction.

To help resolve the difficult question of meat offered to idols, Paul uses the 'weaker brother' argument (1 Cor. 8). His contention is that mere knowledge of the irrelevance of idols to the Christian is not an adequate basis for action. The 'stronger brother' may know that for the Christian there is only one God and therefore idols are 'nothing', but if he eats the food, he may offend the conscience or sensitivities of the 'weaker brother', i.e., the Christian who has not reached the stage of maturity of the 'stronger brother'. This may be to the spiritual detriment of the 'weaker brother'. In other words, to neglect the foreseeable consequences of one's action for one's brother is to sin against him, and to sin against him is to sin against Christ (1 Cor. 8:12). 'Knowledge' produces an attitude of arrogance which excludes concern for others, while 'love' leads to spiritual maturity, communion with God (8:3) and concern for other people (8:9).

What is interesting in this passage is that for Paul the inadequacy of knowledge-motivation as a criterion is demonstrated by the ethical consequences of acting out of knowledge alone and not out of love.[63] The corollary is that love-motivation is superior—and is judged superior in terms of the ethical consequences of 'acting out of love'. For Paul obviously *agape* is not a *purely* motivational term: when we act out of love *as a motive*, we do consider *the consequences*.

In 1 Cor. 10:23–24 and 6:12, the principle that 'all things are lawful, but not all things are helpful' operates in terms of consequences: 'let no one seek his own good, but the good of his neighbour'; 'all things are lawful' he repeats, 'but not all things build up', i.e., not everything promotes spiritual maturity. Paul's concern for the 'weaker brother" is of a piece with his concern for the edification of the Church. In Romans 14:1–4 and 15:1–3, he stresses the need to accept the man who has scruples (about what he eats), 'for God has accepted him'(14:3); and 'each of us must. . .think what is for his neighbour's good and will build up the common life'.

A similar concern for consequences runs through his discussion of spiritual gifts in chapters 12 and 14 of 1 Corinthians (between which the hymn of love is strategically placed). Although it is good to 'earnestly desire the higher gifts' (like prophesying, teaching, healing, working miracles . . .), the more excellent way is to recognise love (*agape*) as the greatest gift of all and to 'make love your aim' (14:1). This exhortation suggests that Paul thinks of *agape* not simply as a motive but as something to be aimed at—in other words, a *telos*. Consequences of actions are therefore much in his mind. Prophecy is elevated above speaking in tongues (*glossolalia*) on the ground of the consequences of each: 'he who speaks in a tongue edifies himself, but he who prophesies (expounds the gospel) edifies the church' (14:4).[64] Individual inspiration has to serve for the benefit of the community (14:13–16). Throughout this argument, there is a strong utilitarian ring: 'how shall I benefit you . . .?' (14:6) and 'let all things be done for edification' (14:26). In 1 Cor. 9:1–23, his action in renouncing certain rights that he could legitimately claim (3–7) is 'for the sake of the gospel'. He imposes certain limits on his Christian freedom to the extent of being the slave of all in order to make more converts than other men (19). His goal is clearly regulative of his conduct.[65]

Such examples, however, only serve to show that New Testament moral teaching can assume a teleological aspect in certain cases; it does not necessarily or even characteristically take that form. Teleological theories relate particularly well to cases where we are not sure what the right course

---

[63] Kant used the same method of abstraction to show the moral superiority of the motive of acting for duty's sake and for no other reason; cf. H. J. Paton, *The Moral Law*, 1948 (r.p., 1969), p. 19. As Paul used the same dialectical method in his ethical reflection 1700 years before Kant, any view that suggests that Paul is not worth studying for his ethical procedures needs revision.

[64] Cf. 14:3–4, 5, 12, and 19.

[65] Cf. the teleological perspective in N.T. teaching on the upbringing of children— esp. Col. 3:21.

of action is. There may be a conflict of duties, or a large number of factors to take into consideration. Different ethical procedures may seem to be relevant, e.g., shall we keep the rule? shall we consider moral principles, and which one? what are the likely consequences of this action and that? what different reasons would justify one in acting this way and that? The situation may be novel in that no precedents can be provided for our guidance. In such a case, the ethical procedure most likely to commend itself is perhaps to weigh up the situation, deliberate on alternative policies of action—considering their likely, foreseeable and reasonably-to-be-expected consequences—and decide on the one which seems to be for the best. Forms of teleological ethics that speak of 'maximising the good' gain their plausibility from this kind of situation.

Eschatology provides another teleological perspective in Christian ethics. The Jesus of the gospels bids us seek first God's kingdom and his righteousness (Matt. 6:33).[66] Many passages in Paul have a teleological orientation of this kind.[67] A well-known example occurs in Philippians, in which he speaks of pressing on 'toward the goal for the prize of the upward call of God in Christ Jesus' (3:14). This eschatological metaphor, if we may call it such, must not deceive us into thinking that Paul's outlook is wholly or typically teleological at this point. There is a sense in which Christ represents for him a state of perfection or completion towards which he is moving and which he has not yet attained (3:12; cf. Eph. 4:13–16). But the entire context indicates that he is no longer striving for perfection by his own efforts but wants to attain the perfection that comes through faith in Christ, and is from God and based on faith (cf. 3:7ff.). The language of eschatology must be handled with care: the total context in which it occurs is important when establishing its precise meaning.

The same observation applies when dealing with the subject of reward. The background of the 'reward' sayings in the gospels is that of Pharisaic Judaism, in which the language of 'reward' or 'pay' was considered appropriate to moral and spiritual endeavour.[68] Thus, the hypocrite 'has his reward': public acclaim is the only satisfaction he will know (cf. Matt. 6:1–18). The true man of God acts disinterestedly without hope of reward, though his reasons for action—to please God, not man—bring their own reward. Actions done with that motive have an intrinsic and eternal worth,

---

[66] Matthew also records the metaphor of treasure: 'where your treasure is, there will your heart be also' (cf. Matt. 6:19ff.).

[67] For example, metaphors from various athletic contests (1 Cor. 9:24–27), including the metaphor of the prize or wreath.

[68] Cf. M. Smith, *Tannaitic Parallels to the Gospels*, 1951, pp. 54–73, 161–184. The converse of reward is punishment: reward belongs to the normal situation, punishment to the abnormal. 'The Judaic-Christian tradition reflects the long process of training the instinct of vengeance for wrongs suffered': U. E. Simon, in D.C.E., art. 'Rewards and Punishments', p. 297. Thus the 'law of retribution' (*lex talionis*) served to restrict the penal consequences of misdeeds to an appropriate limit and to effect an element of restitution.

'the reward from your heavenly Father, who sees in secret'.[69] In Matt. 5:46ff., the insistence is upon the fact that the transcendent father does not recognise the limitations and restrictions of conventional morality (e.g., that one's neighbour is simply one's fellow Jew) and that therefore true children of God will radicalise their morality till it far exceeds such conventional boundaries. The ensuing conduct will bring its own reward. Again, in Matt. 5:11f., the metaphor of reward expresses the 'nevertheless' of faith, sounded in contradiction to the seeming futility of steadfastness in the face of persecution. In fact, the whole notion of reward in Christian ethics is paradoxical. If one attempts to make this reward into a goal, something that can be grasped like a material prize, then it vanishes. The 'reward' is a by-product of a way of life that has renounced rewards:

'for whoever would save his life will lose it;

whoever loses his life for my sake and the gospel's will save it'

(Mk. 8:35).

Conclusions

Many statements that appear explicitly teleological—especially where metaphor or eschatological imagery is used—are tantamount to statements of intrinsic value and could conceivably be classed as deontological.[70] Christian faith and action, like any reflective human activity, are purposive and make appropriate use of goal-language; but this does not mean that the ethical perspective is exclusively teleological or utilitarian. If teleology is helpful in some cases—e.g., in social ethics, or in cases involving a degree of moral perplexity—its limitations must also be frankly recognised. Teleology in itself, as we have seen, may be of doubtful ethical significance. Again, it does not sufficiently fit the New Testament data. In particular, it is unable to express adequately the prime New Testament concept of grace, the

[69] Phrases like 'intrinsic worth' and 'virtue for virtue's sake' were foreign to Jesus—partly, no doubt, for cultural and linguistic reasons. One of the former may be that, as Bultmann suggests, such phrases presuppose a later humanistic concept, viz., 'the conviction of the intrinsic worth of the human'. For Jesus, 'the actual reward for kindness shown is not the kindness itself, but the joy and gratitude which are awakened by it and enrich the giver': *Jesus and the Word*, Eng. tr., 1958, p. 62f. Intrinsic value, for Jesus, lay in doing God's will, and the language of eternal reward was his way of expressing this concept. As Bo Reicke put it: 'What the servant receives in reward is nothing but communion with God—but as the service of God is just a form of communion with God, there is an intimate relation, if not identity, between this service and this reward': 'The New Testament Conception of Reward', in *Aux sources de la tradition chrétienne* (Mélanges M. Goguel), 1950, p. 196; cf. J. I. H. McDonald, "The Concept of Reward in the Teaching of Jesus', *Expository Times* 89, 9, 1978, pp. 266–73.

[70] Cf. the question, 'Is moral action done for duty's sake or for the desire for some good goal?' That question contrasts two different motives for action, one in non-goal language, the other in goal language. But the first could be put in goal language, too, viz., 'My goal is to do my duty for duty's sake, and in this I have no other goal!'

nuances of agapism or the 'ethic of perfection', or the complexities of the connection between Christian faith and conduct.

No one ethical theory seems to fit every moral situation, despite the claims made by rival protagonists. Each points to the faults in the other. The deontologist asks, 'How can you calculate consequences?' while the teleologist asks, 'How can you really know a person's motives?' But the field is not divided between these two. Don Cupitt points to a large class of situations—involving decisions about one's marriage, career, political or religious allegiances—which relate to one's whole scheme of values, and cannot be conveniently subsumed under either teleology or deontology.

> 'In this area of moral thinking the emphasis is more upon the whole
> moral life than the motives of the agent or the consequences of the act.
> A *Weltanschauung*, a whole way of thinking is at stake. In this sense
> morality does in the end lead us to ask metaphysical or religious
> questions.'[71]

The variety of moral procedures found in the New Testament seems to confirm the view that no one neat theory fits all our moral experience.

[71] 'How we make Moral Decisions', in *Duty and Discernment* (ed. G. R. Dunstan), 1975, p. 88.

3

IS MOTIVE THE MEASURE?

A. MOTIVE THEORIES

'. . . when we praise any actions, we regard only the motives that produced them . . . The external performance has no merit . . . all virtuous actions derive their merit only from virtuous motives'.[1]

Does the external performance have no merit? Is virtue only in the motive? To take a simple example: children playing on an electric railway line. Should other children tell their parents or teachers, or remain silent? If a child informs out of concern for their safety, then (according to Hume) we are to praise the action on account of its motive. If, however, the child informs because he bears a grudge against one of them and wants revenge, or because he wants to become the teacher's favourite or to feel important, then (on Hume's terms) we find the action blameworthy on account of its motive. The action is the same, but the motives are different. 'The external performance has no merit'; it is the motive that is the major factor in our moral judgment.[2]

Motive suggests to most people the springs of human behaviour, the impulse that comes from one's true being, so to speak. Accordingly, 'the heart' is frequently used in religious, poetic and everyday language to denote this inner dimension. Someone has my interests 'at heart'. He speaks 'from the heart'. He espouses a cause 'with all his heart', and pursues it 'with heart and soul'. Clumsy and ineffectual he may be at times but 'his heart is in the right place'. In the New Testament, 'blessed are the pure in heart' (Matt. 5:8). To counterbalance Pharisaic scrupulosity in rituals such as handwashing, the New Testament points to the over-riding importance of inner dispositions: '. . . out of the heart come evil thoughts, murder, adultery, fornication, theft, false witness, slander. These are what defile a man . . .' (Matt. 15:19f.).

There is, however, a certain vagueness about such language, and before

---

[1] David Hume: *Treatise on Human Nature*, Book III, Pt. II (opening of Sec. I).

[2] The first two chapters of this work have discussed two main traditions in ethical theory, *viz.*, deontology or a concern for right action and its motives, and teleology or a concern for consequences. Here we give motive separate treatment for reasons that will emerge.

we can discuss further the question of motive as a criterion of moral behaviour, it is necessary to clarify what is meant by reasons and motives.

1. *Reasons and motives*[3]

How do we know what a person's motives are? There is a problem here, for a person's reasons and motives seem (almost by definition) to be 'inside his head'. How then can we discuss reasons and motives at all?

There is a basis for discussion if three factors come together fairly easily, viz., observation of the person's past and present behaviour, his reputation with other people, and what he says about himself. For example, a person's motive will be obvious if, in the past and present, we have frequently observed him acting without any concern for others; if he has the reputation for acting in this self-interested way; and if he says his motto is 'Always take care of Number One'.

In many instances, however, one or other of these factors is absent. We may not have observed the agent's behaviour except in the present instance. We may not know what others say about him, and they may be mistaken anyway. We may not know what he says about himself—and even when we do, he may mistake his own motives (this will be particularly likely when he acts from mixed motives, or when he rationalises[4]). Again, he may have an ulterior motive and therefore the motive he presents to the world may not be his real motive. He may be acting out of some unconscious or irrational 'drive' (e.g., some form of neurosis or psychosis). Thus, although many reasons may be given by the agent or by outsiders for his behaviour, none of these may be his genuine reason or motive. In moral discourse, we are concerned only with the agent's genuine reason or motive, and this must be both freely chosen and rational if the behaviour is to be counted as morally responsible.

Is there an important distinction between reason and motive? In some cases, even when the agent gives us a genuine reason for acting, he may not be giving his motive. For example, Smith tells us quite honestly that he mended the door because he likes working with his hands, but his motive may be that he desired to stop the door banging and keeping him awake. This can serve as the basis for a general distinction between motives and reasons. Reasons often make great play of dispositions; for example, if we ask Smith why he mended the door, he could give a variety of reasons, all expressed in the form of dispositions (i.e., tendencies to act in certain ways in certain contexts):

'because I always do things myself. . .' (habits)

---

[3] The following works are useful for their treatment of motive or intention: Gilbert Ryle, *The Concept of Mind*, 1949; G. E. M. Anscombe, *Intention*, 1957, 1972, and 'Intention' in *Proc. Arist. Society* LVII, 1956–57, reprinted in D. F. Gustafson (ed.), *Essays in Philosophical Psychology*, 1967, 1970; R. S. Peters, *The Concept of Motivation*, 1960; A. Kenny, *Action, Emotion and Will*, 1963, 1969; Roy Lawrence, *Motive and Intention*, 1972; C. Diamond and J. Teichman (edd.), *Intention and Intentionality* (Essays in Honour of G. E. M. Anscombe), 1979.

[4] See p. 7 above.

'because I'm useful with my hands. . .' (skills, competencies or capacities)

'because I've always been inclined to be practical. . .' (propensities)

'because I'm a considerate man and my old neighbour couldn't do it herself. . .' (traits of character)

Motives, on the other hand, are reasons of a particular kind which refer or allude to goals; for example, if Smith were to give his motive for mending the door, we might find it on the following list:

'to stop it banging and disturbing my sleep'

'to prove to myself that I could do it'

'to prevent further damage and therefore to save money'

'to forestall complaints from the neighbours'

'to show off my skills as a handyman'

'to help my neighbour who could not do it for herself'.

Careful scrutiny of these lists will show that, while all the reasons given in the first list are in terms of dispositons, all the motives given refer to goals that the agent wishes to achieve. Most of these are not in terms of dispositions, for a motive may be a particular reason in a context for a particular action and have no reference to how the agent acted in the past. On the other hand, there is some resemblance between the final examples on both lists. Where precisely is the difference here? Are some motives dispositions? At this point we need to distinguish between directive and non-directive dispositions, i.e., those which refer to the pursuit of a goal, and those which do not.

Apart from the difficulties that attach to explanation from the outside, is motive explanation simply explanation in terms of dispositions? Motive is a reason of a particular kind; and it is fairly obvious that some instances of motive (perhaps all—we shall have to see) have a reference to a goal:[5]

'He married her for her money'.

'He works hard to beat his rivals'.

'He joined the Cubs, even when he was scared, to please his Mum'.

'He bought an expensive car to keep up with his rivals'.

'The firm paid his wife's expenses when she went with him on his business trip abroad, to beat the Government's pay policy'.

'He wrote a letter to warn Jones his life was in danger'.

'He did it to keep his friends'.

'He did it to show off and feel important'.

[5] Broadly speaking, there seem to be two types of context in which people give *explanation* in terms of motive (though these do not cover all instances of motives as *reasons*). One is when a person's reasons seem disreputable or his behaviour otherwise inexplicable. Why did Smith, earning a good salary and trusted by his firm, embezzle £50,000? Answer—to pay his gambling debts. Now we begin to understand, for we know that in tight corners people may adopt desperate measures. The other context is when a motive explanation serves to rule out misunderstanding or blocks other interpretations of the behaviour. Thus, a comment such as 'She is wealthy' or 'They are both artists' may be offered to throw light on a relationship such as marriage which we might have interpreted otherwise.

All these examples involve what may be called directive (as opposed to non-directive) dispositions. A directive disposition is a general tendency to pursue a certain goal and is related to motive because of the reference to a goal. Ambition, greed and curiosity are directive dispositions and indicate goals, though not necessarily explicitly. Directive dispositions (as in 'Macbeth murdered Duncan out of ambition'; 'Smith took over the other firms out of greed'; 'He studied the subject out of curiosity') are a kind of short-hand for referring or alluding to motives linked to intentions[6] (as in 'Macbeth murdered Duncan for the throne'; 'Smith took over the other firms to make more money'; 'He studies the subject to discover and know more'). In the first example, the intention is to kill, while the motive is to get the throne. *Explanations in terms of directive dispositions are motive-explanations.*

Non-directive dispositions, on the other hand, do not describe or even allude implicitly to goals, but describe ways in which a man pursues whatever goals he has: examples include discretion, honesty, meanness, sincerity, sympathy and punctuality.

'Do you think he stole the money?'—'No, I don't; he's too honest'.

'Do you think Smith sent the anonymous donation?'—'No, I don't; he's mean'.

'Do you think he'll put his foot in it?'—'He's unlikely to; he usually acts with discretion'.

It seems inappropriate to use the term 'motive' for this kind of explanation, where appeal is made simply to habit. The question at issue here is not so much the goal as the means by which a man normally pursues his goals. In any theory of motive as the measure of morality we must distinguish motives from non-directive dispositions. *Explanations in terms of non-directive dispositions are not motive-explanations.*

Some words, however, can indicate either directive or non-directive dispositions, depending on the context. Patriotism is a case in point. If we ask, 'Why did he join the army?' and receive the reply, 'He is very patriotic', the explanation is perhaps being given in terms of how he has tended to behave in the past. But we can still ask, 'What was his motive?' He may have wanted glory, a good job after the war, or simply to serve his country. All are motives consistent with 'being patriotic', but only the last is an explanation in terms of the motive of patriotism.[7] Another example is generosity. At first glance, it does not obviously indicate a goal, but on reflection we see that it includes a large number of goal-directed activities: e.g., to help a beggar, to aid a charity, to give time to a youth club. A man cannot be said to be generous if he does not give himself to others in some goal-directed activity. In some contexts a person may be said to have had a generous motive: e.g., 'He worked hard to make the charity sale a success'. Similarly, gratitude, compassion, mercy, love, hatred and the like can be

---

[6] The distinction between motive and intention is discussed below.

[7] Cf. P. H. Nowell-Smith, *Ethics*, pp. 124f.

reckoned as motives:[8] but they are all too unspecific to indicate the precise goal the agent has in mind, and thus often fail to block further questions of the type, 'Why did Smith do that?'

Fear is something of a special case. Can fear be a motive, as Abelard believed it could? Miss Anscombe threw light on the problem in the following way.[9] We are told that the child did not go upstairs 'because he was afraid'. This may sound like a motive-explanation but in fact it is not one since we remain puzzled and want to ask more questions of the 'Why' type: 'Why was he afraid?' 'Of what was he afraid?'. If we are told, 'A bit of stuff on the stair', we are still puzzled and ask, 'Why was he afraid of that?' Then we get the real reason. 'He misunderstood his mother's remark that it was a bit of satin: he thought she said "a bit of Satan"'. In other words, to understand the child's behaviour, we have not only to know the 'motive' (viz., fear), but also to know both the object of his fear (the bit of stuff) and the reason for his fear (viz., he has misunderstood his mother's remark etc.). 'Motive' (if we are to call it such) here fails to be an explanation. To say that this child was motivated by fear—'he refused to go upstairs out of fear'—may throw no light on his behaviour unless we know the object of and the reason for his fear. It is only then that his behaviour is explained. This would seem to suggest that fear is not a motive: it does not explain behaviour as motives do.

But there is another side to the coin. Fear is a rather hazy notion which may attach itself to any object. Whereas ambition, for example, suggests at once a few clear goals—getting a better job, marrying 'well', outsmarting one's rivals—fear tends to inhibit certain kinds of behaviour and certain goals (such as the objective of going upstairs); and it is as a by-product of that inhibiting that it produces certain positive forms of behaviour (such as remaining downstairs). Thus, fear acts primarily to give negative reinforcement and only derivatively to give positive reinforcement, while ambition and the like operate the other way round. Viewed in this way, fear is a directive disposition and may appropriately be called a motive since it directs to rule out certain goals.

People in fact tend to run to form, to act consistently from certain motives, such as considerateness, kindness and compassion or their opposites, selfishness, jealousy and malice. Others tend to act from mixed motives, and perhaps all of us do at times. Then there are ulterior motives, which need not always be mercenary or self-interested: hiding one's real motive may be done to save another's pride or to prevent parading one's altruism. The point is that there can be a connection between motives and character, good or bad. Even when a motive is an isolated reason for a specific act, and not connected with a disposition, this simply means that we cannot read this reason off the person's character as known to us. It

[8] Cf. also, politeness: generally speaking, it is non-directive (e.g., force of habit); when we want to suggest motive, we tend to call it 'thoughtfulness', 'considerateness': cf. Nowell-Smith, *op. cit.*, p. 127.

[9] In her article, 'Intention', reprinted in D. F. Gustafson (ed.), *op. cit.*, p. 32.

does not imply that it has nothing to do with his character in the present (perhaps something is now being disclosed for the first time about his character), far less that this reason will not affect his future character as it is being built up in response to situations and people.

Whether or not a disposition is involved, a motive is a particular kind of reason the agent has for acting, viz., one directed to a goal. This is why in ordinary speech and popular thought, *motive* and *intention* are interchangeable terms. When we ascribe a motive (as when we say that a Trade Union leader representing the mine-workers is against nuclear reactors because he believes they are contrary to the interests of the miners), there is an appeal to the intended consequences of the person's behaviour (e.g., an intention to defend the interests of his members): it is reference to a goal that makes 'motive' and 'intention' share so much common ground. If I give food to a beggar, my *motive* may be the desire to achieve a goal, viz., to relieve the man's distress, the *action* may be the giving of food, and the *intention* comprises both the achievement of the goal and means of achieving it. In this example, as in many others, the means of achieving the goal may be more or less identical with the action (e.g., if the beggar is at my door and the food is already in the house); hence, intention may narrow down to the motive plus action. It is thus easy to see how the popular mind thinks of motive and intention as logically and morally interchangeable.

In other contexts, however, there is a much sharper distinction between the terms. *Prima facie*, a specific motive and an intention may stand in a relationship of tension or contradiction, which is resolved only through fuller understanding of how they are in fact linked. Why did I go out of the house just now, if my motive was to get on with drafting this book? You are understandably puzzled. But my motive becomes clear and reasonable when I give you my intention, viz., to buy a refill for my ball-point pen or a fresh type-writer ribbon. Motive here seems the more fitting term to use with reference to the long-term objective, and intention for the short-term objective, which is also the means to the more ultimate one.

Further, the means to the main end may be undesirable in themselves, but are accepted for the sake of the deferred consequences embraced in the motive—like the pain of the dentist's drilling for the sake of preserving the tooth. A Chancellor of the Exchequer may be totally committed to the goal of a higher standard of living for most people in the country, together with greater social benefits and services. But in order to achieve such an aim he may have to impose a cut-back in public expenditure, a wage freeze and credit restrictions or tax increases which in the short term seem to conflict with the ultimate objectives. He thus intends the immediate consequences of a lower standard of living and the ultimate goal of an enhanced living standard. The motive, however, always gives the reason for acting, as the intention may not, and is related to the final objective.[10]

---

[10] This account of motive has been held to be defective (by G. E. M. Anscombe in 'Intention' *op. cit.*) in that some motives are said to be backward-looking, and not to allude to goals: e.g., in revenge and gratitude, the agent's action is said to look

In law, the distinction between motive and intention may be of critical importance. Murder always presupposes intention to kill, although motives for murder are many and varied: to eliminate a rival, to get rid of an undesirable character who is threatening one's daughter, or in revenge for a previous death. In some instances of abortion, killing may be done with the motive of love. In cases of homicide or manslaughter, the reason or motive for killing is crucial. If the accused acted out of self-defence, that reason or motive (if borne out by the evidence) may be ground for acquittal; or, if some blame attaches to him, it is still adequate to rule out a charge of murder. Here the difference-in-law that the motive makes to the act is based on moral considerations. In general, the 'better' the motive, the more justified the action appears. What has to be watched here is tautology, viz., that our motive-explanations are not just ways in which we approve or disapprove of certain actions in certain situations. In other words, language which may seem to be about motives may have nothing to do with motives as the criterion of moral worth but may be just a way of describing or expressing our moral approval or disapproval.

It is to the question of motive as a moral criterion that we now turn. Are actions justified solely by their respective motives? Is the same action right if done from one motive, and wrong if done from another? Does the motive always make that degree or kind of difference? To answer these questions in the affirmative is to hold that motive is the *sole* measure of morality, and we shall call this the strong form of this type of theory. To hold, on the other hand, that motive is an important, but not the sole, measure of right and wrong is to adhere to the weak form of the theory. We shall discuss these positions in turn.

2. *Is motive the sole criterion of morality?* (*The strong form of the theory*)

The view that morality is concerned solely with motives was examined in a paper given by Donald M. MacKinnon to the Malvern Conference of 1941. It was not a view that MacKinnon himself advocated; indeed, he subjected it to severe criticism.

(*footnote* 10 *continued*)
back to another's past deed, while in remorse, the action looks back to the agent's deeds in the past. But we reject this analysis of these motives as inadequate. Though revenge is not some further concrete state of affairs obtained by (say) killing, 'to get rid of the bounder' describes a goal; if revenge and remorse were totally backward looking, no act of revenge nor remorse would ever be deliberated upon nor planned. In gratitude, there is a goal in mind, if there is an intention to repay, but gratitude, friendship and obedience require separate treatment along the lines suggested by A. Kenny (*op. cit.*). While other actions can be explained in terms of a pattern they exhibit, these are done to display a pattern. Miss Anscombe's account may be further evidence of the inadequacy of merely regarding motive as an outsider's explanation: for, the explanation 'He was full of remorse' for Smith's behaviour may appear to be in terms of Smith's past deeds, whereas from his own point of view his motive directs him to goal-related activities, such as 'I shall make it up to Jones' and 'I shall show him by this gesture that I'm sorry for what I did to him'.

'There is a sphere of human activity that is ethically and therefore religiously irrelevant. Not what we are, and therefore what we do matters, but rather the motive that determines our action. The ultimate, if not the proximate, motive of British nationals engaged in this conflict with Germany, is the pursuit of justice. Therefore it matters not what they do. The propriety of means is a matter for the military expert. Now, if morality is concerned solely with motives, it follows necessarily that there is no problem of the means, and, if for the religious critic only moral considerations (in this sense) are relevant, questions of means inevitably fall without his purview. They become "technical" matters. If religion is a technique for achieving the determination of one's conduct by moral motives, then—cadit quaestio. Its concern is with the disposition of the individual . . .'[11]

It is true that MacKinnon's immediate interest derived from the fact that this sort of thing was being thought and sometimes said by some Christians in Britain in 1941. But he made it perfectly clear that the view need not be confined to Christians nor indeed be expressed in religious terms at all. As an ethical view, it can be stated without religious presuppositions and entirely stripped of its religious dress, and it is as an ethical, not a religious view, that we wish to examine it in this section.

MacKinnon's presentation brought out sharply the basic ethical issue involved, *viz.*, is morality solely concerned with motives and the disposition of the individual, and not with actions at all? It is one thing to condemn an action because its motive is not good. We hardly admire Smith who refrains from stealing or ill-treating his children, only because he fears imprisonment or what the neighbours will say. But it is quite another thing to suggest that any action, however bestial or inhuman, can be made good by its motive. We hesitate to justify murder simply because a man claims that his motive was good, *viz.*, a desire to do the work of God by killing degenerates who did not deserve to live. In other cases, however, the same act of killing is justified by its 'good' motive, e.g., if done in self-defence.

Things, then, are not so simple as the strong form of the theory suggests. For one thing, it condemns itself by its distinction between morally good and bad motives—a distinction which it is difficult to see how it can avoid introducing. This implies that some measure *other than motive* by which motives themselves are judged 'good' or 'bad' is being surreptitiously or at least illicitly applied. If this distinction is introduced, motive cannot be held to be the sole measure of morality.

Secondly, it is much more plausible to hold that moral judgements are made *both* about actions *and* about motives. We can do the right thing from the wrong motive or reason. For example, we can help those in need from a desire to show off, to be praised or admired. In such cases, we can say that the act is right, but that the agent is not morally good or virtuous (a version of the weak form of the theory). Indeed, once we introduce this distinction between rightness and virtue, Hume's words sound more plausible: 'all

[11] *Malvern, 1941: The Life of the Church and the Order of Society*, 1941, pp. 84f.

virtuous' (rather than right) 'actions derive their merit only from virtuous motives". On the other hand, we can do wrong from a good motive. For example, Youth Club leaders, organising a sale for some needy cause, may have to watch lest some Club members with the best of motives go shop-lifting in the supermarket and bring their loot to be sold for charity. 'Robin Hood stole from the rich to give to the poor' describes actions usually considered morally wrong, but done from a generous motive. The unreflective moral judgement is often sent into confusion by such cases; hence the popular admiration for Robin Hood and his Merry Men.

The base motive does not make the action wrong, nor does the generous motive make the action right.

3. *Is motive an important, but not the sole, criterion of morality? (The weak form of the theory)*

While no prominent philosopher in modern times has held the view in its strong form, various thinkers have proposed some version of the weak form—the most notable being Kant.

Kant maintained that the consequences of an *action*, such as happiness or unhappiness, were not to be taken into account in assessing moral worth. Instead he adopted two other criteria, viz., the action itself as an instance of the moral law and its motive.

Let us take motive first. Actions have moral worth, he held, only if done for the sake of duty, and for no other reason. In doing our duty, we are not to be impelled simply by some natural inclination, such as generosity, sympathy or self-interest. We are to do our duty, not because it will bring happiness, but simply because it is our duty. Kant did not mean to condemn motives such as generosity or sympathy, but to maintain that these motives are not sufficient to give any action moral worth. He held that both the act and the agent are morally good when the act is done *because it is our duty*: that an act happens to be *in accordance with duty* only makes the act right, not morally worthy.

Kant's emphasis on motive is brought out in the phrase often used to sum up his ethical position—'duty for duty's sake'. He gives an example of what he means. It is a duty to preserve one's life, but, because each of us has an immediate inclination to do so, the precautions we take to survive often have no moral worth. We protect our lives in

'*conformity with duty*, but not *from the motive of duty*. When on the contrary, disappointments and hopeless misery have quite taken away the taste for life; when a wretched man, strong in soul and more angered at his fate than fainthearted or cast down, longs for death but still preserves his life without loving it—not from inclination or fear but from duty; then indeed his maxim has a moral content'.[12]

Was there in Kant's view some residue of the 'Puritan conscience' whereby one's duty can never be to do what one likes doing or what gives one

[12] Kant, *Groundwork of the Metaphysic of Morals*, ch. I pp. 9–10: as in H. J. Paton, *The Moral Law*, 1948, 1969, p. 63.

pleasure or happiness, but must always be disagreeable to contemplate and difficult to perform? While it is difficult to deny that at least in certain circumstances actions done from the motive of duty have moral worth, the question remains whether Kant has established what he meant to establish—*viz.*, that moral worth is to be *confined* to agents acting from, and actions done from, a sense of duty, and not extended to acts of sympathy, generosity and *agape* or love.[13]

Kant, however, balanced his emphasis on motive by an appeal to the nature of the action itself. He held that 'there is nothing good without qualification except a good will'. Other things are merely *good for* some purpose, as a sharp knife is good for cutting: or their goodness is *conditional on* seeking a particular end, such as happiness. In other words, these things are good in virtue of a *hypothetical imperative*, i.e., a command of the form 'Do *x*, if you want *y*'—e.g., 'Walk fast if you want to catch the train' or 'Cultivate the boss, if you want promotion': they are *good for* this or that, or *good if* you want such-and-such. The good will, on the other hand, is good without qualification, for it obeys a *categorical imperative*, which is a command with no condition attached, i.e., of the form 'Do *x*'.

The goodness of the will, then, depends on two factors: first the motive, *viz.*, respect for the moral law or doing our duty because it is our duty; and, secondly, on the maxim, rule or principle on which the will acts, and this takes the form of a categorical imperative, such as 'Act only on that maxim which you can at the same time will to become a universal law'—i.e., a law with no qualifications attached to it. The maxim or principle on which the act rests must be capable of being universalised. Acts, then, have moral worth when they are (a) conformable to law—i.e., where their maxims are universalisable, and (b) done because they are conformable to law.

Kant gave only a *formal* criterion for deciding which actions have moral worth, and he believed that it was the great merit of his theory that it did not prescribe the *content* of the moral law. The categorical imperative for him had only form (e.g., 'Act only on that maxim which you can at the same time will to become a universal law'), but no content. Kant does not tell us what actions in particular would be right, i.e., what specific actions would be in accordance with the categorical imperative. Instead he supplies a test by which we can discover for ourselves this content. He believed that he had found an objective criterion for assessing moral worth that could be applied by all agents in all circumstances and cultures, irrespective of subjective factors such as tastes and inclinations.

Kant has sometimes been accused of violating his formal criterion in the illustrations he gave of wrong actions.[14] It is also suggested that he

[13] We shall have in mind Kant's distinction between natural affection (= 'pathological love') and the 'love that can be commanded' (=love of neighbour) and its implications for Christian ethics in section B of this chapter.

[14] Four in particular: (i) suicide; (ii) the making of false promises; (iii) failure to develop one's faculties; (iv) the refusal of a rich man to give to those in distress. He can be defended on two counts. First, he gave each of these actions a particular context, and this can be taken to imply that he did not intend to

contradicted himself by making an illicit appeal to consequences in certain of his arguments.[15] While attempts have been made to save Kant from his failure to state his case clearly and cogently enough, it is important to note that he never intended to exclude consideration of consequences from his ethical system. He is willing to argue that some *maxims*, when universalised, would result in forms of society which are unacceptable to rational and feeling beings. But the consequences of an *action* are not to be taken into account in assessing moral worth.

There is always a danger that moral theories are set over against one another in too naive a way—a danger that may arise when the teacher is trying to emphasise the distinctive features of each. Kant can include a consideration of consequences in his moral theory in his own way.

While the strong form of the theory that motive is the *sole* criterion of morality has to be rejected, Kant was correct in believing that both the action and the motive have to be taken into account in assessing moral worth. There are situations where the motive makes at least some moral difference to the same outward act. To tell a lie about a patient's condition

(*footnote* 14 *continued*)
suggest that all instances of these actions were morally wrong. It is extremely doubtful, however, whether Kant had thought of this reply. The second defence is that Kant was merely illustrating the sort of actions whose *maxims* (at least on occasions) violated the categorical imperative. Some claim that Kant condemned suicide on the ground that if everyone committed suicide there would be no one left to do so!—cf., H. J. Paton, *op. cit.*, p. 130 (also, notes on Ch. II, p. 54, n.1). There is no hint of this argument in Kant's text; he never meant to suggest that the criterion of non-universalisation was to be applied to specific *actions*, such as suicide and promise-breaking. It was to be applied only to the *maxim* on which actions were based. In other words, by the use of his four examples Kant is merely illustrating how his doctrine of the non-universability of some *maxims* could be applied in practice. Is Kant's doctrine therefore consonant with the view that stealing, for example, is in certain circumstances morally right, if the maxim for the action can be willed to become a universal law? A man can will that everyone placed in exactly similar circumstances should steal to feed his wife and children (see above, Ch. 2, on G.U. and R.U.). Kant's view would then either be consonant with situation ethics or approximate to it in some respects. It is, however, extremely doubtful if Kant had thought of this implication of his position, and he would probably have recoiled from it.

[15] For example, in his argument that the maxim upon which stealing rests cannot be universalised: if everyone stole, the result would be such a degree of social mistrust that successful stealing would be impossible! Kant probably never intended to suggest this. In some instances, e.g., lying promises, Kant in fact argues that universal false-promising is self-contradictory: the moral law for him is rational and issues in *maxims* free of inconsistency. But in other cases, e.g., failure to be beneficent, he admits that universal non-beneficence is not self-contradictory and is consistent with the continuance of human society. Here he falls back on another line of argument, which he does not sufficiently distinguish from the other, viz., that no one could *will* universal non-beneficence because this would rob a man of the love and sympathy he is bound to want for himself at some time. This is a prudential justification, seeming to depend on the agent's own future happiness, and so on a hypothetical imperative to which he has no right to appeal.

from the motive of concern for his welfare is morally different from telling a lie out of self-interest: indeed except in the cases of atypical stress (e.g., resulting from inadequate parent-child relationships) or of mentally abnormal behaviour (e.g., that of a psychopath), a lie is never told without a reason or motive and, therefore, the reason or motive as well as the act has to be taken into consideration in our moral judgement. If you are a situationist, you will say that telling a lie can in some circumstances be the right thing to do, if it is justified by some kind of consequences or by motive. If you are not a situationist, but hold that there is an element of situationism in many moral decisions, you may still want to hold that in certain circumstances telling a lie can be the right thing to do, though you must not say the same thing about cruelty. Your position, therefore, is that in some cases the motive makes some moral difference to the outward act.

4. Beyond motive

We have noted the connection between motive and character. Motives go with an ethic of 'being good' rather than 'doing good'. It is not the action, but only the agent that is good; and one of the ways of deciding whether a person is good is to examine his motives. It may be well to remind ourselves that goodness has no independent existence (if we leave out metaphysics and theology for the moment). Goodness exists only in good people: strictly, 'good' is a quality attributed to people. A theory about motives, therefore, takes us beyond motive into character, virtue, being good—i.e., into a more general theory of moral value. As this seems to take us far from motives being particular reasons for specific actions, how can this position be justified?

Motivation occupies a central place in personal growth and development as well as in the acquisition of at least some of the social skills. While there is an immense range of reasons and motives for human behaviour, there is much empirical evidence to suggest that all or most of these are comprehended in two basic motivations from which much behaviour in children and adults springs:

(1) the desire to be important in others' eyes or to be recognised or approved by others, including one's group (e.g., doing things for show or exhibition, to show off, to impress someone; doing things to get others' approval or favour; doing things to be socially acceptable; doing what the group or gang says or demands)

(2) the desire to be important in one's own eyes (=self-respect, self-esteem): e.g, doing things because one's honour is at stake; because 'what will others think of me, if I don't?'; retaliating because one's sense of worth is threatened or has been diminished; acting because one feels threatened in some way by some person or group.

It is clear, of course, that these two motivations are often directly connected: one's self-esteem is enhanced when one is esteemed by others. One of the reasons why people join groups (e.g., the tennis club) is to gain recognition from others. Further, the need to gain self-esteem is integral to the search for identity. For example, when a child discovers he is good at football, he forms a picture of himself as a footballer and so acquires a worth in his own eyes. Of course, we can get a sense of self-importance in all sorts of ways: e.g., by knowing more than other people about some subject (the motives of curiosity and the thirst for knowledge); or by developing skills which others do not have. Failure to get recognition is equally significant for personal development; children draw attention to themselves and get noticed by others simply by appearing to be more stupid or less well-behaved than anyone else. The desire to make more money (an instance of greed), or to get a better job (an instance of ambition) are forms of the desire to be important in one's own eyes. We feel jealousy and envy and may act from these motives when we feel our own sense of worth or value threatened or diminished by the talents, property or success of others. Further, the desire for self-esteem may lead people into finding it in co-operation with others; or, if they cannot so find it, it may lead to withdrawal into a fantasy self or may express itself in aggression, where the fantasies spill over into action so that the agent develops a sense of power and self-importance.[16]

Hence in personal growth and development and the acquisition of some of the social skills, it can be claimed that awareness of our motives plays an important part. Recognition of our motives promotes self-understanding and understanding of others; e.g., why people behave as they do, why they are withdrawn or self-giving, destructive or creative, deviant or conforming, and why they join or refuse to join groups. People who have this kind of self-understanding are more likely to achieve a 'balanced and well-adjusted personality' and a measure of socialisation.

Such realities of the human situation have importance for moral be-haviour and education as well as moral theory. As Gordon Kirk claims, pupils 'cannot be expected to build the house of their moral understanding on the sand of psychological and sociological ignorance'.[17] The two basic motivations we have noted are connected with a person's ego-ideal, the ideal picture a person has of himself. This operates to inhibit him from some forms of behaviour and to encourage him towards others: 'I am/am not the sort of person who would do that'. The ego-ideal is an important ingredient in the final stage of moral development where the rational, autonomous adult takes as his sanctions self-praise and self-blame, and no longer the praise or blame of others. Kant's ethical position with its emphasis on motive can easily be transformed into such a morality: 'I am the sort of person who does my duty because it is my duty and for no other reason (such as the approval of others)'. This seems to be confirmation enough that the motive of duty for duty's sake is a moral motive of a fundamental kind. But are there others? Can we probe further?

[16] Examples of fantasy include imagining that one is a great star, or the last of the big spenders, or a notorious gang leader. When fantasy spills over into action, one may commit successful crimes, enjoy reading of one's anti-social exploits in the press, make anonymous telephone calls, or carry out disruptive hoaxes.

[17] *The Structure of the Curriculum in the Third and Fourth Years of the Scottish Secondary School*, 1977, p. 70 in his Note of Reservation ('the Munn Report').

The motive that many people would desire to put alongside duty for duty's sake goes by many names—e.g., consideration or caring for others, beneficence, love in the sense of *agape*. But what about other virtues? Contemporary ethical writing has a revulsion against an old-fashioned catalogue of virtues, such as that bequeathed by Plato and Aristotle to medieval thought.[18] Thomas McPherson[19] rightly explains this revulsion on the ground that ethicists are aware there is something artificial about the isolation of specific virtues, as if one could be attained without the others; and there is much discussion in contemporary writing as to whether the over-all or supreme principle of moral evaluation is justice or beneficence.

The doctrine of a plurality of virtues also proved a difficult plant to cultivate on Christian soil. Thomas Aquinas apparently wanted it both ways. He maintained that love alone makes an action good, but he also taught a doctrine of individual and independent virtues, based on Aristotle's doctrine of the four cardinal virtues: these do NOT become virtues through love alone, but have an independent existence, so that it *is* possible to possess one and not others. Aquinas' doctrine, however, is open to criticism. Wisdom, courage and self-control do not appear to be morally good except when exercised on behalf of others and for their welfare or advantage. The physical courage of Sir Francis Chichester and Sir Alex Rose in sailing single-handed round the world seems to have nothing to do with moral goodness (though some may have felt their lives 'ennobled' by the example of such heroism); whereas the sacrificial courageous act of Captain Oates does seem morally good, simply because it was exercised for the welfare of his fellow-explorers. Further, courage and self-control would be useful dispositions even in a 'bad' man—a man dedicated to pursuing relentlessly his own long-term evil interests, such as the attainment of power to dominate and enslave his fellows or to amass wealth. To be good in a moral sense, then, courage and self-control must be exercised for the benefit or advantage of other people. They are only 'virtues' when practised by someone whose life is related to others and lived for them. Goodness cannot be atomised into 'virtues' independent of each other nor severed from the person as a whole, his motives, goals and character. The qualities of a person cannot be turned into independent 'virtues', conceived as quasi-substantival entities.

Thus we seem to be left with two basic motives for moral behaviour: doing one's duty because it is our duty and action done for the welfare of others. Can these be further reduced to one? There is an important sense in which they can—a sense in which there is only one final motive for moral

---

[18] The list consisted of the four cardinal virtues, wisdom or prudence, courage, temperance or self-control and justice, and the three theological virtues of faith, hope and love: cf. 'Christian virtues' in *Proc. Arist. Soc.*, Supplementary Vol. XXXVII, 1963, pp. 51f.

[19] Justice as a virtue is different from justice as a moral principle: as a virtue, justice is a habitual disposition to act in accordance with the principle of justice: a virtue is a quality of a person, while a moral principle is what someone tries to embody in his actions. A man's sporadic just acts hardly entitle him to be called 'just' or to be said to possess the virtue of justice.

action.[20] Let us scrutinise the kinds of reasons which we identified as important in the first two chapters of this book to see if we can arrive at this basic motive. Take the case of the man who acts in a certain way because he desires to obey a rule or law, the point of which he understands. Our cross-examination might proceed as follows:

'Why do you desire to do action X?'

'Because action X is an instance of a rule and I desire to obey the rule'.

'Why do you desire to obey the rule?'

'Because I see the point of the rule (e.g., it has a safety value)'.

'Why do you desire to obey a rule whose point you see?'

'Because it embodies concern for other people'.

'Why do you wish to act out of concern for others?'

'Because I desire to do what is right'.

'Why do you desire to do what is right'?

'Simply because it is right; and in this situation I believe that action X is right'.

It is only the last answer that blocks further questions. If at any point in the dialogue the question is asked, 'Why do you desire to do the right?', the only answer than can be given in the last analysis is 'Because it is right'.[21] This is the case no matter where the dialogue takes its starting-point—e.g., 'I desire to act in accordance with the moral principle of justice or beneficence' or 'I desire to act out of kindness or compassion—to be of service to my neighbour'. It is the same when we question the man who desires to do an action whose likely, foreseeable and intended consequences he has considered and weighed against other possible policies of action. The action he chooses will produce, he says, the maximum good all round. In the last analysis, he is doing what he believes to be right. Here we reach the terminus of this kind of interrogation.[22] There is no way of going beyond it in terms of moral or ethical discourse. This does not mean that other reasons and motives for moral behaviour do not count , but it does show why 'because it is right or my duty' has a special, indeed unique, place among moral motives.

B. HOW FAR IS NEW TESTAMENT MORALITY ONE OF MOTIVE?

Sweeping claims have been made for the place of motive in Christian ethics. E. F. Scott, for example, took motive to be one of the marks of originality in

[20] While we shall argue that love or *agape*, not justice, is the pre-eminent moral principle, we are not convinced that this is the basic moral motive.

[21] Unless we go into metaphysics or religion, and, if we do, we must be careful not to impugn the autonomy of morality in such a way that this moral motive is eliminated. See chapter 4.

[22] Indeed, this kind of interrogation *assumes* not only that the proposed action is right, but also that some reasons for its being right have been advanced. Our argument works only on these two premises. Peter Geach's argument (*God and the Soul*, 1969, pp. 121–122)—that an appeal to a so-called sense of duty, regardless of the content of the alleged duty (cf. a Nazi sense of duty) is irrational and immoral—therefore does not count against our analysis.

the teaching of Jesus and further claimed that, in Jesus' teaching, 'the good and evil of an act consist *wholly* in its motive'.[23] Are such claims to be accepted? If not, how are we to describe the place which motive properly holds in Christian ethics?

1. *The emphasis on motive is not original to Jesus*

As has been noted already,[24] the popular notion that the ten commandments, with the exception of 'Thou shalt not covet', are concerned only with outward acts and not with motives or intentions, is to be rejected. Little reflection is required to see that the act of murder denotes killing with a particular intent—it is murder rather than manslaughter or accidental killing. Such a wholesale prohibition inevitably condemns intentional killing no matter its motive and rules that no motive can ever morally justify it. Motive is an important element in the actions of stealing, adultery, bearing false witness, and honouring God, one's promises, one's parents and the sabbath.[25] Indeed in Deuteronomy 6:4ff., the definitive response of the Israelite to the one true God who has entered into covenant with his people is to love him with all one's being. Reverence and love for God are the marks of the righteous man in the Psalms and provide motives for his actions. The rabbis, although they often appeal to popular notions of rewards and punishments, know that at the highest level 'love to God should be the sole motive'.[26] Following the inner logic of the Torah, as in the injunction 'You shall be holy, for I, the Lord your God, am holy' (Lev. 19:2), the rabbis developed a doctrine of the imitation of God. In responding to God, men must grow like him in character and 'walk in all his ways' (Deut. 11:20). And the Lord who is the pattern for men to follow is 'a God merciful and gracious, slow to anger and abounding in steadfast love and faithfulness . . . forgiving iniquity' (Ex. 34:7). The doctrine of the imitation of God is 'not only the actual foundation of Talmudic ethics but its motive and inspiration'.[27] It is not surprising, therefore, that R. Akiba could take Lev. 19:18—'you shall love your neighbour as yourself'—as the great principle of the Law, on which all the other commandments and teachings are based; or that R. Hillel, when challenged to teach the whole of the Torah while he stood on one foot, replied, 'What is hateful to yourself, do not to your fellow man'. As T. W. Manson remarked on the rabbinic teaching on love:

'. . . the law of love in some degree ceased to be itself a commandment

---

[23] Cf. *The Ethical Teaching of Jesus*, 1924, pp. 17–19; our italics.

[24] See our discussion of rule deontology or rules-ethics in chapter 1.

[25] A relevant comment on sabbath observance is found in the saying contained in Codex Bezae (D) at Mk. 3:4. 'On the same day, seeing one working on the sabbath, he (Jesus) said to him: "Man, if you know what you are doing, you are truly blessed; but if you don't know, you are accursed and a law-breaker"'.

[26] G. F. Moore, *Judaism*, vol. II, p. 100. See Moore's entire chapter on 'Motives of moral conduct', pp. 89–111.

[27] A. Cohen, *Everyman's Talmud*, 1932, r.p. 1949, p. 212. It was, however, recognised that certain qualities were uniquely divine and were not to be copied by man: e.g., divine 'jealousy' (Ex. 20:5), divine wrath and vengeance (Nahum 1:2).

and has begun to be the motive from which all other commandments should be obeyed. It is obvious that we are here very near to the Christian way of looking at the matter'.[28]

2. *Motive in New Testament teaching*

Motive has an obvious importance in New Testament teaching, and it is not surprising that some commentators have tended to see it out of perspective. According to gospel tradition, Jesus constantly rebuked the Pharisees for their preoccupation with external observances:[29] 'first cleanse the inside of the cup and of the plate...' (Matt. 23:26); 'pray to your Father who is in secret...' (6:6); 'out of the abundance of the heart the mouth speaks' (12:34). Jesus appears to place maximum emphasis on the elements of motive and intention in the Torah. The law against murder is interpreted as a prohibition of anger against one's brother (5:21f.); that against adultery is applied to lustful desire (5:27f.); that against excessive retribution is interpreted in terms of total non-resistance to evil (5:38–42). Jesus and a scribe, who was subsequently declared to be 'not far from the kingdom of God' (Mark 12:34), agree in taking love to God and neighbour as the supreme commandments, 'much more than all whole burnt offerings and sacrifices' (12:33). Probably at this point they were going beyond R. Hillel, who would have added 'The rest is commentary. Go and learn it'.[30] Jesus' attitude seems to be: 'These are the great commandments. The remainder are superseded'. The Law is reduced to three simple commands: love God, love your neighbour, and do as you would be done by.[31] The fact that the language of commandment is retained in this context is not without significance and raises the question of whether love *can* be commanded: a problem to which we shall return in due course.

Prominent as motive may be in the New Testament, it is clearly not the sole criterion of right action. Jesus stresses motive and action. He is concerned that the tree and its fruit should be wholesome (Matt. 12:33). Intention must be translated into action, as the parable of the two sons indicates (21:28–32). Besides, the nature of the Sermon on the Mount must be borne in mind in relation to much of the teaching in question. K. Stendahl has written:

'The point is not inner motivation compared with pharisaic casuistry, or warm concern for human values as opposed to hair-splitting legalism.

We are faced with Mt.'s collection of statements concerning the superior righteousness and its roots in Jesus' messianic restoration of the Law'.[32]

In the Sermon, Jesus' teaching brings the Law to full expression and reveals the full dimensions of its meaning and implications.[33] Hence the criterion of

---

[28] *On Paul and John*, 1963, p. 103.
[29] For example, Matt. 23 *passim*.
[30] Cf. Shab. 31a.
[31] Cf. T. W. Manson, *op. cit.*, p. 105.
[32] *Peake's Commentary on the Bible*, 1962, p. 776.
[33] See above, chapter 1, pp. 25ff.

motive is no more adequate than any other single criterion to represent the nature of New Testament teaching.

The motivation of New Testament morality is never simple. There is a parallel with the rabbinic notion of the imitation of God in the Sermon when Jesus bids his hearers identify with God in his concern for both good and evil: thus they will be sons of their Father (5:43–48). The morality of worldly detachment is made possible by the God who cares (6:25–34): the underlying notion is that of the covenant of the gracious God with his people. The covenant made through Christ is taken by Paul to supply a new motive power in the life of the believer (cf. Rom. 12:1f.). Henceforth the Christian is not concerned with mere outward conformity to the world. Rather, in responding to God's grace, he undergoes a transformation of mind and spirit, so that he is able to discern and give effect to the will of God in his life—knowing 'what is good, acceptable and perfect' (Rom. 12:2). He is 'strengthened in the inner man' (Eph. 3:16), a 'new creation' (2 Cor. 5:17). This transformation, however, is not automatic, nor does Christian conduct follow automatically from Christian profession. As I. T. Ramsey comments,

> 'No behaviour precepts, no theological conclusions follow incorrigibly from a moment of vision . . . we must certainly see to it that Christian convictions arising in disclosures, win a constant explication in behaviour and thought'.[34]

The kind of procedure indicated by Ramsey is well illustrated by Paul himself in the second chapter of Philippians. Rhetorically, he points to the appealing power of Christ, a power which brings conviction and inspiration and moves one to sympathy and compassion (2:1). He then underlines the quality of response he expects of the Philippians, viz., the creation of a loving community (2:2). He reinforces the response by pointing to the model presented by Christ himself (2:5–11): a model of humility, self-giving and obedient service. Finally, he exhorts his followers to obedience: indeed, to work out their own salvation, but with the assurance that 'it is God who works in you, inspiring both the will and the deed, for his own chosen purpose' (2:12f., N.E.B.). Here indeed is theological ethics, in which belief, motive and overt action are moulded into an integral whole.

3. *Can motives be commanded?*

This is a particular problem for ethics in the New Testament. What are we to make of such imperatives as "love your neighbour as yourself' or 'love God with all your heart. . .'? Can motives be commanded? In particular, can love (*agape*) be commanded?

The problem may be stated thus. If motives are feelings or emotions, as Locke, Bentham and J. S. Mill appear to have held, or even if they are personal tastes or involve emotional accompaniments, it is obvious that they cannot be commanded. Either I have an emotion or I do not have one. I cannot choose to have an emotion, and thus I am not free to command

[34] *Christian Discourse*, 1965, p. 26.

emotions even in myself. For the same reasons, if *agape* is an emotion, then it cannot be a moral motive—i.e., it cannot be a criterion of moral worth.

There is a fairly common position which holds that love can be commanded.[35] C. H. Dodd wrote about *agape*:

'It is not primarily an emotion or an affection; it is primarily an active determination of the will. That is why it can be commanded, as feelings cannot'.[36]

It is thus in effect argued that since we are commanded to love God and neighbour, *agape* cannot be an emotion but is a fixed disposition of the will—though how we can be commanded to have a disposition is never made clear.

This position can be criticised on several grounds.

First, it is not consonant with scripture. Dodd cites I John 3:17:

'But if anyone has the world's goods and sees his brother in need, yet closes his heart against him, how does God's love abide in him?'

Yet this does not support the view that *agape* is bereft of all emotional accompaniments (even if it is not itself an emotion). The 'heart' was regarded in Hebrew thought as the seat of the emotions, and so passed into the thought-world of the first century A.D. as an acceptable metaphor both for the affective element and for man's inner life. To 'close one's heart' against a brother will be to dam up one's compassion, to cease to allow an empathetic identification with the man in his trouble.

Secondly, Dodd's position is not self-consistent. He wrote again of *agape*:

'In the end it is not a virtue among other virtues to which men can aspire. It is that total attitude which is *brought about* by exposure to the love of God as it is expressed in Christ's self-sacrifice'.[37]

But if it is so brought about, it cannot be said to be commanded, unless in some paradoxical sense. Dodd, however, does not indicate that he intends a paradox, and so lays himself open to a charge of being confused. Further he comments on I John 4:19, 'We are capable of love, of *agape* at all, only because we are first its objects'.[38] This also appears to contradict the view that *agape* can be commanded. In the end, Dodd appears to support the view we wish to advance.

Thirdly, there was a considerable body of opinion, even before Wittgenstein, that *agape* cannot be commanded. T. W. Manson, for example, held that love can never be legislated, '. . . for it is of the very essence of love that it should be freely given, spontaneous, and not the laboured response to an external requirement'.[39] The commandments to love, consequently, are

---

[35] It has been held by Kant, C. H. Dodd and Joseph Fletcher. For Kant, see Alastair MacIntyre, *A Short History of Ethics*, (2), 1968, p. 194 and H. B. Acton, *Kant's Moral Philosophy*, 1970, pp. 11–13.

[36] *Gospel and Law*, 1951, p. 42. Fletcher borrows Dodd's phrase 'an active determination of the will' in *S.E.*, p. 105 (cf. *M.R.*, p. 21) and argues to the same effect: cf. *S.E.*, pp. 79 and 103 where F. agrees that love is not an emotion or feeling.

[37] *Op. cit.*, p. 42 (our italics).

[38] *Loc. cit.*

[39] *The Sayings of Jesus*, p. 36. Cf. Joseph Sittler, *The Structure of Christian Ethics*, 1958, e.g., pp. 40, 46 (cf. p. 25).

unenforceable: and that is another way of saying either that they are not commandments or that love cannot be commanded.

'If they are to be fulfilled at all, it must be by the willing obedience of men. A man can be compelled to abstain from work on the Sabbath, but he cannot be compelled to love God with all his heart'.[40]

There is, however, a more attractive and more biblical solution to the problem than that of Kant, Dodd and Fletcher. This is to regard the response of love *not as commanded, but evoked*, and the 'commands' to love God and one's neighbour, not as commands, nor even an obligation to have the motive of love but as an indication of the kind of response expected to the covenantal love of God. The love-imperatives in the Bible are not orders, although both Jews and Christians have always been in danger of misinterpreting them as such. But they are not optional recommendations either. They are indications of the response man will give if he apprehends or is apprehended by the divine grace and love. The fact that the language of response adopts the imperative mood shows the importance attached to the response to the divine initiative—a matter of life and death, of salvation and judgement. This means a relational view of Christian morality, where the behaviour is a response to, and evoked by, the divine grace. What arguments can we advance in support of this view?

First, though *agape* is not an emotion, our view refuses to divorce *agape* from union with the affective element. Paul Tillich was too balanced to fall into that error. Though he wrote,

'Semantically speaking, love, as faith, must be purged from many distorting connotations. The first is the description of love as emotion',[41]
two pages later we read:

'The emotional element cannot be separated from love; love without its emotional quality is "good will" towards somebody or something, but it is not love. This is also true of man's love of God, which cannot be equated with obedience, as some antimystical theologians teach'.[42]

But even God cannot *command* human *agape*, if it has any emotional overtones at all. Love is a response of the entire person and so has an emotional quality. To make response to the Gospel a mere matter of the intellect is a mistake commonly condemned; for the same reason it is not a mere matter of 'an active determination of the will'. Is there not in the love of Mother Teresa an affective element, as she cares for the homeless dying on the Calcutta pavements? And is she not a more appropriate model for *agape* than Kant, who interprets Christian love by means of the categorical imperative?

Secondly, we must guard against the assumption that what is grammatically in the imperative mood is necessarily and inevitably a command or order. This is an insight we owe to Ludwig Wittgenstein[43] who taught the

---

[40] *Op. cit.*, p. 305.
[41] *S.T.* III, p. 143. Cf. *Love, Power and Justice*, pp. 4–6.
[42] *S.T.* III, p. 145; cf. pp. 142–47.
[43] *Philosophical Investigations*, 2nd Ed. 1958, reprinted 1963.

wide variety of uses of language and not to mistake the grammar of words for their logic or meaning. The imperative mood in English has a wide variety of uses and to express a command is only one of them. Much depends on the context, including tone and inflexion. 'Give me a pencil' may be a request; 'Put the kettle on and I'll put the car away' may not be an order to my wife, but a suggestion for the division of labour. The language of prayer and hymns is full of imperatives addressed to God, and most of us believe that it is presumptuous to give orders to God: 'Send down Thy Holy Spirit' and 'Come down, O Love Divine' is the language of urgent beseeching,[44] whereas a less direct form with more words would sound tentative and insincere.[45] The teacher-and-pupil context provides many examples of the use of the imperative not as a command: e.g., 'Read such-and-such a book' (helpful suggestion), 'Try dividing by 4' or 'Try translating by x', when a teacher is helping a pupil to solve a mathematical problem or see the sense of a bit of text in another language. When a father is teaching his son to play chess and says, 'Move your bishop', he is making a suggestion or recommendation in short-hand which means, 'If you wish to win the game, I recommend you to think about moving your bishop'. The son knows that his father is not giving an order. He will consider the suggestion and make up his own mind whether he will act on it or not.[46] We must, then, look carefully at the love-imperatives in the Bible before we decide that they are orders. Some recent writers[47] who appear to take the love-sayings as simple commands seem unaware of the immense difficulties that thus arise and even of how their own writing soon contradicts their view. Joseph Sittler was at least aware of the problem:

'The believer is commanded to love . . . (For) faith alone can rescue
from nonsense the command to love. Nothing is more certain than that
love cannot be commanded'.[48]

But Sittler's solution to it is itself a nonsense! There is no need to create a nonsense from which faith alone can rescue the 'command to love'. Can even the action of God in Christ remove a nonsense in our terminology? Surely it is one thing to claim that God's action transforms and makes us capable of loving where before we were incapable of love, and quite another to claim that the absurdity in the 'command to love' can be removed by faith alone.

---

[44] It is arguable that the petitionary language of prayer and hymns is not in the imperative mood at all. But the Latin, the source of much of this language, uses the imperative, and even the German (usually a more polite language than English) retains it, as we see from e.g., Luther's version of the Psalter. While such inflected languages may settle the grammatical question of the mood, they do not settle the meaning, which is a matter of logic and hermeneutics.

[45] For example, 'Would you send down your Holy Spirit' sounds as if we are not sure either whether God wants to do this or we want it!

[46] We are indebted to Professor J. A. Whyte of St. Andrews for this illustration.

[47] V. P. Furnish, *The Love Command in the New Testament*, 1972 appears in his Introduction and first two chapters (e.g., pp. 19, 23) to stress the word 'command' in such a way as to press its literal meaning, but in Chapter III, entitled (*footnote* 48 *on page* 86)

Thirdly, Kant is right if a command-theory of ethics is the only one available, but a relational view delivers us from the difficulties. New Testament morality is characteristically of this relational type, because it has behind it the model of the covenant between Israel and Israel's God. In the covenant model, our response (e.g., gratitude, trust, dedication, love . . .) is evoked by the realisation of God's acceptance of us, and this response gains expression in behaviour. It is not a case of saying, 'You ought to be grateful and live lives of thankfulness because of what God has done for you'. That would be to resort to a command-theory of ethics. The difficulty is that 'ought' implies 'can', and we are not free to command even ourselves to be grateful. Gratitude is something that is evoked by what is done for us: then we *are* grateful. Similarly, we cannot love unless we are first loved (I John 4:19); love is evoked in us.

C. MOTIVE IN CHRISTIAN ETHICS

We are now in a position to look beyond the New Testament. It is sometimes suggested[49] that there is a central tradition in Christian ethics which emphasises the importance of good motives as compared with the consequences of action. Augustine and Abelard are among those who come to mind as likely candidates[50] for the position of main protagonist of this allegedly central tradition, and a consideration of their ethical positions should help to clarify the place of motive in Christian morality.

The famous saying of Augustine (A.D. 354–430),[51] '*Dilige et quod vis fac*', is sometimes taken to be the basis for this tradition, especially when translated as 'Love and do what you like'. But this saying has often been misunderstood, because people have lost the key to its understanding. Hebrew morality sprang from a response to the Exodus, which received definitive expression as God's mighty act of graciousness to which Israel was expected to respond in thankful praise and willing obedience to God's Torah. Its sanction was, therefore, relational, though its form tended to be prescriptive. But in the Judaism of the inter-testamental period it became increasingly a morality of obedience to a code, and that alone. Thus, despite the efforts of the best of the rabbis, Jewish morality became legalistic in the proper sense of the term. To counter such a tendency,

(*footnote 47 continued*)
'Paul: Faith Active in Love', his exposition of Paul's view of the relation between Christian behaviour and the Gospel is not consonant with a command-theory of ethics. Whether the author is entirely aware of the implications of this for his earlier use of the term 'command', the readers may never be quite sure, but at any rate he never examines the question whether the love imperative is simply a command. P. S. Minear, in his *Commands of Christ*, 1972, also fails to distinguish the imperative from command.
[48] *Op. cit.*, pp. 62–3.
[49] Cf. Beach and Niebuhr, *Christian Ethics*, p. 240.
[50] Luther is also a candidate in this context. His position is discussed in chapter 8.
[51] For a further discussion of Augustine, see below, pp. 134, 247.

Matthew presented Jesus as the bringer of the Messianic Torah,[52] and Paul risked the charge of antinomianism in order to set out a fully relational understanding of Christian conduct.[53] Yet the Church of the 2nd. and 3rd. centuries tended to follow Judaism into the captivity of legalism, and it was not until Augustine that the relational motif was effectively revived.

How then are we to interpret *Dilige et quod vis, fac*? To begin with, it does not mean that Christian love abrogates the use of rules in the Christian moral life. It 'in no way advocates doing the loving thing in spite of the rules'.[54] Nor does it mean that, if you have the motive of love, it does not matter what you do, however bestial. It is not an antinomian slogan, and Augustine did not intend to provide a latter-day charter for euthanasia or 'sexual freedom'. Joseph Fletcher fails to make this clear.

'Augustine was right again, as situationists see it, to reduce the whole Christian ethic to the single maxim, *Dilige et quod vis, fac* (Love with care, and *then* what you will, do'.)[55]

Fletcher rightly says that Augustine's saying does not mean *Ama et fac quod vis*, i.e., 'Love with desire and do what you please'. But there is more to it than this. In the context of the saying, the background is the use of arms against the Donatists,[56] and the saying has at least the flavour of 'Do in love what needs to be done, whether it *looks* loving or not'.[57]

The saying, however, must not only be taken in its immediate context; it must be set within the context of Augustine's theological position. When the self is transformed by the divine initiative, the person responds in love to God, and he will do so without fear, for he has been redirected by love. If the self is so redirected by love to God, then man can do what he wills. In that kind of situation, overt acts will take care of themselves, and rules are irrelevant. People misread Augustine because the tradition of a relational morality has been lost; the proper key to his understanding was thrown away long ago.

Motive, then, in a Christian setting is part of a wider question of the whole self and its inner life (including dispositions and traits of character) which have been transformed: it is part of the new man or the new creation. Moral sensitivity has an inner source; the criterion of morality is another question.

Peter Abelard (Abailard) (A.D. 1079–1142), was an attractive teacher, pursued by crowds of students, wherever he settled. He probed the accepted answers of his time in several fields, but he was probably never so unorthodox as his critics held, although at times there seemed justifiable grounds for suspicion. He was a little careless in the formulation of his views, especially as a young man. St Bernard of Clairvaux (1091–1153), a man of deep piety and even well-justified influence, finally accused Abelard

---

[52] See above, chapter 1, pp. 25ff.
[53] See above, chapter 1, p. 29f.
[54] *Teaching Christian Ethics*, 1974, p. 42.
[55] *S.E.*, p. 79.
[56] Homily VII, 8, on the First Epistle of John.
[57] *Teaching Christian Ethics*, loc. cit.

of heresy[58] and had him condemned by the Pope unheard, because he was afraid of being shown inadequate in public debate with this master of dialectic.

Indeed, Abelard was not afraid to think boldly in the field of ethics. In his *Scito te ipsum* and his *Commentary on Romans*, he put forward a view that was surprisingly original for the age in which he lived, although he did not bring his work on *Romans* into any kind of synthesis with his views expressed in *Scito te ipsum*. We believe that it would be fairer to Abelard to attempt the synthesis he failed to provide himself.

His doctrine of the Atonement has at least the promise of a relational view of Christian morality. In his *Commentary on Romans*, he declared that the death of Christ was not a ransom paid to the devil. To take it as if it were would be to imply, wrote Abelard, that the devil had man in his power, but this was never so. Rather the love of Christ shown in his Passion arouses or enkindles a love in us which conquers sin and is the ground of Christian behaviour.[59]

Unfortunately, Abelard sometimes presented his view as if Jesus had merely set an example of love and sacrifice that influenced people to imitate that love and self-sacrifice. While the Church has never made any theory of the Atonement authoritative, there has been widespread agreement that such an exemplarist or moral-influence view is unsatisfactory, as it makes the death of Jesus the Christ no different from that of any Christian martyr, nor perhaps from the death of Socrates, and it fails to do justice to the New Testament understanding of the death of Christ, as effecting a new relationship to God and, therefore, to our fellows. Abelard was rather careless in how he expressed his view, but it is unfair to credit him with a moral-influence theory of the Atonement. For him, the death of Christ did not merely influence people to imitate that life and death, but changed them in their inner life, so that their outward behaviour was changed.

Abelard's interest was in how man's inner life could be nourished, and not just in the demand of outward obedience. In the view prevalent in his day, sin was regarded as an outward act, in respect of which expiation had to be made in the form (as it were) of a fine, just as a murderer paid a definite fine for killing a nobleman, a clerk or a serf, and, of course, the fine was graduated according to the rank of the victim. Expiation in this form was easily made, for it left the inner man untouched—his dispositions, intentions, motivation, his moral sensitivity were all alike unaffected and unchanged. This kind of penance bore no relation to *metanoia* (repentance) in the New Testament.[60]

For Abelard, sin was not an outward act, a factual transgression of the law of God, a transgression conceived as possible even when that law was

---

[58] St. Bernard wrote of him: 'When he discusses the Trinity he sounds like Arius, when grace he sounds like Pelagius, when the person of Christ, like Nestorius'.

[59] Cf. (ed.) A. D. Galloway, *Basic Readings in Theology*, 1964, VII, pp. 102–7: the final paragraph of the excerpt from Abelard's *Romans* shows clearly his view of the Atonement.

[60] See above, p. 27.

unknown or misunderstood. Sin was rather contempt for God—not merely an action, but a total orientation of the self. Thus he located moral goodness, not in the conformity of an act with the will of God, but solely in the intention and will of the agent. Further, he taught a complete separation of actions and intentions. A good intention and a good act are two radically distinct goods, each sufficient for itself. It is, therefore, impossible to add the one to the other. The good act adds nothing to the good intention.

It follows from this that a person can do a materially blameworthy action with a good intention. So it was, wrote Abelard, with those who crucified Christ and those who put the martyrs to death. The former, for example, did not recognise and, therefore, did not intend to put to death, the 'Lord of glory'. People are not guilty of sin, if they act deliberately from a sense of duty—i.e., if their intention is to do their duty. Similarly, he held that a person can do a materially blameworthy action with a bad intention. But, in both cases, the action matters little, since in the eyes of God the intention alone counts. Such an ethical position we have already dismissed. If motive or intention (and for Abelard the two terms were interchangeable) is the sole criterion of moral worth, the most anti-social, licentious and bestial acts may be justified.

Abelard's view had very practical consequences in his own time. He struck at the financial foundations of many twelfth-century monasteries. They depended for their endowments on the numerous, large benefactions from wealthy people of high rank, whose motivation was, not love for God, but fear of divine punishment in the after-life. Large gifts of money were believed to expiate for sins committed, and religious houses grew wealthy on this doctrine. If the Christian life depended on an inward change of heart, a genuine *metanoia* or repentance, what (asked medieval churchmen) would happen to these 'good works'? Abelard believed that such a doctrine was not true to the New Testament. But to his critics, Paul's 'faith active in love' did not provide the strength of motivation for ordinary Christians which was given by a 'fire-escape' morality.

But it was not merely materialistic abbots who felt threatened. For Abelard, love was a good motive, while fear and desire for power and for honour from God or man were unworthy ones (even if they represented the motives of not a few medieval prelates). Abelard presented the Pauline view of the new man, transformed and transfigured by Christ, capable of love to God and man, without ulterior motive or prudential reason—not even the desire to make one's monastery wealthier, to achieve an archbishopric, or to rule the more lowly diocese. Further, Abelard commanded the young to love with all their beings, and to love with passion; and it was little wonder that even the pious were alarmed. Clearly whatever motive Abelard thought was supreme, many people had many different motives for silencing him.[61]

---

[61] One conclusion affecting Abelard's private life could be drawn. As we have already seen, his position was that in the eyes of God the intention alone matters,

The best that can be said for Abelard's ethical position is that he had grasped that in Christianity motive is part of a wider view, a morality of response evoked by God's grace, a response that includes the inner man. But he overstated the relational view as if it were setting out, not the source of moral awareness for the Christian, but the sole criterion of moral worth (the strong form of the motive-theory). We suggest that he was striving after a relational view and trying to speak of the source of Christian living as deep within a person's being.

Abelard indeed pioneered views which became later ethical common-places when they were incorporated into scholastic moral theology. It was agreed, for example, that a person at the moment of action must choose deliberately and freely what seems to him to be right. It became also a respectable claim that, by so doing, he performs right action, even though, had he had greater moral insight or a more thorough understanding of the circumstances, he would have acted differently. But scholastic moral theology did not, as we do not, accept the view that *any* action is justified by its motive.

Conclusions

In this chapter we have discovered some important features of the Christian life that have to be encompassed in the shape we give to Christian ethics. *Agape* is a motive for behaviour but in no ordinary sense as one motive among others; it is a continuing response to the divine love which affects the whole person—motives, dispositions, traits of character—and constitutes a new life. For the Christian, there cannot be a plurality of independent moral norms, for what unites the various norms is the pre-eminence of *agape*. Or, to put it another way, *agape* is the pre-eminent 'virtue' because the archetypal Christian response is *agape* and the archetypal fruit of Christian faith is *agape*. Partial failure in wisdom or prudence, in justice and moderation will never seem so appalling to the Christian as a complete failure in love; and a first-class mark, so to speak, in wisdom will never compensate for a failure completely to relate to people.[62] *Agape* is more like a total orientation of the self than one of the many motives that one may choose for conduct.

It is 'the heart . . . that makes us right or wrong'.[63] But while this must not be emphasised so exclusively as to give the impression that a person's

<hr>

(*footnote* 61 *continued*)
and that every act, even one wrong materially, is innocent if dictated by the sentiment of pure love. Perhaps even Abelard did not mean to push his argument to that length, but it was certainly how many understood him in his day. On this view, Heloise could have held that her premarital affair with Abelard, though technically wrong, was innocent because she acted out of pure love. Heloise would appear to have drawn this conclusion, but, then, the genuineness of her letters has been questioned this century, and their authorship even attributed to Abelard.
[62] Cf. 1 Corinth. 13:1–13.
[63] Robert Burns, *Epistle to Davie*.

'heart can be in the right place' even when he never acts beneficently, it is equally myopic in a Christian understanding to emphasise the outward act alone. Any view of morality, no matter from however august a source,[64] that fixes attention solely on the outward act or even gives the impression of so doing, does an injustice to a Christian understanding of morality as well as a grave disservice to the growth of responsible personhood. If the moral judgement is focused on certain acts—e.g., premarital sex, homosexual practices and masturbation—the impression is given that the important thing in morality is the doing or refraining from certain actions that can be listed. Further the impression is given all too easily that morality is concerned with only a few acts, usually with those to do with sex. Again, if moral teaching is linked to a form of the divine-command theory which seems to suggest that all that God has commanded is restricted to refraining from these few actions and that these are the only ones covered by the divine command, then this teaching is likely to discourage the young from taking the initiative in their own behaviour, and from doing what they believe to be right, simply because they see it needs doing and they are willing to help someone in need. A too narrow view both of morality and of God's claim on people's lives will probably be taught, however unintentionally, and probably be learned, however subconsciously. Roman Catholic moral theologians are increasingly aware of this defect in past teaching, and are drawing attention to the vast area of living, not covered by such rules and prohibitions, where people's free and responsible actions and initiative are called for.[65] In Christian ethics, we must seek a model for decision-making, the use of which will not create a generation of zombies.

[64] Cf. the Vatican pronouncement, *Declaration on Certain Questions Concerning Sexual Ethics*, given in Rome at the Sacred Congregation For the Doctrine of the Faith, 29 December, 1975. Roman Catholic writers have observed how different this *Declaration* (1975) and the encyclical *Humanae Vitae* (1968) are from the views on marriage and the family expressed in the documents of Vatican II and in the Majority Report of the 'Papal Commission for the Study of Population, the Family, and Birth'. For example, in the U.K. the psychiatrist Jack Dominian in *Proposals for a New Sexual Ethic*, 1977, p. 20 is highly critical of both the *Declaration* and the encyclical, demanding that 'the whole basis of Christian teaching on sexual morality needs fundamental reconstruction' (p. 21) and suggests that the basis be 'the concept of person, in terms of human wholeness, and love . . .' (p. 10)—cf. our chapter 10 below. In the U.S.A., A. Kosnik and others (edd.), *Human Sexuality: New Directions in Catholic Thought* (A Study Commissioned by The Catholic Theological Society of America), 1977, is mildly critical of the encyclical (pp. 48–49) and places emphasis on the more personalistic, positive and pastoral notes in the *Declaration*, but says the *Declaration's* 'treatment of specific issues (premarital sex, homosexuality and masturbation) appears to be exaggeratedly absolute and legalistic' (p. 52). To us, the *Declaration* seems strangely ambivalent: the doctrine that certain acts, irrespective of situation, consequences, motives etc., are intrinsically right and others intrinsically wrong seems to be held (e.g., pp. 7 and 14); yet, alongside this, there is at least an incipient relational view of Christian morality (e.g., pp. 17, 20 and the last page, where Vatican II is quoted).

[65] See chapter 7 below, pp. 165–9.

Some important features of such a model seem to be emerging. It will promote moral insight rather than expect people to act on rule of thumb. It will cover new situations for which authority provides no law. It will enable the agent to give reasons for his behaviour—other than mere authority. It will centre on *agape* which, as we have seen, is a continuing response in the whole of a person's life to the divine love.

Part Two

FROM MORALITY TO CHRISTIAN ETHICS

4

MORALITY AND RELIGION

As soon as the topic of religion and morality is raised, we are in danger of being engulfed in ideological warfare. 'Morals without religion' has been the battle-cry of secular humanism.[1] If religious teaching is used as a means of bolstering morality, then—it is suggested—rejection of religion may result in young people rejecting morality as well. It is better, therefore, to have a form of moral education that does not make appeal to religion in this way.[2] The opposite ideology assumes that morality depends wholly and directly on religion and therefore cannot be taught or caught unless religion is taught or caught. 'No morality without religion' is its slogan. So strongly is this view held in some quarters that any denial of it is regarded as tantamount to joining the humanist or atheistic camps. But this is not the only view that Christians have held. They have held several, and there is no reason for regarding this one as the norm of orthodoxy; nor is it held by any major theological figure nowadays.

The way forward, however, is to ignore all propaganda and to subject the different viewpoints to critical analysis. We examine four views: (1) that morality is dependent on religion; (2) that religion is dependent on morality; (3) that morality and religion are distinct and independent; and (4) that morality and religion are distinct but interdependent.

1. *Morality is dependent on religion*

The view that morality depends directly and wholly on religion takes three main forms.

(1) There is the view that one cannot be moral without holding some form of religious belief or making some religious confession of faith. In its strongest form, this view holds that no moral concept can be understood and no moral awareness or insight is possible without understanding or awareness of religious concepts, including religious faith. The moral distinctions we normally make, e.g., between right and wrong, good and bad, have no *meaning* apart from religion.

---

[1] Cf. M. Knight, *Morals without Religion*, 1960.
[2] Cf. *Religious and Moral Education:* a pamphlet containing some proposals for County Schools by a group of Christians and humanists (circulated privately). The same difficulty seen from the standpoint of a professional philosopher is stated by W. G. Maclagan in *The Theological Frontier of Ethics*, 1961, p. 186.

This view claims to be stating a *fact*, *viz.*, that people are not moral unless they are also religious. Now there is one way of settling a factual claim, *viz.*, by appeal to experience. We have *in fact* known people who were not only moral (as distinct from a-moral) but were capable of the highest degree of moral sensitivity and activity (i.e., were far from being immoral) and who made no religious confession of faith. Moral awareness in their case was not directly dependent on religious awareness. Others tell us that they have met these people too. This view then does not square with experience, nor do Christian theologians today lend any support to it. A modern theologian writes in characteristic vein:

'We shall defend the view that plain men, including unbelieving and non-religious plain men, can *discern* the difference between right and wrong and can act dutifully'.[3]

(2) There is the view that, while one can be moral without being religious in the above sense, the moral distinctions we make have no *justification* apart from religion. Moral concepts, indeed our very moral awareness itself, need justification in terms of religion.[4]

This view is not so easy to deal with as the first, with which it is often confused. The argument is sometimes met that if there be no God and if this space-time universe be the whole of reality, then our value-judgements would be no more than expressions of our own subjective tastes, and, in practice, might would be right, and the last word would lie with the dictator. This point of view was expressed by Professor Leonard Hodgson in his Gifford Lectures.[5] H. D. Lewis piquantly and rightly replies:

'I am sure that if he lost his faith he would not in fact side with the dictator or regard questions of good and bad as matters of mere subjective taste'.[6]

Yet Professor Lewis knows that the argument only begins at this point.

For Hodgson did not mean that he could not be moral without holding his religious faith (version 1 above). He meant (version 2) that, when morality is understood in its full implications, it cannot be *justified* without holding a religious position. The case for ethical objectivity, as opposed to subjectivism, depends upon such a religious justification. This is one form of the view that there is some kind of logical relationship (of dependence or derivability) between religion and morality. Another form would be that the whole moral quest raises the question, 'Why be moral at all? Why be good?', and that this question cannot be answered save in religious terms, i.e., morality itself requires a religious justification.

Does the case for ethical objectivity depend upon holding a religious

---

[3] J. Richmond, *Faith and Philosophy*, 1966, p. 96.
[4] H. D. Lewis, *Philosophy of Religion*, 1965, p. 258. A corollary of this view is that, if religion is denied, then morality will be denied also. In the words of H. D. Lewis, 'What is right, it is argued, is what God has ordained, and if religion is without substance' morality 'in any proper sense must be found wanting too'. This is also a corollary of version (1) above.
[5] *For Faith and Freedom*, Vol. I., 1956, pp. 130–1.
[6] *Op. cit.*, p. 258. Cf. the same author's *Our Experience of God*, 1970, pp. 325–6.

view? Even at this early stage in our discussion we can give a confident 'no' to that question. Of the many philosophers who have argued for objectivity in ethics, some have been humanists and others have used arguments that showed no dependence on a religious position (for example, G. E. Moore and W. D. Ross).[7] Besides, to argue that morality cannot be justified[8] without religion is to claim too much. The most that might be claimed is that morality requires some kind of ultimate justification in terms of either religion or philosophy. Whether this would be to claim that morality depends directly and wholly on religion or philosophy is another matter. 'Direct dependence' and 'ultimate justification' do not sound like similar concepts.

Of course, any form of the view that morality is dependent on religion may be defended by making the definition of religion so wide that nothing is excluded: '. . . everybody is religious. To be human is to be religious. So therefore I am religious!' In this way, the data of the historical religions of the world are drowned in pools of watery meaning. Another common device is to smuggle in the word 'ultimate'. This needs careful handling. Consider this argument for the dependence of moral education upon religious education:

'. . . morality involves at least one ultimate valuation—*viz*., your answer to the question, What do you count as of ultimate moral worth?—and to make such an ultimate valuation is to make a religious assertion'.

Exponents of such arguments fail to realise that people, including non-religious philosophers, bestow ultimate valuation on various objects: some may even bestow it on 'clarity of thinking'! The argument, of course, only works if there is a suppressed minor premiss: something like, 'Only God is of ultimate worth'. There is also an equivocal use of the term 'ultimate', *viz*., as meaning now 'normative' or 'without qualification', and now 'transcendent' of this world, man and all his achievements, 'The Beyond'.

Another example of the view that morality is dependent on religion is the not uncommon approach which advocates, in effect, 'no morality without Christianity'. Thus the Earl of Selborne, when moving the passage of the Education Bill of 1944 (England and Wales) in the House of Lords, spoke of the beginning of a pilgrimage which he claimed, would lead to

'. . . an England which avows as never before the principles of liberty, justice, toleration and discipline, on which this realm depends, and which themselves are founded on the teaching of the Church of Christ'.[9]

A connection is assumed between on the one side the moral concepts of liberty, justice, toleration and discipline, and on the other Christianity on which they are claimed to be founded. This is historically false. Aristotle had much to say of justice in his *Nicomachean Ethics*, as well as Plato in the

---

[7] Cf. H. D. Lewis, *op. cit.*, p. 325.
[8] In any case, 'justification' is a very slippery term and a full discussion would require some consideration of its different meanings.
[9] Cf. Official Reports in Parliamentary Debates (Lords), vol. 132, cols. 970–71.

Republic.[10] It could be argued that liberty and toleration are founded as much on the eighteenth century *Aufklärung* as on the Church of Jesus Christ, while discipline is by no means an exclusively Christian concept. Christianity borrowed some of its moral ideas both from the Jews and Greeks, and moral ideas and principles are found in many cultures and religions. Paul appears to recognise this fact clearly enough in Romans 2:14f. And most Christians believe not in a God who keeps aloof from the world as a whole and intervenes only in Christianity, but in the one transcendent God who is immanent in the world and in all human life, and gracious towards all men in all nations.

(3) There is the view that no moral action can be achieved, no duty done, without divine assistance; that grace is required if we are to act morally; that without the help of religion, it is impossible for us to do what morality requires.[11]

We must ask first what the phrase 'without the help of religion' means. Does it mean that God the Creator, whose Spirit works in the hearts of all men, enables them to act morally—just as he enables men to write books, paint pictures, and so on? The trouble is that when God's activity is pictured on so vast and general a scale as this, it ceases to have any value for the argument—as well as being impossible to check against experience at all. In terms of theism, since we cannot even exist without God, it follows that we cannot be moral without him; but that is the truth of an axiom, not much better (if at all) than a tautology.

Does it mean that men cannot attain virtue without a religious motivation (e.g., hope of heaven, fear of hell, or love towards God)? As a factual claim, that is simply false. It is untrue to experience to hold that non-believers cannot attain to moral virtue without religious motivation, unless we give a special sense to 'virtue'—but that is not the issue here. And it would be a little far-fetched to suggest that the phrase means that God provides certain conditions without which morality would not be possible—intelligence, nurture by other human beings and freedom from disease which might, for example, entail brain damage. When we contemplate such cases, we might say, 'There but for the grace of God go I', but this is not what people usually mean when they say that one cannot lead a truly moral life without the help of God.

Nor is it adequate to hold that the divine assistance, while essential to moral progress, is an activity of which we are unconscious. There can be no empirical evidence for this, let alone empirical confirmation. On the other hand, if we hold that the activity of God is one of which we are conscious, we must face the fact that there have been and are atheists and agnostics who live out in their lives high moral standards.

Is there, then, nothing to be said for the view we are discussing? Clearly, it claims too much and requires modification. By its extravagant claims it

---

[10] See below, pp. 150f., 163f.

[11] The meaning of 'grace' for Christian faith and life is discussed in a later chapter: see pp. 116ff. Here the question is how it relates to the moral discernment of the plain man (including the unbelieving and non-religious plain man).

succeeds in obscuring important empirical evidence, which consequently must be brought forward into new prominence. The fact of moral failure is important:

'I do not understand my own actions. I do *not* what I want to do, and I do in fact what I detest' (Rom. 7:15).

Paul's kind of moral frustration was known also to Aristotle, who described it as *akrasia*, incontinence: one knows what is right but does not do it. But as well as the fact of moral failure there is the fact that Paul and many others have experienced a new factor, which they have identified as the operation of divine grace and which has enabled them to make the transition from the old life of moral failure to the new life of moral strength. This awareness of grace, or encounter with grace, is thus a factor which is relevant for our consideration of the relationship between religion and morality. It does not change the nature of morality: duty remains duty, right remains right, even if one calls it 'God's will'.[12] But such an awareness of God's grace can enable us to do our duty in a way we might not have otherwise done. It makes sense to claim that religion is, or can be, a great help to moral achievement. It may provide 'an insight not otherwise obtainable'[13] into worth and duty, and especially about the course to be followed on particular occasions.

'Our characters are modified and our interests transformed and elevated . . . But what we attain in this way is not strictly moral worth, it is virtue perhaps, there being a precedent for using the word "virtue" to designate admirable traits of character, such as a brave or charitable disposition'.[14]

The use here of 'virtue' is a different use from that of 'right', 'duty' and 'obligation'. Iris Murdoch has written:

'It is significant that the idea of goodness (and of virtue) has been largely superseded in Western moral philosophy by the idea of rightness, supported perhaps by some conception of sincerity'.[15]

However this may be, it is clear that the relation between morality and religion (or Christianity) needs to be carefully stated. This problem is discussed below.[16]

2. *Religion is dependent on morality*

This is the view that the relationship between religion and morality is to be explained in terms of the dependence of religion on morality: i.e., it is derivable from or is based on morality. It is thus the exact contrary of the view discussed above.

Matthew Arnold (1822–88) thought that religion was very little more than morality.

'Religion, if we follow the intention of human thought and human

---

[12] That is, the autonomy of morality is not impugned; see below, pp. 109f.
[13] H. D. Lewis, *Our Experience of God*, 1970, p. 331.
[14] *Ibid.*
[15] *The Sovereignty of Good*, 1970, p. 53.
[16] See below, pp. 107–11.

language in the use of the word, is ethics heightened, enkindled, lit up by feeling; the passage from morality to religion is made when to morality is applied emotion. And the true meaning of religion is thus, not simply *morality*, but *morality* touched by *emotion*'.[17]

In the twentieth century, the philosopher R. B. Braithwaite created a stir in Cambridge by becoming a Christian 'on terms' worked out like a special concordat between himself and the Church of England authorities. The terms were understood to be at least consonant with the lines indicated in his essay 'An Empiricist's View of Religious Belief'.[18] He held that to make a *religious* assertion was equivalent to declaring adherence to a policy of action, i.e., affirming an intention to act in a particular sort of way; and to make a Christian confession of faith was to declare an intention to live an agapeistic way of life (from *agape*, the outgoing love for the other as represented in the New Testament). He did distinguish religious from moral assertions, in that the former are accompanied by particular stories, while the latter are not. In the case of Christianity, these stories include the biblical (and Braithwaite meant what are usually indicated by such terms as myths, legends, sagas, fables, parables, allegories, doctrines) and are drawn from the Christian tradition. But it is not necessary for the person making a Christian confession of faith to believe that the stories are true; they simply give him psychological support to follow a pattern of behaviour he might otherwise spurn.

According to this view (in whatever form) religion is an aspect of, but not (quite) the same as, morality. Religion is dependent on morality and is more or less reducible to it. What criticism can be advanced against this contention? In the first place, the view gives a false phenomenological picture of each of the major world religions, with the possible exception of Confucianism.[19] They are each a complex of beliefs, practices and structures, and in these complexes morality is an interlocking factor, but only one factor. Each of the others[20] is important and interlocking also. Secondly, it is untrue that religious adherents have understood their doctrines in the way that Braithwaite does.

---

[17] Matthew Arnold, *Literature and Dogma*, 1888, p. 15f. (Arnold's italics). Such a view was more than a nineteenth century liberal aberration. H. D. Lewis claims that, among other theologians, John Baillie, in *Our Knowledge of God*, came very near to equating God with the moral order itself: see H. D. Lewis, *Our Experience of God*, 1959, 1970, p. 334.

[18] This essay has been reprinted in a number of publications, e.g., Ian T. Ramsey (ed.), *op. cit.*, and Richmond and Bowden (edd.), *A Reader in Contemporary Theology*.

[19] Of course, many hold that Confucianism is in fact more like a moral system than a religion.

[20] As a recent study puts it, the data of Christianity are set within a historical context which provides the framework within which the main subdivisions may be conceptualised in terms of eight dimensions. These are: (1) the communal—the church and her denominations; (2) worship; (3) the cultural—church, state and society; (4) the ethical—ethics and Christian ethics; (5) the scriptural; (6) the doctrinal; (7) the philosophical—incl. apologetics; and (8) spirituality. A similar model could be applied to other religious traditions. Cf. F. Whaling, 'Christianity as a world religion', in *Education in Religion*, The Journal of the Scottish Working Party on Religions of the World in Education, I, 2, 1977.

If the first criticism is turned by holding (as we do not) that all these complexes can be reduced to, or are unimportant and incidental accompaniments of, the main moral theme, the second cannot be so easily refuted. In the Christian tradition, for example, doctrinal statements have not been used merely as psychological support for moral action (though attempts are made today thus to secularise them), but have been treated as (however inadequate) symbols of the nature of the one, transcendent and gracious Being, who draws near to each of us. Of course, we know that some hold that Christians are mistaken in so treating their doctrines, but the grounds for this position would have to be more broadly based than the (near) reduction of religion to morality.

3. *Morality and religion are distinct and independent*

The view that morality and religion are independent takes two main forms, corresponding to two main senses in which philosophers argue for the 'autonomy of morality'.[21] The first holds that morality and religion are distinct and autonomous realms of discourse. The second takes moral actions to be the expression of an autonomous rational will. Consequently, on both of these senses of autonomy, the relation of morality and religion is understood to be an external or extrinsic one. While their concerns may coincide or overlap at certain points, they are essentially independent of each other. In particular, morality is a complete realm of meaning in itself; it has no need of any assistance that religion might offer it, as this would make morality heteronomous or under the control or jurisdiction of religion.

How are the advocates of a religious morality or a theological ethics to respond to this double-stranded challenge? Must a religious morality always impugn the autonomy of morality, or are there some forms of theological ethics that do not impose a heteronomy on morality? Is there any possibility of an intrinsic relationship between a religious morality and general morality? We shall scrutinise the two main forms of the argument in turn.

1. *Morality and religion are two distinct and autonomous realms of discourse.* This view is supported by philosophical writers in the field of education, such as P. H. Hirst and R. S. Peters, who hold that morality and religion are two distinct 'forms of knowledge', on the ground that the content of morality and our ways of knowing in morality are different from the content of religion and our ways of knowing in religion.[22]

There are two main philosophical grounds for this view. The first is to

---

[21] Also called 'the autonomy of ethics'. We shall treat both phrases as interchangeable in their various senses, except that 'the autonomy of ethics' is more often used in the context of ethical discussion by philosophers and theologians (though not to the exclusion of the other phrase) than in other debates concerning secularisation and moral development.

[22] *The Logic of Education*, 1970, pp. 63f.; cf. also Peter McPhail *et al. Moral Education in the Secondary School*, 1972, p. 20; P. H. Hirst, 'Liberal Education and the Nature of Knowledge', in R. D. Archambault (ed.), *Philosophical Analysis and Education*, 1965; P. H. Hirst, *Knowledge and the Curriculum*, 1974; cf. P. H. Phenix, *Realms of Meaning*, 1964.

the effect that no evaluative term, such as right or good, can be defined in non-evaluative terms. This argument concerns the meaning of evaluative terms. One formulation of the 'autonomy of morality' is 'the contention that ethical and indeed valuation concepts generally are quite distinctive and cannot simply be reduced to those of any other branch of knowledge (or any combination of them)'[23]—whether science, metaphysics or theology. Those who infringe this principle and define moral concepts in non-moral terms are said to be guilty of committing 'the naturalistic fallacy', i.e., analysing an ethical concept such as goodness in terms of a natural or non-moral quality.[24]

There are, however, some terms which carry an evaluative as well as a factual meaning: e.g., 'humanity', 'rationality' and 'God' when taken in the context of the world's religions and not divorced from them as a pawn in a philosopher's argument.[25] If the fallacy is restated thus:

'If a term carries an evaluative meaning, it must not be reduced to a non-evaluative meaning',

then no difficulty is raised for a religious morality or a theological ethics.

The second philosophical ground for the view that morality and religion are two autonomous realms of discourse concerns not the meaning of evaluative terms, but inference from any empirical or factual premiss. Moral judgements, it is held, cannot be formally deduced from statements of fact: e.g., 'x is good' cannot be inferred from the premiss, 'People approve of x'. Some writers have reformulated 'the naturalistic fallacy' in these terms. This argument is to be traced to David Hume's famous words:

'In every system of morality which I have hitherto met with, I have always remarked, that the author proceeds for some time in the ordinary way of reasoning, and establishes the being of a God, or makes observations concerning human affairs; when of a sudden I am surprised to find, that instead of the usual copulations of propositions, *is* and *is not*, I meet with no proposition that is not concerned with an

---

[23] A. C. Ewing, 'The Autonomy of Ethics' in I. T. Ramsey (ed.), *Prospect for Metaphysics*, 1961, p. 33, and quoted by Ramsey himself in 'Moral Judgements and God's Commands', essay no. 9 in his edited work, C.E.C.P., p. 156. Cf. H. D. Lewis, *Morals and the New Theology*, 1947, pp. 33–40; and D. M. Emmet, *Rules, Roles and Relations*, 1966, pp. 36ff.

[24] G. E. Moore (in *Principia Ethica*, 1903, chapter I) was the first to write on the naturalistic fallacy: he held that, as goodness was a non-natural, simple (i.e., unanalysable), and therefore indefinable quality, it could not be reduced to a natural quality. Moore's particular formulation of the fallacy has not met with wide acceptance, partly because he was open to criticism in calling goodness a simple unanalysable property, and partly because there may be other kinds of definition than the ones he described. There has been much philosophical discussion as to the correct way or ways to formulate the fallacy. Cf. the question of 'is' and 'ought' below.

[25] 'Human' may mean (a) a member of the species *homo sapiens*, as distinct from the other animals—descriptive use—and (b) what a fully human life *ought to be like*, as when people say that the aim of moral or Christian activity is 'to make human life fully human'. The descriptive and valuational uses of 'rational', 'rationality' are given later in this chapter, pp. 105ff.

ought, or an *ought not*. This change is imperceptible; but is, however, of
the last consequence. For as this *ought*, or *ought* not, expresses some new
relation or affirmation, it is necessary that it should be observed and
explained; and at the same time that a reason should be given, for what
seems altogether inconceivable, how this new relation can be a deduction from others, which are entirely different from it'.[26]
Hume's argument may be generalised into the form that factual statements
cannot entail evaluative or regulative principles. Does this argument deny
the possibility of any religious morality or theological ethics?

Much depends, again, on how precisely the naturalistic fallacy is to be
formulated. Does it deny—

(a) that statements about the created order entail evaluative or regulative principles (as in natural law doctrine[27] or the 'orders of creation')?[28]

(b) that the attributes of God entail evaluative and regulative principles?

(c) that historical statements (e.g., the history of Israel and the life of
Jesus) entail evaluative principles?[29]
No doubt each of these statements involves different kinds of facts, and each
would need different treatment, but if the naturalistic fallacy makes all
three denials, there can be no theological ethics at all; while if it does not
make any of these denials, or only some of them, the way is open to some
form(s) of theological ethics.

The whole issue of theological ethics centres on how the naturalistic
fallacy is to be formulated. The fallacy seems to point to something
important which can be formulated in the following hypothetical way:

'If a factual statement contains no evaluative or regulative principles, it
cannot entail any such principle'.

This formulation can be wholeheartedly accepted, while leaving open the
question whether there are not some kinds of factual statements that do
involve evaluative or regulative principles: for example, in our discussion of
natural law we claim that in one sense there are. On the other hand,
there are some forms of theological ethics which do appear to commit the
naturalistic fallacy, e.g., the divine-command theory of ethics as usually
formulated. This formulation makes two assertions: first, that the divine
will always comes in the form of a command: in the last chapter, we
directed criticism against that assertion; secondly, that an action is right or
wrong, *if and only if and because* God commands or forbids it: we are
concerned here only with this second assertion.

The naturalistic fallacy restates in terms of twentieth-century discussion
an ancient objection to the divine-command theory of ethics.[30] As Socrates

[26] *A Treatise of Human Nature*, 1739, Book 3, Part I, Section I, (Everyman Edition,
Vol. Two, pp. 177–78).

[27] Cf. chapter 7 where there is a full discussion of natural law.

[28] Cf. chapter 8 for discussion of the orders of creation.

[29] A. D. Galloway in 'Fact and Value in Theological Ethics' (*Religious Studies* 5,
1969) raises these three questions regarding the naturalistic fallacy.

[30] For our definition of a divine-command theory of ethics, see p. 14f. above.

asked in effect in the *Euthyphro*,[31] is something right because God commands
it, or does God command it because it is right? Euthyphro gave the answer
that most people would still give, *viz.*, that God commands it because it is
right. Socrates points out that in that case Euthyphro must give up the
theory he had in effect advanced, *viz.*, that what makes an action right is
the fact that God commands it. For Euthyphro's answer implies that what
is right is so independently of whether God commands it or not—in other
words, God does not make it right or create its rightness *merely* by
commanding it. The divine-command theory appears to commit the naturalistic fallacy because *the mere fact* that God commands an action can entail
no evaluative or regulative principle.[32]

There is another and related objection to the divine-command theory. It
is contended that, if what is right is simply what God commands, then if
God were to command, for example, cruelty or injustice, such things as
cruel and unjust actions would be right. The reply might be given that God
would or could not command cruelty because that would be against his
nature, which is good. But this is to desert the divine-command theory as
we have formulated it, for it is introducing another reason for action than
the mere fact of God's command, *viz.*, his goodness. Again, we see that the
theory appears to commit the naturalistic fallacy, but if reference is
introduced to God's moral attributes, then they may entail evaluative and
regulative principles, and in that case the fallacy is not being committed.

We are prepared to acknowledge that any religious morality or theological ethics is not credible if it impugns the autonomy of morality as we
have understood it above. The thesis, however, that morality and religion
are two distinct and autonomous realms of discourse need not imply that
there is a complete dichotomy between the two and that there can be no
relationship between them, other than that religion may give a reinforcement to morality. To rule out a divine-command theory of ethics (which we
rejected in the last chapter on other grounds) is not to rule out every form
of religious morality or theological ethics, nor to eliminate the kind of
Christian ethics for which we shall argue in due course.

2. *Moral actions are the expression of an autonomous, rational will.* If moral
action issues from *the autonomy of the rational will*, what implication does this
have for a religious morality or a theological ethics?

The term 'autonomy'[33] is frequently used in the sense of 'not imposed

---

[31] Plato, *Euthyphro*, 12, 10.

[32] Peter Geach, in *God and the Soul* (1969), discusses in chapter 9 the relation between
religion and morality. It is not clear whether he accepts the divine-command
theory as we have expounded it, but he rejects the view that 'all our appraisals of
good and bad logically depend on knowledge of God'—e.g., our knowledge that
lying is wrong is independent of any revelation.

[33] This version of the autonomy of morality goes back to Kant for whom autonomy
had two aspects: action to be moral, as distinct from immoral, (a) must not be
imposed by an external authority (whether God, society, the church or the state),
and (b) must not be dictated by emotion, desire or pleasure, but proceed from the
practical reason or will. This is the origin of two shades of meaning in modern
discussion of 'the autonomy of morality'—i.e., 'autonomous' means (a) 'not
externally imposed' and (b) 'done for a reason', 'rational'.

by some external authority, but self-imposed by the rational will'. This is said to be a mark of the final stage of moral development when the mature adult accepts standards for himself, and no longer are they imposed by parents, society or whatever. Does this rule out all forms of religious morality? N. H. G. Robinson answered in a clear negative in the following exposition of the autonomy of morality in this sense:

> 'Morality by its very nature involves a law or a standard or a norm which is independent of the desires of the individual agent; and the problem of autonomy and heteronomy arises in connection with this standard, for it may be conceived as self-imposed or as imposed from without by another. Thus by autonomy is meant a conception of the moral life as one lived in accordance with a law which proceeds from within and is imposed by the self upon itself. . . '.[34]

As Robinson pointed out, this problem arises for any ethical system, and not only for a religious morality. It must not be assumed that all religious-based ethics are inevitably heteronomous and that all secular-based ethics are inevitably autonomous. If the latter recognises a norm of any sort, then the question arises, 'Is the norm conceived as externally imposed (as with children at certain stages of their moral development), or is it conceived as self-imposed?'

The term 'rational' also requires scrutiny. It is clear that Kant who is the origin of this sense of autonomy meant that an action to be moral must be rational in the sense of issuing not from desire, emotion or pleasure, but from the practical reason or will. If reason is to be the only source of action that is morally autonomous, then action proceeding from any other source will be heteronomous. Is a morality proceeding from religious faith inevitably heteronomous in this sense? For Kant an action to be rational must be in accordance with law[35] and for him the marks of the moral law and, therefore, of rationality were the categorical imperative and universalizability. We noted[36] that Kant believed that it was the great merit of his theory that it did not prescribe the *content* of the moral law. The categorical imperative has form only, no content. What reason, then, prescribes are purely *formal* characteristics: they give no concrete guidance as to what to do in any given situation. Only when we have proposed to ourselves a policy of action as a candidate for implementation, can we apply Kant's two criteria of the categorical imperative and universalizability. Kant's theory of the moral law, then, does not rule out a religious morality: indeed it seems to invite rational, human beings to find the content of morality elsewhere and then bring it to the bar of reason.[37] That source, of course, need not be religion. But whatever the source, the law, standard or norm has to be imposed by the rational will on itself, and not be imposed from without by another. As Robinson freely admitted, it is generally agreed that

[34] *The Groundwork of Christian Ethics*, 1971, p. 149: cf. p. 172. The whole of chapter 7 of Robinson's work has a valuable discussion of the relation between autonomy and heteronomy, and the issues raised for a religious morality.

[35] Cf. chapter 3 above, p. 73f.

[36] Cf. chapter 3 above, p. 74.

[37] See above, n. 34.

curtains for their lounge.[41] The matter of colour, shade and texture have to be considered (aesthetic questions). That settled, there is the question of whether the material is long-lasting, i.e., what it is made of (scientific questions). Then there is the matter of the cost, and whether they can afford it (economic questions). Well, they have the money or can raise it on budget, but the question arises whether, if they make the outlay on the curtains they can afford a holiday in the sun this summer (still economic questions). But they have been working hard and need a holiday before another winter, and the question is: ought they to spend the money on the curtains or on the holiday (moral questions)? If they decide to buy, there is the question of whether mother or the neighbours will like them (if we care about such things): here the matter of awareness and understanding of other people may come into the picture. Someone buying curtains for a National Trust property or the like may have to ask historical questions: e.g., what decoration is appropriate for a fifteenth century Scottish house, or an eighteenth century English manor? Finally, has the assistant calculated the cost correctly and added up the bill correctly (mathematical questions)? The adult mind moves quickly from one autonomous realm of discourse to another, quite aware that the ways we know in each area are different: e.g., we cannot settle the moral questions in the same way that we settle the arithmetic bill. In an external relation, the autonomous realms of discourse impinge on each other, but they do not interpenetrate one another.

Perhaps our very familiarity with external relations between autonomous realms of discourse inclines us to take for granted that the relation between morality and religion will be of that kind (whether or not we can articulate the question in these terms). This, however, is the issue: is this the proper way to conceive of the relation between morality and religion? Certainly that relationship cannot be settled *seriatim* by looking at particular moral issues, but only in terms of each of them *per se*. Can this be done? We believe it can, and we offer some arguments in support of our view. As we believe the relation is a particularly complex and multiform one, we shall select arguments which bring out different aspects of that many-sided relation.

We begin by asking what are the religious questions in the curtain-buying situation. If we are right, it is a fair question. It is not that we cannot plot the religious questions on the logical map, but we have doubts as to whether we can provide serious examples of an external relation between morality and religion,[42] and this difficulty inclines us to the view that the relationship is an intrinsic one. Religious questions are questions of

---

[41] The example of buying curtains we owe to Professor Hirst at a Conference: he uses it for a variety of purposes among which are to uphold the autonomy of the various 'forms of knowledge' and to show the extrinsic relations between such autonomies; we have developed the illustration in our own way.

[42] A humorous (or perhaps tragic) example of an extrinsic relation would relate to the ethos of parts of Ulster or the West of Scotland, where it might be a matter of 'religious' concern whether one's curtains were green, orange or blue.

ultimate meaning, whether the meaning of ourselves ('Who am I? Do I matter? Where am I going? Has man any worth or significance? How should I live my life?'), or the meaning of the universe and ourselves against that backdrop ('Is the universe meaningless so that it will explode with a bang or run down to a whimper?'). Some people say that these are existential questions or philosophical ones—or give them some other name. Call them what you will, but let us beware of a linguistic hang-up that may prevent us from recognising how significant these questions have been regarded by people in all ages. Such questions do not conveniently fit into a separate compartment of knowledge, as at least some of the others *appear* to do: e.g., number into mathematics, and atomic and chemical structure into the physical and chemical sciences. Indeed, religion does not easily separate from the rest of life, though many have tried in all ages to separate it.[43] When people buy curtains, the religious questions are those of life-style and raise issues such as 'On what sort of goods and services should we be spending our money to attain or reflect our particular life-style?' and 'If man is not just another animal, but an artistic, reflective and moral being who needs to live as a "person" to realise his full "humanity",[44] how should we live?'

In other words, religious questions are related to all the others and raise questions about the significance and justification of all the other questions and activities: e.g., why engage in scientific activity at all? why bother with art? must financial considerations always override questions about the quality of human life? why find out about the past?[45]

Further, these religious questions do not relate to all others, in the same way as the other autonomous realms of discourse relate externally to one another. The relation of religious questions to all others is a special one, in that they pervade all the others and cannot simply be conceived in terms of external relations. This is what is often meant by saying that religion has an integrative or synoptic function.

How does this affect our view of the relation between morality and religion? On the one hand, we are not to impose a heteronomy of the one on the other. Duty is duty, and right is right; and it does not *become* our duty

---

[43] Tribunals are sometimes set up to determine whether a person has a genuine religious reason for refusing to join a Trade Union. Such tribunals, as in war-time with conscientious objectors, seem to work on the principle that a genuine religious reason must be of a narrow and compartmental sort, unrelated to the rest of life, thus misunderstanding what religion is.

[44] For the meaning of these terms, see chapter 10, pp. 238–43ff.

[45] These questions are raised by all the world religions—and not only by Christianity. Not all of them, however, return the positive answers to which we are accustomed. Hinduism, at least in one of its many traditions as commonly understood even in India, appears to have spurned history and science, but in another of its traditions to have spawned a wealth of *objets d'art* as well as large-scale sculptures. This is not evidence for Hinduism not raising these kinds of questions: it is only evidence that it has answered—in one of its traditions at least—that some human activities have no religious significance, or are a hindrance to the union of the self with the ultimate reality (Brahman).

brings liberation from it. They need reconciliation with their victim—in this case, generously offered, but that might not always happen. The victim may end up not merely physically disabled but a moral cripple as well—consumed by resentment, bitterness, frustration and the like, just as the others could well be obsessed with remorse, or brittle indifference, or the determination to escape and forget. What all parties need is atonement: at-one-ment with each other and, perhaps above all, at-one-ment with themselves.[2]

It is at this point that the dimension of faith comes into play in a particularly telling way. If through the perspective of faith the parties can find an assurance that forgiveness is a reality for them, then the at-one-ment becomes an immediate possibility. Not that one is suggesting that faith provides some kind of magical exit from the dilemmas of moral experience. The forgiveness that is mediated through Christian faith, for example, is manifested through suffering—Christ's suffering in his life and on the Cross. Anyone who lays hold of this forgiveness is not spared the pain of at-one-ment, for it is not easy—even with the resources of faith—to live with the past, which tends to pursue one like a demon that does not recognise defeat. Nor is it suggested here that religious faith is the only approach to an 'in depth' treatment of guilt.[3] Still less is it asserted that the conventionally religious can readily resolve their moral problems in this way; the dimension of faith represents a deeply personal pilgrimage. What we are concerned to do is to follow up the insights gained in the last chapter concerning the intrinsic relationship between religion and morality and to do so particularly by highlighting the way in which the person of faith understands the moral situation itself.

1. The perspective of faith provides a *wider picture of morality* than is found in some contemporary philosophers who do not write from the standpoint of faith. Morality might be thought of in terms of successive tiers or levels. One level is the 'common sense' stage, at which moral issues are fairly clear-cut and responses largely those of habit: such a person has a morality of rules and may not even distinguish 'legal' and 'moral'. The next level is that of the reflective person who thinks about morality and is ever ready to revise habitual and past responses. He perhaps operates with the devices we discussed in Part One: considerations of rules, consequences and motive may lead him to see that there is more to morality than toeing the line, obeying orders and commands, more even than outward acts. This level should not be despised by Christians on the ground that this is not the whole of Christian living. It should be welcomed as the beginning of moral sensitivity, and therefore an important aspect of moral education.[4]

This level, in turn, shades into an area where things are still more

---

[2] Cf. G. E. Clinton Gardner in *Storm Over Ethics*, 3, 1967, pp. 47–8.

[3] Thus, in much of this discussion, there may be considerable common ground between Christians and humanists. It is to be hoped that there is, even if there are necessary divergencies on the sources of insight and reasons for acting.

[4] Especially for moral education with the age groups 10–14 yrs. approx.

complex, and where it is realised that all sorts of factors—prejudice, myopia, ego-centricity, plain selfishness, pride, jealousy, ambition, the desire for power or the retention of it (to name but a few)—hold people in chains so that they are not free to do the rational thing.[5] This is what traditional theology calls 'sin'. The word itself, of course, is much less important than the reality it denotes. Here, importance attaches to the inner life, *both* in as far as it is concerned with pride, prejudice, ambition, power, chips on the shoulder, inferiority complexes and the rest, *and* in its aspects of providing a vision of goodness or virtue, of perfection towards which we grow and strive, to which we never fully approximate, but which is not practically irrelevant.

The next level might be described as the deeply personal. It is *people* who are caught in this web of irrationality. Therefore, our moral judgements upon them must be at best provisional and liable to error, while in many cases we cannot make moral judgements at all. But we retain our moral seriousness, and continue to struggle, believing that, when we think and act as Christians, we are potentially free from the spider's web. The demons have lost their power over us, but we have still to fight. Here metaphor and symbol are necessary, for the literal is now inappropriate to experience.

But though in many cases we do not make moral judgements about other people, we believe that we *ought* to try to understand them, not by an intellectual effort, but through accepting them as they are. Thus they get back their dignity from at least one fellow human being. We stand beside them, seeking to understand, listening rather than speaking, yet aware of their immense power to deceive themselves as they try to deceive us. We seek to identify with them—our own self-awareness illumining for us the mysterious corridors of their selves. It is not a matter of understanding them in order that we may love them. It is love seeking to understand them . . . and understand why people behave so oddly and strangely towards other human beings.

And if this is true of our dealings with people we count as normal, what of the neurotic or the psychotic? We may believe that we can and must leave the latter to the expert, but we cannot do so in the case of the former. He or she may be our uncle, aunt, mother, husband, wife. And if none of our relations belong to this unfortunate group, the odds are that we meet at least one or two of them, for they are fairly common in the community; one or two may be working with us, or meeting us in our leisure-time. We may be blind and not recognise them, but they are there. Again it is a case of love seeking to understand and perchance to heal.

It would not be difficult, even if it might seem melodramatic, to give many further illustrations of the human predicament. Ask any social worker, any G.P., any psychiatrist, any clergyman . . . We can, perhaps, leave such cases to the imagination and recollection of the reader and simply presume to remind him of the human need to draw a veil over such

---

[5] See previous chapter.

intense pain and conflict—to escape from it for a while. In self-protection, we remember the fun we had, the happy side of life—and forget the pain. But a wider, balanced view of life must reckon with both sides—must take *all* the evidence into account. It was for such reasons that we rejected the attempt to depict man as having, or as able to cultivate, the free, rational will. *That* is a-typical, untrue to life.

The faith perspective, then, combines a variety of elements in its wider purview of the moral situation. Curiously, while much popular religion suffuses the realities of human experience with a sugary coating of sentimentality, genuine people of faith are enabled to face up to the threat to their existence with a relative objectivity that comes from having points of reference beyond the elements of any one experience and that enables them to transcend and discount unreal interpretations of the situation. They are similarly moved to act, not out of detached aloofness but with loving concern. They seek to love and so understand, and if not to understand to love all the same. But this is made possible by yet another element in their experience: the vision of goodness towards which they are drawn and which enriches their living. This we discuss in the following sections.

2. In the perspective of faith, morality is seen as the *outcome and outworking of the human relationship to God:* in Christian terms, as part of *the response of humanity to the grace and goodness of God:* therefore, as something *evoked and engendered by the divine initiative.* All this receives classical expression in the concept of the covenant of God with mankind.

The word 'covenant' today is used of an agreement or sealed contract between two parties.[6] For example, a Deed of Covenant is an agreement and promise to pay a certain sum of money (say, to our favourite charity) over a certain number of years (usually a minimum period is stipulated by law nowadays). You covenant (in an agreement which is legally binding unless one party exercises his option to break it) for x years to pay £y. Again, in the Christian marriage service, the language of covenant occurs. In both cases, there are two parties to the bond, agreement or covenant. Thus, Christian marriage is regarded as a covenant or bond between two people whereby 'in the presence of God' each makes vows to the other and each acknowledges duties and responsibilities to the other.

Moral activity in both Old and New Testaments (i.e., Old and New Covenants) is set within the structure of covenant response. A tiny nation, Israel is the object of God's love, which is supremely expressed in the events of the Exodus. She is chosen to be God's people, not for any merit of her own but out of God's grace (cf. Deut. 7:6–8). As in all covenantal discourse, the relationship involves responsibility for both partners, and Israel's response to God's gracious initiative was to bind herself with corresponding faithfulness to God, whose requirement was made known to her in the Torah.[7] To fail to obey the Torah was to break the covenant and

---

[6] This and our following example are not intended to provide the archetypal meaning for the biblical covenant, which is discussed in the succeeding pages.

[7] Torah, often translated 'Law', primarily meant divine instruction or teaching. Hence it included commandments, covenant codes and the detailed requirements

incur God's judgement (cf. Deut. 7:9–11). As it transpired, the covenant relationship—characterised as a marriage by Jeremiah (2:2)—was repeatedly broken by unfaithful Israel (cf. 31:32), and the divine judgement was felt all too keenly in her history. But Jeremiah looked forward to the making of a new covenant, through God's gracious initiative once again: a renewal and revitalisation of the covenant relationship effected through the internalising of God's requirement and sustained by God's forgiveness (Jer. 31:31–34). In this way, Israel's whole life would be a response of gratitude and obedience, expressed in worship and in everyday living. Her way would reflect that 'righteousness' and 'mercy' or 'covenant love'[8] which characterised God's own nature. Religion and morality are thus brought together. A similar covenant-model operates in the New Testament. In his discussion of the great commandment, Jesus appears to underline the element of covenantal response which it presupposes (cf. Mark 12:28–34). Jesus himself seems to have internalised the covenant relationship and characterised it not so much in terms of marriage as of the 'I-Thou' relationship of father and son (cf. Matt. 11:25ff.). For Christians, the new covenant—fulfilling Jeremiah's expectation, for example, and thus bringing Israel's covenant with God to a new and full expression—is spelled out in the last supper and the sacrament which looks to it. The covenant love of God receives new and final expression in the self-giving of Christ on the Cross.

'For the love of Christ holds us in its power, once we have made the decision that one has died for all and that therefore death applies to all. And he died for all so that the living should no longer live for themselves but for him who for their sake died and was raised' (2 Cor. 5:14f.).

Thus Paul strongly emphasises that the love of Christ[9] stands at the heart

---

(*footnote 7 continued*)
which the God of the covenant laid upon Israel and which comprise a description of the life of God's people. It also included teaching on the covenant itself and God's election of Israel. This teaching, like the covenant, was a gift of God. Hence the term Torah came to be applied to the first five books of the Hebrew Bible, in which the whole story of God's election of Israel is set out.

[8] Two quotes from J. Muilenburg are apposite here: 'To be righteous is to fulfill the demands of the relationship. Yahweh is righteous because he is faithful to his covenant and fulfills what is required in the relationship. Thus the righteous deeds of Yahweh are his saving acts, his victories, all that he does to create and establish and perpetuate community. He who obeys the Torah, the revealed Law implementing the covenant, is righteous': *The Way of Israel: Biblical Faith and Ethics*, 1962, p. 60. Muilenburg describes 'mercy' (*hesed*) in this way: 'It can mean kindness, covenant love, steadfast love, devotion, fidelity, even grace. It bears the connotation of stability, strength, and firmness, and is associated not infrequently with truth (*'emeth*), which also bears this connotation. It is the strength which gives stability to the relationship, and it is therefore the gift of God to his people': *op. cit.*, p. 59.

[9] The phrase 'love of Christ' admirably illustrates the covenantal relationship: it denotes both Christ's love for us and our love for Christ. The verb *synechei* may mean 'constrain', i.e., to set the bounds beyond which man may not go in the direction of self-centred behaviour, but it clearly means more than that here: controls us and holds us in its power so that it provides us with a powerful dynamic or motivation: those who live in response to him 'no longer live for themselves but for him . . .'

of Christian motivation and effects behavioural change. No longer do we view people simply from a human standpoint.[10] Another dimension has been added to the picture. The new dynamic of faith in Christ transforms our inner life and outward action—transforms *us*, makes us new creatures— so that, having experienced reconciliation with God through Christ, we ourselves become reconcilers. And all this is God's doing . . . (2 Cor. 5:18). To put it another way: to respond to God in Christ is liberating (cf. Gal. 5:1), so that there is no possibility of defining the Christian life in terms either of legalism (cf. Gal. 2:21) or antinomianism (cf. Rom. 6:1ff.). Christian freedom means to 'walk by the Spirit' (as opposed to 'the flesh'). It means not only fellowship with God but genuine community with one's neighbour. It enables man, in response to God's grace, to develop those qualities which are prompted by the Spirit of Christ and are presupposed in all authentic relationships (cf. Gal. 5:22).

Thus the person of faith can see morality in the broader setting of fundamental relationships and can find the solution to the problem of motivation in the faith perspective itself. The difficulty is that such perspectives and relationships are relatively sophisticated. There is nothing instant about them. They do not provide a 'ready-mix' type of solution to the problems of morality. Obligation, duty, responsibility, motivation, prescription and prohibition are all contained within the covenantal relationship and derive their cogency from it. Frequently, when the response of Israel has been markedly deficient in one particular aspect, the prophets—those redoubtable champions of the covenant—may single out that one aspect as if Israel was in simple breach of prescriptive law. But, always, the logic of the covenant is presupposed. What the Lord of Israel requires is not only righteous conduct and merciful and compassionate action but also humble piety, 'to walk humbly with your God' (Micah 6:8): the full dimensions of covenantal religion are assumed. Similarly, in the New Testament Paul can speak paradoxically of the 'law of Christ', for Christ indeed teaches us what is required of the children of God: there is no question of the Christian way being antinomian. But neither is there any question of its adopting a law-model of ethics. Paul knew—better than most!—that there is no salvation by works of the law.[11] The writer of the Fourth Gospel is well aware of the paradoxical nature of the 'commands' of Jesus when he represents him as saying, 'You are my friends, if you do what I command you' (John 15:14). If you said to someone, 'You're my friend, if you do exactly as I tell you', you might well expect to be given the answer. 'It's not a friend you want; but a slave'. But the author of the Fourth Gospel anticipates our thinking. His next words are, 'No longer do I call you servants (slaves), for the servant (slave) does not know what his master is

[10] The phrase *kata sarka* is a well known *crux interpretum*. It must be taken closely with the verb: 'to know in a purely fleshly (i.e., human) way'. To know Jesus in this way is to reckon his life's work and his cross as a stumbling-block or as foolishness; whereas those who have come to faith find him to be 'Christ the power of God and the wisdom of God' (1 Cor. 1:24).

[11] See above, chapter 1, pp. 29f.

doing. I have called you friends . . .' (15:15). There is an implication that the Christian is in a relationship to the Master ('know') that makes the language of command inappropriate. The author of this Gospel has clearly given deep thought to this problem. Earlier he has written, 'If you love me, you will keep my commands . . . He who has my commands and keeps them, he indeed it is who loves me . . . He who does not love me does not keep my words' (14:15, 21, 24). The point is that love can only be expressed in action and that the Christian who says that he loves his Lord and does nothing about it does not genuinely love him (14:21, 24). And, as 14:15 clearly implies, the man who is genuinely committed to Christ in love will keep his 'commands': i.e., he will express that love in his life in ways appropriate to his situation. The language of 'command' suggests that a new force, a dynamic, has come into one's life and experience and must not be denied. If it is denied, the entire relationship with God through Christ is negated.

It is important that we do not short circuit New Testament meaning by attempting to impose the specious utility of a command theory (or law model) of ethics at this point. The nuances of presentation and argument in John and Paul are essential, and they are readily comprehended within the structure of the covenant relationship. As we have seen already,[12] love is spontaneous and freely given. It cannot be compelled by legislation, nor does it belong within a rules-ethics. It belongs to the personal realm of discourse, to the relational model of ethics.[13] Consequently, it is evoked by the love which is directed to us. It is responsive. It is engendered. In the covenant, God takes the initiative in love. He does 'the redemptive and restorative deed';[14] consequently he 'creates the response',[15] for he makes it possible for people to respond. The covenant concept at its most mature is therefore no contract. Thus God may be said to engender love in human minds and hearts. Here we reach the deeply personal roots of experience, and humbly acknowledge the element of mystery where the human spirit touches the deep things of God. But the mystery, although it always remains such, has meaning for the person of faith.

What we are suggesting, therefore, is that the concept of covenant is focal to a proper understanding of the relationship between faith and morality, at least as understood in Christian terms. Covenantal insights, so to speak, are required of all who would discuss Christian ethics—whether from the inside or the outside. Thus, to the person of faith, the ten commandments, the great commandments to love God and neighbour, and the imperatives of the Sermon on the Mount are all to be regarded not as commands from God but as clear and uncompromising indications of the kind of life expected within the covenant relationship and of people within the covenant community. They are delineations of a life-style, rather than final absolutes. In

[12] See above, chapter 3, pp. 83ff.
[13] This question is discussed further in chapter ten.
[14] Cf. J. Sittler, *The Structure of Christian Ethics*, 1958, p. 40.
[15] *Ibid.*

this realm of discourse, the only 'absolute' is the divine claim on people to respond in love in the situation in which they are.[16]

Almost inevitably, the secular world will take the biblical imperatives as heteronomous rules—i.e., rules imposed externally by authority, divine or ecclesiastical. And the fact that Christian ethics has been represented so often by Christians (both catholic and reformed) as a rules-ethics does not make for elucidation of its true nature. The imputation of a heteronomous view—emasculating the biblical context as it does—should not be accepted without demur. However, while there is an obligation on all who discuss Christian ethics to come to terms with the covenantal realm of meaning, Christians need not be over-anxious when the religious grounds of their behaviour are not fully understood.

This leaves the question of how humanists, for example, can understand the Christian's view of morality, and how Christians can co-operate with non-Christians in, for instance, the tasks of community service and moral education. Is there any common ground? The covenant concept suggests the notion of *relationships*. The covenant between God and Israel becomes in today's thought-forms a relationship between God and man that involves relationships between man and his neighbour. Relationships can be broken. Not only are they less than perfect, but they do not spring up all at once complete and entire. They have to be 'worked at'. Thus they grow towards completion. This is a universal human concern. Here is common ground.

We may take an example from relationships between the sexes. The Christian position is often represented (not too unfairly) as 'no sex before marriage and chastity within it';[17] and this may seem like a rule—a heteronomy—from which some claim to have been 'liberated'. These critics may thus imply the pursuit of hedonism, or experience for its own sake, or sheer antinomianism. Are personal values, and personal relationships, thus enhanced? Christians would wish to scrutinise any such claims or assumptions. They have nothing to fear from the challenge of contemporary *avant-garde* fashions: how quickly they fade! But they have nothing to gain from exaggerated reaction to them or strained approximation to them! Here, the 'moral majority' and the situationists appear equally at fault. To have recourse to a rules-ethics on the one hand or to a 'liberated' Christian ethics on the other (delighting in standing traditional Christian virtues on their head and capitalising on extreme examples) is equally wrong-headed, for both deny, or take insufficient account of, the covenant concept. The liberation which the Christian knows is that effected by the grace of God alone—not by a brittle secularism. Hence Christians would want to ask about the quality of the relationships involved—what makes for a full or complete relationship, for truly personal responsibility?—and about what is

---

[16] Cf. the 'unconditionedness' of the moral imperative (in Tillich's terms). This must not be confused with a rule, law, or command to do an action that is considered always right, i.e., absolute in the other sense of 'context-invariant'.

[17] When this slogan is promulgated as 'chastity before marriage, and fidelity within it', this may imply a limited concept both of chastity (= no sex) and of fidelity (= in marital sex only).

involved in commitment to the other person, and whether fidelity to a personal commitment means anything. They would want to talk about life-style and a quality of life beyond the merely sexual, biological and materialistic levels (e.g., food, drink, clothes and material goods); to talk even of *choosing* a life-style. The aim of such a discussion is not to do battle from an entrenched position (even though the Christian recognises the covenant as the archetypal relationship, he might not mention it explicitly in a discussion of this kind) nor simply to make converts to one's viewpoint, but rather to explore the moral situation and in particular all that is involved in relationships: to share insights and seek new perspectives. One thing is clear. Such a discussion is not possible on the basis of a rule-model. 'No sex before marriage' does not correspond to any biblical imperative. In as far as it represents the general tendency of Christian teaching, it is part of the pattern of a developing relationship moving towards the commitment which marriage denotes and seals.[18] The nature of the relationship—one of total commitment—sets its own bounds. Adultery or unchastity represents the negation of the relationship; hence it is excluded from the expected response of the agents (cf. the seventh commandment). The one-in-a-thousand exception beloved by situationists and their followers—the case of 'sacrificial adultery' would be an instance—has only a very limited application; and while the logic of such examples is defensible (grace or *agape* takes precedence over mere convention or institution), tacit assumptions are often made about other aspects of the situations in question, and in consequence the examples may end up as red herrings rather than disclosures of ethical insight.[19]

Perhaps two comments might be added. Provided Christians renew their grasp of covenantal thinking, there is no need for them to feel insecure in the face of the challenges of secularism; still less, to allow such insecurity to drive them into the cul de sac of rules-ethics or the specious delights of a libertarian position. Christian morality, relationally and covenantally understood, possesses great inner strength. Let believers draw upon its resources as deeply as they can. In the second place, the Christian can feel confident in co-operating with non-Christians in the social and moral sphere, in as far as all participants have a genuine concern for human welfare, for good relationships and for social cohesion. It would be unthinkably arrogant to suggest that Christians have nothing to learn from their secular counterparts, or that non-Christians have no concern for, or insight

[18] It is not our intention here to discuss in detail the various stages in this development, such as the place of the engagement or betrothal. These are conventions which interpret the relationship in a particular way and are culturally determined.

[19] It is relevant to raise also the question of the breakdown and failure of the relationship: cf. Israel's constant breaking of her covenant with God (Jer. 31:32). Churches which adopt a law model here find themselves in a straitjacket. Does their strong defence of the permanence of the marriage covenant always allow them to minister in *agape* to the alienated partners who have come to see the solution of their problems not in renewing a bond now utterly broken but in keeping apart or perhaps in building a new life and a new set of relationships?

into, morality. It might be that the non-Christian will learn from his Christian fellow citizen also.

3. To the person of faith, life is characterised by *conflict, change, transformation* and *growth*. These indeed are the matrices of the Christian view of man, life, world and God.

Change and transformation. Christians believe that, as they respond *to* God's grace *in* their love to others, they grow in moral sensitivity (grace); consequently, they have a greater awareness and understanding of others, a truer appreciation of their own true selves (as distinct from their fantasy and counterfeit selves), and heightened sensitivity to 'What is good, acceptable and perfect' (Phil. 4:8). Of course, that is not to claim that Christians have a monopoly of moral sensitivity—any such claim would demonstrate a marked lack of sensitivity! Nor is it a proud assertion of Christian achievement (what Paul would call 'boasting'). Moral sensitivity is the outworking of the grace of God in us; its absence is testimony to our failure to respond adequately to God's grace.

The living of the Christian life involves self-knowledge or self-awareness. The motorist who constantly drives through the amber-to-red sequence of lights, or who cuts in on another vehicle and forces it off the road, or who recklessly overtakes, or who intimidates other road users, is not likely to be 'straightened out' simply by being told about correct driving procedure. To be given again the rules of the Highway Code will not cure his lack of consideration for other road users. He does not relate—at least in these driving situations—to other people. There is an important sense in which he is not free to care, and needs liberation (redemption, salvation). Thus contemporary experience can help us to understand such concepts as the bondage of the will and liberation from it which occur in the Christian tradition (e.g., in Paul and Luther).[20]

In other words, the Christian acknowledges *a problem of the self.* Moral transformation is not achieved by keeping rules, reflection on the consequences or consideration of motives (though these must not be despised in the process of moral education). Only the loved can love, only the forgiven can forgive. It is by accepting the divine acceptance of us that we are released from ourselves. 'Sin' needs to be interpreted today in such terms as estrangement from the core of our being, and failure to relate to others—a breakdown in relationships because there is a breakdown in the self's relatedness to others and to its own essential being. The self's existential being is in conflict with its essential being. 'Redemption' and 'reconciliation' can be seen (as Tillich has taught us) as a union of the separated and estranged, and a transformation *from* failure *to* concern for others. People become new beings, new creations.

This transformation, however, does not take place all at once or overnight. In the old phrases, salvation must not be divorced from sanctification. Sometimes young people expect to have a complete relationship with another person all at once, and are disappointed when this does not

---

[20] See p. 173.

happen. But the Christian sees the self as always in process of being re-made: he sees himself being constantly turned again to others, as he responds to God's address.

This means that the self cannot be statically understood. Our picture of the person must be of one to whom the call of *change and transformation* can be addressed: of one who is always a person-in-the-making. Categories drawn from Greek philosophy, such as 'substance' and 'essence', that suggest permanence and invariability, will not be so appropriate as those drawn from existentialist philosophy that suggest the self is always in process of coming-to-be.

Further, this self-knowledge is a continual catharsis for people of faith. They do not pretend that they are morally better than they are, or morally superior to other people. They do not fail to be aware of the beam in their own eye. They are less open to self-deception and self-justification. They know that people rationalise their conduct. They are aware that sometimes we project ourselves on to others, so that we 'see' them as *we* are. They know that people play roles, and tend to present not their real self, but a counterfeit. For example, they tend to present themselves in a more favourable light than circumstances warrant, or they play 'the big guy' or 'the wise guy' or 'the hero'. Christian worship will have an important place in this catharsis—confession of sin and the asking for forgiveness, obviously; but their praise and adoration of the God who constantly transcends them, the constant address of God through ordinary events, and the constant challenge to do what is right in each situation, will also promote this continual cleansing and remaking.

Growth and conflict. For the Christian, morality is not simply a case of doing right actions, but also a growth towards some ideal of goodness or virtue (cf. sanctification). But nothing grows, if it is paralysed. A theory that simply said that we were all sinners acting in our own self-interest would lead to moral paralysis. But 'being accepted' by the divine love, we are released from this; and we accept others because of that divine acceptance. The response, therefore, that is the Christian life involves a continual response to people and events, not an obedience to a static and final set of absolutes (rules and commands). There will be no final rejection of others, nor any facile belief that growth is easy. How do people grow towards a more desirable life? Not by lolling in the sun, but through encountering a hard, resistant world, through conflict with people, events and situations. We grow by and through response to people and events—and that embraces conflict.

In the Christian tradition, there is a place for meditation, quiet, silence, mysticism, and 'seasons of refreshment' when we retire from ordinary life, yet there are no 'distracting' objects as in Eastern faiths. Most of us desire to repudiate the notion that grew up in the fourth and fifth centuries in the West—out of which emerged the hermits with their odd behaviour—that people were a distraction from achieving the perfection of the Christian life and union with God. Christians cannot retire completely from others, and still be entitled to the name, for they cannot forget the divine pressure on them through their own ordinary lives, the events that happen to them, and their encounters with other people.

The challenge of perfection, as presented in the Sermon on the Mount, is not to be regarded as useless, because it is unattainable. It presents the challenge to grow in grace, to move towards that goal. The Christian life is a life-style that raises eyebrows at permanencies considered inviolate, for it knows that no human structures ever incorporate either perfect justice or love. No nation-state and no human institution is perfect, and none acts except from self-interest. Christians, though a minority, will continually try to improve the social services, to create a greater approximation to justice within the state and the international community. Yet they will not be naive idealists, for they know that people do not always act from the highest motives or with the best intentions. They will not be surprised at the chronic complexity of social and political issues and at the current examples of human intransigence, whether of nations or groups, whether in industry, between nation-states, or with ignored and disaffected minorities. They will not underestimate the enemy and so misunderstand the enormity of the problem—because they hold some too optimistic view of humanity.

Christians, however, will not turn their backs on the problem through despair of its ever being solved. They will not separate themselves from others either in an attempt to live a more desirable life on their own or in the hope that the problem will go away. Christians believe their own existence is historical—lived enmeshed with the lives of others and their groups—and that they cannot repudiate history. For them the road to holiness lies through village, town or city, through industry and commerce, through life as it is lived in the world of the everyday.

Community and maturity. While not entirely endorsing Lehmann's position on *koinonia*-ethics, we agree that 'Christian thinking about ethics starts with and from within the Christian *koinonia*'.[21] There are three notes we wish to sound here. First, the growth of the person also starts with and from within small groups: e.g., a family, a school group, a neighbourhood; and in such groups we include the local Christian *koinonia* which, of course, itself embraces the family.[22] Such growth continues to be so nourished from childhood through adolescence to adulthood. Physical structures need to be provided whereby neighbourhoods *can* be formed and flourish and where persons *can* develop: i.e., such structures must not inhibit the growth of persons. People who are not positively formed in this sense by and within the community may be said to be disadvantaged in their personal development. But even where appropriate structures are provided, other sources of conflict may inhibit their growth. No physical structure can guarantee the growth of persons to full maturity, nor can conflict be eliminated from the growth of persons.

Secondly, we agree with Lehmann that, to the person of faith, morality is more about relations and functions than about principles and precepts.

[21] *Ethics in a Christian Context*, p. 124.
[22] Lehmann, however, does not equate his *koinonia* with the empirical church.

People have to be considered before such principles and precepts,[23] and this is what we mean by the importance of *ethos* in Christian ethics.[24] We would, however, place greater importance on norms, especially in social ethics, than he appears to do.

Thirdly, we take it that one important stage towards the goal of Christian maturity is the ability of adult Christians to make free, responsible decisions for themselves in the light of their faith. Whether this is called autonomy (in a good sense) or theonomy, does not appear to matter so much as the reaching of this stage.[25] Autonomous Christians, however, will be aware of the claims of the Christian community so that their autonomy does not descend into the antinomianism of doing as they please. In this sense, *koinonia* balances autonomy.

[23] Cf. Lehmann's example of the hospital patient, *ibid.*, p. 132f.

[24] See chapter 10 below.

[25] Autonomy is used in many different senses in ethical discussion. While we have maintained the autonomy of morality in various senses, we have refused to accept moral autonomy in the sense that religion and morality could not be internally related. What we are maintaining here is yet *another* sense of autonomy.

6

ETHICS AND CHRISTIAN ETHICS

We now turn to a completely different question, 'What is the relation between Christian faith and morality outside such faith?' We desire to ask whether there is anything in Christianity that determines the Christian's attitude to such morality. How ought a Christian in virtue of his being a Christian to regard the 'ought' that comes from outside faith? This is a question that has always been on the agenda of Christian ethics, but it is surprising how often writers on Christian ethics have failed to discuss it:[1] perhaps this is due to the divorce of Christian ethics from theology.

Christians have often been divided on their answer, and have held views with a degree of inconsistency—sometimes to an alarming degree. Some method is required by which we can look at these various views and examine them in depth, yet relatively quickly, to bring out their advantages and disadvantages. The method we have chosen is to set out what the options are, rather than to classify the views that have been held. These five *possible* ways of understanding the relationship between ethics and Christian ethics are to be taken primarily as ideal types and only secondarily as the views of the authors cited, which should be regarded merely as illustrations of or near approximations to the type. Probably no author has held to any of the first four types wholly consistently and that too should tell us something about the complexity of the relationship we are trying to grasp.

A. FIVE IDEAL TYPES OF THE RELATIONSHIP

Here then are the five ideal types of the relationship between ethics and Christian ethics.

1. *They are completely distinct*

This ideal type may be represented by the model of two circles on a page—not intersecting at any point—the one circle representing Christian

---

[1] Paul Ramsey's *Basic Christian Ethics* is a case in point—an omission described by N. H. G. Robinson as 'the main weakness of what is otherwise a notable contribution to Christian ethics'; cf. Robinson's own work, *The Groundwork of Christian Ethics*, 1971, pp. 145f., which is perhaps the only recent full-length study which does discuss this question.

ethics, the other ethics. In this ideal type, there is a divorce between the two: Christian theology and ethics stand in a negative relation of separation and rejection to morality outside Christian faith, and, therefore, to philosophical ethics which claims to be an inquiry into morality without making any religious presuppositions.

This ideal type goes back historically to Tertullian (c. 160–200 A.D.), the first major writer of Christian theology in Latin. He became a Christian comparatively late in life, which may account for his rather extreme attitude to the culture from which he came. Despite his debt to Stoic moral teaching, he assumed a negative answer to the question: 'What has Jerusalem to do with Athens?', and understood the Christian as set apart from and hostile to the world around him and its culture. Christianity has nothing to do with culture from whatever source it comes.[2] The implication of such a view, of course, is that Christianity has to adopt a negative attitude to all morality outside Christian faith.

The most famous twentieth century representatives of this ideal type are Karl Barth (at least in some of his early writings), Emil Brunner, Hendrik Kraemer and in some respects Dietrich Bonhoeffer.[3] The ethical question (as Barth called it in his early writings)[4] is genuine but brings into question man himself and destroys him. All expressions of good are questioned, all proximate and finite goals of conduct are queried, with the aim of leading man on to the ultimate goal, viz., his relationship with God. Man's conduct and his living are all in critical question: man, that is, is confronted with a question about himself. 'The problem of ethics contains the secret that man as we know him in this life is an impossibility. This man in God's sight can only perish'.

But while in Barth's early writings, the ethical question is genuine, serious and cannot be escaped, there is in his later writings, from the Church Dogmatics onwards, a change of view. Ethics or rather the multifarious ethical systems, 'the attempted human answers to the ethical question',[5] result from man's desire to give the answer himself and of himself, and so be like God, knowing good and evil. Ethics and its various answers result from the Fall and the prolongation of the Fall. General ethical discussion is a work of human pride and presumption, an attempt of human beings to justify themselves before God, and so must be set aside by theology and Christian ethics as a 'presumptious intruder'.[6] Such ethics is not genuine, but illegitimate.

But not only is such ethics a work of human presumption, Christian theology and Christian ethics must meet the enemy and destroy it.

'To this iniquity' (sc. ethics) 'and all its answers, theological ethics must simply say "No", and if—by grace—it also says "Yes", it does so by

---

[2] Cf. E. LeRoy Long, Jr., A Survey of Christian Ethics, 1967, pp. 34f.
[3] See chapter 9 below, pp. 181–86, 189–97.
[4] For example, The Word of God and the Word of Man, Eng. tr., 1957, consisting of addresses given by Barth when he was a pastor in a Swiss parish.
[5] Church Dogmatics II, 2, p. 516f.
[6] Cf. N. H. G. Robinson, op. cit., p. 52.

completing its own answer to the ethical problem in active refutation, conquest and destruction of all human answers to it'.[7]

Nothing could be plainer than Barth's rejection of morality outside Christian faith and of philosophical ethics: 'revelation and the work of God's grace are just as opposed to these attempts' (sc. to solve the ethical problem) 'as they are to sin'.[8] Yet Barth is far from consistent (as can be seen from his 'No' and 'Yes' above). For him, 'general ethics' may become a clue to the inherent features of the divine command, though no particular sort of ethical reflection does this adequately.[9] The only true ethics is christocentric; 'general ethics' is transmuted and subsumed under theological ethics.[10]

Under the influence of Barth, some Protestant theologians have denied any value to morality outside the faith, and have even regarded philosophical ethics (as Barth did) as a kind of human arrogance. This view was due to a particular understanding of the doctrine of justification by grace alone, which denied any value to 'works'. Dogmatic considerations determined this view of general ethics. For example, Emil Brunner worked out, in *The Divine Imperative*, a Christian ethics more explicitly and fully than Barth did, yet he supported Barth in his view of the relationship between morality and ethics, on the one side, and Christian faith on the other. The differences and the break between Brunner and Barth did nothing to affect fundamentally the views of either on this relationship. Theologians, however, have not been the only defenders of this view of the relationship between ethics and Christian ethics. Some philosophical writers on ethics have insisted on the autonomy of morality, as we have seen in our discussion above,[11] in such a way as would prevent any relationship either between morality and Christian faith or between general ethics and Christian ethics.

This view has important implications for education. Christians who take Barth's line cannot in principle engage in or support moral education which is not (or not always) explicitly and fully Christian education. Nor can there be any stages in moral education, as we suggested earlier, marking a developing moral insight. Indeed, it is difficult to see how *education* (moral, Christian, or any other) can proceed at all on this position. Is education also a work of human arrogance, on Barth's view; and if not, why is it not?

---

[7] *Church Dogmatics* II, 2, p. 517.

[8] *Op. cit.*, II, 2, p. 517.

[9] *Op. Cit.*, III, 4. Further discussion of the positions of Barth and Brunner will be found below in chapter 9.

[10] Consequently, Barth could condemn the evils of Nazism only by the Word of God, not on purely human moral grounds. Taken to its logical conclusion, this gives the astonishing meaning that the Jews could not morally disapprove of their own persecution: or rather if they did, their 'moral disapproval' would be merely human and subjective. Jews apparently could have no objective concepts of justice. Barth modified his attitude to human culture, but only to some extent. The modification did not alter this view of ethics, for in *The Humanity of God* he wrote 'ethics according to our assumption can only be evangelical ethics' (Eng. tr. p. 85).

[11] Cf. chapter 4, esp. pp. 104–7.

Can he really make an exception of education in his rejection of human 'works'?

We have given reasons against the view that only the religious man (and *a fortiori* the Christian) has any moral awareness, and it seems obdurate to deny any insight into morality outside the practice of the Christian faith (as we have already argued above).[12] It seems a denial of the Christian doctrine of creation to reject man's moral insights outright. The doctrine of redemption and that of creation must not be allowed to fall apart in the way implied by this view. If man were an a-moral being, or one whose moral endeavour was a work of human presumption, we might well ask how the Gospel could ever appeal to him, and how God could address such a man with his Word of freedom from self. The symbol of the two non-intersecting circles is meant to suggest the ideal type where morality is self-contained and its proper doctrine totally independent of theology. If one holds to this ideal type, then Christian morality and morality outside Christian faith are two wholly separate and independent realms of discourse. And if one holds that, one denies that morality is self-consistent, for the 'ought' has one meaning in ordinary morality and another in Christian morality. We then have two rival claims, a moral claim and a divine claim, and both are unconditional in the sense of brooking no rival. In that case, human life is a desperate and tragic affair, in which we are continually asked to serve two masters. This ideal type is not appropriate to the relationship between ethics and Christian ethics.

2. *They are fully equivalent*

This is the precise contrary of 1. Instead of two circles, the one completely outside the other, this model is two circles, the circumference of the one completely superimposed upon that of the other, so that from above they appear to be one circle. The one circle represents ethics, the other Christian ethics, and the view of their relationship is that there is no distinction of any kind between them.

That we have not found a thinker who has held this position consistently probably indicates that the odds are very high against this view. But the fact that Barth himself did not hold his view consistently indicates that ideal type 1 is likely to be wrong. The second position (2) is, however, an ideal type of some importance to discuss, since there is a popular view that Christianity is reducible without remainder to moral teaching, or else that the remainder is of no significance and may be ignored. The logic of this view is that ethics and Christian ethics are fully equivalent.

As an example of a thinker who has approximated to this ideal type, we cite A. C. Knudson, who held[13] that philosophical discourse about morality (ethics) and theological discourse share the same methodology, and differ only in subject matter, the latter emphasising 'the ethical teaching of Scripture and of the Christian Church'. On this view, the two are not fully

---

[12] See above, pp. 96ff.
[13] *The Principles of Christian Ethics*, 1943.

equivalent, but they are being brought too near to equivalence. Knudson was wrong both on methodology and subject matter. On method, as Edward LeRoy Long remarks somewhat acidly, 'to adopt the religious point of view in confronting moral questions may well entail something a bit distinct from philosophical reasoning'.[14] Knudson wrote of Christian ethics:

> 'It approaches the whole moral problem from the religious point of view, and hence deals with . . . questions . . . in a way and to an extent that would hardly seem fitting in general ethics. Its standpoint is that of the church. It concentrates attention on those moral problems in which the church has been and is primarily interested . . .'[15]

But if Christian faith affects the whole of life—a thesis which is almost axiomatic in Christian thinking nowadays—Christian ethics cannot be restricted in subject matter to 'those problems in which the church has been and is primarily interested'. Rather it is more plausible to hold that ethics and Christian ethics share considerable, if not all, content in common, but look at morality from different perspectives, and with rather different methods. It seems that Long is correct in suggesting that 'the complexities of theological discourse as actually used defy their simple classification as completely distinct from' (as in 1) 'or fully equivalent to other forms of ethics discourse'.[16]

Joseph Fletcher argues that ethics and Christian ethics share the same procedural approach (*viz.*, the use of situationism and of a supreme principle of moral evaluation), and differ only on the choice of that principle of evaluation, Christian ethics taking *agape*, love and only love, as the ultimate valuational principle, while other ethics take pleasure, happiness, the greatest good of the greatest number or whatever as the ultimate principle.[17] Fletcher's position that ethics and Christian ethics share the same methodology and differ only in content, can be taken as a near-example of the 'equivalence' view, but perhaps it is better to regard him as belonging to our next ideal type.

3. *Christian ethics is subsumed under general ethics*

The model for this ideal type is one circle only, representing general ethics, with a segment representing Christian ethics.

This ideal type is represented by the view, for example, that Christian ethics simply replaces the norms of general ethics with *agape*. This may be taken to be Fletcher's position in so far as he fails to exhibit how his Christian convictions (other than that *agape* is the only supreme valuational principle) inform his Christian ethics.

Another example of this ideal type is the view that Christian ethics is a supplement to general ethics. 'Origen' (c. 186–c. 252) 'could be classified as a supplementalist, who added Christian vocabulary to systems borrowed

[14] *Op. cit.*, p. 30f.
[15] *Op. cit.*, p. 33.
[16] Edward LeRoy Long, Jr., *op. cit.*, p. 31.
[17] Cf. above pp. 19–21.

from the thought world of his day'.[18] In modern times, A. B. D. Alexander[19] exemplified in some respects this ideal type, though not wholly consistently. He believed that dogmatics and ethics are really aspects of one subject, though for convenience they may be taught separately. This is a respectable view, if by 'ethics' is meant 'Christian ethics' but this is not what he meant, for he wrote, 'Christian ethics is a branch of general Ethics'.[20] He did hold that Christian ethics is 'Ethics in its richest and fullest expression—the interpretation of life which corresponds to the supreme manifestation of the divine will' in Jesus Christ.[21] Yet as N. H. G. Robinson pointed out, Alexander's treatment suggests that, so far as ethics is concerned, all that Christianity contributes is additional content and further material: 'if Christian ethics is held to be but a branch of general ethics, the implication seems to be that Christian ethics *is* general or philosophical ethics coming to grips with some new material of a Christian origin . . .'[22]

Again Christian ethics is subsumed under general ethics if Christian ethics is regarded as another type of moral theory alongside all the others. Frankena raised the question, 'Is pure agapism a third type of normative theory in addition to (and therefore alongside) deontology and teleology?' If it is not, then it has already been covered by these other two types.[23] But, if the assumption is rejected that Christianity simply supplies another theory of the moral standard, then Christian ethics is not a branch of general ethics, nor does it provide simply another solution to the problem of general ethics, on a par with either hedonism and utilitarianism or deontology and teleology. If religion in general and Christianity in particular, are not reduced to morality, then Christian ethics cannot be contained within ethics.

4. *General ethics is subsumed under Christian ethics*

This ideal type hardly needs exposition beyond the description of its diagrammatic model. It is represented by one circle only, representing Christian ethics, with a segment representing general ethics.

This is an even less attractive option than the type we have just discussed, but, though it is not held by any serious thinker, it is put forward at the popular level today and one often hears it implied in sermons. In that form, it is the popular and confused view within the Christian community that all morality is derivable from religion and from Christianity in particular (often when religion and Christianity are confusedly treated as equivalent) and that one cannot be moral without being Christian. It is a kind of Christian take-over bid for all moral experience and insight. We

---

[18] Edward LeRoy Long, Jr., *op. cit.*, p. 35.
[19] *Christianity and Ethics*, 1914.
[20] *Ibid.*, p. 22.
[21] *Ibid., loc. cit.*
[22] N. H. G. Robinson, *op. cit.*, p. 27.
[23] Cf. Paul Ramsey, *Deeds and Rules in Christian Ethics*, 1967, pp. 2 and 96.

have dealt with this view in a previous chapter,[24] where its cogency was denied, and nothing need be added here.

5. *General ethics and Christian ethics cover the same ground, but from different perspectives*

For this ideal type, no two-dimensional model will do. On one plane, there is a rectangle representing the moral life and its problems, while on a second plane we have a circle, representing the perspective of ethics, and on a third plane we have a second circle, representing the perspective of Christian ethics. Both circles 'look down' on the rectangle which is life and morality.

A representative of this type is Aquinas who taught that the theologian and the moral philosopher use rather different perspectives in considering morally bad acts.[25] This is the most plausible view so far, and it involves some description of the distinctively Christian perspective—and this we postpone to our next section.

B. THE TRANSVALUATION OF MORALITY

Does any more tenable view of the relation between ethics and Christian ethics emerge from our discussion so far? We suggest that a much more dynamic model is required than any of those used in A1 to 4 above, so that the relationship is not of rejection of morality outside Christian faith, nor of the dominance of either over the other, but of both interaction and non-interaction. Christian faith is not *at all points* in conflict with such morality (as in A1), nor *at all points* are they equivalent (as in A2). On the one side, Christian faith does not deny moral insight outside the profession of Christian faith, as if the atheist can be excused the murder of his wife or the ill-treatment of his children. On the other side, Christian ethics does introduce 'a radically different conception of the moral life',[26] so that Christian ethics cannot be subsumed under general ethics (as in A3), nor can general ethics be subsumed under Christian ethics (as in A4).

Having indicated our preference for the last type, we now have to indicate something of the distinctively Christian perspective on life. The Christian life, it is claimed, is the fulfilment and transformation of *all* life, but not its destruction. In Christian morality, then, there is a transvaluation, but not the rejection, of morality outside Christian faith. It is one of the functions of Christian ethics to describe in what this transvaluation consists.

1. *There is a transvaluation of moral discourse*

As we have argued, there is in reality only one claim on us, not two competing claims—a moral and a divine claim. The absolute claim on the

[24] See chapter 4 above, pp. 96–9.
[25] Cf. chapter 7 below, p. 144.
[26] N. H. G. Robinson, *op. cit.*, p. 172. Cf. p. 171.

Christian to will and to do whatever he ought is God's claim on him. The moral claim is autonomous, and cannot be denied by any alleged higher claim, but the Christian *interprets* the moral 'ought' as God's claim on him. This is not a declaration that we ought to do X, *because* X is the will of God, but a transvaluation of the 'ought' in Christian terms without denying the ultimacy or unconditioned nature of that 'ought'—indeed it is the ultimacy of the moral claim that constitutes for the Christian the divine element in that claim.

Christian ethics, therefore, includes in its investigation an analysis of obligation, duty, rightness or 'oughtness' (such as we conducted in chapters one to three), for this notion has immense importance for it. The moral 'ought' is seen in a new perspective and moral discourse is itself transvalued. If 'ought' involves the notion of obeying a rule or law (as N. H. G. Robinson held in his valuable study), then there is a *prima facie* case for adopting a rule or law model for Christian ethics, i.e., for taking obedience to law as our model for understanding the Christian life. If, however, 'oughtness' can be distinguished from the obligation to obey a rule or law and can be understood in some other way, e.g., as a sense of constraint, of unconditional claim, of bindingness, then the case for a law-model will be considerably weakened and the choice of model will be decided on other grounds.

2. *There is a transvaluation of the moral situation and of moral concepts and motivation*

The transvaluation of morality involved in Christian faith is more than a transformation of moral discourse: it also transforms the moral situation and moral concepts and motivation.

We shall turn presently to H. Richard Niebuhr who among writers grasps well this relationship of the transvaluation of morality outside Christian faith.[27] Can we, however, catch glimpses in the past Christian tradition of this understanding of the relation? Since Schleiermacher was always aware of the dangers when the presentation of Christianity involved a rift with culture, we expect him to struggle with this question. Believing that philosophical and Christian ethics were parallel enterprises, he held that in the last resort no contradiction was possible between them, and that 'each must include within its own concern what is central to the ethical reality and integrity of the other'.[28] Schleiermacher's view of the relationship has much in common with the one we desire to advance, and we

---

[27] Modern writers do not agree either as to how the various views on the relation between ethics and Christian ethics are to be classified, or which past figures should represent each class. For example, Paul L. Lehmann in his *Ethics in a Christian Context*, p. 254, classifies such views into revisionism, synthesis and dia-parallelism. He takes Augustine of Hippo to be a revisionist, Aquinas as the classical example of synthesis, and Schleiermacher of dia-parallelism. H. Richard Niebuhr would adopt a different classification: see below.

[28] P. L. Lehmann, *Ethics in a Christian Context*, p. 266; cf. N. H. G. Robinson, *op. cit.*, p. 162.

would place him broadly in the category of those who understand the nature of the problem, but failed (as we all must to some extent) to formulate the relationship correctly.

Paul L. Lehmann places Augustine of Hippo (fifth-century A.D.) into the class of revisionist, but we take him as a classic example of one who tried to formulate the pattern of transvaluation. The moral outlook of the average educated non-Christian in his day comprised an adherence to the four Greek virtues—wisdom, courage, temperance and justice. Augustine did not reject nor despise these virtues, but radically transformed them by claiming that 'their worth is determined by the total intention in which they are cultivated'.[29] We have to ask, not how a man behaves overtly, but what he loves implicitly, or on what he places supreme valuation: is it the self or the transcendent God?

> 'When sought for the sake of self-love, they' (sc. the four cardinal virtues) 'are self-defeating. They become "splendid vices". When these virtues are transformed by the love of God, turned from their temporal and merely human context in which the Greeks conceived them to an eternal and transcendent object, they become highly worthful. The conversion of the Greek ideals of wisdom, courage, temperance and justice by the Christian ideal of love typifies sharply a motif that runs through all of Augustine's thought; his belief that Christianity is not to be laid alongside Greek wisdom, or put on top of it as a superstructure, but is to convert and permeate and redeem it'.[30]

Augustine was putting forward a novel view for his day, viz., that the best of Greek culture was to be transformed for Christian purposes.

The solutions of Augustine and Schleiermacher serve to underline that the question of the relation between Christian faith and morality outside such faith (and, therefore, of ethics and Christian ethics) is simply one facet of the larger question of the relation between Christianity and culture. We propose to use the terminology which H. Richard Niebuhr[31] coined to identify the various types of view held on the Christianity-culture relation, for these types illuminate the relation between ethics and Christian ethics. If we hold, for example, that Christianity rejects culture ('Christ against culture' in Niebuhr's phrase, exemplified in Tertullian and Tolstoy), we shall be inclined to the view that Christian faith must deny all morality outside such faith. If we hold, on the other hand, that Christianity is to be accommodated to culture ('the Christ of culture'—as in Gnosticism), then we shall look to some equivalence or near-equivalence between ethics and Christian ethics. If, when God is conceived as wholly transcendent and other than sinful humanity, the relationship is understood as one where Christianity is to dominate culture in the manner of a heteronomy or one where Christians are to withdraw in a superior manner from culture

---

[29] *Christian Ethics, Sources of the Living Tradition*, (edd. Beach & Niebuhr), p. 109.

[30] *Ibid.*

[31] In *Christ and Culture*, 1952. Like the various types of relation between ethics and Christian ethics that we sketched in A1–5, Niebuhr's can also be called ideal types, since quite different views are gathered under one type.

('Christ above culture' as in later medieval times, in Calvinism, or in the Desert Fathers and early monasticism), then we might hold both that Christianity rejects all 'secular' morality and that Christian dogmatics incorporates any genuine ethics, which by definition is Christian ethics.[32]

The type of relation we are proposing is one which Niebuhr calls 'Christ the transformer of culture'. He sees examples of it in Augustine of Hippo and F. D. Maurice. He discerns some degree of truth in all these types, and in *Christ and Culture* leaves the choice to the reader.[33] But in his later work, *The Meaning of Revelation*,[34] he presents a pattern of transvaluation to which he is obviously committed and which is relevant (as he holds himself) to the relation between ethics and Christian ethics. Both the source and the content of morality are transvalued.

First, the *source* is transvalued. This is simply in different dress the view we have proposed that moral discourse is transvalued in Christian faith.[35] The moral 'ought' is not denied but its source is traced to the transcendent God who has revealed himself in the person of Jesus Christ.[36] The moral claim, therefore, is seen not as what we demand of ourselves in order that we may become what we ought to be, nor as what the best reason of the best people demands, nor as what society requires. It is now seen as the demand of one from whom there is no flight and who makes no exceptions in favour of any of his creatures. This is what we have called the ultimacy or the unconditioned nature of the 'ought' which Christians interpret as the divine claim on them. Niebuhr, however, claims that it is only 'when God reveals himself' that we recognise the unconditioned nature of the 'ought'. But it is an open question whether it is only prophetic religion, which Jesus inherited, that can recognise the 'ought' which brooks no rival (the view to which Niebuhr appears to incline), or whether the modern agnostic's and atheist's recognition of it (the alternative more in accord with our experience) is their inheritance of prophetic religion or God's revelatory activity in their lives, despite their overt beliefs. Some resolution of this conflict is discerned in Niebuhr's conviction that God's revelation as event, not propositions, liberates people from the evasion of the 'ought', i.e., the creation of self-interested and corrupted moralities. All this is the divine side of what Augustine described from the human side as the transforma-

---

[32] Our examples of 'Christ above culture' Niebuhr might or might not accept, but accurate exposition of Niebuhr's views is not the purpose of this paragraph.

[33] 'Our examination of the typical answers Christians have given to their enduring problem' (sc. the relation between Christ and culture) 'is unconcluded and inconclusive' (p. 229); and he refuses to say of any of them 'This is the Christian answer' (p. 230).

[34] *Op. cit.*, pp. 164–72.

[35] In section B.1. of this chapter.

[36] In *The Meaning of Revelation*, 1960, p. 164–72, Niebuhr writes in terms of the transvaluation of 'the moral law', but we have presented his view (except in quotations) in terms of 'moral claim' which, without loss of meaning for his argument, seems a more precise and less ambiguous form of expression, i.e., clearly without the implication that moral experience is best described on the analogy of positive law or best understood in terms of a law-model for ethics.

tion of a morality of self-love by one of love to God. In the terms we have used earlier, it is also the transvaluation of a deontological morality (whether or not conceived in terms of rule-deontology or of moral law) and of a teleological morality conceived as the promotion of the good (however defined, or declared with Moore to be indefinable) into a morality of response and of persons-in-relationship.[37] Transgression, wrote Niebuhr, no longer merely goes against one's conscience or some people's idea of value or of society's standards (though it does all this), but it also goes against 'the grain of the universe',[38] and does violence 'to the body of God; it is his son who is slain by our iniquity'.[39]

> 'As the prophets did not declare to Israel a new morality but directed attention to the eternal imperative behind a nomadic morality, so Jesus Christ gives us, first of all, no new ethics but reveals the lawgiver whose implacable will for the completion and redemption of his creation does not allow even his most beloved son to exempt himself from the suffering necessary to that end'.[40]

Secondly, in Christian faith the *content* of morality is transvalued. God's revelation in Jesus Christ has transformed the moral claim in several ways.

(1) Revelation brings about an extension of social relations: 'love your neighbour' cannot be confined any longer to one's fellow-citizen or one's blood brother.

(2) Nor can the moral judgement be confined to the overt act, but is extended to the inner life, i.e., to 'the implicit movements which occur within the privacy of the individual organism'.[41]

(3) Nor can the will of God be taken as restricted to the world of rational beings, but has to be extended to non-human life: 'sparrows, sheep and lilies belong within the network of moral relations when God reveals himself; now every killing is a sacrifice'.[42]

(4) Indeed, the moral claim cannot be restricted within the boundary of life, for now the earth is cultivated as the garden of the Lord and the stars are reverenced as God's creatures.

Not only are there these *extensions* of the moral claim, but also that claim is *radicalised:* it is changed to its very roots. 'There is no possibility now of restricting moral obedience to the circle of the good, so that we love those who love us or who share our principles and do no harm to our values'.[43] The moral claim is freed from all limitations which circumscribe its range in any way, so that it is universalised and intensified: it is indeed reborn. It is now the claim

'of a living contemporary being, new in every new moment and there-

[37] See below, chapter 10.
[38] *Op. cit.*, p. 166.
[39] *Loc. cit.*
[40] *Loc. cit.*
[41] *Op. cit.*, p. 167.
[42] *Loc. cit.*
[43] *Loc. cit.*

fore forever changing in its specific form. No merely traditional way of doing things is right in the presence of the living authority'.[44]

'. . . this revelation must erase the boundaries of all the successive moralities, of Christendom as of Jewry and paganism . . . A revolutionary transvaluation occurs not in addition to the personal revelation but because of it'.[45]

In the presence of this revelation of the person, we realise (claims Niebuhr) that all our moralities were self-interested, wishful, idolatrous and corrupted. Our moral norms were used prudentially—in the service of the creature or some man-made idol rather than the creator. When we took pleasure as the standard, it was *our* pleasure; if perfection were the measure, it was *our* perfection; if benevolence, it was a benevolence restricted to 'those of our own kind, from whom we might expect some return of our kindness'.[46] We would or did not 'look at things from the viewpoint of a universal person'.[47] In self-deceit, we continually invent new moralities to evade the performance of our duty. The prophetic and Christian transvaluation of the moral claim enables us to talk correctly of an absolute moral claim that transcends all relativities, because it crosses all restricted boundaries.

Thirdly, not only is there a transvaluation of the source and content of morality, but also God's revelation of himself in Jesus Christ converts the moral claim from the imperative to the indicative mood.[48] It no longer meets us simply as 'thou shalt love', but is embodied as a living reality in Jesus. It thus meets us, not as a law externally imposed, but as a free love of God and man. It meets us in a personal way and in the context of grace, so that, as we respond to Jesus, we are set free to love God and man. Our response is never total in this world, and so we discern this feature as a potentiality rather than an actuality, 'as a promise of what the law shall be for us when the great travail of historic life is past'[49]—but, at the same time, it is the beginning of a new understanding of the moral claim and the beginning of a new life. God does not reveal to people, apart from their reasoning, new moral truths otherwise unknown. Revelation is not the giving of a new law or morality, but 'the beginning of a revolutionary understanding and application of the moral law'.[50]

[44] *Op. cit.*, p. 167f.
[45] *Op. cit.*, p. 168.
[46] *Op. cit.*, p. 169.
[47] *Loc. cit.*
[48] *Loc. cit.*
[49] *Op. cit.*, p. 171.
[50] *Op. cit.*, p. 172.

Part Three

THE RE-MAKING OF CHRISTIAN ETHICS

7

NATURAL LAW AND MORAL THEOLOGY

An important and influential way of locating social and personal norms both in and outwith Christian ethics is that of natural law. Contemporary Roman Catholic interpretation of it takes us into the centre of modern controversies, such as abortion and contraception and the debate stemming from Vatican II (1962–65) and the subsequent Papal Encyclical *Humanae Vitae* (1968). Further, the doctrine has been revisited in the second half of this century not only by moral theologians but also by political theorists, jurists and philosophers to discover whether it provides a justifiable basis for positive law in newly-independent secular, sovereign states as in Africa. We shall argue that its interest today for Christian ethics derives from the hope that it may provide a justification of the Christian's co-operation with the non-Christian in social and moral concerns in a multi-faith society.

Natural law has had an important place—indeed a central one—in both Roman Catholic and Anglican moral theology (Hooker was a staunch protagonist for it). The scholastic period in general and the views of Aquinas in particular have greatly influenced moral teaching in both these traditions. Whatever its difficulties, natural law did not in the past come under such severe fire as it has in the twentieth-century bombardment from Karl Barth and others. It was not summarily rejected by the Reformers but lurked in the background of the teaching of Luther and Calvin on 'the orders of creation', though it has not received much favour among their followers. Whatever our views or prejudices on modern controversies surrounding marital ethics and on the way Church authority has used the doctrine in the past, natural law doctrine is worthy at least of initial respect on account of its long history and is worthy of re-examination with an open mind and an eye to its possibilities for dialogue with non-Christians in areas of shared concern.

A. THE DOCTRINE OF NATURAL LAW

1. *What kind of ethical doctrine is natural law?*

What, then, is natural law? At once we encounter difficulties. Natural law has had a very long history both before and after Aquinas.[1] Indeed, the

---

[1] For the long history of the doctrine in European thought, see, e.g., E. Troeltsch, 'Review of Natural Law in the Ancient World', E. Wolf, 'The Law of Nature in

doctrine has taken so many different forms from the Greeks to the present day, that we cannot speak of *one* doctrine of natural law. Rival protagonists have embraced the term 'natural law' for their respective theories or ideologies, e.g., Aquinas, Hobbes, Locke, the Nazis, and newly constituted secular states—even when their theories have been inconsistent with one another or even diametrically opposed. It is, therefore, difficult to provide a definition which brings together what is common to all such versions of natural law, and in current textbooks a variety of definitions is found. We have to be alert to this difficulty of definition at the beginning, for we shall make little progress in understanding natural law if we fail to grasp that one of the items on the agenda in any thorough discussion is 'What precisely is a doctrine of natural law? What would constitute an argument in natural law? What kind of ethical doctrine is it meant to be?'

To offset this difficulty at least to some extent, we propose to use two strategies. The first is to offer two definitions which are to be taken as suggestive indications of the nature of the doctrine, rather than as definitive statements. The first is from a philosopher:

'In so far as any common core can be found to the principal versions of the natural law theory, it seems to amount to the statement that the basic principles of morals and legislation are, *in some sense or other*, objective, accessible to reason and based on human nature. But so vague a specification tells us little until we decide the sense to be put upon these phrases'.[2]

The second is from a distinguished barrister, expert on jurisprudence and a professional philosopher. H. L. A. Hart describes the Thomist tradition of Natural Law as the clearest, if perhaps the most extreme, expression of the view that there is a necessary connection between law and morality.

'This comprises a twofold contention: first, that there are certain principles of true morality or justice, discoverable by human reason without the aid of revelation even though they have a divine origin; secondly, that man-made laws which conflict with these principles are not valid law'.[3]

Our second strategy is to list some fairly common-sense questions which a doctrine of natural law normally claims to answer:

'How can what belongs to common morality be distinguished from what belongs to the way of life of a particular religion?'

'How can what is moral be distinguished, if at all, from what the law of the land requires?'

'Can the law be justified on the ground of morality? Can we say that there are unjust laws which we have a moral right to disobey and which should not be laws at all?'

(*footnote* 1 *continued*)

Thomas Aquinas and Luther', and E. Brunner, 'Fall and Revival of Natural Law', all three in H. Thielicke and H.-H. Schrey, edd. *Faith and Action*, 1970, pp. 225–273.

[2] D. J. O'Connor, *Aquinas and Natural Law*, 1967, p. 57.

[3] *The Concept of Law*, 1961, p. 152.

We have listed these fairly common-sense questions in order to bring out the questions in ethical theory that underlie both them and the above tentative definitions. What kind of doctrine is natural law meant to be? In other words, what ethical question does natural law claim to answer?[4] There seem to be three main possibilities.

First, the doctrine might claim to give *a justification of the objectivity* of at least *some* (perhaps the basic) moral judgements. In other words, it might claim to settle the debate between subjectivism and objectivism in ethics by holding that *some* of our moral judgements are made independently of our own tastes, feelings, inclinations and even religious beliefs, and independently of the laws and majority-views of others or the *mores* of any particular society.

Secondly, the doctrine might claim to settle the question of what is the moral criterion, norm or standard: for example, to settle the question we discussed in our first two chapters, i.e., between deontology and teleology. Added to this might be the claim that such a norm or norms hold independently of people's religious beliefs, though they may have a divine origin.

Thirdly, the doctrine might claim to do both of the above, i.e., both to give a justification of ethical objectivism and to provide a moral norm or norms. Indeed, some writers make this claim. For example, T. E. O'Connell[5] claims that natural law is (a) anti-subjectivist and (b) not a form of legalism, but of consequentialism, i.e., a form of teleological ethics. Of course, this need not be a confusion, for there may be a connection between the two claims. If we hold that moral judgements are justified as objective on the ground that they refer to some objective value, then the moral norm can hardly be a subjective one.

These two claims taken together have received much attention in this century. It has been argued that natural law is a way of avoiding ethical subjectivism and relativism by the appeal to a standard above positive law and all culturally determined moral norms. Hart's definition above narrows the issue of ethical objectivism to that of some objective moral principles which provide a non-arbitrary basis for man-made positive laws. It is in this sense that natural law has been claimed as the justification of the human law of secular, sovereign states. Hart cites the saying of Augustine quoted by Thomas Aquinas: *lex iniusta non est lex*, 'an unjust law is no law at all'.[6] Thus Martin Luther King and all who appeal either to 'natural justice' or to human rights over against the pretentions and arbitrary dictates of human law made by the ruling power in its interests or the interests of a powerful minority or even majority—such people *may* be using an argument in natural law doctrine and *will* be doing so in so far as they hold that the principles of justice and of human rights are norms of natural

---

[4] Cf. P. J. McGrath, 'Natural Law and Moral Argument' in (ed.) J. P. Mackey, *Morals, Law and Authority*, 1969.

[5] *Principles for a Catholic Morality*, 1976, 1978, p. 144f; cf. Franz Böckle, *Fundamental Moral Theology*, 1980, pp. 233ff.

[6] *Summa Theologiae*, I–II, Q. 96, art. iv (hereafter contracted to *S.T.*)

law discoverable by reason, or can be derived therefrom. If these claims alone were justified, i.e., if natural law were an adequate and cogent answer to legal positivism (which holds that there is no necessary connection between law and morals), it would be a valuable ethical doctrine.

Such claims for natural law have not always been made in their Thomist form. Hart, for example, has formulated a modern version of natural law based on human beings' desire for survival and their known dependence on others for such survival—a version which he maintains is free from any metaphysical and theological presuppositions.

Since we are primarily interested in natural law as a doctrine within Christian ethics, we now turn to its classical formulation in Thomas Aquinas.

2. *Aquinas on Natural Law*

The teaching of Thomas Aquinas on Natural Law cannot be studied in abstraction from his total outlook and treated as if it were a philosophical doctrine on its own, as has often been attempted. As far as space permits, we shall introduce aspects of his ontology, divine teleology and theology that bear upon natural law.

It does not follow, however, that his version of natural law is of interest only to Christians. His version does have a theological foundation—for example, he teaches a divine teleology whereby man's ultimate end is the vision of God—and so natural law is for him a doctrine within Christian theology. Yet natural law is for him also a doctrine about man as a moral being, whether he be a Christian, a Muslim,[7] an atheist or whatever. He realised that the theologian and the moral philospher use rather different perspectives or standpoints in considering morally bad acts—the former considers sin principally as an offence against God, whereas the latter considers it as being contrary to reason.[8]

Further, though Aquinas's ethics is theological, it preserves the non-religious meaning of the concept 'good'. He defines 'good' not in religious terms, but as 'that towards which all things tend'.[9] To say 'God is good' is to give *a reason* for obeying his commandments, but 'good' is not *defined* in terms of God's commandments, nor indeed does his definition confine 'good' to 'morally good' but indicates that he is using a more general value term.

(1) *Essential criteria for moral action.* Aquinas is aware that, when expounding any ethical theory, it is necessary to give an analysis of human action. First, he described the essential criteria of the human act that is to be regarded as morally right or wrong. These he gives as freedom and rationality. Action that is involuntary, such as purely reflexive action, falls outside the scope of morality. He rejected the claim later made by some

[7] Aquinas was aware of Islam: his *Summa contra Gentiles* was a kind of theological handbook for Christian missionaries among the Moors.
[8] *S.T.* I–II Q. 71, art. 6.
[9] *Op. cit.*, Q. 94, art. 2.

nineteenth century liberals, 'we needs must choose the highest when we see it', for no good, not even God, is ever presented in such a way that the will is compelled to choose it. As for rationality, a morally right or wrong act is one wherein the will is directed towards an end grasped by reason. But this end need not be objectively good. In accordance with his teleological view of nature, he holds that all created beings tend towards the actualisation of their potentialities, i.e., to their final end and good, but, whereas other beings are (as we might say today) programmed so to do, human beings do so by means of intellect and a will which is free to reject their ultimate end, and choose something else that they take to be good.[10]

Aquinas thought that the moral philosopher, even though he knows nothing of man's ultimate end, understood as the beatific vision of God in heaven, is capable of seeing that some acts conduce to the development of his nature as a free, rational being and that others are contrary to it. Thus Aquinas was led, in addition to describing the essential criteria of a human act that was to fall within the scope of morality, viz., freedom and rationality, to outline the considerations to be taken into account when deciding if a human act is morally right or wrong, viz., its immediate consequences, its intention and the circumstances in which it was performed.

We can only select some aspects of these considerations. For example, an act that is not deliberate (such as stroking the beard or moving a hand or foot) is not properly speaking a moral act, but morally indifferent:[11] but an act which is morally indifferent (e.g., taking a walk in the garden) may be in other circumstances a moral act, if the intention, for example, is to quarrel with the gardener.

He was not talking of outward acts alone for he regarded the interior act and the external act as components of a single whole. On the one hand, intention belongs to the interior act, but informs the whole act. For example, 'to give alms for the sake of vainglory is bad'.[12] The absence of a good intention and the presence of a bad intention render the whole act morally bad. An interesting example of an attempt to apply this teaching to a modern issue is found in the 1976 pastoral letter which the Roman Catholic bishops in the U.S.A. addressed to their people:

'As possessors of a vast nuclear arsenal, we must also be aware that not only is it wrong to attack civilian populations but it is also wrong to threaten to attack them as part of a strategy of deterrence',

meaning that it is as wrong to intend to commit an evil as it is actually to commit it.[13] On the other hand, intention alone does not make an exterior act good. There are some actions which cannot be justified by any alleged good intention, and so Aquinas rejects the view that the end justifies the means. Stealing, for example, is not justified by the good intention of giving

[10] Op. cit., Q. 1, art. 17.
[11] Op. cit., Q. 18, art. 9.
[12] Op. cit., Q. 20, art. 1.
[13] Cf. St. Matthew 5:21–22 and 27–28 where it is said that anger and insults are as evil as murder and lust as evil as adultery.

the money to the poor.[14] The exterior act is morally good only in terms of its consequences for the good life for human beings—i.e., it must be compatible with the attainment of the ultimate end. A human act, therefore, considered as a whole, is morally bad, if either requisite component is defective—either the intention or the external act.

To this analysis, Aquinas added that we have finally to decide whether an act is right or wrong by reference to whether or not it conforms to law. He cannot be called a legalist in the strict sense, for 'conformity to some law', as we have seen, was for him only one of several criteria by which the act was to be judged morally right or wrong.

Aquinas distinguished four different kinds of law—eternal, natural, positive divine law and positive human law, both civil and ecclesiastical. The essence of law is that 'it is nothing else than ordinance of reason for the common good, made by him who has care of the community and promulgated'.[15] This sounds like a slightly idealised version of civil law, rather than a definition covering all four kinds of law.

(2) *The eternal law.* It is, therefore, surprising that he starts with the eternal law and not with human law. The eternal law is the order, the ideal type, the model or plan of the universe pre-existing in God, the final cause in the mind of God, which continues to direct all his creatures to the attainment of their ends.[16] As we have seen, all creatures below the human participate unconsciously in the actualisation of their potentialities, i.e., in the eternal law, which is reflected in their various natural tendencies. But human beings, as rational and free beings, are capable of acting in ways which are incompatible with the eternal law. They must, therefore, somehow know the eternal law in so far as it concerns themselves. But 'no one can know the eternal law as it is in itself, except God and the blessed who see God in his essence'.[17] While human beings cannot know the eternal law as it is in itself, they can know it as they see it mirrored in their fundamental tendencies and needs, and when they reflect on these, they can come to some knowledge of the natural or moral law. In this sense, human beings are not left in ignorance of the eternal law: '. . . the natural law is nothing else than the rational creature's participation of the eternal law'.[18]

As law is defined as an ordinance of reason, we cannot literally speak of irrational beings *obeying* a natural law, for irrational creatures cannot recognise and promulgate to themselves any such law. Similarly, 'natural law' (as Aquinas uses it) does not denote scientific law, which is descriptive, while the moral law is prescriptive. While we cannot expect Aquinas to make this modern distinction, he would have had an answer to any objection from this direction. He was using the term 'law' not literally, but analogically, and the basis of the analogy was not with scientific law (which is not a law at all, since it is descriptive), but with human law (hence his

[14] *Op. cit.*, Q. 20, art. 2.
[15] *Op. cit.*, Q. 90, art. 4.
[16] Cf. *op. cit.*, Q. 93, art. 1.
[17] *Op. cit.*, Q. 93, art. 2.
[18] *Op. cit.*, Q. 91, art. 2.

definition of law). He might have argued that what the moral law and human law have in common is the sense of constraint, bindingness and obligatoriness. For these reasons, today we might substitute 'moral awareness' or some such phrase for 'natural law'.

To the other modern objection that we cannot derive an 'ought' from an 'is', a prescription of value from a statement of fact, Aquinas would probably have replied that the term 'natural law' is applicable, not to the natural tendencies and inclinations of human beings, but to the precepts which they enunciate as a result of reflection on these tendencies and inclinations. He might have admitted that there was a sense in which he *argued* from the facts of human nature to the values embodied in human conduct, but not that he was *deducing* or *deriving* value from fact. Value, he might have said, is already found in human beings, for it is human reason that enunciates or promulgates the precepts of the natural law. Though this moral law is a reflection of the divine plan or eternal law, we can speak of the autonomy of morality, in so far as the moral law is thus promulgated by the human reason.[19] The moral law is not externally imposed on human beings by God, but human beings discern its inherent rationality and binding force and promulgate it to themselves.

(3) *The precepts of the natural law.*[20] There are several precepts of the natural law, not just one. Aquinas holds that there is an analogy between the precepts of practical reason and the first principles of theoretical reason (as in mathematics and the sciences). Just as there are several first principles of theoretical reason, so there are *several* precepts of the natural law.[21] And the first principles of theoretical reason and the precepts of practical reason are self-evident.[22]

The first thing that a human being grasps is *being*, for without understanding *being* he can apprehend nothing else. The first self-evident principle of the theoretical reason is that 'the same thing cannot be affirmed and denied at the same time' and this principle is based on the meanings of *being* and *not-being*. This is the well-known principle of contradiction, sometimes called the principle of non-contradiction, and commonly expressed nowadays in the form 'The same thing cannot both be and not be at the same time and in the same respect' (e.g., 'a piece of paper cannot be both red all over and green all over at the same time'). On this principle, claims Aquinas, all other principles of theoretical reason are based.

Now as *being* represents our first intuitive discovery about anything we are to know, so *good* represents our first intuitive discovery of the practical reason, which is reason directed to any sort of action. Now every agent acts for an end, and such an end is grasped or understood as 'good'. Consequently, the first principle of the practical reason is founded on the meaning of 'good', and this meaning is 'good is that towards which all things tend'

---

[19] On this ground, Aquinas has been called a Kantian before Kant. For Kant's position, see p. 104, n.33 above.

[20] *Op. cit.*, Q. 94, art. 2.

[21] *Loc. cit.* Cf. Q. 91, art. 3.

[22] *Loc. cit.*

(sometimes translated as 'good is that which all things seek'). Hence the first precept of natural law is that *good is to be done and promoted, and evil is to be avoided*. All other precepts of the natural law are based upon this first precept, in the sense that these precepts are grasped as things-to-be-done, or things-to-be-avoided, and such things practical reason naturally grasps as human good or their opposites.

Aquinas did not mean, as is sometimes alleged, that we all *ought* to do and promote whatever we *in fact* seek, for he admitted that many people seek what is evil. 'Good is that which all things seek' has to be understood as meaning 'Good is that which all things *by nature* seek' (hence our translation 'towards which all things tend'). Hence his definition of 'good' is already a statement of value, if not one of moral value in the narrower sense.[23] Again, Aquinas can be freed of the charge of deriving an 'ought' from an 'is'.

Since good has the nature of an end (i.e., something to be pursued), and evil, the nature of the contrary (i.e., something to be avoided), all those things to which a man has a natural inclination are grasped by the practical reason as being good, and consequently as objects of pursuit, and their contraries as being evil and so as objects of avoidance. 'End' here must not be reduced in meaning to 'goal', as if good has the nature of a goal and evil (its contrary) has not. We would be nearer Aquinas's meaning if we said that in the case of human beings, good has the nature of a goal to be pursued, and evil that of a goal to be avoided.

Indeed in the thought of Aquinas, the notion of *end* is as fundamental as that of *being*. Everything has its end. Every being has a nature or form, according to which it acts (*actio sequitur esse* or *operatio sequitur esse*), and that action is good in so far as it tends to fulfil its end, i.e., as it tends to the perfection or full actuality of its nature.[24] What then is the specific end of human being?

Aquinas made a three-fold distinction among the inclinations which human beings possess:

(a) the inclination to good which human beings share with *all beings*, *viz.*, the preservation of their own being. So human beings seek the preservation of human life.

> 'In virtue of this inclination, there belongs to the natural law the taking of those means whereby the life of man is preserved, and threats to life are warded off'.[25]

(b) the inclination to good which human beings share with *the other animals*.

> 'In virtue of this inclination, those things are said to belong to the natural law which nature has taught to all animals, such as sexual intercourse, the education of offspring and so forth'.[26]

---

[23] The point of this distinction will be clear below: cf (a) and (b) with (c).
[24] Cf. M. C. D'Arcy, *Thomas Aquinas*, 1930, p. 228 and E. Gilson, *The Elements of Christian Philosophy*, 1963, p. 264.
[25] *S.T.*, I–II, Q. 94, art. 2.
[26] *Loc. cit.*

(c) the inclination to good which human beings do *not* share with any other beings, but which is distinctively human, i.e., 'in accordance with the rational nature which is proper to human beings'.[27] Thus man has a natural inclination to know the truth about God and to live in society. To paraphrase Aquinas, in virtue of this inclination, there belongs to the natural law such things as the shunning of ignorance, the avoidance of giving offence to other people and 'other such things'.

All these precepts flow from the first precept of natural law—*viz.*, *good is to be done and promoted and evil is to be avoided*. In other words, this multiplicity of precepts is not a disorganised and unrelated collection, but an ordered and unitary whole.

So far we have three primary precepts—or more precisely, three sets of such precepts—which relate to human beings considered as vegetable, animal and rational creatures. Aquinas believed that, from these primary precepts, reason reflecting on experience can discover, by a process of deduction, secondary precepts which are less general and more particular. But the truth of the first principles or primary precepts is known intuitively (i.e., they are self-evident), and not by deductive reasoning.

(4) *Are all sins or virtuous acts prescribed by the natural law?*[28] In this rather technical discussion, something important emerges for our understanding of natural law. Sometimes in the past in the Roman Catholic Church natural law has been understood as if the 'nature' referred to were biological nature: for example, artificial means of contraception have been held to be 'unnatural' in this sense. But Aquinas carefully distinguished two senses of 'nature'—*viz.*, (a) the human nature proper to man as a rational being; and in this sense *all* sins, as being against reason, are also against nature: and (b) the nature common to man and the other animals; and in this sense *some* sins are said to be against nature; e.g., he writes, 'contrary to sexual intercourse, which is natural to all animals, is unisexual lust, which has received the special name of the unnatural crime'.[29]

Aquinas himself on the basis of this and other passages has often been charged with sometimes identifying the demands of natural law with physical and biological processes.[30] Is this charge fair to Aquinas? To determine this involves an interpretation of the text which is admittedly ambiguous. But we offer the following rebuttal on the principle that, on such vexed questions of interpretation, any author must be given the benefit of the doubt. In other words, could Aquinas have defended himself without giving up what was basic to his position?

---

[27] *Loc. cit.*

[28] *S.T.*, I–II, Q. 94, art. 3.

[29] Aquinas is referring to homosexuality, not to that other 'unnatural offence', human intercourse with animals, which he would no doubt have condemned as well.

[30] The charge has been supported by reference to the inclinations which humans share with all beings and with the other animals (see p. 148 above) and by his reference to natural law as 'common to all animals' (*S.T.*, I–II, Q. 95, art. 4). The charge has been made by such Roman Catholic writers as T. E. O'Connell (*op. cit.*, pp. 138–9) and Charles E. Curran (see O'Connell).

doctrine. It was now looking at the world from a Christian perspective, and seeing indications of the Transcendent in man's moral experience. Further, Aquinas, as distinguished from his later 'followers', did seem to attempt to frame a doctrine that was free from the charge of historical and cultural relativism.

We suggest four criteria for a reformulated doctrine of natural law. First, natural law will point to some characteristic of human moral experience that avoids introducing some element of historical and cultural conditioning. Second, natural law will provide grounds for the Christian's co-operation with the non-Christian in a multi-faith society. Third, natural law will look within human moral experience for indications of its dependence upon a transcendent reality. Fourth, natural law will be a doctrine of man on a par with other doctrines of man.[60] We now attempt a formulation of natural law which meets these four criteria.

The doctrine of natural law simply points to man's moral awareness, the sense of 'ought' and moral constraint, the demand that will brook no other claim, the sense of the unconditioned nature of the 'ought' which in this sense is not historically conditioned, but can appeal against any institution or rule.[61] It is in this sense that Aquinas's 'first precept of natural law' is to be understood, *viz.*, 'that good is to be done and promoted, and evil is to be avoided'.[62] Fletcher ridicules this precept on the ground of its lack of content.[63] This shows how far he has misunderstood Aquinas's intention, though he should not be singled out for pillorying, since others have made the same mistake. Though Aquinas presents the argument in terms of ends to be pursued and to be avoided, we might put it today in other terms: e.g., that man is a being who recognises a moral claim, even though its content varies according to culture, century and society. As A. D. Galloway has argued,[64] while the basic, universal (moral) constitution which is the human condition finds concrete expression in a wide variety of rules and institutions in different cultures, these all arise out of the same basic constitutional facts.

> 'The belief that this is so is implied in all inter-cultural and all
> reforming discourse. One appeals against the "ought" which is valid
> only within a special institution to the "ought" which arises out of the
> basic constitutional facts of human existence . . . It is also along these
> lines that I think one could develop an account of the fact/value nexus
> within a theory of natural law'.[65]

---

[60] For example, man as machine (mechanism), an organism (e.g., a naked ape), behaviourism, materialism, an economic view of man, a Freudian view, a rational view and an existentialist view.

[61] Cf. Enda McDonagh, *Invitation and Response*, 1972, p. 34.

[62] See p. 148 above.

[63] Quoting the late Bishop Pike with approval, Fletcher uses the term 'platitudinous' of this precept of natural law in *M.R.*, p. 71.

[64] In 'Fact and Value in Theological Ethics', in *Religious Studies* 5, 1969.

[65] Galloway, *op. cit.*, p. 176. It would be unfair to conceal from the reader that Galloway adds in brackets, 'using "natural law" in a loose sense'. In the context

This conception of natural law is, according to McDonagh, that 'which identifies nature as the human capacity of recognising man's inescapable moral condition'.[66] Galloway argues that the human condition has this basic (moral) constitution on the ground that fact and value are already related for the child before he learns to distinguish them, and that in the *ordo cognoscendi* we learn to make evaluative judgements before we learn formal regulative principles.

> 'The real problem of the moral life—the problem of attaining moral maturity—is not that of ascertaining how to relate fact to value, but how to distinguish and separate them. The problem of the growing child is not how to associate fact and value, but how to separate his perception of value from his perception of his parents or whoever his "heroes" may be'.[67]

On this view of natural law, the grounds of the Christian's co-operation with the non-Christian in a multi-faith and pluralist society will be the former's belief that all human beings have in this sense a basically moral constitution and that (as we shall argue) such a belief is a presupposition of the whole Christian framework of creation and redemption. Such a doctrine of natural law is needed for Christian theology and ethics, as soon as one abandons the untenable view that there is no morality outside the Christian faith. God relates himself to all human beings—and in the same way. He does not relate himself differently to an atheist and to a Christian, or differently to a Hindu and to a Muslim. Each of us may have a different *view* of the relationship, but in the *ordo essendi*[68] the divine-human relationship is the same. From the human perspective, the world is multi-religious or pluralistic: from the point of view of God's activity, it is one world of people responding and not responding (to greater or lesser degrees) to that activity.

There may be exceptions to this universality of the moral consciousness (e.g., the psychopath), but because some people are blind, we do not define humanity as all people who have lost or never had their sight. In other words, it is characteristic of human nature as such to be morally aware. Today we can produce empirical evidence as grounds for this view: from anthropologists and sociologists who show that human beings are social creatures with a need to fulfil a social role, and from psychologists with their theories of moral development. Some may consider that by arguing

(*footnote* 65 *continued*)
of his paper, he was right to be circumspect in view of the history of the term, and he was not attaching it, as we are, to Aquinas's first precept of natural law, but arguing in much more general terms. This merely highlights once again that perhaps we would be better to avoid both 'natural' and 'law' and speak simply of 'morality'.

[66] McDonagh, *op. cit.*, p. 34. The other possible view, *viz.*, that all 'morality' is sufficiently and exhaustively explained in terms of cultural and historical conditioning, is inconsonant with a Christian doctrine of God. Cf. chapter 10 below.

[67] Galloway, *op. cit.*, p. 176.

[68] *Ordo essendi* refers to the nature of being rather than the way we come to learn (*ordo cognoscendi*).

from such empirical statements, we are committing the naturalistic fallacy, but we have shown that a doctrine of natural law based on the universal human condition does not require to derive value from fact by a process of logical entailment, but recognises that there is a primary 'ought' which arises out of the basic constitutional facts of human existence. Such a doctrine does not, in our view, commit the naturalistic fallacy.

If, however, natural law is to be a doctrine in Christian ethics, it will go further than simply quote anthropology, sociology and psychology, and in addition will ground man's moral awareness in a theological understanding of man. For the Christian, moral awareness is a pre-condition of the divine-human dialogue. Whether Rudolf Otto[69] was correct or not in holding that there can be in some religions a characteristic experience of the 'numinous' that is isolated from moral awareness, this is not how God's address to human beings receives classic expression in the Bible.[70] The whole Christian framework of creation and redemption presupposes the moral constitution of human beings. The divine address presupposes that human beings can make a response in faith to God's gracious, loving activity (notice the moral-laden terms) and that response includes one in moral behaviour.

The intention of this conception of natural law is not to provide norms of behaviour, social or personal, but to offer a justification for their being any norms at all. But it is a justification of a special sort. It is not an inference, for example from some feature of moral awareness to the divine. It is different from some forms of the moral argument for God's existence, where there is an inference from the moral law to a (divine) lawgiver. It is simply an *indication* of where the Christian sees the moral condition of mankind impinging upon the transcendent and opening towards it. On the boundaries of our knowledge and experience, we are aware of the mathematically provable at one end and of the inexplicable in terms of present knowledge at the other. But over the great range of our knowledge (in the physical sciences, the social sciences, in history and the law-courts), the test of truth is tested experience sifted and embraced within a coherent sequence, hypothesis or theory—in this case, human moral experience embraced within the coherence of a doctrine of natural law, in which there is an understanding in Christian terms of humanity's moral condition. Christians see natural law as a reflection on humanity of the divine light. This is the point of Aquinas's claim that 'the natural law is nothing else than the rational creature's participation in the eternal law'.[71] It is not, therefore, a doctrine that will be acceptable to atheists, agnostics and humanists. But it does seek to provide an understanding in Christian terms of man's moral condition, whether that man be a Jew, a Muslim, a Hindu, a Christian or of

[69] In *Das Heilige*, 1917, Eng. tr. *The Idea of the Holy*, 1923.
[70] Cf. our discussion of the divine-human dialogue in chapter 10 below, pp. 222–26.
[71] *S.T.* 1–11, Q. 91, art. 2. In this connection, Aquinas quotes the *Gloss* on Romans 2:14 ('When the Gentiles, who have not the law, do by nature those things that are of the law'), 'Although they have no written law, yet they have the natural law, whereby each one knows, and is conscious of, what is good and what is evil'.

no religious faith-community at all. It, therefore, justifies for Christians co-operation on moral and social issues between them and non-Christians in a multi-faith society. Aquinas was quite clear that, though his doctrine had a theological basis, he was distinguishing what belongs to the human moral condition (in the first precepts of natural law) from what belongs to the way of life of a particular religion: for example, only the moral precepts of the divine law belonged to the natural law and to its secondary precepts at that,[72] and so those precepts of the divine law (as in the decalogue) that were not precepts of the natural law are not known or recognised by, or binding on, non-Christians.

While the doctrine of natural law in Aquinas was related to a Christian doctrine of creation, there is no need today to divorce it from redemption. Once we have grasped that in a doctrine of natural law we expect some indication of the dependence of human moral experience on a transcendent reality, we shall make an analysis of that experience to discern its common features and to determine whether any of these indicates such dependence. In particular, in such a doctrine within Christian ethics, our concern will be to determine whether there is a correlation between any of these features and a theological understanding of humanity. As we shall provide a fuller analysis presently, we select here only three features of moral experience. (a) In moral experience, we are aware of a moral *claim* or obligation to *respond* to the other person or group. (b) That claim is an *unconditional* demand on us, despite the personal inconvenience and cost involved in making a positive response to it. (c) In the very experience of the unconditioned character of the demand, we are aware of our *freedom* to respond either positively or negatively to it—i.e., to accept the claim upon us or deny it. These three features correlate with a theological understanding of humanity, and a fuller analysis might reveal other features with a similar correlation. (a) God's address comes to us as a divine *claim* to *respond* to his gift of grace. (b) God's address is *unconditional*, in the sense that it will brook no rival. (c) Despite the unconditional character of that claim, we are aware of our *freedom* to respond either positively or negatively to it—either to accept or deny it—to make what has been called in moral theology the fundamental option.[73] Further, as we have argued,[74] there cannot be two rival claims on us—a moral and a divine claim. There is only one claim. What all human beings experience as a moral claim is God's claim to respond to his gift of grace. Again, in all his activity, and not just in creation narrowly conceived, God relates himself in the same way to all human beings, whether Christians or not. Creation and redemption must not be divorced. As Creator, God calls us as creatures to respond to his continual creative activity in the world. As Redeemer, who makes new creatures, God calls us *simul justus simul peccator* to respond to his gift of new

[72] *S.T.* I–II, Q. 100, art. 1.
[73] The doctrine of the fundamental option is discussed in Franz Böckle, *op. cit.*, pp. 106f. and pp. 108ff., Charles E. Curran, *A New Look at Christian Morality*, pp. 203–7 and Bernard Häring, *Free and Faithful in Christ*, Vol. 1, Chapter Five, 1978.
[74] See above pp. 129 and 132f.

life in a life continually reshaped and renewed. In this way, the doctrine of natural law can be related to a Christian doctrine of redemption, as well as creation, and can be formulated in terms not of a law or rule model, but in terms of a response or relational model for ethics.

Such a doctrine of natural law has been criticised on the ground that it is too abstract. In emptying the 'ought' of any historical conditioning, we have deprived it—so the argument runs—of any moral content and so of any meaning appropriate to the doctrine. It is, however, possible, as we have said, to give an analysis of the 'ought' in such a way as to clarify how the doctrine is immune to this charge of over-abstractness. Various philosophers of education in Britain, especially John Wilson, R. S. Peters and Paul Hirst, have worked more or less independently in the provision of a conceptual framework for moral education in a secular and pluralist society, and have produced lists of the common features of the 'ought' or of the principles that lay down what constitutes the moral judgement. They all agree broadly on the following seven principles:[75]

(1) Moral judgements must be *freely held*, not made as the result of pressure; in other words, people shall in general be free to act as they determine.

(2) Moral judgements must be held *for a reason*, and for *a reason appropriate to morality* (e.g., the desire to do the right, because it is right; the desire to act because this action is just or because I am concerned for others; and NOT because everyone agrees, because I am under pressure or because I do it for kicks).

(3) They must apply to all *in an impartial way:* i.e., in the making of moral judgements, there is implied a principle of fairness, equity or impartiality by which all people are treated the same, unless there are relevant differences between them: e.g., that people are black and poor is not a relevant difference; that some people are handicapped in some way is. (See (5) and (6) which attempt to indicate which differences are and are not relevant.)

(4) They must adhere to a *general principle of truth-telling*, without which determining actions by reasons would be necessarily vitiated.

(5) They must adhere to a *general principle of the consideration of other people's interests:* i.e., there must be a recognition that the interests of others are as significant to them as one's own interests are to oneself.

(6) They must exhibit *concern for people as having a value in themselves*, and not simply as valuable for a prudential reason, such as being rich aunts, luscious blondes, V.I.P.'s or whatever.

(7) They *prescribe action* (as aesthetic judgements do not), i.e., once one has said 'This is right', one is committed to action determined by that moral judgement: and further, *they cannot be overriden by non-moral considerations* (e.g., one's own personal benefit), i.e., (to use our previous language) they make a claim on us to respond, and that claim will brook no rival.

---

[75] The three features of moral experience mentioned above p. 161 are incorporated here in (7) and (1).

There is more to a full analysis of moral experience than this, but these are the principles to be used in the settling of moral issues, or the principles that lay down what constitutes the moral judgement. There is greater agreement on the principles to be selected than on how they are derived. Some speak (e.g., Paul Hirst) of a gradual refinement of morality—i.e., a gradual agreement among civilised people as to what principles are to be used in the settling of moral issues. Others, without necessarily disagreeing with that view, take the line of R. S. Peters when he claims to infer such fundamental principles by a process technically known as 'transcendental deduction':[76] by this he means that these are the principles involved and implied in the very process of giving reasons for moral beliefs, actions, dispositions and so on.

Christians may see in this refinement of moral insight evidence of God's movement of grace among all peoples over many centuries. It can be seen as a way of reformulating an up-dated version of 'natural law'. That it proposes a concept of growth or development not only in the individual but in the species need not be an argument against it. Our first conception of natural law in terms of the basic, universal moral condition of humanity is consonant with a Chomsky-type genetic preprogramming,[77] but need not involve the notion, nowadays untenable, that moral awareness is literally innate, i.e., that babies are born with a ready-made conscience. We know from psychological research that moral learning takes place through a number of broad stages of development, and indeed this is more consonant with Chomsky's ideas than with behaviourism. In other words, the moral condition of humanity is consonant with a doctrine of natural law. The common features of human moral experience, as we have outlined them above, can be correlated with a theological understanding of humanity, one aspect of which is that the human being is not at any moment complete and entire. (To deny this is to deny the possibility of repentance and renewal.) Human existence is always in-the-making. So are children and young people. Further, the self-understanding of Christians will embrace an awareness of how incomplete they are as persons: e.g., the more they relate to others, the more they sense how incompletely they relate to them, and yet their existence is always in the making, and they are growing in grace as they relate more and more completely to others.[78] Our present stature in Christ is as nothing compared to what it shall be when God has finished his work in us and his full glory is revealed.

If natural law needs to be related in this way to redemption and the *eschaton*, it can be related to creation also, if humanity's moral possibilities have been set in certain basic directions which suggest pre-programming. We are aware, of course, that these directions are difficult to formulate with any degree of precision without involving some historical conditioning, but the seven principles indicate these directions, for they are *constitutive* of

---

[76] The term is no doubt meant to recall and is suggested by Kant's 'transcendental deduction' of the categories in his *Critique of Pure Reason*.

[77] Noam Chomsky, *Reflections on Language* and *Language and Mind*.

[78] See chapter 10 below.

morality, i.e., they lay down criteria for what constitutes a moral judge-ment, irrespective of culture or century. The case for cultural relativism is strong, as we argued in chapter one,[79] but this version of natural law teaches that normative relativism is false. Further, while these principles give us the basic directions for the mature, morally autonomous person, the four main broad stages of moral development, which are again independent of culture and century,[80] indicate the basic directions in which humanity moves towards moral maturity. Natural law in this form testifies to there being glimpses of God's creative and providential activity in all peoples. Certainly this outworking of his movement of grace to all peoples is seen more clearly in some individuals than in others—e.g., in the lives of teachers and prophets, saints and martyrs of many generations, including our own, for they have lit torches on the way and suffered for the light they gave—a light, however, that has never been extinguished—or was it not so much a light they gave as a revelation they received and acted on?[81] Conflict and growth, suffering and development can be encompassed within this version of natural law.

Criticisms that this or any other version of natural law doctrine pro-duces only tautologies or truisms may sound convincing if we expect from it more concrete norms than it supplies, i.e., something more specific than the fundamental principles of morality, which are also very difficult to formu-late precisely. For example, the third principle, i.e., of fairness, equity or impartiality, is one formulation, and one basic meaning, of justice, but justice, even as a basic constitutive and/or regulative principle of a civilised state, is constantly changing in meaning: e.g., what was considered just even 50 years ago or less is considered unjust today, as can be seen from some modern states undertaking functions that were not in the past considered functions of the state at all—e.g., in making provision for the unemployed, the sick, the handicapped and the old. Natural law doctrine in this form need hold only that, irrespective of the differing conceptions of justice in various societies and cultures, and the changing views of what constitutes justice in the same society, *all* civilised human beings seek justice in the sense that they seek a better understanding of it and a greater approximation to it in law and social practice. It is often the manifest failure to achieve justice that stimulates a better intellectual grasp of it. In any case, the Christian with his eschatological perspective believes that in the full humanity in Christ, man's moral constitution—including his con-ception of justice—will be transformed and fulfilled.

Finally, while we have concentrated on human moral experience in our reformulation, that cannot be divorced in a doctrine of natural law from human existence and our understanding of it as a whole. This is recognised

---

[79] Cf. chapter 1 above, pp. 11ff.

[80] What research exists on the moral development of non-Western peoples confirms this. Cf. p. 13 above, n. 30.

[81] Cf. *Hebrews* 11:33–40.

by James P. Scull, S.J., when he writes:[82]

> 'Put very succinctly, the natural law is nothing else than the demands which flow from the dignity and needs of what one is as a human person and hence from God as the author and creator of the human person in the divine image'.

Thus when we say that children *need* security and care, or that they *need* to be loved by parents and teachers, we are using an argument in natural law. When we point to *agape* as the basis of nurture in the family, we are again appealing to natural law. There is too the evidence of various 'secular' arguments as to how people *need* to be treated, if they are to change their life-style: for example, the argument that prisoners *need* to be treated with dignity, if their self-esteem is to be restored and their rehabilitation achieved; and the arguments that appear even in *avant-garde* writers that non-physical factors in a sexual relationship are important. All this is seen by Christians as confirmation of the need for *agape* in human relationships generally, for without it people are aware of a want, an emptiness of spirit, a lack of joy. We may adapt the saying of Augustine: people are restlessly empty, until they find their fulfilment in God who is *agape*.

C. THE SHAPE OF MORAL THEOLOGY TODAY

Prior to Vatican II, the purpose of moral theology in the Roman Catholic Church was to train priests for the conduct of the Sacrament of Penance. The Penitential Manuals of the seventeenth and eighteenth centuries—based on models of earlier centuries—provided the correct penance to fit the offence of the penitent. This was casuistry which understandably was a system whereby moral norms (rules or principles) were applied to concrete cases, conflicting obligations were weighed and exceptions classified—all with the aim of helping the priest to recognise the mortal or venial sin committed by the penitent and then to specify the appropriate penance. The casuist was an expert in moral theology: it was the critics of the system who used the term in a derogatory manner to mean 'sophist' or 'quibbler'.[83]

Though this view of moral theology was much narrower than that held in the medieval period (roughly 500–1545 Trent) when by the use of the scholastic method the aim was to produce a systematic statement of Christian moral teaching (as we have seen in Aquinas), its origins go back even before that period began. When 'the Christian faith had emerged from its minority status and had become the commitment of the masses',[84] the needs of the newly-converted barbarians required a new pastoral approach.

---

[82] In 'Roman Catholic Moral Theology (Contemporary)', article in *A Dictionary of Christian Ethics*, (ed.) John Macquarrie, 1967.

[83] Moral theologians taught rival methods for resolving doubtful cases, e.g., probabilism, probabiliorism and equiprobabilism.

[84] T. E. O'Connell, *op. cit.*, p. 12.

retribution for a sin committed (and so the greater the sin, the greater the penance), Christian forgiveness was thought to be a matter of retributive justice, rather than of mercy and grace.

Now a more personalist moral theology is taking shape with the focus of attention on the personal values of distributive and creative justice and mercy—'the weightier matters of the law'—which are impossible to reduce to a code of permitted and unpermitted actions for all in every circumstance anyone is likely to meet. As a result of this kind of moral theology, the laity are more likely to see God's forgiveness, not as a due penalty for a sin committed, but as the activity of God's grace to create the believer's life anew.

(4) As a result of the approach and content of the manuals, moral theology became associated with what has been called 'Christian minimalism'. The laity were led to believe that the Christian life consisted in the *avoidance* of the sins listed, and that successful avoidance of these justified confidence in one's moral righteousness. There was no call to 'perfection'— to 'go the second mile', 'to forgive forty times seven', to be 'perfect as your Father in heaven is perfect'—and the insight that this call was addressed to *all* Christians, and not just to priests and monks, was lost. In the new approach, there is an insistence that all Christians are called to perfection.

(5) The manuals were based on the view that the human essence or nature is fixed, static and, therefore, common to all human beings. The new moral theology recognises the significance of historicity. Both Fuchs and Häring have espoused a Christian ethics which gives due importance to the historical, the temporal and the personal aspects of Christian existence. Not only is greater flexibility thus given to the concept of nature with consequences for natural law doctrine, but also, with a view of human existence as always in-the-making, a greater consonance is achieved with biblical teaching on repentance, renewal and growth in grace.

In this last connection, contemporary Roman Catholic moral theology is giving renewed attention to the principle and use of *epikeia*, by which one sincerely in conscience[90] judges exceptions to general norms (laws or rules). In the past, there have been two traditions on *epikeia*, an earlier and Thomistic one, and a later and voluntaristic one. The first can appeal to Aquinas in two ways. First, he taught that secondary principles hold only in the majority of cases, and that they are found to be less and less binding, the further one descends towards the particular.[91] Secondly, he taught that any human law, which is incompatible with natural law, is no longer a law but a perversion of law.[92] While just laws are binding on conscience, unjust laws are not. A law is unjust, wrote Aquinas, (1) if an authority imposes burdens on the citizens, not for the common good, but rather for his own

---

[90] Aquinas called the act of applying moral principles to particular actions, *conscientia*, while he called the inborn grasp of general moral principles *synderesis* (sometimes written *synteresis*)—cf. *S.T.* I, Q. 79, art. 12–3—a word which may have originated in a copying error for the N.T. *syneidesis*.

[91] See above p. 150.

[92] *S.T.*, I–II, Q. 95, art. 2.

cupidity or vainglory; (2) if in enacting a law, the legislator goes beyond the powers committed to him; and (3) if burdens (e.g., taxes) are imposed unequally.[93] Laws are also unjust when they are contrary to divine positive law: such unjust laws are 'the laws of tyrants inducing to idolatry . . . (and) must in no way be observed, because, as is stated in *Acts* 5:29, "we ought to obey God rather than man"'.[94]

'Most manuals of theology' however 'actually adopt a very restricted . . . understanding of *epikeia*',[95] and this is because they follow the voluntaristic tradition of Scotus and Suarez, rather than the rational one of Aquinas. In the latter, all law is primarily an ordering of reason, while, in the former, positive law (whether human or divine) is primarily an act of the will of the legislator. There is need, therefore, for recourse to the legislator to determine if a particular law is still obligatory—before using *epikeia:* and, if it is impossible to consult the legislator, then the individual may act according to the presumed will of the legislator. Here there is some suspicion of *epikeia*, because it goes against the letter of the law. The Thomistic teaching on *epikeia* demands recourse to the legislator *only* in doubtful cases where there is need for interpretation of the law. It holds that, if the law does not contribute to the common good, then it no longer obliges, and, in cases where the meaning of the law is clear, the individual may disobey the law. Aquinas asserts that *epikeia* is a virtue,[96] an aspect of the virtue of justice, precisely because of the imperfection of all human law. It is not an attempt to escape one's obligations, but is a response to a higher law, the law of justice.

Some moral theologians[97] are teaching the need for a more extensive use of *epikeia* to-day. The role of the individual in society has changed greatly since Aquinas's time: now people are citizens rather than subjects; everything does not now come from the command or will of the ruler; the citizens are not the 'unlettered masses' of the past; modern society depends for its proper functioning on people's free and responsible actions and initiative, and on the creative contributions of individuals and institutions. If Christians are to be encouraged to live the Christian life in this kind of society, then moral theology, if it is to be culturally relevant, requires a renewed understanding of the place of *epikeia* in that life.

---

[93] *S.T.*, I–II, Q. 96, art. 4.
[94] *S.T.*, *loc. cit.*
[95] Charles E. Curran, *A New Look at Christian Morality*, p. 138.
[96] S.T., II–II, Q. 120, art. 1.
[97] E.g. Bernard Häring and Charles Curran.

8

LEARNING FROM THE REFORMERS

At first sight, the Reformers seem to belong to a different world from that of Thomas Aquinas and the schoolmen: to a world in which natural law has been displaced by revelation, the authority of the Church by that of the Word, and a doctrine of 'works' by one of grace. In fact, all such over-simplifications contain an element of caricature as well as truth. Both Luther and Calvin were indebted to their upbringing in the late medieval disciplines. There was continuity, as well as discontinuity, in the Reformation. The philosophical tensions and conflicts in which they were involved, and the solutions they put forward, were either known or foreshadowed in earlier ages of the Church. There is something of Augustine,[1] as well as later scholasticism, in both Luther and Calvin; and when we come, as we do now, to discuss how far the Reformers' view of Christian ethics was relational in character, we may well hear echoes of Paul and Augustine, and even be reminded of Abelard.[2] Since the place of law is a recurring problem in a relational theory of ethics, it is not surprising to find Luther and Calvin wrestling with it, as Paul, Augustine and Abelard had done before them. We might be encouraged to take historical studies in ethics all the more seriously if we were to perceive—as is very probable—that such dilemmas remain an essential part of ethical discourse today.

A. LUTHER: FAITH ACTIVE IN LOVE

In Luther's time (he lived from 1483–1546), a caricature of Thomas Aquinas's thought was widely accepted: *viz.*, that virtue is to be acquired by performing virtuous acts. F. S. Carney has called it the 'acquirement view of virtue'.[3] Theologically expressed, it is the view that a man receives

---

[1] With B. Häring, we pay tribute to Augustine as one of the greatest moral theologians of all time, yet at the same time acknowledge the negative influence (perhaps from Manichaeism) of his rigorist perspective on his own and later views of sexuality and marriage: *The Law of Christ*, Vol. 1 *General Moral Theology*, 1961, p. 8 and *Free and Faithful in Christ*, Vol. 1 *General Moral Theology*, 1978, p. 42. Cf. Timothy E. O'Connell, *Principles for a Catholic Morality*, 1978, p. 11 and footnote 4; and A. Kosnik and others (edd.), *Human Sexuality*, 1977, p. 37.

[2] See above, pp. 87–90.

[3] 'Deciding in the Situation: What is required?' in *Norm and Context in Christian Ethics*, p. 14.

recognition from God if he performs good works. It could equally be called the 'acquirement view of *salvation*'.

When a monk, Luther accepted this view so whole-heartedly that he paid frequent visits to the confessional on what seemed to his superiors trivial matters. To them, this was evidence of an over-scrupulous conscience: he was to come back only when he had something worth confessing! But in terms of the view held by Luther and his father confessor, there was no answer but confession of one's sins as often as the sinner believed he had failed—with the consequent despair at ever attaining peace of mind. Luther reacted against this view when reading Paul's letter to the Romans. He could achieve no peace through the 'acquirement view'. He found his own experience mirrored in Paul's. Saul the Pharisee tried to keep the whole law to get recognition from God. Luther the monk tried to live up to the demands of the Gospel as a way of achieving salvation. 'In place of self-justification through works Luther affirmed God's gracious justification through faith'.[4] He condemned the works-righteousness inherent in what was taught in his day—a position that was (to be fair) itself a misunderstanding of Aquinas.

This doctrine of justification by grace through faith implies an alternative theory of virtue—the relational theory. Man's virtue is not a product of his achievement—of his virtuous acts—but of 'his acceptance in faith of the justifying relation God freely offers him and of his consequent acceptance in love of a servant-relation with his fellow-men'.[5]

In Luther's experience, a modestly rigorous system of works-righteousness was supplanted with a theology of grace, and the chief significance of the law for Luther ever afterwards was *as a goad to repentance*, to bring a man to Christ. He seriously distrusted the law *as a source of moral guidance*.

One explanation for legalism in religious morality is a soteriology of works of the kind Luther had tried to make work.[6] Religious legalism is the combination of two factors—a code-morality and a doctrine of salvation by works—so that the fulfilment of a moral code is made the condition of gaining recognition or favour from God. Such a legalism need not accompany an ethic of norms. It occurs only when the fulfilment of a code becomes a means of ensuring one's salvation.

This kind of 'law-righteousness' was rejected by both Luther and Calvin, as well as by Paul. In the less complex and more authoritarian society of the day, the moral problem for Luther was not one of knowledge, but of the will. Man's need was not so much to know the good, or the law, or the rules, but to experience a forgiveness which would release him from his self-concern (including concern about his past sins), and turn him outwards to a life of service. And so the ethical watchword of the Reformers

[4] *Ibid.*, p. 14.
[5] *Ibid.*, p. 14.
[6] Cf. Edward LeRoy Long, Jr., 'Soteriological Implications of Norm and Context', in *Norm and Context in Christian Ethics*, p. 265ff.

was 'Faith active in love'. Important among the theological and moral ideas which run through all of Luther's writings, is

> 'the principle that "good works do not make a good man but a good man produces good works". In common with a central tradition in Christian ethics Luther emphasises the importance of good motives as compared with the consequences of action. While careful calculation of consequences is necessary in technical action when men deal with things, such calculation is misplaced when it is applied to persons and to personal relationships. There everything depends on the spirit, the source of action. Luther illustrates the point in his *Treatise on Good Works*.[7]

> 'When a man and a woman love and are pleased with each other, and thoroughly believe in their love, who teaches them how they are to behave, what they are to do, leave undone, say, not say, think? Confidence alone teaches them all this and more'.[8]

By faith the inner being of a man is set right, so that he brings forth good fruit in action. It is the motive or disposition of the heart that determines whether or not acts are expressions of devotion to God. This ethic is on the way to situationism.

> 'Luther's ethic makes it possible for the Christian man to respond in liberty to the demands of the situation in which he finds himself and to relate creatively to the problems that arise'.[9]

There might be thought, then, to be little support for legalism in Luther's *basic relational position*. He eschewed such ideas as intrinsically right actions, and unalterable moral norms existing independently of the man-God relation. Yet the Christian man has a duty to his neighbour. His faith has to issue in love, and he has to become 'a Christ to his neighbour' because for him Christ offered himself. Further, when faith is weak and incomplete, laws of church and state are useful as guidance.

Luther, then, was more ambivalent than Calvin in his attitude to the law. The former held a basically relational position in ethics and distrusted the law as a source of moral guidance, yet he did not abandon it completely as a norm for social ethics. This is where he may be charged with inconsistency. He did not carry a relational position to a consistent conclusion over the whole field of morality. Calvin, on the other hand, was aware that there was a problem here and tried to find a place for law within a relational position.

For Luther, there are two uses of the law. The first use is to serve as an instrument of civil order (*usus civilis*), restraining sinful men from transgression. It is a 'dyke against sin'. 'The restraint of the law holds in check the consequences of evil from both the Christian and the unchristian segments of the social order.'[10] This civil function of the law was taken by Luther in a

[7] Beach and Niebuhr, *Christian Ethics*, p. 240.
[8] Luther, *Treatise on Good Works* in *Works of Martin Luther* I, 1915, p. 191; cf. Beach and Niebuhr, *loc. cit.*, and Long, *Survey of Christian Ethics*, p. 132.
[9] Long, *ibid.*, p. 133.
[10] Long, *Norm and Context*, p. 266.

basically negative sense. The second use of the law (*usus theologicus*) is to enable a man to see and understand his sinful rebellion against God. It is a goad to repentance: '. . . this use of the Law' writes Luther in his *Lectures on Galatians*, 'is completely unknown . . . to all men who go along in the presumption of the righteousness of the Law or of their own righteousness'.[11]

For Luther, the chief function of the law was the second (*usus theologicus*). The use of the law as guidance paled into insignificance beside its value in bringing men to salvation. Once a man has experienced the grace of God in Jesus Christ, he is no longer under the law. He is a new being who has no need of moral guidance from a code. On Luther's *relational* view, the Christian's criteria and motives for moral behaviour come from a new and different source. His view is not unlike Augustine's *Dilige et quod vis fac* ('Love God and then do as you will')—itself often misunderstood.[12] The Christian lives his life trusting in God's grace. Therefore, standing in this relation to God, he can do what has to be done freely and spontaneously, not with the objective of gaining merit and accumulating good works, but because it is the good pleasure of his will to please God. His will is being transformed to the divine will: '. . . a Christian has no need of any work or of any law in order to be saved', writes Luther in his *Treatise on Christian Liberty*, 'since through faith he is free from every law and does all that he does out of pure liberty and freely, seeking neither benefit nor salvation, since he already abounds in all things and is saved through the grace of God because of his faith, and now seeks only to please God'.[13]

Yet this teaching was modified by Luther's position on the two realms, both established by God—the spiritual realm of faith, and the secular or worldly realm of institutions.

'God's kingdom is a kingdom of grace and mercy, not of wrath and
punishment. In it there is only forgiveness, consideration for one
another, love, service, the doing of good, peace, joy, etc. But the
kingdom of the world is a kingdom of wrath and severity. In it there is
only punishment, repression, judgement, and condemnation, for the
suppressing of the wicked and the protection of the good. For this reason
it has the sword, and a prince or lord is called in Scripture God's wrath,
or God's rod (Isaiah xiv)'.[14]

The spiritual realm 'has no sword, but it has the word, by means of which men are to become good and righteous, so that with this righteousness they may attain eternal life'. The other realm 'is worldly government, which works through the sword so that those who do not want to be good and righteous to eternal life may be forced to become good and righteous in the eyes of the world'.[15]

[11] Jaroslav Pelikan (ed.), *Luther's Works* (American edition), Vol. 26, p. 309.
[12] Cf. pp. 86f. above.
[13] *Works of Martin Luther* II, p. 331f.
[14] Luther, *An Open Letter Concerning the Hard Book against the Peasants*, quoted by G. W. Forell, *Christian Social Teachings, A Reader in Christian Social Ethics* etc., 1966, p. 162.
[15] Luther, *Whether Soldiers too can be saved*.

There are four institutional structures, according to Luther: the family; the state; one's occupation or 'calling' (*Beruf*); and the church. The last belongs to the spiritual realm, the other three to the secular. It is through these structures that the Christian carries out his duty to God, but the first three are called 'orders of creation' because they are part of God's creative design, and therefore they are part of the life of all men, not merely Christians. These 'secular' realities, then, are linked to the Christian doctrines of creation and the law: 'created by God both as the channels of service and as restraints against sin', they 'stand alongside the "sacred" aspect of life known in the Gospel'.[16]

But the Christian is no less obligated within these orders of creation. His political duties are given him by God through the state, and Luther enjoins the strictest obedience to the orders of secular authority. The Christian's responsibilities as an individual on the one side, and as a citizen, a soldier, an official of the state, on the other side, are quite different. The Christian acting *as an individual* towards other individuals must act out of pure love, but when he acts *as an official of the state*, though he must still have the motive of love, he must do his duty as defined by the state, however distasteful personally it may be. Out of love he may have as a judge to mete out the sentence called for by the law, and as such he is the divinely appointed instrument for preserving society from disorder, injustice and wickedness. This was the doctrine that became standard Lutheran practice in Germany, so that even in the days of the Nazis many Christians believed their political duty was given them by the state.

But is this a correct interpretation of Luther himself? 'Luther often expresses himself rather unguardedly',[17] differentiating too sharply between the temporal kingdom and the Kingdom of God, and suggesting that the Christian 'surrenders, as it were, the identifying marks of his Christianity the moment he enters the worldly sphere'.[18]

> 'It' (sc. the kingdom of the world) 'should not be merciful, but strict, severe and wrathful in the fulfilment of its work and duty ... It is turned only against the wicked, to hold them in check and keep them at peace, and to protect and save the righteous'.[19]

Is he aware of the over-sternness of his position and of its failure to face the radical demands of the Sermon on the Mount, when he adds a little later that 'in the exercise of their office, worldly rulers cannot and ought not to be merciful, though out of grace, they may give their office a holiday'?[20] Perhaps too his choice of examples was unfortunate, because time-bound— the judge, the hangman and the soldier—for those carry out the punitive functions of public office. His point would have been better made if he had been able to choose an official who carries out more positive functions of

[16] Long, *A Survey of Christian Ethics*, p. 187.
[17] Helmut Thielicke, *Theological Ethics*, Vol. I, (Eng. tr.), 1968, p. 362.
[18] H. Thielicke, *loc. cit.*
[19] Luther, *An Open Letter Concerning the Hard Book against the Peasants*, quoted by G. W. Forell, *op. cit.*, p. 162.
[20] G. W. Forell, *op. cit.*, pp. 162–3.

welfare: e.g., the food-rationing officer who must limit the food he gives to the first mother in the queue in order to provide the next mothers with their fair share. Since Luther's day, the state has assumed more and more positive functions: it is no longer simply a 'dyke against sin', in the sense of restraining sinful people from transgressing.

On the other hand, the three 'orders of creation' are also channels of service. God works and rules in every sphere: e.g., the state is ordained in order to repel the forces of chaos, for God wills the preservation of the world in the face of the destructive consequences of sin. Political authority is 'a sign of the divine grace, of the mercy of God, who has no pleasure in murdering, killing and strangling':[21] by the peace which the state establishes, its divine purpose is to make possible the proclamation of the gospel.[22] Indeed, all occupations (e.g., those of father, maid, politician and judge) involve the service of God and of our fellows which must be rooted in and determined by the motive of love. Love is not confined to relations between individuals but is exercised also in the orders.[23]

This two-fold character of the orders is seen also in marriage. While for Luther marriage is a means whereby man's sexual appetite is kept in control, echoing the monastic view of marriage as legalised lust,[24] it has also its divine purpose in the procreation of children and for Christians their education in the faith.[25]

What is the relation of the orders to natural law? The order of the church apart, they are expressions of God's rule in creation. But this is not to justify current structures. For Luther, the secular orders are governed by natural law: i.e., they are reasonable orders and have to be interpreted by the use of reason. While the spiritual realm was controlled by faith, the worldly or secular orders were seen in terms of the reason. Specific historical institutions, therefore, such as the German princes (whose power it was in Luther's interest to accept: cf. the principle, *cuius regio, eius religio*), were not absolutised, and could in theory be exchanged for something more nearly, as reason conceived it, an expression of the divine creative will.

A danger if not a weakness in Luther's position is that it is, as he expresses it, too liable to misunderstanding. It encourages too radical a discontinuity between private and public life, with an ethic of love for the one, and an ethic of one's duty to God given by the state for the other. Further, Luther's ethical position, while giving a justification of general norms for social morality, betrays an inner inconsistency between his relational-model for relationships between individuals and his law-motif for

[21] *The Table Talk of Martin Luther*, tr. William Hazlitt.

[22] *D. Martin Luthers Werke: Kritische Gesamtausgabe* (1883–), vol. 16, p. 339.

[23] Luther, *Whether Soldiers too can be saved*. Cf. H. Thielicke, *op. cit.*, p. 377.

[24] Cf. R. W. Southern, *Medieval Humanism and other Studies*, 1970, p. 95.

[25] Luther, *The Large Catechism*, Exposition of the Ten Commandments, The Fourth Commandment; and *Sermon at Marriage of Sigismund von Lindeman*, 1545, in *Luther's Works*, American Edition, vol. 51, pp. 357–367. On the other hand, Calvin emphasised the relational aspects of marriage, as Luther did not: in Calvin's teaching, woman was seen primarily as a companion to her husband and only secondarily as concerned with procreation.

social ethics. But he cannot fairly be charged with legalism (though that set in with his followers, as we shall see). He was too great an enemy of a soteriology of works to fall into the trap of religious legalism.

B. THE ETHICS OF CALVIN (1509–64)

How does Calvin's position compare with that of Luther? First, both accepted a basically relational position, because both gave a central place in their theology to the doctrine of justification by grace. The basis of the Christian life for Calvin was gratitude to God for his gifts. If a man wants assurance of being accepted by God as righteous, then he must place no weight on 'works of the law'.

The doctrine of justification was set in the context of the themes of divine sovereignty and creation, human depravity and the obedience of the Christian. Calvin did not teach that man in his depravity can know and do nothing good or worthwile. His genuine humanist interests prevented him from going to such an excess.[26]

> 'Total depravity does not mean that God has left no goodness to man, but that the total man—in reason, will, religion, politics, etc.—is infected with corruption. Despite the depravity many excellent gifts are left to man so that he is enabled to regulate the community life, to pursue arts and sciences, to direct thought into logical channels, to develop medicine and law'.[27]

Man is corrupt, but he has not lost the use of his reason for the purposes of the world, where it proves a most useful tool:

> 'Since man is by nature a social animal, he is disposed, from natural instinct, to cherish and preserve society; and accordingly we see that all men have impressions of civil order and honesty. Hence it is that every individual understands how human societies must be regulated by laws, and also is able to comprehend the principles of those laws'.[28]

This doctrine of the natural law lies behind the *usus civilis* and affects even how Calvin understands the *usus theologicus*.

Secondly, Calvin's understanding of the uses of the law was different from Luther's. The former followed Melanchthon in adding a third use to Luther's two uses of the law; he put Luther's second use into first place numerically (again, following Melanchthon), and he made the third use of the law primary. Calvin's order then, was as follows:

(a) *usus theologicus:* the law was a pedagogue to repentance: it convicts of sin and brings a man to the new life in Christ.[29]

(b) *usus civilis:* not all men find the law leading to repentance, and for them positive law with its sanctions operates to hold them in check; but

---

[26] Brunner here follows Calvin. See our discussion of Brunner in chapter 9.
[27] Beach and Niebuhr (edd.), *op. cit.*, p. 271.
[28] Calvin, *Institutes of the Christian Religion* II, ch. ii, paras. 12–14.
[29] Cf. Calvin, *Institutes* II, ch. vii.

even Christians are no 'less subject to human laws'.[30] This function of the law provides social norms and sanctions. Calvin went further than Luther in noting the more positive reasons for political authority: government was necessary for social, free and rational men, who could not live together without laws. Men do not keep such laws merely because of fear of punishment, but because men are capable of some degree of moral discernment.[31]

(c) *usus didacticus:* the third use of the law instructs Christians each day in the will of God which they are committed to obey. Christians need the law, which teaches, exhorts and urges them to good, consequent on their justification, though the law does not give them acceptance with God. Believers are not to oppose the law, which they need for their gradual growth in grace—but they must reject the notion that salvation is earned through works of righteousness.

Thirdly, then, Calvin rejected a soteriology of works rather than the law itself. He tried to find a place for law in a basically relational position, without falling into legalism. Calvin was aware of the potential dangers in the use of the law to attain security before God—as when, for example, he wrote with sarcasm of the over-scrupulosity that led into legalism.[32]

Fourthly, the primary use of the law for Calvin was the *usus didacticus.* Despite his adherence to the doctrine of justification, he saw the law as a source of normative guidance for Christian behaviour. He saw no conflict, as Luther had done, between law and gospel; and believers are subject to both.

For Calvin, love is the sum of the law of God, which is contained in Scripture, and especially in the Ten Commandments and the Great Commandment. (His interpretation, however, of the Ten Commandments, for example, is a highly extended and deepened version, going far beyond what these Commandments actually *say:* it is an interpretation of a Christian man). Calvin expounded God's law as one of self-denial whereby a person leaves all aspects of his life to be governed by God's will, including his reason and will.[33]

'The great point is, that we are consecrated and dedicated to God, and, therefore, should not henceforth think, speak, design, or act, without a view to his glory'.[34]

When we are enjoined to lay aside concern with self, we are divested of excessive longing for wealth, power or human favour, and all ambition and thirst for worldly glory are eradicated.[35] The lordship of Christ is to be expressed over the whole of human life—not just over the church and in the church, but, for example, through politics and economics.

But, at the same time, the law in its third and principal use is the gift of

[30] Cf. Calvin, *loc. cit.*
[31] Cf. above pp. 172ff.
[32] Calvin *Institutes* III, ch. xix, para. 7.
[33] Cf. Calvin, *Institutes* III, ch. vii.
[34] *Loc. cit.*
[35] Cf. *loc. cit.*

God to his people—to help them live in gratitude to God. Nor is the biblical law an imposition on man, but a decisive statement of 'natural law', the law of our human nature and one which we must obey to attain our proper end and good.

> 'Calvin understands very clearly what is obscured in some Christian thinkers: that the reconcilation of man to God through the work of Jesus Christ does not result in an automatic, effortless change of man's whole moral and spiritual nature. It is rather the beginning of a new and intense activity. The Christian life, as Calvin sees it, is a continuous and hard struggle to realise in every sphere of existence the consequences of the new beginning'.[36]

Fifthly, we have to understand the theological framework of Calvin's ethics—the doctrine of Creation (e.g., natural law is implanted in man by the Creator and is known by man's conscience) and, behind that doctrine, that of election. Church and state, spiritual life and economic life, are expressions of God's one, unchanging purpose: e.g., the rulers are instruments of God intended by him to rule, as the private citizen is intended to obey. Calvin's view may be regarded as a 'one-realm' view—unlike the two-realm view found in the medieval church and in Lutheranism. Further, while for Luther the gospel set one free from the law, for Calvin law and gospel alike are willed by God and have a continuing place in his scheme. To abrogate the law would be to impugn the sovereign decree of the transcendent God.

Sixthly, Calvin allowed a right of rebellion against the unjust ruler, though not on the part of the private citizen. Yet the Christian can live in any set of conditions and under any laws, for 'the spiritual kingdom of Christ and civil government are things very widely separated'.[37] He will not allow the Christian to adopt an archaic and antinomian position in civil affairs. The freedom of the gospel is not to be construed as involving for the Christian the overthrow of all forms of power (courts, laws and magistrates). Nor does the distinction between civil and spiritual government justify the supposition that the former is so polluted that Christian men can have nothing to do with it. Indeed Calvin's understanding of the distinction sounds archaic to modern ears, for civil government has the functions of fostering and maintaining the external worship of God, defending sound doctrine and the condition of the church, and upholding civil justice and peace—'its object is . . . in short, that a public form of religion may exist among Christians and humanity among men'.[38] He holds that there is no contradiction in holding that the spiritual kingdom of Christ is beyond and outside the will of men to create by their civil laws and that the task of constituting religion arises from human polity, for civil order is directed 'to prevent the true religion, which is contained in the law of God, from being with impunity openly violated and polluted by public blasphemy'.[39]

[36] Beach and Niebuhr's introduction to Calvin, p. 272.
[37] Calvin, *Institutes* IV, ch. xx.
[38] Calvin, *loc. cit.*; cf. *The Scots Confession*, Art. XXIV.
[39] Calvin, *ibid.*

The private citizen is to obey the civil ruler, and suffer, if need be. He is not to rebel under any circumstances. The Lord takes vengeance on unbridled domination, but that vengeance is not committed to the ordinary citizenry.[40] But neither the prince nor the people can lay claim to supremacy, since both are subject to God, the almighty sovereign. As far as the civil magistrate is concerned, however,

> 'so far am I from forbidding these officially to check the undue licence of kings, that if they connive at kings when they tyrannise and insult over the humbler of the people, I affirm that their dissimulation is not free from nefarious perfidy, because they fraudulently betray the liberty of the people, while knowing that, by the ordinance of God, they are its appointed guardians'.[41]

Further, in the obedience due to the commands of the rulers, we must be careful that it does not conflict with the obedience due to God 'to whose will the wishes of all kings should be subject'.[42]

> 'We are subject to the men who rule over us, but subject only in the Lord. If they command anything against Him, let us not pay the least regard to it, nor be moved by all the dignity which they possess as magistrates'.[43]

It is not clear whether Calvin means that here is a circumstance where the private citizen may rebel either by active resistance or by some form of passive disobedience.

These ideas were adopted by John Knox and by the French Huguenots, and were later appealed to by the Confessional Church in Germany in its resistance to Hitler's claim to supreme authority in church and state, over life and liberty, the universities, the press and the courts. They were developed into powerful arguments for the right of rebellion against tyrants and the unjust ruler, though in the Reformed tradition rather than the Lutheran. *The Scots Confession* (1560), of which John Knox was perhaps the chief author, has much to say about tyrants. Among the works of the second table of the law, it acknowledges both obedience to the commands of rulers (so long as they do not impugn the commandment of God) and the repression of tyranny.[44]

C. FOLLOWING LUTHER AND CALVIN

Lutheranism lost whatever elasticity there was in Luther's own position; rigid legalism crept in with Luther's later followers. Luther had allowed, as we saw, for rebellion against the state in certain circumstances, however unclearly he had made this point.[45] But the right of rebellion receded into

[40] Cf. Calvin, *loc. cit.*
[41] *Ibid.*
[42] *Ibid.*
[43] *Ibid.*
[44] Article XIV, 'What warkis are reputit gude befoir God'.
[45] In Luther, *The Large Catechism*, Exposition of the Ten Commandments, The Fourth Commandment, there are hints of this possibility. Cf. p. 175 above.

the twilight. Moreover the worldly realm was understood apart from the work of salvation, so that in Lutheranism the doctrines of creation and redemption became divorced. Luther had understood the three (secular) orders of creation as the 'left-hand' work of God, while the kingdom on God's right hand was made up of Christians who did not need coercion by the state to keep the laws of the land, but obeyed by God's word alone. The former was called God's 'strange work'. But presumably Luther did not mean this to be understood as if God's right hand didn't know what his left was doing! Since Nazism exploited this kind of interpretation, the leaders of the confessing church (and especially K. Barth, living in exile in Basel) had the task of dissolving the dualism and recreating a unity of the two poles.

Calvin's teaching was also misinterpreted by his followers. In Calvinism generally, certain structures of justice and order have been regarded as instruments for enforcing standards within the community of the church, though this is a misunderstanding of Calvin's third and principal use of the law. For example, the role of the Kirk Session became in Scotland a coercive sanction, though this third use of the law was normally confined to a few rules, usually concerning sex (e.g., the prohibition of 'ante-nuptial fornication'), and interpreted in a legalistic way.

The teaching of Luther and Calvin has deeply influenced the ethical teaching of classical Protestantism, whether in Lutheranism or Calvinism. There is some artificiality, therefore, in treating them separately, and in this regard Calvin is better treated as the systematiser of Luther's teaching than as a separate figure representing a different tradition. One reason for treating them together is that this whole 'tradition' gives an important place to norms for social ethics in the *usus civilis* and the three institutional structures (family, state and one's occupation or profession), the orders of creation.

9

SOME TWENTIETH CENTURY RESHAPING

A. THEOLOGICAL ETHICS

At the turn of the century, liberal Protestantism dominated Christian ethics, just as Roman Catholic traditionalism directed moral theology. It was an age, in Protestantism, which found its values in eternal truths such as the Fatherhood of God and the brotherhood of man; which emphasised the historical experience of mankind and the development of human culture, as well as the moral sense of the individual; and which found the natural focus of its religious and moral interests in the life and personality of Jesus. It was a time of optimism, when belief in human progress came readily to the educated and cultured European bourgeoisie. But with the dawning of the twentieth century, the first tremors of cultural and theological upheaval were beginning to be felt. Already M. Kähler had rejected life-of-Jesus research as the central concern of biblical scholarship and had pointed to the *kerygma*, the proclamation of Christ, as the proper focus for Christian preaching, theology and ethics.[1] What consequences would this bring for Christian ethics in general and Christian social ethics in particular? Would Christian ethics continue to be essentially bourgeois, or did the rediscovery of the kerygmatic emphasis herald a new and critical, even revolutionary, approach? If the latter, what would be the gain and loss, and what the cost, for Christian ethics?

For an answer, we turn to examine some twentieth century attempts at the reshaping of Christian ethics.

1. *Karl Barth (1886–1968)*

When the First World War broke out, many liberal theologians (including Harnack, Schlatter and Hermann, Karl Barth's teachers) were parties to the 'Manifesto of the Intellectuals', endorsing the Kaiser's war policies. A 'German war-theology' was replacing the truth of the gospel. The young Barth was completely alienated. As John Bowden has put it

> 'This, then, was the consequence of their theology and ethics, their
> understanding of the Bible and history. If that was what the great
> cultural synthesis, in the climate of which Barth had been brought up,

---

[1] *Der sogenannte historische Jesus und der geschichtliche biblische Christus*, 1892 (Eng. tr., 1964).

meant in practical terms, then there was no point in following the road any further. It was time for something new'.[2]

This 'something new' was seen clearly when Barth's *Commentary on Romans* appeared in 1918. The focus was no longer anthropocentric: it was on the Word which encounters us in Christ: it was on God's action and man's dependence on God's grace.[3] Throughout Barth's writings, this emphasis never varied, and the corollary of it was a political attitude. As God in Christ espoused the cause of the needy and helpless, the believer is summoned to take up the cause of all who suffer wrong.[4] God in Christ challenges the existing order and calls mankind to the Christian revolution. For this reason, Christians should stand well to the left in the political spectrum,[5] and Barth's own commitment to socialism never wavered.[6] Even in his parish ministry, he was known as 'the red priest of Safenwil'. As Dietor Schellong has put it, 'In the thought of Karl Barth theology appears as a critique of the "bourgeois world-view" for the first time in recent theological history'.[7]

Barth's christocentric emphasis has important consequences for his whole approach to ethics. The divine grace always has priority, the human response is one of obedience. Gospel always comes before law, never law before grace as in the Lutheran order. It is not simply a matter of the law leading man to despair because he finds it incapable of achievement, or of the law making people ready to receive the divine grace. The law itself proceeds from grace. On christocentric premises, he replaces the opposition of law and gospel with the synthesis of gospel and law. For the Christian, even the law is a form of the gospel, wherein God addresses us with the gospel of grace. Hence there is no question of either natural law or the orders of creation being independent sources of moral guidance apart from the gospel or the grace of God in Christ.

Barth had a second reason for ruling out all generalised norms, including the orders, as independent sources of guidance, *viz.*, his view of the divine freedom. No law, no set of rules, not even the law in the Old Testament or in the New, can encapsulate the freedom of God who speaks to us in a way always consonant with that divine freedom. The command of God, therefore, is not a generalised command, but a particular command to me in my situation, embracing norm and context, so that neither of these, as it were, speaks for itself.

'The question of good and evil is never answered by man's pointing to the authoritative Word of God in terms of a set of rules. It is never

---

[2] *Karl Barth*, 1971, p. 34; cf. K. Barth, *The Humanity of God*, Eng. tr., 1961, p. 12f.

[3] Cf. his effort to translate this approach into ethical terms in *Ethik*, 1928; Eng. tr., *Ethics* (D. Braun, *ed.*), 1981; significantly, this work comes from Barth's earlier period.

[4] *Church Dogmatics*, I/1 (Eng. tr., 1957), p. 387.

[5] *Der Römerbrief*, 1919, p. 24; *The Epistle to the Romans* (Eng. tr., 1968), p. 463.

[6] Cf. James Bentley, *Between Marx and Christ*, 1982, pp. 60–78.

[7] 'A Theological Critique of the "Bourgeois World-View" (Bürgerlichen and Weltanschauung)', in J. B. Metz (ed.) *Christianity and the Bourgeoisie* (Concilium) 1979, p. 74.

discovered by man or imposed on the self and others as a code of good and evil actions, a yardstick of what is good and evil. Holy Scripture defies being forced into a set of rules; it is a mistake to use it as such'.[8] Those who write and speak today as if Christian morality were a set of rules, backed by divine sanctions in the Word, might still learn much from Barth, whose orthodoxy in other ways they would not wish to question.

Barth, however, had a third reason for his positions both on natural law and the doctrine of two realms—this time a political-theological reason. He held that both these doctrines left Nazi rulers free to claim divine sanction for their regime and its 'laws'. That is why there is a triple 'take' in his use of 'law'—it covers natural law, biblical law, and all positive law. In 1934, he had drafted what was to become the charter of the Confessing Church— the Barmen Declaration—and its first article includes these words:

'Jesus Christ, as witnessed to us in Holy Scripture, is the one word of God to which we have to listen, trust and obey in life and in death.

We reject the false teaching that the church can and must recognise any other events, powers, personalities and truths, apart from and in addition to this one word of God as sources of its proclamation'.[9]

Thus, neither the 'secular' realm (e.g., 'the order' of the state) nor natural law is a source of revealed guidance alongside the Word of God; only if they are under the one command of God can they be of use to the Christian in giving him guidance as to the moral claim upon him. This command of God is an event, not a general proposition about right behaviour or good conduct. Barth is no antinomian, but if a place for norms were to be found, it could only be in relation to his christocentric and incarnational premises. In spite of his negative attitude at least in his early writings, Barth admits that general or philosophical ethics may prove useful, so long as it is kept subservient to the ethics of grace.

Related to Barth's evangelical and theological concerns was his life-long devotion to socialism. He renewed his political commitment in face of Hitler's rise to power, and F.-W. Marquardt has argued that the Nazis objected far more to his socialist stance than to his refusal to take the full oath of loyalty to Hitler.[10] For Barth, to confess Christ was an action that had social and political dimensions. He had imbibed the social gospel of Christoph Blumhardt in particular, who had taught him to see that the future which Christ opened up entailed the prospect of an alteration in earth as in heaven.[11] Barth always deplored what J. B. Metz later described as the 'privatization' of religion: the reduction of Christianity to a private matter, and thus its 'depoliticization'. To be sure, his Christian perspective

---

[8] *The Humanity of God*, p. 85.

[9] As in P. Matheson (ed.), *The Third Reich and the Christian Churches*, 1981, p. 46.

[10] Cf. *Theologie und Sozialismus. Das Beispiel Karl Barth* (2), 1972; J. Bentley, *op. cit.*, p. 71.

[11] On Christoph Blumhardt, see Bentley, *op. cit.*, pp. 15–35; and cf. C. Blumhardt, *Gottes Reich kommt!* 1932, p. 58. Barth was also influenced by the Swiss religious socialists, H. Kutter and L. Ragaz, although he frequently criticised their views (as he also criticised Blumhardt) especially when they identified the kingdom of God and the socialist expectation of the future.

modified many aspects of socialist (and Marxist) ideology and *praxis:* its materialism, the possibility of making an idol even of the humble and lowly (the 'proletariat'), and Marxist 'immoralism'. He never believed that by political action one could realise the kingdom of God on earth. But he accepted much of the Marxist criticism of the Church: its collusion with the ruling classes, and its neglect of the economic dimension and thus of 'the whole man'.

> 'So, half a century later, still under the influence of Blumhardt, Barth urged Christians to take the risk of singing "a political and unwelcome tune", since, he believed, the needs of individuals are "decisively, though not exclusively, grounded in certain disorders of the whole of human society". Barth remained convinced that the prevailing social, economic, and political conditions set certain limits to what the Christian diaconate could achieve. Blumhardt had been one to show him the possibility of a Christian social criticism that would open up a new place for and give fresh meaning to Christian social action'.[12]

But how did Barth relate this political stance to biblical interpretation? He realised that it was not simply a matter of citing biblical texts nor of carrying out the normal tasks of biblical exegesis. Nor would the theological treatment of biblical themes, such as Creation and Covenant, Justification, Reconciliation and Redemption, meet the requirement. He therefore frequently resorted to the use of an *analogy of relation.* Generally, he perceives an analogy between Christ, Church and Kingdom on the one side and the affairs of the world on the other. At times, his use of this analogical method is strange and unconvincing, though the judgements he based on them were liberal and balanced. The problem is that the method could be open to abuse, and it might then produce very different results.[13] Even Barth's application of it has been controversial. Some of his critics applauded when from 1933–45 his way of analogy seemed to produce the 'right' views, in which 'assertion and qualification' were 'kept in continual balance'.[14] Even then his method could seem subjective, enabling him to stand aloof from every form of social, economic and political order, and yet to embrace any he chose. But the same critics were nonplussed when, having resisted the Nazi state in the name of the Word of God, he refused in the post-war period to denounce the Eastern Bloc with similar vigour and, indeed, seemed to reserve his sharpest barbs for the West. Here it may well be that he is more sinned against than sinning, for Barth consistently tried to address each situation in the light of the Word. In spite of his personal dislike of communism, he did not accept that the communist state offered an exact parallel to the Nazi state (admittedly, he evinced a certain naivety in relation to Stalin in particular); he saw no virtue simply in denouncing totalitarian states as if they alone were imperfect; and he refused as a theologian to be merely the mouthpiece of Western anticommunism. He

---

[12] J. Bentley, *op. cit.*, p. 68.
[13] Cf. H. Zahrnt, *The Question of God*, Eng. tr., 1963, pp. 179–82; cf. H. Thielicke, *Theological Ethics*.
[14] Cf. E. LeRoy Long, Jr., *A Survey of Christian Ethics*, p. 202.

was only too well aware of the kind of mentality which cries 'crypto-communist' or 'communist lackey' if there is a hint of criticism of Western policy, life-style or assumptions, not to mention oppressive right-wing or racialist regimes supported, overtly or covertly, by Western powers. Living in obedience to the Word provided, in one sense, a more objective stance, a willingness to see the other standpoint. Surely the West must bear some responsibility for 'the painful situation which has arisen since 1945'?

'Did we give the Eastern partner any choice? Did we not provoke him by erecting a massive Western defence alliance, by encircling him with artillery, by establishing the German Federal Republic—which seemed to him like a clenched fist pushed under his nose—and by rearming this republic and equipping it with nuclear missiles? Did we not challenge our former partner to corresponding counter-measures of power display and thus in no small measure strengthen him in his peculiar malice? Did the West finally know no better counsel than to put its trust in its infamous A- and H-bombs? And did it not serve the West right to have to realise that the other side had not remained idle in regard to such weapons? Was there no better diplomacy for the West than the one which now manoeuvres the world into what seems a blind alley?'[15]

It is easy to claim that Barth was inconsistent in his attitude to the state. Sometimes he held that any existing order is bound to be tyrannical (it must enforce its decrees), and therefore Christians ought to submit, for by submitting they will take the tyranny out of the order (freely chosen obedience is not coerced). Yet he drew an analogy between the Kingdom of God and democracy. Elsewhere he can be more positive in his attitude to the state. Of course, different situations demand different behaviour, and Barth has been too unsympathetically criticised here. The question is whether he allowed sufficiently for the twin factors of rational deliberation and the attempt to grasp what the empirical situation is. Sometimes he showed a very clear grasp of the empirical situation, and his argument is supremely rational. At other times he seemed aloof from the mundane tasks of 'fact-finding' and deliberating between different policies of action. As H. Zahrnt put it, 'he crosses the threshold from the kingdom of God to the earthly State in a single step'.[16] He was also afraid to let in 'autonomy' ('each man making his own good'), uncontrolled by the event of Jesus Christ, i.e., by the command of God.

It is notoriously difficult to arrive at a definite assessment of Barth's ethical position. It is many-sided; one of its aspects involves biblical hermeneutics, a problem which Barth can hardly be said to have solved. Some critics like Charles West welcome Barth's freedom from any philosophical system and suggest that this strengthens his free, responsible and empirical ethical thinking. He is guided only by a determination of social conditions and a biblical understanding of the needs of one's neighbour.[17]

[15] *How I Changed My Mind,*, Eng. tr., 1969, p. 64; originally published in *The Christian Century*.

[16] *Op. cit.*, p. 182.

[17] *Communism and the Theologians: Study of an Encounter*, London, 1958.

It is not surprising that the prophetic strain inherent in Barth's position has appealed to some political theologians today. On the other hand, Ronald Preston has observed that, when all qualifications have been made, Barth's position is essentially act-deontology, or (as we have called it) 'divine act-deontology', and so gives no consistent help in making specific moral decisions.[18]

2. *Rudolf Bultmann (1884–1976)*

Bultmann nowhere devotes himself to extended ethical discussion. His 'ethics'—and he probably would have repudiated the term for what he was doing, perhaps because for much of his career it was still unpopular in Germany to undertake this task—has to be carefully reconstructed from various passages scattered through his many works. But when we do so, we find that his views are so remarkably consistent over a large number of years that it is clear that he gave much thought to the subject, and further, that he can reasonably be said to have 'done Christian ethics';[19] for not only does he provide a theological basis for the Christian's moral behaviour, but he subjects New Testament moral teaching to that kind of critical analysis that we associate with the philosopher.

Like Barth, Bultmann was a theologian of the Word, but unlike Barth he had a highly developed and explicit approach to biblical hermeneutics. Much discussion has centred on his programme of demythologising, but what concerns us here is his insistence that the mythology of the New Testament must be interpreted existentially. He found in the existentialist philosopher, M. Heidegger, the key to a phenomenological analysis of human existence which, he believed, enabled him to express the gospel and the Christian life as a live option for modern people. Hence, his understanding of Christian ethics is essentially existentialist, with all the problems which that raises.[20]

Like Barth too, Bultmann saw the theological basis for the believer's moral behaviour in a relational position. The Christian's obedience is a response, in the concrete and particular situation in which one finds oneself, to the Word of God as made known in that situation; and that response is part and parcel of the new situation in which people so addressed find themselves.

---

[18] See *Expository Times* 83, 11, 1972, p. 347f., in a review of R. E. Willis, *The Ethics of Karl Barth*, 1971. For a different but well balanced view, cf. S. Paul Schilling, *Contemporary Continental Theologians*, 1966, p. 35f. Carl F. H. Henry, *Christian Personal Ethics*, 1957, p. 350, holds that the 'significance of the Law is that it inscripturates God's command in propositional form as a fixed rule of life', and so Barth's denial of this view does not suit him. H. Richard Niebuhr, *The Responsible Self*, 1963, p. 66, also holds that Barth is unbiblical in his attitude to law, but for the opposite reason.

[19] Cf. W. Schmithals, *An Introduction to the Theology of Rudolf Bultmann*, 1968, pp. 273, 288, 293f.

[20] See above, pp. 17ff.

'Only he who has been loved can love'.[21]

'In freeing man from himself, God's forgiving grace has freed him from anxiety and so for existence for others, for love!'[22]

Bultmann makes central to his ethics Paul's saying 'faith is active in love' (Gal. 5:6), that is, faith becomes effective or operative through love. Bultmann, however, does not understand God's demand for love as a *concrete* moral demand, nor as *one* such demand among others, nor as a demand alongside God's Word to people, for it is the call of faith itself: 'a faith which realises itself as true faith in concrete existence in the form of love for one's neighbour'.[23]

The call to faith is to an obedience only in relation to the will of God, and not to a human morality, however high. It is, in this sense, a radical obedience.

'And *this* burden is just what Jesus puts upon men; he teaches men to see themselves as called to *decision*—decision between good and evil, decision for God's will or for their own will'.[24]

Radical obedience exists, not when one simply conforms to some moral norm imposed from outside, but when one inwardly assents to what one does, so that the whole person is involved.

'Radical obedience is possible only in unconditional openness for the future, i.e., for what encounters a man in each particular moment . . . If *today* he were to determine the principles of his action for *tomorrow* and were to keep to these principles he would be claiming to have control over the possibilities in which God could encounter him tomorrow'.[25]

Any other ethical solution to the Christian's moral decision-making than what has come to be called pure act-deontology would endanger the nature of the call to faith. The gospel offers no prescriptions or principles for morality: it gives no norms and no concrete guidelines for moral conduct. Bultmann does not understand the command to love as an ethical norm: it does not lay down any pattern which this love will take.

'The command of love explains nothing about the content of love. *What* must a man do to love his neighbour or his enemy? It is said simply *that* he is to do it'.[26]

'Man is trusted and expected to see for *himself* what God commands'.[27]

'A precise *what* love is cannot be specified, but must at any moment be

---

[21] Cf. Bultmann, *Kerygma and Myth*, I, p. 32.

[22] Bultmann, *Glauben und Verstehen*, 2, p. 99; *Essays*, Eng. tr., 1955, p. 112. Cf. *Existence and Faith*, 1964, p. 237: 'For self-surrender through the cross means positively that the man who no longer wills to be for himself exists for others. Since what has been opened up to him in the cross is the liberating love of God, the love of Christ also compels him to serve his fellow men (II Cor. 5:14), and his faith is active in love (Gal. 5:6)'.

[23] W. Schmithals, *An Introduction to the Theology of Rudolf Bultmann*, 1968, p. 280.

[24] Bultmann, *Jesus and the Word*, Eng. tr., 1958, p. 83.

[25] Schmithals, *op. cit.*, p. 283.

[26] *Jesus and the Word*, p. 72.

[27] *Ibid.*, p. 61.

discovered in the historical situation. Since this demand is always
present and new in any present, it does not contain a programme of
cultural or social ideals'.[28]

The command of love does not come performed or prepackaged. While the
obedient person may bring to his/her decision norms from the past—laws,
rules, principles, values—these, like all else, must be questioned in the
moment of obedience to the will of God: one is always open to the future
which must not be taken as predetermined by one's past. The only norm for
the radically obedient person is openness to God's will at a given time.
God's demand 'refers me to my particular situation at the moment so that I
may hear the claim of the other who meets me in it and, as one who loves,
find out what to do'.[29] The chief duty of the Christian, therefore, is to live
responsibly, making use of the same moral insights which are available to
all, but not resting secure in them. One must meet every situation in
trusting faith, which is an openness to the will of God and which leads one
into authentic community with one's neighbours.

From all this, it follows that the Church cannot act as a heteronomous
source of guidance that would invalidate the Christian's authentic existence. The function of the Church is to proclaim the Word of God, call
people to the decision of faith in God's grace and point them to authentic,
responsible existence. It is also a focus of community. However, if the
Church goes further than this by providing answers to social, moral and
political questions, it implies that these answers are mandatory on all
Christians, i.e., that other positions are unchristian. This does not mean that
the preacher is prevented from taking a particular stand on moral questions, for he has to make the same act of faith—like any other believer—
ever and anew in each present. Bultmann took such stands himself, for
example, on the questions of the suppression of free speech and the
treatment of the Jews.[30] But he does not, any more than other existentialists, provide a basis for Christian social ethics. It is remarkable that, while
he insists on placing New Testament utterances in their social context (their
Sitz im Leben), he himself stops short of engagement with the modern world
in the same way. Despite the radical nature of the Word, Bultmann
emerges with a general picture of Christian ethics with which the
bourgeoisie could remain relatively at ease. His 'modern world' is that of
Kant, Heidegger and Marburg, rather than that of Marx, Freud, Einstein
or the industrial Ruhr. As Dorothee Sölle put it, somewhat extremely:

'. . . It is not necessary to belabor the way in which Bultmann defames
concepts like program, theory, principle, organization. On this matter
he thinks in a bourgeois and presociological fashion: in other words, an
essential presupposition of modern political theory is omitted in his
work—namely, the distinction between state and society, a distinction

[28] Bultmann, 'Reply to Interpretation and Criticism', in C. E. Kegley (ed.), *The
Theology of Rudolf Bultmann*, 1966, p. 279.
[29] I. Henderson, article 'Bultmann Rudolf' in J. Macquarrie (ed.), *A Dictionary of
Christian Ethics*, p. 38.
[30] Schmithals, *op. cit.*, pp. 296–99.

which in fact is constitutive of every political theology . . . There can be no place in this pre-democratic way of thinking for participation in decision making, constructive criticism, and political change, not to mention revolutionary transformation of existing structures'.[31]

On another issue, however, Bultmann seems to have been particularly acute. He often spoke negatively of a specific Christian morality or the possibility of Christian ethics. Behind the lack of clarity in the terms he used, his point was that moral norms do not derive solely from Christian sources. Not only does the command to love one's neighbour, for example, occur frequently in non-Christian *paraenesis*, but also human existence is from the outset being-with-others, so that a knowledge of love is part of human life.[32] But he goes even further. The New Testament presupposes that everyone *qua* human being can know what is demanded if one is to act lovingly, without need of 'formulated stipulations': 'the example of the merciful Samaritan shows that a man can know and must know what he has to do when he sees his neighbour in need of his help'.[33] When the New Testament tries to concretise the command to love, it has to resort without shame to moral commandments of the Old Testament or to the catalogues of virtues and vices from the paraenetic traditions of the Graeco-Roman world and Hellenistic Judaism. So far from the command of love being a specifically Christian commandment, Paul describes it as a summary of all the commandments, indeed of the Law.

> 'These commandments can be known to every man before he has heard the Christian message. Every man has a conscience, and can know what is good and what is evil. True Christian preaching does not have special demands to make with respect to ethics'[34]

—we would say 'to morality'. What is new for Bultmann in Jesus' teaching as distinct from Judaism, is not the addition of some new moral norms (laws, principles, values) but the carrying out of the idea of obedience to the will of God radically to the end. Bultmann's central concern is therefore to uphold the distinctiveness of the gospel, rather than to strike common ground with the humanists or to be faithful to existentialism; but his position opens the way to a more positive view of natural law than Barth held.

3. *Emil Brunner (1889–1966)*

Professor of Dogmatics at Zurich, Brunner produced one of the most important works[35] on Christian ethics of this century at a time when most theologians of the Barthian persuasion criticised all such efforts. His position has three main features: (i) it is relational; (ii) it involves a theory

---

[31] *Political Theology*, Eng. tr., 1974, p. 44.
[32] *Glauben und Verstehen* I, pp. 231 and 236.
[33] *Theology of the New Testament* I, p. 19.
[34] *Glauben und Verstehen* 3, p. 125, quoted Schmithals, *op. cit.*, p. 290.
[35] *Das Gebot und die Ordnungen: Entwurf einer protestantisch-theologischen Ethik* ('The Command and the Orders: an Outline of a Protestant Theological Ethic'), 1932.

of divine command; and (iii) it champions the secular orders of creation as providing social norms.

Brunner held that God comes to man *personally* in Jesus Christ. He located what is distinctively human in the I-Thou relation to God which requires response, whether that of faith or revolt. Following Luther and Calvin, he gave a central place to the doctrine of justification by grace for the moral life of the Christian. Christian morality is a life of response to God's gifts.

The English title of Brunner's work, *viz.*, *The Divine Imperative*,[36] expresses the importance of the divine command in his ethics. This is the command of love. But God's command is made known in each concrete situation through the Holy Spirit, and since the situation is unique to each individual, the divine command cannot be known beforehand, e.g., as a universal norm (law, principle or rule).[37] No human category, theory or concept—including a general norm—can encapsulate the divine will for any of us. In this, Brunner is faithful to the dialectical theology of the early Barth.

> 'To wish to know it (*sc.* the divine command) beforehand—legalism—is an infringement of the divine honour . . . We cannot have his (*sc.* God's) love at our disposal . . . It cannot ever be perceived as a universal principle, but only in the act in which he speaks to us himself'.[38]

In thus using a prescriptive motif (*viz.*, divine command) in his ethics, Brunner desired to distinguish his position from legalism; but he seems to confuse law in the sense of some general norm with legalism, which is the theory that we obey law simply because it is law and for no other reason (such as love to God). We have already indicated our hesitation about the appropriateness of speaking in terms of a 'command to love', although the usage occurs frequently in Christian ethics.[39]

Brunner recognised five orders of creation (forms of community); the family based on the sexual impulse; work or the economic community, arising from the need to earn a living; the state, the greatest form of community, setting standards for the others; the community of culture, based on intellectual and artistic pursuits; and, finally, the community of the visible institutional church, arising from faith. These 'orders' are at least partially based on the nature of man and human needs: e.g., the biological distinction between man and woman results in the institution of marriage and the family; the needs of men for minimum subsistence and their quest for a higher standard of living bring forth economic institutions; and 'the dimensions of community and personal enrichment . . . are served by cultural institutions'.[40] But though the orders are 'partially based' on

---

[36] A title 'given with Dr. Brunner's consent and approval', according to the translator's note (Eng. tr., 1937, p. 13). The omission of any reference to Orders in the English title is itself probably indicative of the neglect of the discussion of social norms in the modern Protestant theology of the English speaking world.

[37] Cf. *The Divine Imperative*, pp. 117f.

[38] *Loc. cit.*

[39] See above, pp. 14f., 82ff., 90f., 103f.

[40] Long, *op. cit.*, p. 169.

human needs, they are at the same time given by God: hence, 'orders of creation'.

These situations in life within which we are to act and which are given by God the Creator, must be accepted, before we can do anything to change them.[41] Brunner did recognise a place for transition, even revolution: 'adaptation to the existing order . . . is the *first* point in the Christian ethic, but it is never the *last* point'.[42] He criticised those who held that the orders were not subject to the command of Jesus Christ, but only to nature and reason. He acknowledged that sometimes an existing 'order' ought to be overthrown (and he wrote in 1932, a year before Hitler came to power):

'. . . the will of God does not merely tell us to adapt ourselves, to accept but also to resist, to protest, not to be "conformed to this world". The kind of apologetic . . . by which, with the aid of the idea of Providence, the existing "order" at any given time is justified as that which is willed by God, and every from of criticism and desire to change conditions is suppressed as "godless rebellion", as disobedience to orders willed by God, can only arise out of a condition in which faith has been badly distorted'.[43]

Yet he holds that 'the legalism of those who uphold the existing order is bad; but the lawlessness of fanatics is worse'.[44]

Brunner's attempt to solve this dilemma has been strongly criticised. To Reinhold Niebuhr, who was generally sympathetic to Brunner's approach to Christian ethics, it betrayed an 'excessive fear of chaos' and militated against Christian advocacy of social change by its insistence that such change must be effected immediately and without dislocation. The dynamic of prophetic religion is lacking: 'it neatly dismisses the Christian ideal from any immediate relevance to political issues'.[45] Equally, he maintains, it fails to recognise that 'the more basic moral values are more likely to rest with the standard of the attacking forces',[46] since oppressed people often show astonishing patience and act against authorities only when their sufferings have driven them to desperate measures. Brunner, however, does leave room for political revolution, but he fears that such revolution will not, in the end of the day, produce the social justice it set out to achieve.

A second controversial area was Brunner's attempt to relate the Christian to 'the world of systems'. Brunner followed Luther in his view of the need to fit behaviour to the character of the office. The Christian, he said,

'must, as it were, first of all forget all he ever knew about the meaning of love, in order that he may help to protect and further the life of these "orders" themselves in accordance with their own logic . . . Our "official

---

[41] *The Divine Imperative*, p. 224. For Barth, Brunner's theological grounding of law in the doctrine of Creation rather than in justification by grace was highly dangerous for the Church politically, basically untrue to the gospel of grace, and quite misleading as guidance for the Christian.

[42] *Op. cit.*, p. 214 (Brunner's italics).

[43] *Op. cit.*, p. 217.

[44] *Op. cit.*, p. 218.

[45] *An Interpretation of Christian Ethics*, 1936, p. 167.

[46] *Ibid.*

duty" is "harsh", objectively technical: the human relation which it
requires to men is external'.[47]

and again:

'Within the world of systems, he (*sc.* the Christian) . . . does not cease to
be a loving human being, but he can only find an object for his love
when he is no longer concerned with the world of systems, but with the
individual human being in it, detached from it, where, so to speak, he
can look through the meshes of systems to see and grasp the human
being himself'.[48]

To such an approach Paul Ramsey took grave exception.

'What man nurtured in the Bible can be content with love effective only
through the interstitial spaces? What prophetic voice announced that
"justice" need not flow down like a mighty stream but only as a gentle
spray'?[47]

However, it is to Brunner's credit that he recognised and attempted a
solution to this problem in Christian ethics, even if his disjunction of *agape*
and justice is counter-productive. It illustrates the difficulties presented by
the world of systems to a certain kind of personalist philosophy which works
predominantly through one-to-one relations. The irony is that Brunner was
attempting to avoid the very pitfall to which he fell victim, and many of his
observations are to the point. Love, he says, *must* be expressed in terms of
'the current coin of justice, since that alone is legal tender in the world of
systems'.[50]

If we pursued this line of Brunner's thought, the Christian's working for
justice might take the form of infusing sanity into situations of prejudice, of
building up social mechanisms which incorporate trust and understanding,
or of seeking to modify or even effect radical changes in the system itself in
the interests of individual and corporate fulfilment. But Brunner failed to
associate *agape* and justice consistently and was always in danger of lapsing
into that kind of unreality that has led many to conclude that the gospel has
nothing to say to the industrial situation. As Paul Tillich put it:

'One could say that constructive social ethics are impossible as long as
power is looked at with distrust and love is reduced to its emotional or
ethical quality . . . Constructive social ethics presuppose that one is
aware of the element of love in structures of power without which love
becomes chaotic surrender'.[51]

It is necessary to bear in mind the ambivalence of power groups. It would
be as unrealistic to ignore their own inner logic and their demonic possibilities as to see them as simple expressions of brotherhood. They represent a
challenge to Christians to deepen the element of love and humanity within
them and to find in them a field of service. In the process, Christians might
even *discover* what faith and commitment really mean as they learn to

[47] *Op. cit.*, p. 225.
[48] *Justice in the Social Order*, Eng. tr., 1945, p. 116f.
[49] *Basic Christian Ethics*, 1953, p. 3.
[50] *Op. cit.*, p. 116.
[51] *Love, Power and Justice*, 1954, p. 12.

understand *agape* not simply in terms of one-to-one relations but also in terms of active involvement in the social, economic and political order. We might be portraying here what N. Berdyaev calls 'a new type of saint, who will take upon himself the burden of the complex world'.[52] Certainly, Dag Hammarskjold's dictum applies: 'In our era, the road to holiness necessarily passes through the world of action'.

We cannot leave Brunner without raising one further issue. The *imago Dei* in man was, according to Brunner, never wholly obliterated by the Fall. Man is an answering and responsive being in relation to God.[53] Brunner can even sponsor a doctrine of natural law.

'Every human being has a sense of right and wrong. Every schoolboy feels the wrong done to him by an unjust and partial teacher. Every coolie protests if he is cheated of just wages for his work'.[54]

He goes on to quote Calvin with approval:

'There is no doubt that certain notions of right and justice are innate in the human mind, and that a light of justice shines in them'.

This aspect of Brunner and of Calvin is often overlooked. But just as there is no propositional revelation, i.e., no revelation which reason prior to faith or enlightened by faith can put into positive, undialectical statements, so for Brunner there is no moral norm which can be known prior to God's address to each of us in our situation. It is only the believer, transformed by faith and given new capacities for response, who can make proper use of law in the penultimate sense (i.e., not as the last word, but as the 'second last').

4. *Dietrich Bonhoeffer (1906–1945)*

Bonhoeffer wrote his ethics under a number of influences often thought disparate: for example, the Lutheran tradition, the liberalism of Harnack, Karl Barth who inspired him in his stand against the Nazis as early as 1933, and Rudolf Bultmann whose influence on him also seems considerable. Events forced Bonhoeffer to a reconsideration of Christian ethics—an unfashionable pursuit in some quarters. His work is far from traditional and cannot be given a convenient label. The following themes are particularly relevant to our discussion.

Bonhoeffer sponsored a relational ethic. He used various theological bases in his attempts to formulate Christian ethics; but whether the basis

---

[52] Cited by J. A. T. Robinson, *Exploration into God*, 1967, p. 124. For an appraisal of Robinson's ethical procedures, cf. P. Ramsey, *Deeds and Rules in Christian Ethics*, 1965, pp. 15–40.

[53] *Justice and the Social Order*, 1945, p. 14. His treatment of the *lex naturae* in the *Divine Imperative* is not, we believe, a complete rejection of all versions of natural law; cf. ibid., p. 42, n. 3.

[54] Because of the presence of both relational and law motifs in his ethics, writers disagree as to how to classify his position. Some regard it as over-all relational: others, like Paul Lehmann, assign him to the imperative school of ethics, while H. Richard Niebuhr believed that Brunner overstressed the categories of legal obligation. It seems that his conception of divine command (or imperative), despite his protestations, was too coloured by shades of prescriptive law and compulsion to have a consistent place within a relational ethics.

contemplated was justification by faith or a christology, we are to love our
fellow human beings as Christ loved them and us. The foundation was
never a moral code, based (say) on the Sermon on the Mount, nor yet an
imitatio Christi, as that has ordinarily been understood, but a response to
what God has done for us and all mankind. Bonhoeffer's use of the term
'command' is completely free of any association with obedience to any
general norm, whether law, principle or rule.

> 'God's commandment is the speech of God to man. Both in its content
> and in its form it is concrete speech to the concrete man . . . God's
> commandment cannot be found and known in detachment from time
> and place; it can only be heard in a local and temporal context'.[55]

Here and elsewhere, there is posited a discontinuity between ethics and
Christian ethics which is reminiscent of Barth at his worst and which we
believe is not particularly helpful.

> 'The knowledge of good and evil seems to be the aim of all ethical
> reflection. The first task of Christian ethics is to invalidate this know-
> ledge. In launching this attack on the underlying assumptions of all
> other ethics, Christian ethics stands so completely alone that it becomes
> questionable whether there is any purpose in speaking of Christian
> ethics at all'.[56]

Elsewhere he writes that the object of a 'Christian ethic' 'lies beyond the
ethical', *viz.*, in the commandment of God; and we have seen the philosophical difficulties a position of this kind possesses. Probably Bonhoeffer
was merely reacting against certain views and associations of the term
'ethical': for example, that at every moment of our lives we have to make a
final choice between good and evil, or that every human action has a
specific label attached to it, such as 'permitted' or 'forbidden'. For Bonhoeffer as for Barth, the command of God always comes in a specific context in
a concrete way. The command does not *emerge* from the context, or from the
application of any principle to the situation. He differed, however, from the
situationism of later writers like Fletcher, in providing a theological grounding for his Christian ethics, e.g., in a christology or soteriology.

Bonhoeffer replaced the Lutheran 'orders' with 'mandates'. Certain
spheres of human interest are subject to divine mandates.

> 'We speak of divine mandates rather than of divine orders because the
> word mandate refers more clearly to a divinely imposed task rather than
> to a determination of being'.[57]

He recognised four mandates as named in the scriptures—labour, marriage,
government and Church.[58] These have to fulfil divinely imposed tasks or
purposes.

> 'God has imposed all these mandates on all men. He has not merely
> imposed one of these mandates on each individual, but He has imposed
> all four on all men. This means that there can be no retreating from a

[55] *Ethics*, (Eng. tr., 1955) p. 245; cf. p. 244.
[56] *Op. cit.*, p. 142. See also above, pp. 126–29, where we have replied to this kind of
disavowal of both ethics and Christian ethics.
[57] *Op. cit.*, p. 73.
[58] *Loc. cit.*

"secular" into a "spiritual" sphere. There can be only the practice, the learning, of the Christian life under these four mandates of God'.[59]

Bonhoeffer was striving to formulate the unity of God and of the world in Christ. This unity, founded in redemption, meant that the structures of world had to be taken seriously by the Christian, and that 'thinking in terms of two spheres' was not an open option for the Christian, though it had bedevilled 'a large part of traditional Christian ethical thought'.[60]

A mandate involves the idea of an institution but it is not a way of blessing the *status quo:* 'the origin of action which accords with reality is not the pseudo-Lutheran Christ who exists solely for the purpose of sanctioning facts as they are'.[61] Significantly, Bonhoeffer moved the orders or mandates from the realm of reason and natural law to that of christocentric command. The motive was to counter Nazi claims that God spoke in a natural revelation through the order of the state. He appealed to the logic of the other mandates to confirm his point. 'Labour "in itself" is not divine, but labour for the sake of Jesus Christ, for the fulfilment of the divine task and purpose, is divine'.[62] To get the thrust of the argument, we need to substitute 'the state' for 'labour' in that quotation. The mandates are not divine creations corrupted by the Fall and to be interpreted by anyone by the use of natural reason; they are divinely imposed tasks related to the will of Christ. As we would put it, the mandates function within Christian ethics as spheres of activity in which Christians see that they are to exercise stewardship; they are not independent 'orders' to whose divine ordaining the non-Christian can appeal for his own purposes.

Thus Bonhoeffer broke with the Lutheran tradition in his understanding of the doctrine of the two realms. The words of Jesus in the Gospels, 'render to Caesar the things that are Caesar's, and to God the things that are God's'[63] could easily be misinterpreted to mean that the state, being ordained by God, defined the citizen's political duties; the Christian, therefore, obeyed God in the political sphere by rendering obedience to the state. It was the Church struggle in Germany under Hitler that forced a re-examination of the old Lutheran 'two realms' view. The Nazi state made certain totalitarian claims[64] that Christians of the Confessing Church, such as Bonhoeffer, believed could not be obeyed. He sees a unity between the two realms: not a dichotomy, but a dialectical relationship.

'This unity is seen in the way in which the secular and the Christian elements prevent one another from assuming any kind of static independence in their mutual relations'.[65]

---

[59] *Loc. cit.*

[60] *Op. cit.*, p. 62.

[61] *Op. cit.*, p. 199.

[62] *Op. cit.*, p. 73.

[63] Mark 12:17; Matt. 22:21; and Luke 20:25.

[64] For example, that on grounds of race no Jew was to be employed by the press or the universities, or have a voice on the radio, or hold office in the Church. Any state makes totalitarian claims over its citizens: it is the nature of law so to do. It was the particular nature of these totalitarian claims to which the Christians of the Confessing Church objected.

[65] *Op. cit.*, p. 65.

This unity is in Christ. The relationship of Christianity to the world is not represented either by the monk who typifies a spiritual existence which has no part in secular existence, or by the 'Protestant secularist' (as he calls him) who typifies a secular existence claiming autonomy for itself over against the spiritual sphere.[66] The secular and Christian elements are polemically related, and their true relationship is one of dialogue and conflict.

> 'Just as Luther engaged in polemics on behalf of the secular authority against the extension of ecclesiastical power by the Roman Church, so, too, must there be a Christian or "spiritual" polemical reply to the secular element when there is a danger that this element may make itself independent, as was the case soon after the Reformation, and especially in the nineteenth century German secularist Protestantism'.[67]

Bonhoeffer rejected the notion that the Church should protest only when its own life was threatened, and not be concerned with the worldly sphere. He held that it must protest not only if a person of Jewish blood was excluded from Church office or membership, but also if such racism were imposed on the universities or elsewhere. When today 'Christianity is employed as a polemical weapon against the secular', he insists that this 'must be done in the name of a better secularity and above all it must not lead back to a static predominance of the spiritual sphere as an end in itself'.[68] This, he believed, was the original sense of Luther's doctrine of the two realms. Presumably Bonhoeffer is talking primarily about how *Christians* are to regard the secular and the spiritual in the union of the world and God in Christ. And yet he wrote:

> 'A world which stands by itself, in isolation from the law of Christ, falls victim to licence and self-will'.[69]

Consistently with this point of view, he rules out all political theories of the state (e.g., the social contract) which would make it a human creation, not subject to the divine mandate, but to laws of its own. The state is neither merely an instrument of power, nor merely an agency for the organisation and maintenance of justice. He balanced power with justice, holding the two ideas in tension.

In breaking with the doctrine of the two realms as it had come to be understood in Lutheranism—'pseudo-Lutheranism', as Bonhoeffer liked to call it—he was able to uphold the right of dissent and resistance for the Christian in some situations in the political sphere. The relationship between the Christian and the state, according to Bonhoeffer, is a penulti-mate, never an ultimate, relationship. State officials exercise their roles only under the mandate from above (whether they recognise this or not) and, while the Christian is to obey the state and its government, there are exceptional circumstances when the penultimate relationship is overtaken by the ultimate relation to God.

[66] *Op. cit.*, p. 63.
[67] *Op. cit.*, p. 65.
[68] *Op. cit.*, p. 65.
[69] *Op. cit.*, p. 307.

'His duty of obedience is binding on him until government directly
compels him to offend against the divine commandment, that is to say,
until government openly denies its divine commission and thereby
forfeits its claim. In cases of doubt obedience is required; for the
Christian does not bear the responsibility of government . . . Even an
anti-Christian government is still in a certain sense government. It
would, therefore, not be permissible to refuse to pay taxes to a government which persecuted the Church'.[70]

In spite of citing—no doubt for illustrative purposes—a *particular* action as
not permissible, he remained consistently against an ethics of a universal
norm irrespective of circumstances. It is, he wrote,

'generally impossible to pass judgement on the justice of a single
particular decision. It is here that the venture of responsibility must be
undertaken . . . The refusal of obedience in the case of a particular
historical and political decision of government must . . . be a venture
undertaken on one's own responsibility'.[71]

We know how he put that responsibility into action at the cost of his own
life.

5. *A Further Critique of Theological Ethics*

Further developments in theological ethics may be reviewed under five
headings.

(i) *Personal and social*. Radical critics such as the Roman Catholic
theologian, J. B. Metz (1928–), have faulted theological ethics for its
tendency to operate within the parameters of 'bourgeois' religion: 'turning
into an endorsement and encouragement for the haves, the propertied, for
those in this world who already have plenty of prospects and future'.[72]
Metz attempts further to identify the root of the problem.

'. . . It seems to me that it was, in a certain sense, a fateful event when
the discoveries and conclusions of *Formgeschichte* were at once interpreted
in the categories of theological existentialism and personalism. This
meant that the understanding of the kerygma was immediately limited
to the intimate sphere of the person; briefly, it was privatized'.[73]

However, to speak of the 'intimate sphere of the person' as an essentially
private concern, taken with Metz's strictures on 'the closed circuit of the
I-Thou relation', can lead to misunderstanding and raise the question of
what we mean by 'person'. To emphasise the importance of 'the person' in
ethics is not necessarily to 'privatize' nor to 'depoliticize'. Personal development can take place only in inter-personal terms: i.e., it necessarily involves
social interaction.[74] Hence, to interpret ethics in terms of the person is to

---

[70] *Op. cit.*, p. 66.
[71] *Op. cit.*, p. 307f.
[72] 'Messianic or "Bourgeois" Religion? On the Crisis of the Church in West
Germany', in Metz (ed.), *Christianity and the Bourgeoisie, Concilium* 1979, p. 62.
[73] *Theology of the World*, 1969, p. 109.
[74] See chapter 10.

place emphasis on the correlation of the personal and the social. Neverthe-less, Metz's comments provide a timely warning against any attempt to reduce the interpretation of 'the person' to a narrowly individualistic and 'private' realm of discourse. In similar vein D. Sölle is critical of the tendency to reduce the kerygma to doctrinal propositions or abstract theological concepts which are 'far removed from the worldliness of Jesus as portrayed in his words and deeds'.[75]

> 'In distinction to theological language, which has supposedly been depoliticized but thereby in fact has become subservient to the prevail-ing interests, the language of Jesus is always both religious and political, encountering the whole man in his social environment'.[76]

(ii) *Social and prophetic*. The challenge of social ethics elicited a more complete response from Barth, Bultmann and Bonhoeffer in their lives than in their writings. Other theologians contributed more directly to the question of Christian social ethics. Paul Tillich (1886–1965), who resigned his theological chair and left Germany for the U.S.A. because his religious socialism brought him into conflict with the Nazis, recognised the moral and ethical realm as an important component in religion and theology: and within it, he identified the prophetic attack on injustice as of particular significance.[77] He developed the notion of creative justice, which he found 'expressed in the divine grace which forgives in order to reunite' and which he characterised as 'reuniting love'.[78] It was a notion which could give expression to *agape* in social and corporate life and relate Christian ethics to the structures of power in society. Dorothee Sölle, whose political theology is derived from Bultmann, commented:

> 'A political theology could be developed far more directly from the early writings of Paul Tillich, who understood religious socialism as "the radical application of the prophetic-Protestant principle to religion and Christianity"'.[79]

No less important was the American theologian, Reinhold Niebuhr (1892–1971) who, as we have noted, stood in some respects close to E. Brunner and, with his brother H. Richard Niebuhr (1894–1962), made a lasting contribution to Christian social ethics.[80] Reinhold's previous parish experience in Detroit ensured that his ethics was rooted in the realities of industrial society, to which the optimism of liberal Protestantism bore no

---

[75] *Op. cit.*, p. 33.

[76] *Ibid.* p. 36: cf. Jesus' involvement with the social, political and religious groups of his time; and his use of terminology (e.g., 'King') which had political repercus-sions. All these factors contributed to his death, on an apparent charge of treason.

[77] This prophetic concern is linked with 'catholic substance' and 'protestant principle' in the definition of the essence of pure religion. For a brief review of Tillich's position, cf. A. I. C. Heron, *A Century of Protestant Theology*, 1980, pp. 137–44.

[78] *Love, Power and Justice*, 1954, p. 66.

[79] *Op. cit.*, p. xix; cf. J. L. Adams (ed.), *Political Expectation*, 1971, p. 54.

[80] Richard's position was more consciously Barthian. Reinhold clashed with Barth on a number of issues.

relevance. Critically aware of the Marxist analysis of capitalism and history, he developed in his seminal work, *Moral Man and Immoral Society* (1932), the view that, while individual people may act altruistically and idealistically, the social group was motivated much more directly by self-interest. Hence, he emphasised the empirical reality of sin in human society, which is manifested and reflected in the structures of power and corporate institutions.[81] Human existence, which yields clues to its deeper levels in the awareness of sin and the sense of responsibility, is further illumined by the biblical testimony to the grace of God in Christ and is capable of being transformed by the gospel: for Niebuhr too sought to expound a vital prophetic Christianity. But if living is thus enriched and transformed by God's grace, the task of transforming society is one which must be undertaken in realistic terms: i.e., with a full appreciation of the limitations imposed by the entrenched sinfulness of society and the fact that, whatever change for the better is effected, the kingdom of God is not built on earth by human effort. But Niebuhr continued to emphasise the practical relevance of the impossible ethical ideal: the goal of Christian endeavour is eschatological.[82] Today, many of his writings appear 'time-bound'—part of the cost of being so completely involved in the contemporary political scene; yet there can be no doubting that he identified and responded to recurring central issues in Christian social ethics.

(iii) *Historical and eschatological.* In Germany again, Helmut Thielicke's massive *Theologische Ethik* (1951–64),[83] which relates the Lutheran doctrine of justification by grace to the question of Christian existence and action today, emphasises that human beings are always to be seen in the concreteness of their particular situation *in the world* and *before God.* Much of Thielicke's work is devoted to Christian political action and Christian involvement in the affairs of the world in the name of Christ. The world, though created by God, is alienated from him, yet it is God's purpose in Christ to restore and redeem it.[84] Christians therefore experience the tension between the 'new aeon' which Christ has made a reality in the world and the 'old aeon' which exists in tandem with it until Christ comes again to effect the consummation of God's work. But although the 'old aeon' pursues its apparently autonomous course, the 'new aeon' has broken in upon it like the dawn after a particularly dark night. Christian ethics thus deals with the realities of life, viewed in the new light of Christ. Yet the Christian is not thereby spared the effort and ambiguities of moral decision-making in faith: for we still see through a glass darkly—although we see more clearly than before. Christian ethics cannot proceed by fixed rules or principles which operate as if there were no tension and ambiguity in the Christian's situation in the world: it cannot provide 'the right answers' or painless solutions to the ills of society. At most, it indicates the direction of

---

[81] Cf. *The Nature and Destiny of Man,* 1941.

[82] Cf. *An Interpretation of Christian Ethics,* 1936, pp. 113–45.

[83] Eng. tr., *Theological Ethics* I, II.

[84] Cf. R. Gregor Smith, *The New Man,* 1956, pp. 94–112; *Secular Christianity,* 1966, pp. 141–204.

travel, as well as the motive force, in the Christian's pilgrimage 'between the two worlds'. Hence Thielicke makes a positive evaluation of *compromise*, reflecting both the tension in which the Christian lives and works and the accommodation which God himself effected with worldly existence in Jesus Christ. Nevertheless, all worldly existence is constantly 'under fire' from God: in this way, Thielicke distinguishes his position from that of traditional Lutheranism, which too readily allowed an unqualified autonomy to worldly authorities. Yet there remains the suspicion that Thielicke's model is defective.

> '. . . Does he not strive too much merely to maintain existing institutions and conditions, rather than to improve them, and is it sufficient only to interpret human and historical reality instead of changing it—in short, does Thielicke's *Theological Ethics* give sufficient emphasis to Christian *hope*, and to the necessary redirection of Christian consciousness towards the *future*?'.[85]

As Jurgen Moltmann has suggested, a more adequate model would allow Christian eschatology to operate as the real future hope which defines the bearing of the gospel on the present order.[86] Viewed as critical theory,[87] theology is inseparable from practical concern and a commitment to work in harmony with God's transforming purpose, and is validated by its concrete expression in historical experience.

(iv) *Theoretical and practical*. 'Today theory and *praxis* constitute the nerve-centre of all critical knowledge'.[88] As long as the search for knowledge and truth presupposed cool detachment or pure contemplation, it was possible to hold that it was objective and apolitical. Since, on the whole, neo-orthodoxy was presumed to be of this nature, it either professed itself uninterested in ethics or turned ethics in the direction of supporting the status quo. But as soon as it was recognised that our knowledge of the world comes through a critical reflective activity that changes the world, the relation of theory and *praxis* is defined in a new way. 'Science comes to serve a revolutionary function by proposing alternatives that are very different from the existing reality'.[89] When theology and faith are approached in this way, they find in *praxis* the criterion by which they can claim validation. 'By their fruits you shall know them'. Hence Christian ethics has to embrace human *praxis* as it is, theological reflection on it, and the new *praxis* which arises from the critical process. Thus in a real sense it promotes change.

(v) *Political and theological*. If such an active-reflective or critical approach is once launched, it may well have serious consequences for traditional theology not previously exposed to such a cutting edge. The outbreak of war in 1914 moved the younger Barth to reject the religio-cultu-

[85] H. Zahrnt, *op. cit.*, p. 195f. Our summary of Thielicke's contribution to Christian ethics owes a debt to Zahrnt's fuller discussion, *op. cit.*, pp. 184–96.
[86] Cf. *The Crucified God*, 1975; *The Church in the Power of the Spririt*, 1977.
[87] Underlying Moltmann's position is his dialogue with Marxism, especially with Ernst Bloch (1885–1977): cf. J. Bentley, *op. cit.*, pp. 79–97, especially p. 89f.
[88] A. Fierro, *The Militant Gospel*, Eng. tr., 1977, p. 90.
[89] *Ibid.*, p. 89.

ral synthesis of the European bourgeoisie. Moltmann followed Studdert Kennedy in critical reflection on the battlefields of Flanders. 'For him the war was a struggle between the God who is suffering love and "the Almighty" who blesses the violence and the weapons'.[90] In not dissimilar vein, D. Sölle asserted (at a Church gathering) that the idea of 'the Lord, who o'er all things so wondrously reigneth' was intolerable after Auschwitz. Hence, the scalpel of historical experience was being used to inflict a fatal wound on the God of traditional theism. The 'death of God' acquired a new meaning in theological circles. But what was being killed off was the 'God-talk' that was the projection of the power groups, the rationalisation of their values. How then do we identify the true God? Is atheism the only option, as Bloch believed in his curious way?[91] The God we discern is the God who has chosen to manifest himself in the suffering of war, who identifies with all who are oppressed; who declares his love in the Cross and Resurrection; who opens the way to freedom, responsibility and a new future. 'I have seen the affliction of my people . . . and have heard their cry . . . I know their sufferings, and I have come down to deliver them'. (Exodus 3:7f.)

Christian *praxis* is thus transformational and revolutionary. It is truly personal and truly social; it unites social reality and prophetic challenge; it bridges the historical and the eschatological. In its unity of theory and practice, it identifies God in political as well as inter-personal and inner experience. To illustrate it, we turn to one who by upbringing and theological education was well fitted for the task of critical reflection on the situation he encountered, and who was called upon to translate that reflection into revolutionary action: Dr. Martin Luther King, Jr. In his ministry, he provides a prime example of Christian social ethics as the ethics of liberation.

B. THE SOCIAL ETHICS OF LIBERATION

1. *The struggle for civil rights: Dr. Martin Luther King, Jr.*

Looking back over the momentous events that began with the arrest of Mrs. Rosa Parks and the formation of the Montgomery Improvement Association, Martin Luther King wrote as follows:

'From the beginning a basic philosophy guided the movement. This guiding principle has since been referred to variously as non-violent resistance, non-cooperation, and passive resistance. But in the first stage of the protest none of these expressions was mentioned; the phrase most often heard was "Christian love". It was the Sermon on the Mount, rather than a doctrine of passive resistance, that initially inspired the Negroes of Montgomery to dignified social action. It was Jesus of

[90] J. Moltmann, *The Trinity and the Kingdom of God*, Eng. tr., 1981, p. 35.
[91] Cf. Bentley, *op. cit.*, p. 90.

Nazareth that stirred the Negroes to protest with the creative weapon of love'.[92]

His understanding of Christian love was rooted in the Christian personalism that informed his entire theological understanding; but this personalism was not individualistic nor, as we shall note, subject to the charge of privatization. In his doctoral dissertation at Boston, he had contended against the positions of H. N. Wieman and P. Tillich, both of whom in their different ways chose the less-than-personal to explain personality, purpose and meaning. King wrote:

'The religious man has always recognised two fundamental religious values. One is fellowship with God, the other is trust in his goodness. Both of these imply the personality of God. No fellowship is possible without freedom and intelligence. There may be interactions between impersonal beings, but not fellowship. True fellowship and communion can exist only between beings who know each other and take a volitional attitude toward each other . . . Fellowship requires an outgoing of will and feeling. This is what the Scripture means when it refers to God as the "living" God. Life as applied to God means that in God there is feeling and will, responsive to the deepest yearnings of the human heart; this God both evokes and answers prayer'.[93]

A relational view of this kind underscores the sacredness of human personality, and the worth and dignity of human beings as ends in themselves. Reason and faith provide resources for the moral life and should be employed to make proper use of that degree of freedom which man has for moral choice. This is to live responsibly and to move towards the fulfilment of one's social nature in community with others, for 'a self becomes a person only through social interaction with other persons'.[94] Human beings are essentially personal, responsive beings (having intelligence and freedom), and in that fact lies hope, assured ultimately by the personal God. As Erwin Smith put it '. . . morality gains its fullest expression in its transformation by the transcendent ideal'.[95]

In his exposition of Christian love, King appeared to draw heavily on writers such as Anders Nygren and Paul Ramsey.[96] He frequently distinguished between 'the three loves' (*agape*, *eros* and *philia*). *Agape* is 'disinterested love' which seeks the good of one's neighbour. It does not operate on the basis that other people necessarily merit or evoke one's love; it is love 'for their sakes'. *Agape* is therefore directed toward friend and enemy alike.

---

[92] *Stride Toward Freedom: the Montgomery Story*, 1968, p. 63; cf. p. 104f.

[93] *A Comparison of the Conceptions of God in the Thinking of Paul Tillich and Henry Nelson Wieman*, Boston University Graduate School, 1955, p. 272.

[94] E. Smith, *The Ethics of Martin Luther King, Jr.*, 1981, p. 52f.; cf. W. Muelder, 'Personality and Christian Ethics', in E. S. Brightman (ed.), *Personalism in Theology*, 1943, pp. 200ff. King's personalism was much influenced by E. S. Brightman and A. C. Knudson, his teachers at Boston. Cf. Chapter 10 below.

[95] E. Smith, *op. cit.*, p. 56.

[96] Cf. King, *op. cit.*, p. 105; K. L. Smith and I. G. Zepp Jr., *Search for the Beloved Community*. 1974, p. 63f.; Anders Nygren, *Agape and Eros*, Eng. tr. 1953, esp. pp. 75–81; Paul Ramsey, *Basic Christian Ethics*, 1953, pp. 92–103.

It recognises that people *need* to be loved—with the kind of love the Samaritan showed to the victim in the parable. To love (*agapan*) is to understand, to have redeeming good will for all men (King tended to emphasise the role of the will). It is love in action, love seeking to create, preserve and restore community. To be sure, King emphasised the 'image of God' in mankind, but he did not underestimate the human capacity for evil. Nevertheless, he gave prominence to the divine summons to 'fulness of life' in Christ: a summons characteristically associated with the command 'love your enemies'. 'Our responsibility as Christians is to discover the meaning of this command and seek passionately to live it out in our daily lives'.[97]

King differs, however, from Nygren in refusing to differentiate *eros* totally from *agape*. For example, he suggests on occasion that self-love (a concept akin to *eros*) can have a positive as well as a negative side, *viz.*, self-respect, self-actualization, and the concern to develop one's full potential.[98] By contrast, *philia* means affection or friendship, a complement to rather than the essence of Christian love.

When we turn to the relation of love and justice, three major influences are detectable in his thinking. From W. Rauschenbusch he learned to think in terms of the social expression of the gospel, which is concerned with material and physical conditions as well as with spiritual wellbeing.[99] What King rejected was the simplistic notion that the proper development of democratic processes and the economic programmes of capitalism would lead in themselves to the establishment of God's Kingdom on earth. The 'cult of inevitable progress' was an illusion. Even if one understood the Kingdom as a community of love, peace and justice, the factor of human nature was much too potent and complex to allow a naive optimism of this kind.

The second influence was that of Reinhold Niebuhr, with his keen awareness of the operation of power in national and international societies, and his insistence on a realistic view of human nature. In social ethics, love is the 'impossible possibility', incapable of complete realisation in history.[100] Although King never fully accepted this aspect of Niebuhr's thought, he learned much from him about the operation of power structures which was borne out in his protracted experience of confrontation with entrenched racial discrimination.

---

[97] *Strength to Love*, 1963, p. 48.

[98] *Eros* denotes, in philosophical terms, for example, the desire for beauty and goodness and the yearning of the soul for the divine (cf. Platonism). King is perhaps not wholly convinced that such yearning has no meaning for the Christian, although his view of man is quite different from Plato's. Nygren, however, distinguishes philosophical *eros* from 'vulgar *eros*', which he simply takes to be irrelevant to Christian love. King clearly differs from him at this point.

[99] Cf. W. Rauschenbusch, *Christianity and the Social Crisis*, 1907; *A Theology for the Social Gospel*, 1922. There was also a strong social emphasis in the writings of G. W. Davis and L. Harold DeWolf, under whom King studied.

[100] Cf. *Moral Man and Immoral Society*, pp. 8–22, 266–77; *The Nature and Destiny of Man*, Vol. II, pp. 244–69; *An Interpretation of Christian Ethics* (2), pp. 113–45. See also above, p. 199.

It was from Gandhi, the third main influence on him, that King learned the way to make love effective in social, political and economic matters and so provide the true dynamic of social justice. That meant relating love to power, for power is the possibility of effecting the desired changes in society and implementing the requirements of love. Conversely, the evil of segregation lay in the fact that it denied black people all access to power—even the power to realise their own personhood.

> 'Justice in King's thought is measurable to a significant degree. It is the attainment by each person of those inalienable rights he is due because of the sacredness and inherent worth of his personality. These rights are concretely and correctly identified in the Constitution, the Declaration of Independence, and the Bill of Rights. Most normal men know them. They are life, liberty and the pursuit of happiness. For King, there is nothing abstract about this: "It is as concrete as having a good job, a good education, a decent house and a share of power"'.[101]

There is therefore a positive connection in King's thought between love, power, justice and law. Law encodes human rights and in so doing defines the bounds within which one may live without infringing one's neighbour's rights. It has therefore both a restraining and a didactic function. The self-centredness of human nature and its lust for power must be curbed and corrected by law; otherwise, some groups will deprive other groups of basic human rights, as the study of racial discrimination demonstrated over and over again. It also guides society in the direction of justice and safeguards the rights of all.

But *how*, i.e., by what methods, can love be effective? Gandhi is the best known proponent of non-violent resistance as a strategy for social and political change, and he had pioneered it in South Africa. It became an essential part of Gandhi's philosophy, which he called *Satyagraha* ('the Force which is born of Truth and Love or non-violence'); and this embraced *ahimsa* ('respect for life': it literally means non-violence but he gave it positive meaning, *viz.*, respect for life). He saw it as compatible with and an expression of the Sermon on the Mount. For King, Jesus' teaching on love was basic. He adopted non-violence as a way of giving expression to love in social and political terms and as an expression of his Christian personalist philosophy. It also enabled him to maintain the coherence of means and ends. He recognised that active non-violent resistance was a form of coercion, but one much to be preferred to violent coercion. A coercive element had to be present, otherwise protest would be ineffective and of marginal concern in society; and if no outlet was provided there was always the danger of violence. Boycotts, sit-ins, mass marches and the like are ways of registering protest and non-cooperation with an unjust system. They are ways of embarrassing the authorities, who were the real violators of human dignity: ways of focusing attention on the vulnerable position of those who uphold injustice. They are urgent demands for change. If the opponent

---

[101] E. Smith, *op. cit.*, p. 69. The quotation from King in the passage is from *Where Do We Go From Here: Chaos or Community?* New York, 1967, p. 90.

suffers, his suffering is the result of his recalcitrance. On the other hand, non-violent resistance is an expression of one's own convictions; it requires moral courage and discipline; it is the giving of oneself for freedom and social change, and so involves suffering. King spoke about unearned suffering as creative and redemptive: suffering can be used for positive ends, as in the ministry of Jesus. But whether this is really the key to the success of the civil rights campaign is a matter of debate. It certainly won the sympathy and respect of the wider community, but the successful deployment of economic and political pressure, the appeal to legal authority, and King's insistence on the rational basis of the case were also important factors.

Part of King's bequest from personalism was his view that all reality has moral foundations. According to him, the moral order was created by God: God's moral demand stands beyond all human approximation to it, and this divine demand is the core and heartbeat of the cosmos. Hence God and his moral claims (the language King uses sounds like that of moral law) are ranged on the side of justice. Moral imperatives are part of the structure of the universe. The purpose of non-violent action was to bring particular situations and issues into line with the reality of this divine moral claim. Hence, not only was the black community's struggle for justice authenticated by the objective moral order, but racism, economic injustice, exploitation and militarism are incompatible with it, i.e., immoral. And mankind *can* perceive something of this fundamental moral claim, which King describes in terms of law. An appeal to moral awareness *is* possible. A moral cause generates support. Much of King's effort and campaigning was against unjust laws. But what is an unjust law? Following Thomas Aquinas, he held that it is a human formulation of law which is not properly derived from the objective moral order: i.e., from the 'eternal law' or 'natural law'.[102]

King's understanding of the moral order, like his adoption of non-violence, is rooted in Christian personalism, and in particular in the belief in the personal God who gives coherence to the whole created order. Thus, if a law uplifts human personality it is just; if it degrades it, it is unjust. But he did not insist that all who were attracted to non-violent action had to believe in God, any more than he held that the moral law was known only to Christians: he found the method of non-violence expertly employed by Gandhi, a Hindu. Nevertheless, as we shall see, the code of discipline he adopted for his movement was based on Christian assumptions.

Much of King's effort was devoted to the practical task of campaigning for civil rights. He recognised that his followers required to be trained in the technique of non-violent resistance. In his writings, and especially in *Why We Can't Wait*,[103] King indeed articulates what is in effect a comprehensive methodology of Christian social ethics. In this, six stages can be identified,

---

[102] See above, pp. 142ff., 168f.
[103] New York, 1964.

although these are to be understood as part of a fluid process:[104]

(1) *empirical investigation:* establishing the facts, analysing the social conditions and pinpointing inherent injustice;[105]

(2) *communication with the authorities:* this involves not only relating to the power structure but also a readiness to resolve problems through negotiation and dialogue;[106] if this approach fails to resolve the situation, further disciplined action, rather than simply outrage, is required;

(3) *self-discipline:* careful self-preparation, indeed purification,[107] as an essential preliminary to stepping up the campaign: the purpose being to clarify one's self-understanding, aims and motives prior to campaign organising and planning; King, never one to undervalue personal growth and development, required his followers to pledge allegiance, by means of a commitment card, to a strict code of discipline:

'I hereby pledge myself—my person and my body—to the non-violent movement. Therefore, I will keep the following ten commandments:

1. *Meditate* daily on the teachings and life of Jesus.
2. *Remember* always that the non-violent movement in Birmingham seeks justice and reconciliation, not victory.
3. *Walk and talk* in the manner of love, for God is love.
4. *Pray* daily to be used by God in order that all men may be free.
5. *Sacrifice* personal wishes in order that all men might be free.
6. *Observe* with both friend and foe the ordinary rules of courtesy.
7. *Seek* to perform regular service for others and for the world.
8. *Refrain* from violence of fist, tongue, or heart.
9. *Strive* to be in good spiritual and bodily health.
10. *Follow* the directions of the movement and of the captain of the demonstration . . .'[108]

K. Slack commented: 'Was there ever so godly an army since Cromwell regimented the saints'?[109]

(4) *direct and effective action:*[110] to bring pressure on those authorities who have been preserving the unjust status quo, to focus attention on questions of social morality and the crisis in society, and to press home the need for change; at this stage, the protesters may have to meet and absorb violence with courage and self-discipline, but their suffering is creative and will enhance their campaign;

(5) *negotiation resumed:* for compromise can have a positive use; there must be a restructuring of the situation, a new synthesis embodying justice in society;[111]

(6) *reconciliation and forgiveness:* the black people, a minority group, must

[104] The authors wish to acknowledge their debt, particularly in this paragraph, to the work of Larry B. Lake, doctoral research student at Edinburgh.
[105] King, *op. cit.*, p. 78.
[106] *Op. cit.*, pp. 51–54, 78.
[107] *Op. cit.*, p. 78.
[108] *Op. cit.*, p. 63f.
[109] *Martin Luther King*, 1970, p. 77.
[110] Cf. King, *op. cit.*, pp. 78ff.
[111] *Op. cit.*, p. 26f.

take their place in the nation as a whole: after non-violent conflict, forgiveness and reconciliation must be effected in the interests of multi-racial harmony and integration.[112]

King provides an admirable illustration of the fact that a personalist position need not be equated with the inwardness of private experience nor be conceived in individualistic terms. Being essentially relational, it emphasises human interaction, fellowship and community, and hence human existence in a social and political context. Love, as he understood it in Christian terms, is closely related to justice, which in turn is thereby linked with forgiveness and reconciliation. Love also finds practical political expression through non-violence and is thus related to power. Equally important, however, is the fact that King's Christian ethics was worked out in a critical political and social situation in which Christian leadership was essential. Beginning with the empirical and concrete, he was able to interpret the contemporary crisis in terms of a theological understanding, which his education and training, as well as his own intelligence and judgement, made possible for him. Thus he came not only to express a theologically mature Christian interpretation and analysis of the situation in which he and his people were caught up, but also to outline a programme of Christian action (which could appeal to all people of goodwill) and a practical strategy—embracing motivation and method—for putting it into operation: an organic combination of theory and *praxis*.

As his ministry rushed towards its tragic conclusion, King found himself involved in a number of wider issues: Vietnam, world peace and socio-economic reform at home. Had he not been gunned down, he would undoubtedly have been involved in further struggles and controversy. As it turned out, the quest for social and political freedom passed into other hands and can be viewed as part of a global liberation movement on behalf of the world's poor and oppressed: a movement which has important theological and ethical dimensions.

2. *An outline of liberation ethics*

In the latter part of the twentieth century, much attention has come to be focused on 'liberation theology', a movement which takes different forms in different cultural settings.[113] But all forms of liberation theology are shaped by a consideration of action or *praxis*, which presupposes an *ethics* of

---

[112] *Stride Toward Freedom*, pp. 163–73.

[113] For example, there is the well-known Latin American form, represented by G. Gutiérrez, J. P. Miranda, J. L. Segundo, J. M. Bonino and others, and its expression through education in the work of Paulo Freire; the 'black theology' of James H. Cone and others in the U.S.A.; the South African liberationists, such as A. A. Boesak, Beyers Naudé, Bishop Tutu and others; African theology in the younger countries; Yong-Bock Kim and K. Koyama in South-East Asia; the Pentecostalists in Mexico and elsewhere; the feminist movement, represented by Mary Daly, Rosemary R. Ruether and others. See A. Kee (ed.), *The Scope of Political Theology*, 1978; G. S. Wilmore and J. H. Cone (edd.), *Black Theology: A Documentary History, 1966–1979*, 1979.

liberation. Our purpose here is to outline and comment on the more prominent features of 'liberation ethics'.

(1) *Biblical foundations*. Though informed by different kinds of theological approach (from the Barthian to the liberal humanist), liberation theology characteristically focuses on leading biblical symbols: 'God's liberating deeds'. Old Testament motifs, arising as they do from the historical experiences of Israel, are prominent among them: the Exodus, with its concern for the deliverance of an oppressed people from slavery to a new, God-given future; the prophets, with their dynamic proclamation of the righteousness and justice which the God of the covenant requires, and their critical perspectives on contemporary society; or the exile, with its sense of shock, bitterness and outrage at what has happened to Israel, its acceptance for the time being of a situation that must be changed in the future, and its hope and longing for freedom and renewal. The New Testament, however, also supplies major symbols: not least, the ministry of Jesus himself, with his concern for the poor and the outcast, or the prophetic Messiah, the political Christ. Other motifs include the incarnation as God's identification of himself with alienated and powerless mankind; Christ's defeat of Satan; the cross, as God's act of liberation; the transfiguration, as the symbol of transformation; the love of God, not confined to inter-personal relations but combining with power and justice to overthrow evil and oppressive forces; and the kingdom of God, the *eschaton*, as the goal to which all God's work moves and as the stimulus to change the present evil order in the direction God has indicated.

All these biblical motifs are symbols of revolution. To be sure, important hermeneutical assumptions are implied in this kind of interpretation. While the matter cannot be discussed fully here, two hermeneutical principles stand out clearly. One is that this approach takes seriously the historical nature of the biblical revelation. It is not content to build statements about 'God's acts in history' or 'Christianity as a historical religion' into an ideological scheme which effectively depoliticizes them. To depoliticize them is in fact to dehistoricize them. Historical experiences, whether in Old or New Testaments, are by their very nature social and political encounters. For this reason, the interpreter is alerted to the possibility of dehistoricizing tendencies, whether in biblical tradition or in later theology. Something strange has happened when Jesus, 'who is said to fulfill the most politicized religious tradition in the history of the world',[114] is presented as a politically irrelevant figure, yet is condemned on a charge of treason. Secondly, this approach takes seriously the historical—i.e., the social and political—context of the modern interpreter. It is as historical beings, in our own setting-in-life, that we are brought into dialogue with the biblical message in its ancient setting and in consequence hear the Word addressed to us in ours: in this way we participate in what is often termed the 'hermeneutical circle'. Dorothee Sölle has observed.

'The liberating significance of the historical-critical method is lost

---

[114] A. Kee (ed.), *op. cit.*, p. 20.

whenever one disregards the hermeneutical circle and subjects past texts to historical critical examination, but not one's own present and its problematic character . . .'[115]

But what kind of ethics emerges from liberation theology and its inherent hermeneutics?

(2) *Liberation ethics is situational and contextual.* The ethics of liberation develops both in relation to specific situations and in wider cultural contexts. For example, the Civil Rights campaigns began in the specific situation of Montgomery and segregation on buses, but it was rooted in the cultural context of Negro self-awareness and growing critical consciousness. Black theology provides a good example of this dimension.

'For some black theologians the very first step in coming to grips with self-determination and self-fulfilment is the acceptance of what one is as a black person. This is a very legitimate and logical step. If one denies the very self which constitutes one's own being, it will be contradictory to speak of the determination of this self or the fulfilment of this self. As the centre of consciousness and being, the self must be the starting-point'.[116]

'Education for freedom' is concerned that people should be enabled to recognise and overcome the barriers and forces (economic, medical, cultural and political, as well as moral and spiritual) which prevent them from realising their full potential as human beings. Paulo Freire insisted on the need for people to 'name the world', to engage in dialogue about their situation, to develop a critical consciousness which takes them beyond the role of spectators to become reflective actors and participators: a process he calls 'conscientization'.[117] Black theologians, like liberation theologians in general, insist that since the gospel is a gospel of liberation and since the situation of oppression and deprivation denoted by 'blackness' is the most intractable of social and political problems, the only expression of any Christian theology in the United States (or South Africa) today is 'black' theology. Indeed, only by engaging with such liberationism will Western theology ultimately find its own deliverance from bourgeois captivity.[118] Nevertheless, the danger of using a term such as 'black' theology is that the relevant theology and ethics, instead of being contextualised in the appropriate way, are localised and thereby isolated from a global theology of liberation. Consequently, such theological ethics may be so moulded by the situation, that it actually runs counter to the nature of the gospel itself: for example, it may encourage hate rather than love. Not that structural injustice in the situation can be resolved by any sentimental notions of love. As James H. Cone has put it, 'love means that God rights the wrongs of humanity because they are inconsistent with his purpose for man'.[119] Cone

---

[115] *Op. cit.*, p. 15.
[116] Choan-Seng Song, 'The Black Experience of the Exodus', in Wilmore and Cone (edd.), *op. cit.*, p. 577.
[117] Cf. Paulo Freire, *Pedagogy of the Oppressed*, 1975.
[118] Cf. A. A. Boesak, *Black Theology, Black Power*, 1978, p. 143.
[119] James H. Cone, *Black Theology and Black Power*, 1969, p. 51.

goes on to ask what it means for the black man to love his neighbour, especially his white neighbour. It means that the black man *confronts* the white man as an equal, a Thou who has no intention of becoming an It; and if the white man is accustomed to addressing an It, the black man must be prepared for conflict and confrontation in the name of Christ.[120] Furthermore, white people must never be allowed to forget the interrelatedness of love, power and justice. This means that they must be careful when they tell blacks to love their white neighbour that they are not sounding as if they meant 'Love your neighbour, but don't demand justice from him'.

> '. . . The new blacks, redeemed in Christ, must refuse their "help" and demand that blacks be confronted as persons. They must say to whites that authentic love is not "help", not giving Christmas baskets but working for political, social, and economic justice, which always means a redistribution of power. It is a kind of power which enables the blacks to fight their own battles and thus keep their dignity'.[121]

Cone's ethics and theology attempt to be thoroughly contextual and thoroughly biblical. As in Martin Luther King, the notion of personal worth and dignity, grounded in biblical understanding, is fused with the contextual one of social and political change. Inevitably, the social situation so strongly reflected in Cone's writings localises the message to some extent. This is not to suggest that it applies to Birmingham, Alabama, but not to Birmingham, England; nor is its challenge to Western theology invalid or untimely.[122] But in the Western European situation, though social and political change (including opposition to racism and the need for the recovery of dignity among the underprivileged) are priorities, Christians might not isolate such issues as the major single test of Christian ethics today.

> 'For our generation that test is, I believe, the question of peace and war—and of nuclear disarmament. To support the status quo in arms is, I believe, no longer an open and viable option for Christians. To do so is simply not to have opened eyes and ears to the evidence and to reality'.[123]

There is indeed, the possibility of a clash of priorities within the field of liberation theology and ethics. The middle-class Western woman who advances the cause of women's liberation in a way appropriate to her situation may find herself incurring the criticism of the South African black

---

[120] *Op. cit.*, p. 53.

[121] *Op. cit.*, p. 54f.

[122] This is not to deny that there are real problems in 'exporting' a theological/political approach that has been developed in one specific cultural setting: cf. A. I. C. Heron, *op. cit.*, p. 167. Neither must one assume that it has no relevance to other cultures.

[123] Kenyon E. Wright, interview in the *Scotsman* newspaper, August 1982; cf. the Church of England report, *The Church and the Bomb*, 1982. In the U.S.A., cf. the Pastoral Letter on War, Armaments and Peace, by the National Conference of Catholic Bishops Ad Hoc Committee on War and Peace, the second draft of which appeared in *Origins*, N.C. Documentary Service, Oct. 28, 1982 (vol. 12, no. 20).

woman who has already become an ordained minister of her Church and who sees the liberation of her people, male and female, from political and civil oppression as an overriding priority. Yet, whatever the tensions, these situationally and contextually grounded priorities can co-exist on a global model of liberation ethics which enshrines the liberating gospel.

'The situation is never an entity *an sich* which autonomously determines the ethic of liberation. It has a history, and the results of the action within a given situation will have some bearing on its future. A black ethic will arise in a black situation; it will be determined by the black experience in order to be authentic, but it will not be confined to the black experience, neither will black situational possibilities and impossibilities be its only determinant'.[124]

(3) *Liberation ethics is corporate and personal.* As we have seen, it is concerned with the liberation of people from oppressive systems by which they are manipulated and deprived of meaningful personal existence. 'Education for freedom' (Freire) is thus akin to the more radical type of moral and religious education which aims to promote learning through experience, through the raising of a critical consciousness that involves a new awareness of oneself in relation to one's world. It aims to enable one to become truly the subject, the 'I', rather than the object, the 'It'. It aims, in other words, at personal growth which can take place only in relation to others, through communication, dialogue and the sharing of understanding. It aims at demystifying or unblocking those ideologies, sponsored by the ruling elite, which seek to determine and control one's being and so deny one's worth and limit the possibility of genuine choice or self-determination. It aims at bringing the learner out of 'the culture of silence', the situation of oppression and passivity, so that one can begin to talk again as a personal being, capable of making moral decisions, of participating in community and the reshaping of society. In short, it opens up the possibility of becoming a *cooperator Dei*[125] in the liberation of one's people. Hence, 'the facts of the case'—always an important element in social ethics—have a special significance in liberation ethics. They are not simply 'out there', to be objectively researched and collated (important as this task is), but have a significance for the learner's very being. Engagement with them brings one to a new self-understanding which involves a growing awareness of the world which has shaped one's life and which one is no longer content to view as a spectator. An existentialist and personalist ethics so often only embraced the behaviour of private, a-political individuals; but this kind of involvement with one's cultural context overcomes the equation of existentialism and personalism ('the closed circuit of the I-Thou relation') on the one side with the process of privatization and depoliticization on the other.[126] Liberation ethics is at once corporate (political) and personal. Personal liberation and the liberation of society go together and this is a safeguard against today's revolution becoming the bondage of tomorrow.

---

[124] A. A. Boesak, *op. cit.*, p. 144.
[125] Cf. D. Sölle, *op. cit.*, p. 53.
[126] See above, pp. 197f., and the observations of J. B. Metz cited there.

(4) *Liberation ethics is eschatological and revolutionary.* Eschatology is notoriously open to abuse. It can be made to induce a paralysis of political and social ethics, as in the well-known hymn parody:

'Sit down, O men of God.
His Kingdom He will bring
Whenever He desireth it:
You cannot do a thing'.

Eschatology can be used to postpone necessary social and political activities, to put off the revolution until the End-time, and thus reinforce the imperfections of the present order and power structures. Again, it can be a kind of theological escapism, a drug to anaesthetise people from the painful, hopeless present time. Evangelical eschatology, however, proclaims a challenge to the existing order and a message of hope for all who are oppressed. It is integral to the work of liberation set in motion by Jesus himself. As well as proclaiming and giving assurance about the ultimate completion of Christ's liberating work, it calls the faithful to action as his co-workers now. Liberation ethics, being truly eschatological, finds new insights into the truth of the present position and works for fundamental change in people and society.

'This transformation of society can be called a revolution and this
revolution need not necessarily be violent. We understand such a
revolution to be a fundamental social change. It is a transformation, a
movement from what is to what *ought to be*. For Christians can never
acquiesce in the status quo, but they continually challenge the structures of society where they fall short of the fullness revealed in
Christ'.[127]

Viewed in this perspective, the major criterion of liberation ethics is teleological. Moral action, whether geared to personal, social or political development, is action which is directed to the attaining of certain goals:[128] goals which embody some aspect of the fulness of God's liberating work. This *eschaton* is not attainable simply by human striving yet it gives direction and motivation to human effort. In non-theological terms, this liberation approach can be expressed in terms of utopianism or idealism which, however, commands one's total commitment. Nelson Mandela said as he concluded his speech for the defence at the Rivonia trial:

'I have cherished the ideal of a democratic and free society in which all
persons live together in harmony and with equal opportunities. It is an
ideal which I hope to live for and to achieve. But if needs be, it is an
ideal for which I am prepared to die'.[129]

[127] A. A. Boesak, *op. cit.*, p. 146.
[128] For example, securing basic human rights for all; liberation from discrimination and prejudice, whether in terms of race, sex, religion or minority status; the securing and safeguarding of peace and justice; widening the scope of participation in industrial or economic, political or community affairs; securing a pollution-free environment and safeguarding the welfare of threatened species; in general, giving people the opportunity to be truly responsible for their lives and actions.
[129] N. Mandela, *No Easy Walk to Freedom*, 1965, p. 189.

Or as A. A. Boesak puts it in more theological terms towards the end of his consideration of the quest for a black ethic:

'Blacks want to share with white people the dreams and hopes for a new future, a future in which it must never again be necessary to make of Christian theology an ideology or part of a particular aggressive cultural imperialism. Black theology, by offering a new way of theologising, desires to be helpful in discovering the truth about black and white people, about their past and present, about God's will for them in their common world'.[130]

(5) *Civil Disobedience and Spirituality.* A teleological ethics which places such emphasis on liberation and revolution is inevitably involved in civil disobedience and conflict. This can be regarded as a sound evangelical principle: 'Civil disobedience is an act of protest by the Christian on the grounds of Christian conscience'.[131] It can be regarded also as a reaffirmation of the insights of the Reformers. Beyers Naudé quotes John Knox's controversy with Queen Mary, in which he insisted on the right of the subject to disobey when the ruler contravenes the law of God.[132] The question is, what form is civil disobedience to take?

Most Christians probably agree with Peter Matheson when he says, 'For me personally, the risk and the sickening challenge and the real hope all seem to lie in the non-violent alternative. How can one rescue dignity and humanity by the gun'?[133] Violence is an evil to be avoided at all costs. If coercion is necessary, let it be non-violent, devoid of hatred and constructive in intention. But how effective is non-violence against structural violence? Some make far reaching claims on its behalf,[134] and these should not be dismissed lightly. Yet even Martin Luther King was unable to prevent his campaign from provoking violent reaction. On occasion, the riot police had to be brought in. Under extreme provocation, King armed himself in self-defence. And he knew how near simmering resentment came to violence itself. It must be remembered that non-violence is a form of coercion, and thus the gap between non-violence and violence can be very thin. Long before King, the opposition movements in Southern Africa, such as the African National Congress founded in 1912 to defend the rights of Africans, pledged themselves to non-violent resistance. Yet Nelson Mandela, recounting their efforts to promote non-racial democracy and to avoid anything that might widen the gulf between the races, observed in his defence speech at the Rivonia trial (1964):

'... The hard facts were that fifty years of non-violence had brought the African people nothing but more and more repressive legislation, and

---

[130] *Op. cit.*, p. 152.

[131] B. Naudé, *The Trial of Beyers Naudé*, p. 159.

[132] *Op. cit.*, p. 162. The whole of appendix 1 (Exhibit E at the trial of Naudé), 'Divine or Civil Disobedience?' (pp. 153–63) is highly relevant to our discussion. See also above, on Aquinas and Calvin, pp. 143f., 179.

[133] *Profile of Love*, 1979, p. 152.

[134] Cf. *Non-Violent Action: A Christian Appraisal*, A Report Commissioned for the United Reformed Church, 1973.

fewer and fewer rights . . . It could not be denied that our policy to achieve a non-racial state by non-violence had achieved nothing, and that our followers were beginning to lose confidence in this policy and were developing disturbing ideas of terrorism'.[135]

What can be done in such conditions? Some, like Desmond Tutu and A. A. Boesak, continue to maintain a non-violent opposition. The South African Council of Churches, now the only publicly tolerated official channel of opposition, has refused to advocate violence but does not condemn those who in good conscience take up the gun. Mandela describes a carefully controlled escalation of pressure: sabotage, guerrilla warfare, terrorism, and finally open revolution. The movement Mandela represented—it issued the Manifesto of Unkonto (1961)[136]—opted for sabotage since this did not involve loss of life and kept open the possibility of racial harmony and democratic government: a rational enough procedure in the face of tremendous structural violence on the part of the state. Mandela and seven others were sentenced to life imprisonment.

Against this kind of violence, is it in order for Christian ethicists to prescribe non-violent resistance as the *only* Christian response? Western Christians, with their propensity towards 'law and order', tend to be much more outraged by the violence of protest than the violence of the established system: witness the outcry against W.C.C. Campaign to Combat Racism ('too little, too late' was a typical African comment). White sympathy is often partisan, even among Christians. James H. Cone is characteristically trenchant. Martin Luther King came to be accepted by a great many white people because his methods carried least threat to the white power structure.

'. . . Churchmen and theologians grasped at the opportunity to identify with him so that they could keep blacks powerless and simultaneously appease their own guilt about white oppression. It was only a few years back that King's name was even more radical than that of Rap Brown or Stokely Carmichael. At that time the question was being asked whether civil disobedience was consistent with Christianity. What whites really want is for the black man to respond with that method which best preserves white racism'.[137]

Is our advocacy of non-violence related to the bourgeois captivity of the churches? It is difficult to avoid the conclusion that such a factor may frequently operate. The Christian ethicist must underline the need to take account of *all* factors affecting the situation, including the human tendency to rationalise one's own preferences and self-interest. Nor is the ethicist worth his salt—certainly not in terms of a social ethic of liberation—if he opts merely for general principles (e.g., freedom, justice, love) on the grounds that only those actually involved in the situation can take further steps towards *praxis*. The Christian ethicist must accompany the practition-

---

[135] N. Mandela, *op. cit.*, p. 168.
[136] *Op. cit.*, pp. 170ff.
[137] J. H. Cone, *op. cit.* p. 56.

er step by step along the way of *praxis:* anything less stops short of historical involvement, which is the essence of Christian faith, and would justifiably incur the charge of bourgeois pontification. As Cone observes, living according to the Spirit means that one's own will is brought into line with God's will. And this may mean, as the parable of the sheep and the goats indicates, that God's priorities involve a transformation of ours. This may apply even to the ecclesiastical sphere. The signs of the true Church may not be simply the preaching of the Word and the administration of the Sacraments: it may be where the naked are clothed, the sick are visited, and the hungry are fed.[138]

What kind of civil disobedience does Cone commend? It involves a refusal of white definitions and parameters, and a process of liberation *by any means necessary.* But it is also necessary to point to the kind of society *for* which one is being liberated. Here Cone seems to fall into the trap of general principles, such as 'equality'. As has been pointed out by F. Herzog and A. A. Boesak, if he cannot produce a more definite outline of the new society, Cone himself might be charged with thinking essentially in bourgeois terms. If he is simply extending the power structure rather than amending the system, is 'any means' justified for so limited an objective?[139]

The striving for liberation must be in principle universalizable. It must be in context with the cause of the oppressed throughout the world and therefore, for Christians, an expression of the gospel of liberation. Hence, the problem of the appropriate methods, like the seeing of the vision itself, is inseparable from the question of spirituality. J. Miguez Bonino, perhaps controversially, finds spirituality in the Marxist's militancy.[140] Less controversial is Alistair Kee's plea for a new spirituality that is not in flight from the world but enables us 'to appreciate the realism of the spiritual when we have faced the hollowness of the political'.[141] Thereafter we go forward in faith, groping in the darkness yet knowing the direction of travel. To quote Peter Matheson again:

> 'How can we fail to feel with those who, in their quest for justice, have encountered only the iron hand of repression, and have been driven in desperation to violence themselves? If we would stand on this frontier of the future, if we believe that it is here, in the struggle for justice, that the Christian today must stand up and be counted, if the profile of love is not to be sentimentalised out of recognition, we will need hard heads as well as gentle hearts, we will have to produce the more convincing analysis, the better alternative, the costlier discipleship'.[142]

---

[138] *Ibid.,* p. 59.
[139] Cf. A. A. Boesak, *op. cit.,* p. 151; F. Herzog, *Evangelische Theologie,* 1974.
[140] Cf. *Christians and Marxists,* 1976, pp. 133ff.; cf. A. Kee (ed.), *The Scope of Political Theology,* pp. 114ff.
[141] *Seeds of Liberation,* 1973, p. 6.
[142] *Op. cit.,* p. 153.

Part Four

PROPOSING A MODEL FOR
CHRISTIAN ETHICS

10

THE PERSONAL MODEL

What do we mean by a model? We have used the term at various points already, and the time has come to clarify our use of it. We employ the term in a similar sense to its use in science. Science frames models for understanding reality, e.g., sometimes a mathematical model, sometimes a 'physical' one. No model is ever indispensable; and the scientist always hopes next time to frame a more 'adequate' one, i.e., one that gives a more correct, or less false, picture of the reality he studies. In other words, such models are provisional, never final. The scientist uses his creative imagination in constructing models so that he may be better able to communicate the picture of the world his investigation suggests—better than his mathematical formulae or his dial-readings. Models in science are neither useful fictions nor final truths.

Many Christian doctrines can be looked upon as models in this sense— models of a reality, suggested by such data as evidence of order in the universe or the fact and implications of personal relationships. Religious models, however, evoke distinctive attitudes and, therefore, their function is not the same as that of models in science, but they do function in similar ways. Science sometimes uses complementary models, e.g., the 'wave' and 'particle' models of the electron; for the two models correct one another and together give a more adequate understanding than would be achieved by using either alone. Christian theology uses complementary models (e.g., those of Judge, King and Father) in order to contribute to a total understanding. And the more comprehensive a model can be, whether in science or in theology (i.e., the more data it can cover and the less it leaves out of account), the more appropriate for understanding that model will be.

As far as Christian ethics is concerned, therefore, we do not expect to construct a perfect model, i.e., a model that will in every way do justice to all aspects of Christian living. Some aspects will be hidden from us and from our contemporaries. For this same reason, we do not expect that all Christians will accept the model we propose: no shape of Christian ethics can be normative for all Christians, as if it could become a matter for promulgation as a dogma *de fide* by an Ecumenical Council. But we do expect that some models will be more adequate than others.

By what criteria, then, are we to judge a model to be a 'good' one? It must, of course, have the characteristics that any good model possesses, whether in science, philosophy or theology, e.g., comprehensiveness and internal coherence.[1]

More particularly, the model must bring out some basic *motifs* of Christian faith that are significant for conduct. In other words, a model for understanding Christian ethics must be to some extent at least a viable model for Christian theology. We shall need to decide what these *motifs* are, knowing that there can be no Archimedean point from which we can discern the Christian faith in a pure form, that it is always refracted for us through cultural forms, and that our choice of *motifs* will emerge from our own limited standpoints. Some correction of our relative perspectives is provided by the common experience of the Christian community down the centuries, and by the various attempts that have been made to construct models to express that common Christian experience. No thinker starts *de novo* but, in attempting to furnish a satisfactory model, he both builds on the experience of the past and uses his imagination to express a new understanding. By so doing, he need not deny the experience of the Church in every past age.

A model, however, might be in line with some basic motifs of Christian faith, and still not be a 'good' model. For example, we may find that certain models of the past have extrapolated some aspect or other of Christian faith in ways that did not do justice to what is distinctive about moral decision-making as Christians understand it. This is similar to the charge sometimes made against some types of theology that they make the Gospel subservient to a philosophy, and fail to do justice to its unique character. Clearly, we need other criteria.

A further criterion, we suggest, is the cultural validity of the model. It has to be appropriate to the kind of society we have in the West, and are increasingly finding all over the world, i.e., secularist, pluralist, multiracial, and multi-faith. Moreover, it must have the possibility of having a *global* cultural validity, for we increasingly live in a 'global village', and it certainly must have in it the seeds of a Christian response to the Third World. But if in the last analysis it seems more appropriate to the West than the East, we shall not be surprised, alarmed or dismayed. Indians have recognised for some time the need for an Indian theology, and have been making attempts to construct one. The same logic suggests the need for an Indian Christian ethics. The model must at least be suitable to the kind of society for which it is proposed. A monarchical model for God or ethics, or even one which possessed monarchical characteristics, may once

---

[1] The first of these criteria must not be understood as demanding that a model be all-embracing (and thus getting on for perfection), but rather that it comprehend and illuminate more of reality than other models. For example, a model for Christian ethics must be comprehensive enough to overcome the individual/collective dichotomy and have a place for Christian social ethics. It must also have a sufficient degree of internal coherence, so that, if it is a relational model, it must be careful not to allow such a place to other features (such as a divine-command theory of ethics or a law-motif justifying social norms) as to endanger the congruity of the model.

have been viable in a hierarchical society and even later, but not in the pluralistic, secularised, egalitarian, social democratic society of many Western states today. Obviously, we cannot have a model that will be all things to all men—both to repressive military dictatorships that are appearing in Africa and Latin America and to 'democratic' regimes that are often equally slow to respond to public opinion and majority-interests. This is not a matter of 'being with it' and certainly not of being gimmicky: it is true to what Christians believe about the historical context in which they are to respond to the moral claim.

But can we have a model that is at once true to the Gospel and also viable in a secularised, pluralist, and multi-faith world? We believe that a model for Christian ethics today must embrace, with a measure of self-consistency, what have been taken till now to be apparently irreconcilable antinomies. Indeed, we have already argued for this in our chapter on Natural Law. The Church has to be the Church—but in a secularised and multi-faith world: to improve the quality of human life whether in the West or the Third World involves today co-operation between Christians and humanists, and between Christians and people of other faiths and of none.

But let us add yet another criterion that may reassure some anxious readers. In such a model, basic *motifs* of Christian faith that are significant for conduct must not be presented independently of their context in Christian faith. This error may arise from an over-anxiety to show the relevance of Christian faith to morality or to life in today's world. The warp of Christian faith must be shown to be woven with the woof of the moral claim on us, yet not just on Christians, but on all people. This does not mean that Christians must always make their doctrinal presuppositions explicit in working with non-Christians. The model must be sufficiently tight to make those presuppositions evident to the Christian, yet refined and subtle enough to afford a basis for co-operation with those who, not sharing our presuppositions, desire to improve the lot of mankind, though not just materially. Yet this must be accomplished without some form of theological reductionism that destroys the inextricable connection between the Christian life and Christian faith. A model for Christian ethics must beware lest it make a complete separation of morality from Christian faith, as if the relation between them were purely extrinsic.

It is no new insight that the Christian life is inextricably connected with Christian faith. Text-books on Christian ethics have been saying it for the last 30–40 years—ever since we emerged from the dominance of theological liberalism. But nowadays it is not sufficient to make the statement and argue for it on biblical grounds or grounds of Christian tradition. Indeed, it is unlikely that a new shape to Christian ethics can be consonant with the classical structures of theology, for to some extent the false starts of past shapes of Christian ethics are due to these same structures. A new shape to Christian ethics probably requires a new theology.

We have indeed come full circle back to our first criterion. A model for understanding Christian ethics must be to some extent at least a viable model for Christian theology. In Christian ethics, we need an understanding of the basic *motifs* of Christian faith that bear upon conduct, so that we may discern how theology and ethics are precisely related. We do not aim to give a complete list of such *motifs*—a complete theology—but simply to make a selection that seems to us to be basic for Christian ethics. If some of the *motifs* selected are surprising (as we think they will be to some readers), let us recall that Christian faith is itself unimaginable and unexpected, and that traditional *motifs* are likely to be misleading since they were coined at a time when the connection between theology and ethics was never worked out, but was assumed to be obvious to all.

A. THE BASIC MOTIFS OF CHRISTIAN FAITH THAT ARE SIGNIFICANT FOR CONDUCT

1. *The Hebrew-Christian tradition has a certain morphology of revelation that bears upon ethics*

How is revelation pictured in the Hebrew-Christian tradition and how are we to understand revelation today?[2] While visions of God and angels do appear in the Bible, normally religious experience in the Hebrew-Christian tradition is ordinary experience interpreted in a particular way: even the sense of mystery and awe, of the transcendent numinous, is conveyed through ordinary experience. In this tradition God addresses us in and through his creation, his works—i.e., through the world of man's environment and of other people. Any object or event, any situation, may become my 'moment of truth'[3]—my moment of disclosure—when I encounter God. The Bible is full of concrete things and events—ordinary and extraordinary, but not supernatural—such as a bush, deliverance from enemies, a friendship, an illness, the death of a king, buying and selling in the market-place, the unfaithfulness of a wife, the fall of a nation, a wedding, a piece of bread and a cup of wine, a cross, persecution of others—events that become some person's 'moment of truth' when he becomes aware of God asking him to do something; for, in the Hebrew-Christian tradition, such 'moments of truth' always involve doing something, a task, an action.[4]

In this tradition, therefore, there is no knowledge of God independent of our knowledge of his world. For example, we do not have knowledge of the 'supernatural' separately from our knowledge of the 'natural'. We do not have a 'line to God' independent of all other means of communication with the world and other people: and, if this is true in revelation, it will be true in ethics. There is no private 'hot line', a kind of divine telex, on which we can get directions on what to do in every situation that confronts us, and which relieves us of any obligation to look at the situation ourselves. From the point of view of our human knowledge, we cannot separate the 'Eternal Thou', on the one side, and historical events and moral situations on the

---

[2] Here we acknowledge our debts to many thinkers, especially Martin Buber and Ronald Gregor Smith.

[3] Cf. the humanist Abraham Maslow's 'peak experience' that gives direction to the whole of life in *The Farther Reaches of Human Nature*, 1973.

[4] E.g., Exodus 3:1–12; Isaiah 6:1–8; Acts 9:1–9 and Paul's subsequent life.

other. One cannot speak about God without speaking about man. But, further, one cannot speak *to* God and turn one's back completely on other men and our relations to and with them. We do not know God as he is himself: we do not know some transcendent realm independently of our knowledge of him through his world. Our knowledge of God is mediated through his world. We are not simply talking about our theological knowledge of God—which is reflection somewhat removed from the initial 'encounter'. We are speaking of disclosures themselves in the 'moments of truth'.

To turn this the other way, all genuine knowledge of God must somehow correlate with our genuine knowledge of the world. Here is a control against the fantasies of 'private' revelation. If a man claims to have some knowledge from God which completely contradicts what we know on other grounds, we are free to suspect that either he has misinterpreted his 'moment of truth' or perhaps he has not had such a moment at all (e.g., he may be deranged). We can at least say that, where there seems a disparity between the two, either our understanding of the world or our understanding of God is at fault, or perhaps both are at fault. No proper knowledge of God's world can be a hurdle on the road to God.

Further, there is no way of guaranteeing that anyone will have his moment of divine disclosure. The awareness of God's presence is not to be had on demand in the Hebrew-Christian tradition. 'The wind blows where it wills . . .' (John 3:8). Which event or situation will become our 'moment of truth', no one can say. There is no technique that has been or can be devised whereby we can guarantee that, if people use it, they will have their 'moment of truth'.[5] Awareness of God's presence is not on tap each time people engage in the practices of corporate worship or private prayer. The living God is not subject to people's manipulation.

All this entails the belief that God is continually addressing us through all signs of life and creativity, all human history, every ordinary event, though we do not always 'hear' (i.e., respond to) him. Humans come to their authentic being when they respond genuinely to the address of the 'eternal Thou' which comes in what happens to them, in what is to be observed and felt in each concrete situation. While concrete events may become a person's disclosure-situation, in the Bible no event is taken as an adequate symbol for God. That is ultimately why the commandment against idolatry was so important. God is not to be completely identified with any moment, event, situation, object, with anything of his creatures, anything in 'creation' or 'nature'. God always transcends such. God cannot be equated with any event, object or person in the world. And so, God is not directly observable and demonstrable as true in the same way that events are observable and demonstrable. God is the transcendent—transcending his own world.

---

[5] Here Judaism and Christianity differ from Eastern religions such as Hinduism and Buddhism, where yogic techniques are prescribed as ways of realising the union of the self with Brahman, the ultimate reality (Hinduism), or for attaining the state of *samadhi* (Hinduism), or *Nirvana* (Buddhism).

Further, if God is continually addressing us moment by moment in all that goes on, it is not a matter of revelation finally grasped in a moment and then contemplated the rest of one's life. In no one moment or continuation of moments, are we given a final and complete revelation which forever after we have at our disposal to reflect upon and write down. To think of a 'revealed morality' as of this sort—a set of rules and principles finally delivered at some time in the past—which we have only to 'apply' for the rest of our days without further reference to God, is a denial of the view of revelation we are proposing. Revelation is a living relationship grasped moment by moment, though not at every moment, and grasped only fleetingly and fitfully because of our lack of completion.

There is a gulf between that living relationship and our creeds, confessions and doctrines. We know God only as we meet him continually in dialogue, as he addresses us in this situation and that, and even then we do not have either psychological certitude or logical certainty. Doubt remains the other side of faith, not as its opposite, but as the reverse side of the same coin. Faith and doubt live side by side, or back to back! In the Hebrew-Christian tradition, the renewal of the covenant is a continual 'returning' to the sources of our faith and a 'withdrawal' from the moment of truth to the daily task, to the action demanded, to the response in life to what we recognise as God's claim on us. It is a pattern of 'return and withdrawal'—but not a withdrawal from the world of neighbour, nation, community, or politics. It is here that the Jew and the Christian see the importance of worship and the sermon. But such 'moments' or 'seasons of refreshment' are not achieved (as they seem to be in some Eastern religions) by putting away all 'distracting objects'—by forgetting the divine pressure on us through our ordinary lives and the events that befall us. On the other side, it is true that in some forms of Protestantism there is a dearth of the mystical and meditative side of religion—indeed a lack of emphasis on 'seasons of refreshment' properly conceived.

This morphology of revelation has important ethical implications. We become aware that God is addressing us moment by moment in each new situation—in a dialogue in which we are not only addressed, but remade and redirected. God addresses us through the absolute claim we experience in this situation and that. The claim is absolute, not in the sense that it issues rules that are context-invariant in the manner of rule-deontology but in the sense that it is unconditioned and overrides all other claims. My moral 'ought' becomes a response to that address—to that meeting, that relationship, that 'presence'.[6] We have argued[7] that our Christian life-style

---

[6] It is hoped that the many terms used will make it clear that our view of revelation is not committed to holding that our knowledge of God is univocally, or even best described analogically as, a personal knowledge that exists between a human 'I' and 'Thou'. For important criticisms of the 'I-Thou' view of revelation, cf. John Macquarrie, *Principles of Christian Theology*, 1966, pp. 84–5, and of Buber's understanding of the 'I-Thou' relation itself, cf. R. Gregor Smith, *The Doctrine of God*, 1970, pp. 131–37.

[7] Especially in chapters 3 and 5.

is both a response and a fruit, and that the response is not commanded, but evoked by the divine grace. For Jew and Christian, the moral and the religious cannot be separated. There is an intrinsic relation between them. The moral lives in the religious—to use Buber's phrase—'in faith and service'. It remains true that one can be moral without being religious, and the non-religious man will interpret his moral experience differently. The absolute or unconditioned and overriding moral claim that will brook no rival and that he too experiences will not be to him the claim of God upon him.[8] But within the Hebrew-Christian tradition one cannot be religious without recognising the moral claim as a divine claim—without making a moral response to God. The Christian sees his total life as a response to the God who addresses him, a response to the God who graciously shows his presence in every situation.

The underlying *motif* is the covenant one. It is not, therefore, surprising to find a Jewish thinker with a similar understanding of morality.

'In Buber's view, responsibility is the basic notion of every genuine ethics, but then the term is to be taken in its literal meaning: genuine responsibility exists only where there is real responding. This respond-ing and answering presupposes someone who addresses me primarily from a realm independent of myself and to whom I am answerable. "Our answering *for* ourselves is essentially our answering to a *divine* address". This address, however, does not come to me in the form of a universally valid law or norm; it rather comes over me in the "lived moment" of existence and takes place in the concreteness of each situation in which I find myself. Responsibility thus means listening to the unreduced claim of the hour and answering it out of the fulness of one's being'.[9]

Two points are of importance in this. First, for Buber there are not two claims, a divine and a moral one, but only one claim interpreted differently by the non-religious person and the religious believer. Secondly, we have come to a theological reason for an element of 'situationism' in ethics. The divine address, meeting, presence 'does not come in the form of a universal-ly valid law or norm', and the response we make is not obedience to laws or rules, nor even an application of principles given 'in revelation'. The form of a universally valid law or norm erects a protective structure behind which people evade the absolute claim on them to be responsible in each existential situation in life. It is much easier to have such a universally valid norm, for then it is not the self that makes the decision: the general norm decides for me. How often we have heard people argue that Christian love tells them what to do, as if they wanted to evade the responsibility of answering the divine presence in each situation. This is not to say that we

[8] As on our view God relates himself in the same way to all men, believer and unbeliever, the Christian will expect to see signs of this relation in the unbeliever's life: e.g., the humanist's apparent unease in not being able to leave God alone in talk and discussion, and perhaps his attempts to escape subjectivism in ethics.

[9] Joseph J. Kockelmans (ed.), *Contemporary European Ethics: Selected Readings*, Intro-duction to the chapter (15) on Martin Buber, 1972, p. 418 (italics ours).

may throw away all norms and become antinomian. We shall discuss this matter later,[10] but in the meantime we note that for the responsible person the absolute claim—contained, but hidden, and never encapsulated (so to speak) in the norm—never becomes a rule (in our sense of the term), and the fulfilment of the norm never a habit. Such people are constantly open to revise their habitual responses: nor do they adopt some stereotyped responses to the people they meet (responses based perhaps on the first impressions and superficial judgements), for they are ever ready to respond in the situation. If we define the Christian moral task as the application of moral principles, then it will be too narrow to come to terms with such hang-ups as stereotypes and superficial judgements.

2. *It is characteristic of Christian faith to regard human existence-in-the-world as historical: Creation and history*

The correlation of creation and history may seem paradoxical to some readers; but in Christian theology it is important that creation and history should not be divorced as they are on a deistic view of the universe or a docetic view of the Person of Christ. We saw creation and salvation falling apart in Lutheranism: but creation passes almost perceptibly into providence, and providence into reconciliation. These technical theological terms are always in danger of breaking up the one movement of the grace of God in creation, providence and redemption.

A doctrine of creation gives us primarily an understanding of our own existence in the world rather than a speculative piece of Jewish cosmology about how things began, or a Christian piece of metaphysics. There has been too much emphasis on the Aristotelian concept of the First Cause, as if God were the first cause in the same series as the cause-effect relationships in nature, and not sufficient emphasis on how both creation stories in Genesis provide (different) self-understandings for the people of the time, i.e., how they understood themselves in the world. Creation is not about what God did at a particular point in time. He did not create *in* time, for God transcends the whole space-time continuum and so created time. Creation is about God's eternal relationship to the creation which gives meaning to human existence. A Christian doctrine of creation is not about origins, but about meaning. In deism God relates himself to the world or universe only at its origins, and in rebutting it we must be careful not to be infected by the same deistic disease. God is *semper Creator*, creating then and now, holding the universe in being all the time, and creating as he urges the cosmos to move out in new creative ways, building upon previous phases in evolution but ensuring at moments the emergence of quite new developments—e.g., from inanimate to animate, from plant life to animal, from animal to human life.

---

[10] Cf. below pp. 250f., where we argue that an ethic of the principle of *agape*, while inadequate for Christian ethics for other reasons, would not be inconsonant with the nature of the act of faith. In both these contexts, we are arguing that *agape* does not tell us in advance of the situation what precisely to do in it.

What understanding of our own existence does Creation give? First, we notice that we as human beings have a peculiar insight into creaturely existence, for it is only we who have any firsthand knowledge of creaturely being.

Secondly, we can put together a scientific understanding of human existence and a theological one.[11] Strictly, there is no such scientific understanding: what we mean is that we can put together an understanding of the creation suggested by modern science and an understanding that derives from Christian faith. In human beings the cosmos has become aware of itself, because only they can look back on the whole process of evolution and understand from what they have come, and only they are aware of the paradoxical and tragic character of their existence whereby their incompleteness and biological death seem to deny their desire for completeness and their infinite longings. As Dr. A. R. Peacocke has remarked, only they bury their dead with rites of passage; for them, death is more than a biological fact. Human existence is aware of itself as a paradox that needs an answer. Yet human existence is unique, if only because of the human ability to transcend the whole universe and human history and because of its own self-transcendence: no other animal has these characteristics. The results of scientific research and the scientific search itself suggest this view of human beings as a paradox.

Alongside this 'scientific' view of human kind, we place a view derived from Christian faith, wherein creation, christology and eschatology are all interconnected. Humans are created to respond to their creator as self-conscious, responsible beings: their answerability is for all creation and history. A Christian doctrine of creation teaches that humans are responsible for their natural environment. As soon as we say that, we realise what they do to that natural environment, so that 'nature' and 'artifice' cannot be separated. Consider also those things that we believe God wills that humans should create—television sets and typewriters, telephones and refrigerators, biro pens and colour film, washing-machines and dish-washers, calculators and computers, overhead projectors and video-cassette recorders: the list of their technological devices seems almost endless. Human beings share to some small extent in God's creativity, and this is also a response to the Creator. The creation has, therefore, a certain independence; God allows human beings really to be themselves even with regard to God, and this independence is the other side of human freedom. They can rebel, disobey, fail to respond to God: the dialogue between them and God is real, not sham.[12] They must answer God's Word to them in

---

[11] For a fuller discussion, see A. R. Peacocke, 'The Nature and Purpose of Man in Science and Christian Theology' in *Zygon*, vol. 8, nos. 3–4 (September–December 1973) in which he has a most useful correlation of 'scientific' and theological views of man. Cf. also his *Science and the Christian Experiment*, 1971, and *Creation and the World of Science*, 1979.

[12] We must not over-intellectualise this dialogue—it is better seen as a matter of existence-in-relation than as *merely* conscious and 'religious' responses, though, as human beings are thinking animals, at its higher levels it embraces such responses.

their own way: they can harden their hearts and resist the Spirit, or they can be genuine co-workers with God in the drama of history.

Christology and eschatology take us a step further. Christ reveals God and also humanity as it is meant to be. We can conceive of human beings in terms of their future as this is revealed in Christ: in Christ we see the revelation of what we really are, i.e., of what we may become. Christology and eschatology are united. The love of God, expressed in creation and in his incarnation, is active in the life of humanity to make a new creature.

Putting the two perspectives together (from science and from faith), we can regard the evolution of the world as *towards Christ*. Here is the ontological goal of the movement of creation as a whole. In human beings the cosmos has become aware of itself, and more and more they take over direction of the movement. Now evolution depends not on mutations, but on human activity. By means of the provision of a healthier environment and modern medical techniques, human beings have enormously reduced infant mortality rates, so that far more people reach their 'natural' life span and beyond it. They can control the size of their own family; why should birth-control not be used responsibly, even if it was once considered 'unnatural'? By the same token, human beings have the power to blow their environment—natural and artificial—literally 'sky-high' and bring life to an end on this planet. The next stage of evolution depends on their responsibly responding, on their being the new humanity that we see in Christ. For Christ is 'the first-born of all creation' (Col. 1:15) in that he shows the new humanity, i.e., what humanity (Adam) was meant to be and never was— the mystery of God's will for human existence (cf. Eph. 1:9), hidden for ages and generations but now made manifest (cf. Col. 1:26). God's purpose is 'to sum up or gather up all things in Christ' (cf. Eph. 1:10). What Christ is in his perfect response and humanity, human beings are meant to be in the intention of God, and indeed shall be when God has completed his work in us.

While all the beings that go to constitute nature share in basic human creatureliness, there is clearly a hierarchy of beings (e.g., matter, life, mind and spirit), culminating in that answerability that belongs to human existence as responsible being. There is no reason, therefore, why creation should not be understood relationally. Tendencies that work blindly in nature come to self-consciousness and take over responsible self-direction in human beings.

Much of what we have said could have been expressed in terms of history. History is neither process nor occurrence, for these are natural events, describable in terms of natural causality. Historical events, on the other hand, are the result of human agency, whether it be ambition or acquisitiveness, aggression or greed, fear or distrust, hunger or other material want, or whether we express it in terms of the deliberate decisions of human beings. Of course, history has a mixed character in that, on the one hand, it is the product of human creation, arising from humanity's relative independence, freedom and decision, while, on the other, it is the result of circumstances. Yet these circumstances need not coerce human action, though it is always in the context of them that human decisions have to be made. Circumstances are outwith human control to change, but they do not necessitate human action in the sense of ruling out all options: they have to be taken account of in arriving at a decision. It is as if human beings have to play the system, for they cannot fly in the face of 'nature'. They have to adapt their decisions to it, and so co-operate with nature. A Christian doctrine of creation has to embrace both the element of facticity in human existence—the 'givens' such as intelligence, heredity, race, nation, country of birth—and the possibilities of human existence. The former is the measure of 'thrownness' (*Geworfenheit*) in human existence—a metaphor which may have been suggested to Heidegger by the act of 'throwing down' cards when they are dealt: though human beings cannot choose the cards they are given, they can play them as they please, so that their freedom is not impugned.

Human existence has a radically historical character. Animal existence is not historical in this sense, for animals do not make decisions, nor can they respond in the conscious and self-conscious ways in which human beings do. What people have done to the natural environment and how they have created an artificial environment (e.g., houses, theatres, art, industries, schools, universities) is part of history, of the responsiveness of mankind in the widest sense. On a Christian view of morality, the relation of behaviour to empirical situations, including social and political issues, is crucial. The historical context in the widest sense in which we have to act—whether it be the population-explosion in the East, or techniques of birth-control and their dissemination, or the appallingly low standards of living of the majority of people—should never embarrass Christians in debate, as if they wanted to get away from them in order to get on to 'real issues' of 'Christian' morality. On the contrary, it is precisely in all these empirical and historical situations that Christians believe God addresses us with an absolute claim. But in many of these situations, God's will is not a clear and unmistakeable will, available, for example, to those who submit themselves to Church authority, or read their Bible daily, or pray daily, or are people of goodwill. Nor is God's will encapsulated in certain rules or even principles. For information about the context of action does affect our judgements as to what ought to be done.

History for Christian faith is neither abstract nor primarily a concept, but a form of human existence-in-the-world. History, is, therefore, never complete, never final, but a continual movement. No form of past guidance, however revered, will necessarily fit successive centuries. God's will is creative: he wills his children to do his will in the present. The human form of existence-in-the-world is not static, but changes—e.g., from a hierarchical society to the technological, but highly individualistic, age of today. It follows that man's being is not static.[13]

Christian social ethics must nowadays be immensely interested in how changes in the form of human existence-in-the-world can illumine the moral

---

[13] Cf. chapter 5, pp. 123ff. where we saw this from another perspective.

situation of mankind today. There is the argument which runs: 'Modern technology is morally neutral: it's how you use it that's morally significant. The aeroplane can be used either as a bomber or an air ambulance—an instrument of death or of life. Television is morally neutral, but you can use it for the communication of *trivia* or purely for entertainment on the one side, or you can use it to give information, to educate, and genuinely to promote understanding between peoples and nations'. There is truth, of course, in this argument, but we suggest that it fails to appreciate the moral significance of the changes in the form of man's historical existence-in-the-world. If one looks at an historical drama on TV, one is immediately struck with the total dependence of Queen Elizabeth or James VI and I on their courtiers for news, and with how the nobles could filter the news reaching the monarch for their own purposes. Monarchs were the prisoners of the intrigue of their nobles: they could not reach for the telephone, or turn on the radio or TV or institute a survey and find out for themselves. Faster means of communication, open to all, ended court intrigues of that sort at least. Technological devices can and have introduced a new dimension into how citizens are treated by authority, from the state downwards.

Of course modern technology does not guarantee an inevitable moral progress, but it introduces for good or ill ways of treatment that were not available before. The bomber can kill more people in a shorter time than was ever possible before (not to speak of the nuclear and H bomb). The small light aircraft and the helicopter can lift people from remote places, such as the Scottish islands or an oil-rig and take them to hospital, whereas previously people in such places could not have been conveyed to hospital in time and would not, therefore, have been taken to hospital at all. A change has taken place in the form of human existence-in-the-world, and that change means that for good or ill, a new dimension is introduced into human relations. For good, there is an extension in our treatment of disease, in our care for others; limits on medical care have been reduced. Similarly, radio, television and communication satellites can do what was not possible before—they can reduce limits on our knowledge of people in 'distant' parts of the world. In former days, news of a famine would never have reached us—or not until it was too late to take action. Now when we hear about a famine in Ethiopia, a drought in India or Pakistan, or flooding in Bangla-Desh, the money flows in to help meet the need. In remote areas too, people can hear the news as soon as people in the large cities. This is perhaps so obvious that we fail to realise its moral significance. If we are to talk intelligently in the area of social ethics, we must understand human existence as historical.[14]

Christian ethics, therefore, cannot be thought of as a fixed, unalterable system. When we ask about a shape for Christian ethics today, we are

---

[14] Nixon failed to understand this when he ordered all conversations in the White House to be recorded. No doubt he intended to prevent intrigue against himself and his party, but, instead of catching others, he became 'the first man ever successfully to bug himself' (Headline in American magazine *Time*).

reflecting on our Christian life-style in the twentieth-century world: and that means, among other things, understanding that world—what makes it different for behaviour from previous 'worlds'—and attempting to discover an appropriate shape of ethics for that world. It will be no obedience to the transcendent God who acts in our history today to have an excellent shape for ethics for a previous stage of human existence-in-the-world.

On the other hand, if we take history seriously—as we must as Christians—we cannot simply dismiss the past history of the Christian community. That was why we devoted the last three chapters to a historical survey. If we can understand the forms of historical existence of Christians down the centuries, i.e., how people were related to one another structurally in society (such as lord to serf in a feudal society), then we shall be on the way to understanding the connection of such forms with the shapes given to Christian ethics (e.g., heteronomy). Nor shall we ever understand what is significant in our form of historical existence, if we have no idea how we came to be where and what we are: they know not the present, who only the present know—to adapt famous words. But we shall also learn from the mistakes and from the insights of the past. Our attempt will be to evolve a shape for Christian ethics in dialogue with our past as a control over merely following a current fashion.

To sum up, to think in terms of a definitive Christian ethics—including even a definitive shape for Christian ethics today—is to be disloyal to what we claim is Christian ethics' own understanding of the moral and historical context in which every society stands—and in which the Christian community stands. N. H. G. Robinson was right when he wrote:

'The task of Christian ethics is never finally accomplished. Each generation has to work at the problem as best it can . . .'[15]

3. *It is characteristic of Christian faith to have certain experiences of freedom and transformation that bear upon ethics: Cross and Resurrection*

Our discussion will be brief, as we have already written on this *motif*.[16] Easter has many facets, and many of them have a bearing on ethics: e.g., God's victory over evil in Christ; the continuation of Jesus' work after his death in the lives and labours of his followers with whom his presence remains; and Jesus Christ as Lord and King, with a claim to rule the whole of life. But, because of its centrality for Christian ethics, we select here the theme of being freed from the old life to live a new life. It hardly needs establishing that the Christian movement in its origins had much to say about the human need for a transformation of the self, involving freedom from one's old self and release to live a new kind of life. Indeed, we wrote in the last section about the new Adam and the new creation. Baptism meant for Paul a passing from the old life to the new; and he saw in the actions of baptism, whereby the candidate literally went down into the water and was raised again, the symbolism of dying to his old self (or being buried to sin)

---

[15] *The Groundwork of Christian Ethics*, p. 224.
[16] In chapter 5, pp. 122ff.

and being raised to new life, of being freed from sin and redeemed to live no longer for himself.

Theological language that uses terms such as freedom from sin, redemption and sanctification is apt to be meaningless today because it fails to evoke the appropriate experiences of transformation of the self that once gave the language significance. There is certainly a need today to exhibit the experience in which religious and theological language is rooted. For example, sin may be a meaningless *term* to most people today, but it is not a meaningless *experience*, if it is presented as a lack of relating to other people and an incompleteness in the self rather than little naughtinesses and breaches of rules and laws. Or sin may be presented as treating our incompleteness as if it were a form of completeness, as if one were to say, 'I have no need of a physician' (cf. Mark 2:17).

The point we want to make here, however, is that these experiences of freedom and transformation have an important bearing upon ethics. Christian ethics cannot be simply an ethics of applying the principle of *agape*, for it is also about what inhibits people from a fuller realisation of their 'new humanity' in Christ, or (in secular terms) that prevents human beings from growing into their personhood. Once put that way, we see that the new Adam or the new creation is not an individual, however new, torn from his social context in history. What inhibits the new humanity in the Third World (for example)—i.e., what prevents people there becoming persons, or reaching that quality of life that is really personal? The elements of facticity (e.g., housing, economic status, education, occupation) restrict the possibilities of human existence to an extent that they fail to provide the likely minimum conditions for the emergence of personal life. It is like trying to win at bridge when neither partner has a face card—it is not impossible but it is extremely unlikely. Whether it be the woman somewhere in S.E. Asia who spends all day in the paddy fields with a child strapped to her back and returns in the evening to her bare hut with a mud floor, or the woman in a city slum in the U.K., the U.S.A., or anywhere in the Western world, with six children under seven years, whose husband drinks and gambles most of his pay, an environment of this kind is totally against the growth of personhood. Indeed, people may be caught in one of the 'cycles of disadvantage' and never have 'known anything better'. If we are concerned (*agape*) that people in the Third World or the Western world reach this new humanity, we shall be concerned with development in the widest sense—not just economic growth (important as that is) but with an overall social process which has economic, social, political and cultural aspects and all of them inter-dependent.

Thus, our model for Christian ethics must be sufficiently elastic to be culturally relevant, embracing a concept of development that includes moral values, and sufficiently tight to do justice to those motifs of Christian faith that bear upon ethics. We shall suggest[17] that this is possible using a model that centres on the person. Such a model must be realistic in its

---

[17] In section C of this chapter.

treatment of the person. Christian ethics is not just about applying the principle of *agape*, but about what prevents people ever applying it. The requirement of a transformation of the self and a new humanity bears upon this issue.

However, before we reach this climatic point in our discussion, we must finally come to terms with what has been, after all, the dominant position in Christian ethics, *viz.*, the law-model. In our discussion of it, the question of the fundamental *motifs* of the Christian faith will be of critical importance.

B. THE LAW-MODEL: AN ATTRACTIVE FAILURE IN CHRISTIAN ETHICS

The law-model has been so prevalent in Judaism, Christianity[18] and Islam that religious morality and theological ethics are inevitably associated, if not identified, with it, especially at the popular level. It, therefore, deserves great respect and cannot be lightly laid aside. It will have been obvious to the reader that we mean to reject it finally and to propose another model in its place. Our critical appraisal, however, must do more than give reasons against it (as we have already done). It must include some attempt to discover why it has been so attractive and why it has persisted so long. We shall confine our attention to the Christian tradition. Did this model point to some basic *motif*(s) essential to Christian morality or theological ethics? Or is its long history to be attributed to sheer inertia—a reluctance to change models? Or was it rather a matter of powerful sociological and ecclesiastical structures that the model reflected and that ensured its continuance? And were these structures reinforced by ethical and theological reasons to give it such a long innings in Christian thought and practice?

---

[18] In ch. 1, we gave an indication of the extent of rule-deontology in theological ethics, although our list of examples was far from complete. In discussing the law-model here, several important additions and qualifications have to be made. Though the law-model is absent from Jesus and Paul, it is increasingly found in later ethical strands in the N.T. It is prominent in the writings of the *Apostolic Fathers* in the 2nd and 3rd centuries, including the manuals, *Didache* and *Doctrina*: while the *Didache* shows some allowance for circumstances, the latter seems to have hardened into a strict code-morality. Despite the position of Thomas Aquinas, it is present in the medieval period, as evidenced by the penitential manuals and by popular religion as pictured by Chaucer. It is found in the whole Catholic tradition, both Roman and Anglo-Catholic, though that tradition is being increasingly questioned today, especially since Vatican II. See chapter 8 above for the mixed model (relational and law) found in Calvin, and how the law-model passed into Calvinism and the Reformed Churches. In effect, the Puritans (e.g., Richard Baxter and Jeremy Taylor) worked with a similar mixed model, and certainly it is the law-model that is associated in the popular memory, however mistakenly, with Puritanism. Similar mixed models in the writings of several 20th cent. theologians are reviewed in ch. 9 above; to whom may be added more recent writers of such contrasting backgrounds as Fr. Herbert McCabe, Paul Ramsey and Norman H. G. Robinson.

1. *Sociological and ecclesiastical structures*

Since the post-Constantine identification of Christianity with the establishment in the West, the law-model has echoed the view that the relationship of the Christian faith and the Church to the non-Christian world should be one of domination, heteronomy or paternalism. It has taken the basic concept of Christian ethics to be the law, rules or commandments (whether or not in the manner of a narrow rule-deontology): its approach may be broadly described as prescriptive,[19] giving expression to a heteronomous morality.

The use of this model, then, and its persistence must be seen in the context of the kind of society and church in which it was prevalent at any one time. It arose and became accepted in the centuries of conflict and persecution because of the kind of church this was: there was a need to give concrete guidance in a code to recent adult converts who were immature in the faith and had not been nurtured in Christian living since birth. Further, it had become accepted by the second century probably by default rather than as a result of any profound Christian ethical discussion. Such reflection and debate had not yet begun in the church because of its preoccupation in the early centuries with resistance to persecution from outside and with the formation and elaboration of doctrine within—particularly the doctrine of the person of Christ.

When we turn to the medieval period (c. 500–1600 A.D.), society had a hierarchical structure, and for centuries the church was a *de facto* authority with the same authority as any modern nation-state. To such a society the law-model was culturally relevant.

With the Reformation, Christian ethics took a new turn. First, ethical discussion passed out of the milieu of moral theology (i.e., an ecclesiastical context) into a scriptural and theological one. Secondly, this was ethical reflection in the proper sense of the term, because Christian ethics was now recognised as having problematic features—e.g., what was to be the relation of Christianity to the state and society? The possibility, then, of a much more profound outlook is seen in the doctrine of justification by grace found in Luther and Calvin, and the basically relational ethical position arising from it, but their attempts to formulate the relation of Christianity to the world (e.g., the family, the state, one's occupation) were much less satisfactory. Further, their initial relational view-point failed to inform the rest of their ethics, and both used the law-model for social ethics, an inheritance from the middle ages and its church.

Whatever might be the doctrine of the Word of God in the churches springing from the Reformation, in practice scripture became like another *de facto* authority, with churches practising discipline backed by their power much in the spirit of heteronomy. This reflected a society that retained its hierarchical structure till the eighteenth and nineteenth centuries, where

---

[19] We do not here mean to use 'prescriptive' in the way that it has come to be used in British ethical writing since R. M. Hare; we use it in a general, wider and non-technical sense.

the plain man knew his position, work and duties, and seldom, if ever, had to make an unprecedented decision for himself. We can imagine that even the ways of caring for one's neighbour (where it might be thought there would be scope for independent decision and action) were limited, restricted and in any case fairly specifically prescribed by convention and precedent. In such a society, a law-model construed in terms of heteronomous rules seemed appropriate for Christian ethics. The churches springing from the Reformation believed as much as did the medieval church in using their power and authority to dominate society. Again, the mixed models of Luther and Calvin were as nothing in strictness to the law-models of their followers in succeeding centuries. The element of authority was nearly always associated with this model in this kind of society. The precept was regarded either as the revealed will of God or as enforceable—and it was enforced—by the Church (Roman, Anglican, Lutheran, Reformed). The only alternatives for most men and women were obedience or punishment and reparation for non-compliance.[20] The options of complete independence of Church authority and of apathetic indifference to its message did not then exist: even those most defiant in the moment of action submitted to Church reproof for their wrongdoing. Few writers within mainstream Christianity till the nineteenth century were entirely free from aspects of the law-model.

It is not sufficient, however, to imply (as the above arguments do) that the law-model is not culturally relevant to the very different kind of society and church we have today. The outsider will only be strengthened in his suspicion that Christianity is out-of-date; and conservative Christians will only be reinforced in their conviction that the law-model must be retained, for (from their point of view) it is the times that are out-of-joint, not the model. The rejection of the law-model must be on the ground that it fails to do justice to some basic *motifs* of Christian faith, as we have tried to show in section A of this chapter. It is from an understanding of its basic *motifs* that we discover why certain models for Christian ethics are inappropriate. The cultural irrelevance arguments can never be final.

2. *Ethical and theological reasons*

The sociological and ecclesiastical structures, however, were reinforced by some ethical and theological reasons, which in turn were bolstered by the former: it was a two-way process of reaction and counter-reinforcement. The ethical and theological motivation for the continued use of the law-model is no doubt complex, and the following reasons are meant to be suggestive, rather than exhaustive.

(1) *The law-model was believed to be the only means to secure the normative character of Christian ethics.* Despite contemporary criticism and disavowal of ethics as a normative enquiry, any ethical theory (even a meta-ethical one)

---

[20] The experience of Robert Burns at Mauchline is simply the best-known example in Scotland of what was the universal practice in the country, as Kirk Session records everywhere testify.

assumes or advocates and so commends some normative judgements, principle(s) or standard. We cannot, therefore, avoid the difficulty by claiming that Christian ethics is not normative. In teaching, the normative character may be at a minimum, as we investigate the nature, difficulties and meaning of Christian ethics—but that is another matter. In the end, it will be normative: e.g., its assumption that unselfish and out-going concern for others or *agape* is the pre-eminent virtue, and yet not a virtue at all in the usual sense, is an implicit commending of *agape*. It may be, however, that the aim of securing the normative character of Christian ethics was confused with the next objective.

(2) *The law-model was believed to be the only means to secure objectivism in ethics.* Perhaps what was really at stake, as far as ethics is concerned, in the retention and continued advocacy of the law-model, was not so much 'Christian norms' as objectivism in ethics over against subjectivism; and some theory of divine law, rules or command was thought to be the only way to secure this. But, as we have already indicated,[21] many ethical writers who defend objectivism in ethics do not do so with religious, let alone Christian, arguments. It may be, then, that the law-model rests intellectually on a mistake, but in practice sociological and ecclesiastical reasons ensured its uncritical acceptance and continuance. Linked to this reason, however, there was a third—an ethical and theological reason.

(3) *The law-model was believed to be the only means to do justice to the absolute element in Christian ethics.* As we have already suggested,[22] the law-model is inappropriate in that it tries, but fails, to do justice to the absolute element in Christian ethics: it tried to enshrine a true insight but gave it wrong expression. It has construed the absolute as a universally valid law or norm, and consequently has failed to preserve properly the factors of 'situation-ism' and so of calculation and deliberation, though historically it did its best to hold these insights through the casuistry of Catholic moral theology.[23] It failed, too, in its emphasis on law to bring out the factors of response and being evoked by the divine love and mercy which must never be obscured in any account of Christian behaviour.

In reality, the absolute is not the context-invariant law, but the absolute claim on us to do what is right and pursue the good in this situation in which we find ourselves. A Christian ethical position must not merely hold that there is an action that is objectively right to do in the situation, i.e., right independently of our desires, tastes, inclinations and interests, though not, of course, independently of our *desire* to do the right. In addition, it must hold that there is a divine claim on us in the situation—a claim that cannot be brooked or gainsaid. As Paul Tillich wrote,

'. . . the religious dimension of the moral imperative is its unconditional character',[24]

[21] In chapter 4, pp. 96f.
[22] Pp. 224 ff. above
[23] Cf. Alexander Miller, *The Renewal of Man*, 1956, p. 94.
[24] *Morality and Beyond*, 1969, p. 14.

and he maintained that the unconditional character did not refer to the content (e.g., a universally valid law), but to the form of a moral decision.

> 'And should anyone be in doubt as to which of several possible acts conforms to the moral imperative, he should be reminded that each of them might be justified in a particular situation, but that whatever he chooses must be done with the consciousness of standing under an unconditional imperative'.[25]

This, of course, is where Christian ethics will part company from humanist ethics—for the Christian, the unconditional character of the moral imperative is the divine claim on him or her. Further, in Christian ethics there will be still additional considerations of an experiential kind undergirding the divine claim—e.g., an element of moral realism that sometimes (indeed, very often) takes the form of contrition that we cannot achieve more in the circumstances and that the human situation, tied up as it is in a mesh of 'sinful' relationships (including relationships between the individual and groups, and between group and group), does not permit more. This alone makes us chary of claiming at any time that we are 'doing the will of God', especially when we know how often that is said by people who desire to claim that God is on the side of *their* point of view.

Indeed, the divine claim that we have been describing has often been represented as the demand 'to do the will of God'. There is truth in this, but the divine will in Christianity is conceived not 'as the revealed rule by which alone we can know his will'[26] but as a personal will, which is pressing on us through all the events of our lives and the lives of others, and this is the will of the same God who is to us grace and forgiveness.

> 'This unity of moral demand and saving grace may be lost when morality is thought of in terms of abstract standards, laws or values, without reference to a personal divine will'.[27]

To know the will of God is at least in many situations not a matter of immediate awareness, but of waiting upon God to reveal himself through the situations in which we are. We have to try to discern the divine will in particular situations and that involves grappling hard with the particular situations—getting to know them from everyone's angle, estimating the likely consequences of various proposed policies, and so on. The liberty of the Christian man or woman has many aspects, but one of them is that we have to judge for ourselves, and that responsibility cannot be evaded by letting a rule, commandment, or principle decide for us, and so it is almost never an easy liberty to exercise. Further, in the Christian tradition, revelation does not come to man (as in Islam) in an infallible form, but 'we have this treasure in earthen vessels, to show that the transcendent power belongs to God and not to us' (2 Cor. 4:7). We can never claim to know infallibly the will of God because God, in addressing us, does not lay aside

---

[25] *Op. cit.*, pp. 15–6.
[26] James A. Whyte, 'Protestant Ethics and the Will of God' in (ed.) G. R. Dunstan, *Duty and Discernment*, 1975 p. 113.
[27] *Op. cit.*, p. 119.

our incomplete humanity. Yet in trying 'to do the will of God', we have a confidence—not the confidence that we shall never make mistakes, but that despite our failures God is the real director, because He is evoking by his love and mercy our response of obedience, thankfulness and praise.

C. THE PERSONAL MODEL

The personal model is difficult to formulate succinctly because of its immense unitive power. The model has the status of a symbol in the sense that it combines several concepts together, e.g., concepts of response and relatedness, of responsibility and relationships, and of morality as the ethos of a community rather than obeying a law, rule or even principle.

Further, the personal model enables us to see these concepts internally related to each other and potentially related to other factors—e.g., to context (including situation and circumstances), to the minimum economic conditions required for the nurture and growth of persons, and to the need to provide appropriately designed physical structures wherein neighbourhoods may be created. So we shall argue. In the meantime, we suggest that it is these features of comprehensiveness, imaginative appeal and relevance to today's society that give this model its integrity, attractiveness and power.

Let us look at some of these factors and how they are integrated.

1. *Description of the person*

Since the personal model involves an ethics of the person and of the persons-in-relationship, the description of the person is crucial for our understanding of it.

The danger in suggesting a minimum cash-value for the person is that by restricting human beings to one or more functions we dehumanise or depersonalise them. For example, under the influence of existentialism, we might define the person as an *actor*, and not just a *thinker*, a doer in contrast to things or objects which are passive. Man is what he is by his own decisions (Jean-Paul Sartre). Man does not have a pre-existent value or an essential nature. Existence precedes essence. *Opto ergo sum*—'I choose, therefore I am'. Man creates himself. He chooses his own values and so makes himself. Choice creates both value and essence. There is, however, an immediate and obvious objection to this kind of reductionism. Man is more than an actor—much more. He has many functions. He is *homo faber*, the smith and the toolmaker, industrial and technological man; he can speak, read and count, because he has universals, and these are the minimum skills for communication; he is social man because he is able to have I-Thou, and not just I-it, relations with others; he is man the aesthete and the artist, able to appreciate and create beautiful objects; he is reflective and theoretical man, scientific and philosophical man, because he is able to ask both scientific and philosophical questions; he is moral man because he is man the agent, and able to make responsible decisions; he is religious man, at once aware of his finitude and apprehending the infinite to which he belongs. To be a person is to be all this: to dehumanise or depersonalise him is to deprive him of one or several of these functions. To develop in isolation one element in this structure of the whole, complete man, and put it, as it were, in control is both to distort the whole structure and to deprive even that element of its power and meaning.[28] If we are to suggest a minimum cash-value for the person, it cannot be by isolating one of these functions, but only by finding some experience that underlies them all and makes them all possible.

Of course, in popular thinking there is no problem with the definition of the person. 'Surely', people say, 'you mean a member of the human race, of the species *homo sapiens*'. We do not mean this. Rather we would suggest that minimally a person is someone capable of communication. A human being, reduced to a vegetable, is not a person in the sense in which we are using the term, while someone who has lost all his limbs or the power of speech might still be able to communicate—e.g., by typing or using some elaborate electronic device which he presses with nose or ear. When Christians say that God is personal (or at least not less than personal), they do not mean that God is a human being, but that God can communicate with people in a manner in some ways analogous to personal communication. If we could never communicate, we would not be persons.

This meaning of the person rules out another often suggested, again under the influence of existentialism, or at least of Martin Buber, *viz.*, that the person is a subject, and not to be treated as an object; or (to get rid of the valuation involved) that the person is the self, the I, who can enter into relations with the Thou. But the difficulty here is how, if we begin with the I as given, we can ever get beyond the I to the Thou. It is not a matter of ready-made persons entering into relations with others: rather we only become persons as we encounter and relate to others. David E. Jenkins misses the point when he writes:

> 'In an attempt at definition we might be inclined to say that an essential feature of being a person is a capacity to enter into, and to appreciate reciprocal and reciprocated relationships with other human beings. But I suspect that a definition of this nature would turn out to have at least some element of circularity in it'.[29]

But this suspicion can only arise, if we do not realise that we do not become persons except as we relate to others. Then such a definition is not circular.

The experience of Helen Keller is significant for our understanding of 'personhood'. When she was freed from her blindness, her deafness and her dumbness—in the sense that she was now free to communicate and receive messages in language-form—she considered that she was freed to be a person. The ability to communicate was merely the basis for a still richer

---

[28] Cf. Paul Tillich, 'The Person in a Technical Society' essay in ed. Gibson Winter, *Social Ethics*, 1968, p. 133. We are indebted to this essay for the substance of this paragraph. It should be noted that 'man' is used in this passage and elsewhere as the Latin *homo*, 'humanity', and no sexist overtones are intended or implied.

[29] *The Glory of Man*, 1967, p. 5.

personal life, in which she had a degree of autonomy or independence of others, and the opportunity to become aware of her own richness. She discovered who she was as a person and what she had to offer. She was awakened to herself, and her tutor had contributed to her becoming a person in her own right. Becoming a person, then, is a process which includes the realising of the possibilities of one's being. The more restricted the range of possibilities open to people, the more stunted personal life will be, and those who can make no responsible decisions because they are incapable of communication, can never become persons in this sense at all.[30]

The ability to communicate in the sense we mean is not simply a matter of being literate and numerate, for we only become persons through our encounter with other people. In Helen Keller's case, it was supremely through her encounter with her tutor that she was freed to be a person— free both to realise her potentialities and to have her own worth recognised by others and so to obtain self-respect. 'Primarily' wrote Ronald Gregor Smith, 'knowledge of the self arises in the world, along with other persons'.[31]

Helen Keller's experience is a particularly dramatic instance of a situation that is not unique, where someone is freed by someone else to become a person (cf. 'salvation'). This is a common, potentially a universal, experience that may take less spectacular forms, but there is nothing banal about its effect. When a girl at a camp was visited by some of her school-mates, she realised for the first time that she *was* someone, she mattered—i.e., she recognised her own value. The experience affected her whole life, enabling her not just to grow up, but to be 'reborn', to have a new quality of life. The experience led to what some call fulfilment and what Christians see as 'transformation' and 'new life'.

We become persons through our encounters with other people and the relations we establish with them. For Buber, it is in the 'I-Thou' relation of subject to subject (not the 'I-It' of subject to object) that the person emerges. For him, the primary relation in which man achieves his authentic being is the 'between-man-and-man'.[32] Of course, becoming a person may take place through the encounter of the child with his parents in the home and out of it. That this does not happen in so many cases either in the home or elsewhere is a tragic comment on much life today.

The transformation of the self is described in Paul's letters by means of the metaphor of death and resurrection: we die with Christ to the old life and rise with him to new life, i.e., to a new quality of life.[33] The analogies with first-century Christian baptism and with the crucifixion and the

---

[30] This is why 'the person' is sometimes cashed in terms of 'creativity'; but we are claiming that the ability to communicate with others is basic to such creativity.

[31] *The Doctrine of God*, 1970, p. 115.

[32] *das Zwischenmenschliche* and *Zwischenmenschlichkeit*—a coinage of Buber's. How far Buber was successful in his account of interpersonal relations is discussed by Gregor Smith, *op. cit.*, pp. 131–134.

[33] E.g., Romans 6:5–11; 2 Cor. 4:7–16.

resurrection must not blind us to the experience—common to the first and twentieth centuries—that lies behind the language.

Then there is the paradox of the person. We only discover our real meaning as persons in a social context—not in isolation from other people, but in relation to them; but the other side of the paradox is that only the man who has become a person can relate fully to others. 'It is in his (man's) togetherness with others that he is truly himself'.[34] We take it that this is what social and moral education is largely about: when such education passes beyond the mere commending of rules and prohibitions, it begins to develop the child's self-understanding as he becomes aware of others, their interests and needs. We only know ourselves as we know others. Indeed adults, as well as children and adolescents, need to discover themselves constantly in a wealth of human relationships and encounters. For a complete relationship with another (whether of the same or the opposite sex), there is needed a process of encounter and transformation. We do not become a person in any adequate sense all-at-once or overnight, but we grow into a person through our encounters with others which influence and change us.

There is a school of social psychology, known as symbolic interactionism, which draws attention to the significance of this feature of human behaviour. It supports much, if not indeed all, of what we hold regarding how we become persons and how we learn to relate to others. We cannot expound the views of this school in any detail here and we confine ourselves to two quotations which typify its doctrines:

'The central idea . . . is that a person's self develops in relation to the reactions of other people to that person and that he tends to react to himself as he perceives other people reacting to him. That is to say, the self-system is not merely a function of a person's manipulation of the environment, but a function of the way in which a person is treated by others. The self is a social product'.[35]

'In short, the self is not inborn, nor could it appear in the individual isolated from his fellows. The self arises from the social experience of interacting with others. The self has an important reflexive quality: it is both subject and object. In interaction, a man learns to respond to himself as others respond to him'.[36]

We are all familiar with the principle in the sciences that for every action there is a corresponding reaction: but this is not often applied to human behaviour. We act; others react; and we in turn react again. Their reaction to our behaviour influences our behaviour.

We have already argued that, within the context of Christian faith, we cannot regard the person as static, with a fixed nature. We are not fully persons at birth, nor do we arrive complete at personhood at some stage of

---

[34] R. Gregor Smith, *op. cit.*, p. 141.

[35] David H. Hargreaves, *Interpersonal Relations and Education*, 1972, 1975, p. 5.

[36] *Ibid.*, p. 7. On the same page, the author quotes John Macmurray's *Persons in Relation*, the first modern philosophical work on the person.

maturation. We *grow* to personhood—not automatically, but only through our encounter with others. On a Christian view we never experience fully what it is to be a person, but we grow in personhood and relate more fully to others, yet never fully in an absolute sense. This is at least one important meaning of 'sin'—a failure to relate fully to others.

Further, for the Christian this interaction of self and others in our world—this interaction which enables us to be persons—points to the existence of community. There is no problem of the individual *versus* the community, of individual or so-called personal ethics *versus* social ethics, for we go back to an experience behind the separation or distinction of self and others. For the Christian, this experience is a call to respond to the other, and to be responsible in the face of the other—something to be developed presently. Again, with his eschatological perspective, the Christian looks forward to growing into the fulness of the stature of Christ—into full Christian manhood or womanhood, into the fulness of personhood.

According to J. B. Metz, theology reacted to the Enlightenment and Marx's criticism of religion by placing the social dimension of the Christian message on a secondary and accidental level and insisting upon Christianity's essentially private aspect.[37] Further, he sees this private, interior version of Christianity as proper to transcendentalist, existentialist and personal theologies. There is truth in the historical interpretation, but there is no need for a personal model for Christian ethics to be guilty of such privatisation. If the process of personal development is fully understood, there can be no question of equating the 'personal' and the 'private'. Metz is right in holding that talk of 'mixing religion and politics' is wrongheaded, for they are not two separate ingredients which require to be mixed: in Christianity they are mixed from the beginning. The person whom God addresses becomes a person in his relation with others and with God himself. Moreover, the person is enmeshed in a web of social and political structures.[38] From the point of view of the personal model, politics is the art of creating and managing the appropriate structures wherein the person may develop as fully as possible. For human beings to assume autonomous responsibility for their own destiny and not to be determined by a heteronomy of class, wealth or regime, a process of democratisation is a prerequisite.

What are the obstacles to personal growth? As there is nothing automatic about this growth, we must hold that it can be impeded—e.g., if in early life we feel insecure and not accepted. If we are afraid that we shall be hurt, if we feel others do not recognise nor accept us and we cannot see ourselves as important in our own eyes, then we react with either aggression (e.g., anti-social behaviour) or withdrawal (e.g., into a fantasy world), with either

---

[37] *Theology of the World*, tr. William Glen-Doepel, 1969, pp. 108f.

[38] E.g. the provision of employment, housing, sanitation, water, light, heat and means of communication—by post, telephone, newspapers, radio, TV—or the lack of such provision; all the provision of the state, local, regional and central, and of the legal system, including such provision as taxation, rules of the road and social security benefits, or again the lack of any of these.

hate or distrust. The fear/distrust/hate reaction becomes a syndrome—directed not just at some people or some section of society, but at all people, whether we know them or not. It becomes an archetype by which we interpret all our experience. *All* people are feared, distrusted or hated. This is a typical example of the stunting of personal growth. People thus affected are never capable of accepting other people and trusting them—or so it seems. There is, however, always the possibility that they will have their 'moment of truth' when they 'find' themselves as they encounter others who treat them as having a worth and give them a measure of self-esteem. For the Christian, it is never true that 'human nature does not change' or that some people are 'irredeemable'. This experience of being counted unimportant—of a lack of value—is, of course, the experience of the socially and educationally deprived, particularly in our cities and urban areas in the West, and almost everywhere in the rest of the world. It is the experience of mass-humanity—of dehumanisation or depersonalisation.

On the other hand, we can grow into persons, if in early life we feel secure because we have been accepted. We are thus encouraged to trust other people, to commit ourselves to them and to accept them as they are; and, when in adult life we find that many people are *not* to be trusted, we do not develop the fear/distrust/hate syndrome. We are 'free' from such attitudes, in the sense that we are not bound to them: we are not their prisoners. There is much talk today of 'freedom' which is empty of moral content. Is a man free who is chained to his aggression and hate or to his inability to relate to other people? Christianity is not a revelation of God who is outside life and the world, but of the transcendent we meet in our world, revealing the truth about ourselves and other people. Christians believe that in Jesus the Christ they encounter the one who re-orientates them in a new direction and enables them to relate to others, as well as the one who gives them a value in their own eyes (self-esteem).

We are, however, not just *freed from* hatred or unrelatedness, but freed to identification and solidarity with other people (instead of either aggression or withdrawal)—i.e., *freed to* acceptance of others because we know that we have the divine acceptance. There is always, of course, the danger that people take themselves too seriously, because they do not have the proper perspective on themselves. Being basically insecure, they seek to magnify their importance (the school-playground exemplar is the bully) in a way that the man who knows he is accepted need not do. The mature person embraces any threats to his being so that they become, as it were, part of his being and so no longer a threat to it.

Neither the transformation nor the divine acceptance are events that once took place in our past and are over and done with. Christian ethics requires a relational model because the Christian's behaviour is a fruit of that relationship with the divine which is continually renewed. As we have seen, the Christian continually returns to the sources of his faith and new life, because the divine acceptance and the transformation are events that take place again and again in those 'moments of truth' of which we have spoken.

2. *Difference between law-model and a personal model*

In proposing a personal model for Christian ethics, we telegraphically characterised this model as an ethics of the person and of persons-in-relationship. Now that we have described what we mean by person, let us attempt to describe one basic difference between a law-model and a personal model.

If, for the advocate of the law-model, the antinomian represents the supreme exemplar of immorality, then the man who fails to respond to people and situations is for the relationist the immoral being. The lowest forms of life respond to light: failure of human beings to respond in the way specified brings them to the inhuman level. Of course, we are not talking of a failure to respond in certain circumstances and for adequate reasons—when one has a responsibility to a group, for example, and cannot abandon it in order to respond to others; or when such responding might be taken for favouritism; or when one is temporarily pre-occupied. We are talking of a more basic failure to respond.

Examples are hazardous, because they may always be explained in other terms as in the cases just indicated. In a crowded street, where parking-space is at a premium, a man sits in his car waiting for his wife to return from shopping; though there is plenty of room behind him, he fails to move back a little to allow a car to park in front of him, even when appealed to. On the one hand, he may be taken as the paradigm of those who fail to react to people and situations and who opt out of active involvement with others. On the other hand, he may be taken as excused on the ground that we do not know enough about the situation—e.g., the empty space behind may have been a bus-stop, or his wife may have been physically handicapped so that he desired to wait exactly opposite the shop. Further, we are all aware at times of some degree of insensitivity to others, occasions on which we feel remorse and distress at ourselves.

The following examples are perhaps more apposite. Someone who was once more than an acquaintance and with whom you have never quarrelled fails to notice you, even though he clearly recognised you. Someone you know fails to respond to innocent banter in such a way that he ignores *you* as well as the banter. Or people fail to consider the interests, feelings and needs of others at all; they drive rough-shod over others in an aggressive way; or you are treated at a purely superficial level, as for example when an acquaintance slaps you on the back, but there is no meeting of person with person. Or there is what appears at first sight to be an attempt at establishing personal relations—for example, one party makes a gesture of goodwill or a token of good faith, but when the other takes this as a readiness (say) to discuss a matter of joint interest seriously, i.e., as a readiness to enter into genuine dialogue, the first party either withdraws or acts aggressively.

The problem of personal relationships is how to achieve the proper balance of genuine dialogue, without either acting aggressively or pretending the other's views are correct when one thinks them wrong or giving the impression that the other person has no value, simply because one thinks his views are unimportant. Those who work with students will know the problem well, and its many other manifestations: e.g., how to motivate a good student who for some reason has ceased to work without giving an over-severe reprimand, or how to help a student who is working hard but fails to do herself justice in the examination because of an anxiety proceeding from a failure to realise that she is capable of reaching the required standard. Sometimes we can use gestures of courtesy and 'tricks of the trade'—e.g., building up a student's position so that it is a respectable position to discuss, or seizing on something that seems correct in what the student has said and giving credit for that, and going on from there, or bolstering the ego of the insecure student. Of such devices, we shall not be ashamed, if we believe in the kind of relating we have been describing. But it does take two to make this kind of dialogue, and it does mean people exposing themselves to some extent.

Whatever other reasons there may be (e.g., upbringing, lack of facility in language, educational deprivation), the main reason for a refusal to relate to others is fear: people are afraid of exposing themselves (e.g., to ridicule, or attack); they fear threats to their being. But the forms of such refusal are many.

3. *The personal model offers the insight that an appropriate action can change a human situation*

The personal model we are discussing involves an ethics of living response to situations rather than one of fixed rules and laws. But while we consider the context significant for moral decision-making, this personal model differs from Fletcher's situationism in that it offers the insight that *an appropriate* action can change a human situation. It is not a matter of always accepting the situation as it is and acting in it; sometimes the situation can and has to be changed. This is indeed the heart of the model: a person or an event may evoke a response whereby the self is given a new direction—indeed whereby we have a new person (cf. the 'new humanity').

We can argue for this approach from three directions—from experience, from psychology and from theology.

First, is the approach true to experience? At a training course, a group of students and teachers were improvising in their Drama Workshop on their understanding of the theme of the Good Samaritan parable. They divided into two groups, recalling the conflict between Jews and Samaritans, with the double-take of two rival gangs today. They used the well-known symbol in such improvisation of rivalry between groups—the one group wore shoes, while the other did not. They represented the conflict perfectly—they fought each other, and they fought again and again and again. It was getting boring: for they could not find a way of improvising 'reconciliation'.[39] The tutor who had been observing closely on the side-

[39] That reconciliation is not a basic theme (or a theme at all) of the Gospel parable is irrelevant to what the students were doing: it would only be relevant if they were *dramatising* the parable in ancient or modern form. Faithfulness to the thrust of the parable belongs to dramatisation, not to improvisation where there can be exploration of issues that may belong only peripherally to the meaning of the parable.

lines stepped into action with his shoes on and for a little appeared to identify with that gang. Then in a lull in the fighting, he crossed to a member of the rival gang, sat down beside him and began to remove his shoes. A new dimension has been introduced—a new direction to action, and the others of both gangs began to respond: some of the shoe gang followed his example by removing their shoes; and shortly one of the shoeless brigade began to don shoes.

What do we learn from this? The students discovered something new—that an appropriate action can transform a human situation and evoke a response whereby people receive a new motivation and new insights into the scope of the moral claim upon them. These students, of course, had not rehearsed: they were simply responding to the new situation. With the response to the action goes a new sense of responsibility: indeed, the response is the recognition of the responsibility. Put generally, a person or an event may evoke a response whereby action is given a new direction.

Secondly, we can argue for this approach from psychology. The school of social psychology, known as symbolic interactionism,[40] which highlights how we react and modify or change our behaviour as a result of how people react to us, is fast gaining ground in the U.S.A. and parts of Europe. It is providing psychological support for the way in which someone's behaviour or the activity of a group can change a human situation. We need a model that reflects this. Long can put the point in secular terms:

> 'When a leader or a group proves attractive and exciting or when an event induces a profound sense of indebtedness or appeal, men are frequently given new motives for their actions and new insights concerning the scope of their obligations'.[41]

Of course, this can be true of any group, party or leader, for good or ill, of a Hitler as well as a Gandhi, of the Hitler Youth or of Alcoholics Anonymous. This does not alter the fact that there is a measure of reflexiveness about human behaviour that needs to be reflected in our model for Christian ethics.

Thirdly, we can argue for this model from theology. In the Hebrew-Christian tradition, gratitude and love are evoked by a living encounter with God as we meet him in ordinary events and people.[42] This relationship of faith, gratitude or love shapes the direction of action. We have already set this down in chapter 5 (*Faith and morality*), and we saw relational views of Christian ethics grounded in the doctrine of justification by grace in chapter 8 (*Learning from the Reformers*) and in chapter 9 (*Some twentieth-century reshaping*). In this respect, our model reflects its theological grounding: but in particular it reflects the morphology of revelation characteristic of the Hebrew-Christian tradition, and those experiences of freedom and transformation of the self characteristic of Christian faith (as expounded in

---

[40] Cf. p. 241 above.
[41] *A Survey of Christian Ethics*, p. 117.
[42] For the theology implied here, cf. pp. 222–33, above, esp. pp. 222–26.

section A of this chapter). So far, our model satisfies one of the criteria for an adequate model—*viz.*, that it should bring out some basic motifs of Christian faith that are significant for conduct.

This approach, therefore, is an older development than Situation Ethics, and it is found throughout the history of the Christian movement. It is evidenced in the concept of covenant-relationship found in the source-documents of the Christian church. It is found in Augustine, Abelard and Martin Luther. It has had a notable revival in the twentieth-century, and many writers have incorporated aspects of the personal model, though often mixed with motifs of a law-model—e.g., Brunner, Bonhoeffer, Barth and Bultmann[43] as well as Anders Nygren, Walter Lowrie, Nels F. S. Ferré, Alexander Miller, Joseph Sittler, H. Richard Niebuhr and Paul L. Lehmann. Most of these writers were motivated in their use of the relational *motif* mainly by biblical and doctrinal considerations: they did not characteristically make use of wider considerations from psychology and sociology to support their theological position, though H. Richard Niebuhr is one of the notable exceptions. Roman Catholic writers today are also making more use of a relational and personal model,[44] and some of them are evaluating data from a wide range of empirical sciences to support their moral theology. We come round again from another angle to the point that Christian ethics has to become, much more than in the past, a multi-disciplinary study.

In many of the writers, classical and modern, to whom we have alluded, the *motifs* were curiously mixed: in particular those who used a relational *motif* failed to hold it consistently throughout their ethics. Indeed, it is striking how a morality of *response* to God's initiative is both affirmed and denied throughout the Hebrew-Christian tradition. Hebrew morality sprang from a response to the Exodus. Its model was, as the concept of the covenant testifies, relational as we should expect: yet since its *form* tended to be prescriptive, its *language* was in time misconstrued as that of divine command. In the Judaism of the intertestamental period, Jewish morality became one of obedience to a code for its own sake: i.e., it became legalistic in what we were at pains to distinguish as the proper sense of the term. We observed a like deterioration in the understanding of Christian morality, a process which had begun in the later strands of New Testament material, and was complete by the second and third centuries A.D.[45] The relational-*motif* revived again in Augustine in his much misunderstood *Dilige et quod vis fac:* when the self is transformed by the divine initiative, then we respond in love to God, and we shall do what we will without fear, for we have been redirected by love; in that kind of situation, rules are not so much unnecessary as irrelevant.[46] But the revival under Augustine did not last, though 'small groups and peripheral thinkers espoused his theological

---

[43] The ethics of these theologians were reviewed in chapter 9.
[44] For some recent Roman Catholic writers, see chapter 7 above, pp. 165–69.
[45] Cf. above chapter 1, and pp. 233ff., esp. n. 18 on p. 233.
[46] Cf. above pp. 86f.

ideas'.[47] For such an important thinker as Abelard there were glimpses of a relational view of Christian behaviour, but apart from him we have to wait till Martin Luther for the reappearance of this approach to Christian morality, and even then it is not consistently held.[48] Can the model be held consistently? The question comes to whether the personal and relational model can embrace social ethics: and to that question we now turn.

4. *The personal model: ethics and koinonia-ethics*

The ethics of this model presupposes a form of life in which true persons, as distinct from human animals, have to grow and flourish. This approach echoes the view that the relationship of Christian faith and the church to culture must be formulated on some basis other than a pattern either of domination or of separation. Instead of making the model one of a rule, command or law that either society or the church must obey, or even a principle or goal to which they should aspire, it places at the centre of attention an *ethos* in which they must live.[49]

We must be on our guard against thinking this merely idealistic. An ethic of relationships, which emphasises how human relations can be poisoned, and how relations of trust can only be built up over a long period in which people come to trust one another, is, for example, more relevant to an understanding of Northern Ireland than one that simply tells people to obey the law, irrespective of the rights of minorities and the history of the province. The context has to be more widely conceived than it has been in some recent contextualism and situationism. It includes the whole fabric of social relations in which the members of a community are enmeshed, by which they are influenced for good or ill, and which can make people turn inwards on their fantasies (including violent and aggressive ones), or turn outwards to see their fellows as persons with claims on their behaviour. This is what we mean by an *ethos* in which people must live. For this reason, this model affords an important place to the life of groups—e.g., the family, the neighbourhood, the peer-group—and to the way of life of such groups; for this is how an ethos is absorbed for good or ill.[50]

The tragedy of Northern Ireland is that the prolonged violence and the polarisation of politics spawn a new generation of distrust, hate, violence and aggression both on the streets and in the political arena, and render a 'solution' still more remote. The politicians who represent the polarised communities are still more disinclined even to talk to their opposite numbers, and in their speeches and actions simply bolster the collective ego and prejudices of their camp-followers. The whole fabric of social and political life is thus poisoned, despite the efforts of Church leaders and lay

---

[47] Long, *op. cit.*, p. 131.

[48] Cf. for Luther, chapter 8 above.

[49] Cf. Long, *op. cit.*, p. 119.

[50] Bultmann's form of existentialist ethics appears to be lacking in social or political awareness. One forms the impression that he had no grasp of how groups, as distinct from individuals, function. Reinhold Niebuhr is a better guide here: see above, pp. 198f.

people, both Roman Catholic and Protestant, to provide the healing antiseptic. Indeed, it can be argued with some cogency that without these efforts the situation would have escalated speedily to full-scale civil war. In this situation the art of politics has been lost, forgotten and killed off, and this is the basic reason why all attempts at a political solution which depends on bringing the two sides together for consultation and agreement have so far failed. Such judgements are those of Christian realism, and, we repeat, to talk of *ethos* is neither vague nor idealistic.

The personal model looks not only to society but also to the church, for it is in the Christian community that people are nourished in the Christian life, by Word and Sacrament, worship and fellowship. There is, therefore, always a sense in which Christian ethics is an ethics of *koinonia*.[51] Yet no aspect of this spiritual nourishment comes prepacked and guaranteed. Within the church, people may learn to live in response to God's love or they may learn countless ways of avoiding any deep response at all. For those who do respond, the result is a many-sided enrichment of the personal: a growing sensitivity to people, a greater degree of self-giving, a readiness to enter into community with others, a more real penitence. For them, the 'practice of the presence of God' sustains their search for Him even when his absence is most marked. Such a response is unitive: it unites sacred and secular, church and world, ethics and theology. Here, insofar as it can be realised in this world, is life more abundant: life lived to the full—in its full dimensions, so to speak. The core of the gospel is expressed in just such response and relational terms in John 3:16. God so loved . . . that He gave . . . that whosoever responds in trust should not perish but have life. Failure to be responsive is to perish as a personal being. Response to God's love in faith and trust is to find the springs of 'life'. That is why the personal model is the most adequate for theological ethics.

5. *The personal model and social ethics*

How does this model unite personal and social morality? We have seen that, in this approach to Christian ethics, the concept of response is internally connected with that of persons-in-relationship. The question,

---

[51] Cf. Paul L. Lehmann, *Ethics in a Christian Context, passim*, and p. 124 above, n. 22. 'The theological factors that are particularly significant for Christian nurture in relation to moral education are faith, autonomy, *koinonia* and *agape* . . . moral education in the Church is for autonomy within the *faith-koinonia* which, when living up to its vocation, is characterised by *agape* . . . Christian nurture takes place within that faith-community, in which they' (sc. children and young people) 'are already participating, and . . . , therefore, the faith-community in its whole life is formative of the child's and young person's behaviour'—James Scotland and I. C. M. Fairweather (edd.), *A Good Education*, pp. 50f.: though the quotation is from a report entitled 'Moral Education in School', it is from a section on moral education in the Church, as distinct from the state school. In the Christian community, *koinonia* balances autonomy: 'If you really care for your brother or sister within this faith-community, you will not be constantly claiming the right to take your own autonomous decisions, even at the risk of tearing the community apart . . .' *ibid.*, p. 51.

however, is whether the model can embrace only 'private' or 'individual' morality and whether in embracing social morality it introduces a notion of prescriptive law or rule that is not consonant with itself as relational. To understand our answer to this question, we have to present a more thoroughgoing account of our model than we have yet done and to do so against the backdrop of basic issues in Christian ethics that have raised their heads in the preceding discussion.

The personal model preserves the basic insights of the relational model. The foundation of Christian ethics is not a moral code, based (say) on the Sermon on the Mount, but a response to what God has done and is doing for us and for all men. Christianity is not a yardstick of what is good and evil, because the non-Christian has a conscience too and can respond, like the Samaritan in the parable, in *agape* to human need. A code is not what is distinctive of Christianity: and we must avoid too easy clichés about preserving Christian values, when we are not sure what these are over against non-Christian, secular, or humanist values.

If this is true, we cannot expect Christian ethics to provide concrete guidance for any particular situation; nor can we suggest a new casuistry and attempt to give such guidance for every conceivable circumstance that the layman is likely to face. Why? Of the many reasons that could be given, we suggest that the basic one is that Christians are given the task of making free, responsible moral decisions for themselves. God treats us, we believe, as mature, adult persons come-of-age, not as children under heteronomous tutelage. This is not to say that we have reached a stage of moral perfection, where our decisions are always right objectively. It is to say that the call to faith is a call to make free, responsible decisions.

But since we obviously need general norms for social morality, is the layman (e.g., teacher, doctor, M.P., Trade Unionist, accountant, town planner) to be left with no further guidance in the many, difficult, perplexing situations he meets today and which call for some action on his part? Granted that Christianity is not a code, i.e., a set of moral rules that give detailed guidance, is Christianity not a set of principles, and above all *agape*? Is an ethics of principles the solution? While rules are meant to *specify* the behaviour commanded or prohibited, principles do not, but apply over much wider areas of living. What, then, precisely is erroneous about Christianity as an ethic of principles?

There is one objection to an ethics of principles that we have met in the last chapter and that is completely misguided; and its rejection takes us near the heart of the matter. The objection is that to follow a principle which tells one what to do is to fail to respond to God who addresses us moment by moment. We must not present Christian behaviour preformed and prepackaged as that would impugn God's freedom in his Word, our openness to God's nature, and the nature of the call to faith. But this objection is wrong-headed for two main reasons. First, it rests upon a misunderstanding of what a principle is, for a principle does not tell us (in advance or at any time) what precisely to do. For example, *agape* tells us to be loving, but not what precise behaviour will be loving in the situation:

that we have to decide for ourselves. Secondly, as we do not know till we come to the situation what behaviour will express *agape*, God's Word is not being prejudged; and in any case, we are only saying that the behaviour will be a response to God who is love. We do not see then how an ethic of the principle of *agape* would be inconsonant with the nature of the act of faith.

Further, we can present our ethics as one of an *agape*-principle in our work with non-Christians. We must avoid a discontinuity between ethics and Christian ethics at this point. We are against Bonhoeffer and with Bultmann on this issue. There is a common foundation in man's moral discernment which gives a justification for co-operation between Christians and non-Christians, as we saw in our discussion of natural law. It is much more important that we work together with humanists, Muslims, Hindus, Sikhs in many public issues and for the maintenance of the social order and mutual understanding than that we try to impose on them the theological foundation of our ethics.

But, of course, Christian ethics is more than an ethic of principles, because, being an ethics of the new humanity and the person, it has more to say than merely, 'apply *agape* in the situation'. Christian ethics has something to say about what inhibits people from applying the principle of love. It is never an easy matter, for it is inconvenient, time-consuming and costly. There is enough of the old Adam in all of us to make it demanding Further, often in social morality where what can be achieved depends on what the group or the community will do, we cannot achieve as much as we would like; and there is a place in Christian social morality for confession, repentance and the acknowledgement of guilt. Again, human beings have the ability to rationalise their actions and to hide the truth about themselves from themselves. They represent what they do in the most favourable light or put themselves in the centre of the picture when often their part was minimal or secondary. At the root of this dissembling is fear and anxiety lest other people will not accept us as we are, lest we shall lose a friendship, and lest we shall despise ourselves and lose our sense of self-esteem. Christians have the resources to be more aware of their own self-deception. In the revelation of the transcendent God who removes all restrictions on our concern for others, and in its place for confession and forgiveness, Christian faith can free people from their self-deception because it frees them from their anxiety. Basically, an ethic of mere principles knows nothing of the ethics of the new man, freed from fear about threats to his being, freed from anxiety about not being accepted by others. Accepted by God, and continually accepting that acceptance, he is freed for existence for others, and has ceased to be careful about others' acceptance, and to be worried about his own sense of importance. As we have just said, this freedom is never a permanent possession, and has to be constantly renewed and realised in obedience to God's love.

How, then, can we find a place for social norms within a personal model, without introducing the prescriptive *motif* of law or rule, that would threaten the consistency of the model? The other side of the same coin is whether we can have a relational model without embracing, with Barth and

Bultmann, a pure act-deontology which in denying general norms gives the layman no help at all? Does any ethical position other than pure act-deontology endanger the nature of the call to faith?

The first thing that has to be said to all this is that God is calling us away from heteronomy. This is easy to see at some levels. Christians cannot hand over all the responsibility for making moral decisions to some heteronomous authority (such as Church, state or statistical survey). And by the same token Christian morality is not conformity to some moral norm or norms imposed upon the Christian from outside, but is inward assent to what one does, so that the whole person is involved. Our discussion of motive in chapter three is vital here. But what has escaped so many thinkers is that we have called divine act-deontology (that is, 'God will tell you in the situation what to do') can be another mode of heteronomy: it can mean to be commanded externally, rather than to be inwardly formed.

It follows that moral responsibility for the Christian involves making up one's own mind. How? (a) We have to look at the situation; and find out about it. We cannot act responsibly unless we undertake a phenomenological analysis of the situation, free from subjective slant, for which the Christian has his own resources. There is need for empirical studies in many areas before we can make responsible moral judgements. (b) We have then to deliberate rationally between policies of action, using the principles and skills of moral decision-making (e.g., considerations of likely and foreseeable and intended consequences; of our reasons and motives; of our 'principles' of justice and love). We agree with Bultmann that the chief duty of the Christian is to live responsibly, making use of the same moral insights (and, we would add, procedures) that are available to all men, but not resting secure in them.

The Christian approaches every situation afresh, not being bound by his previous decisions, actions or attitudes, but meeting every situation afresh in trusting faith which is an openness to the will of God. But God does not expect us to begin again *de novo*, as if we were children learning for the first time. Man's continuing identity as subject and agent under God must not be denied. He can learn from the past, including his own past decisions (and how he arrived at them) and his past mistakes. Further, our knowledge of God is not separate from our knowledge of his world (as we saw in our sub-section on morphology of revelation), a world in which we see that antinomianism in social morality would spell disaster for the emergence and growth of persons, and that social norms are required. To dismiss this as pragmatism and prudence is almost to deny God's working in the world, to deny that we can ever know, with the insight of the O.T. prophets, that some social policies are disastrous for the common life and the public weal. God does not address us *apart* from his world, and so divine act-deontology is not the only position consonant with the nature of the call to faith.

Here, then, is how the model unites personal and social morality. The individual, as we have seen, becomes a person only in encounter with others, and the growth of personhood is nourished in human communities, often small neighbourhoods or groups, rather than huge urban sprawls or large comprehensive schools. On a personal and relational model, norms for social morality, even rules, will be justified on the grounds of the provision of minimum conditions for personal growth. On the level of 'private' morality (i.e., of relationships between individuals), instead of merely commending rules, such as 'Always be chaste' and 'Always keep your promises', we can give the reasons for such rules, by talking in terms of relationships. On the level of social morality (i.e., of the relation between the individual and the group, or between groups), the model enables us to talk about what hinders the growth of persons, what poisons human relations, what creates distrust and hate, and what fails to promote human and personal relationships. We shall talk about what social and political structures deny human freedom and inhibit our fulfilment as persons, what structures alienate us from our humanity and prevent the emergence of the new humanity. From this point of view, politics is the art of providing and maintaining the structures, as well as modifying them according to circumstances, whereby the human situation may be changed, so that the self may be liberated from oppression and alienation and be given a new direction to be free for others and to achieve fulfilment. The words of Gustavo Gutiérrez often echo our approach to social ethics, though we have come to it by a different route, certainly geographically and to some extent culturally and theologically. He is a Peruvian Roman Catholic Priest, who against the background of the Latin American scene has produced a masterly work on Liberation Theology. He writes:

'It is not a matter of "struggling for others", which suggests paternalism and reformist objectives, but rather of becoming aware of oneself as not completely fulfilled and as living in an alienated society'.[52]

'To characterise the situation of the poor countries as dominated and oppressed leads one to speak of economic, social and political liberation. But we are dealing here with a much more integral and profound understanding of human existence and its historical future'.[53]

What we have expressed in terms of the growth of persons, Gutiérrez expresses in terms of self-fulfilment and the achievement of freedom: we regard them as two languages with a single meaning.

'A broad and deep aspiration for liberation inflames the history of mankind in our day, liberation from all that limits or keeps man from self-fulfilment, liberation from all impediments to the exercise of his freedom'.[54]

When we look at human existence in this way in the light of Christian faith, social ethics itself becomes a critique and valuation of current social structures and policies. We then frame our questions differently and see how the model we are proposing is culturally relevant. These questions in their concrete form will always vary according to the circumstances of our community, country and culture. For example, in general terms, we shall be concerned with economic deprivation, employment and industrial relations

[52] *A Theology of Liberation*, 1974, p. 146.
[53] *Ibid.*, p. 27.
[54] *Loc. cit.*

and even pollution. It is not that we cannot expect people to have any moral standards when economic conditions are poor, but that humanity in the sense of mature personhood cannot flourish in these conditions. As John Macquarrie has written, 'The concern for persons leads the Christian to seek such social and political structures as will best allow persons to develop their full potentiality'.[55] Christians should not be surprised to discover that once again the Christian insight of 'wholeness' (the unity of the material and the spiritual, the physical and the personal, the body and the soul) is relevant to the situation of many in our cities, whether in urban centres or in outer housing estates. The great mistake is to regard this as an area of life where only economic arguments prevail, and to make the charge of an unwarranted interference in economics and politics. Christianity's way of valuing covers all areas of life; and its great mistake is to settle for less, *viz.*, the area of the soul or of 'private' views on the meaning of life. Without a sense of personal value, riches and poverty are alike fairly meaningless to human beings, but poverty never comes without an essential connection with personal value. In the Great Depression of the late 'twenties and 'thirties, the worst feature was not the poverty and the squalor consequent on unemployment—terrible as these were—but the loss of a sense of worth by the people themselves. They felt thrown on the scrap-heap of society, as if they had no importance: devalued by society, they lost their sense of self-esteem and felt alienated from themselves.

Poverty, we are maintaining, is *never* merely an economic factor. Material poverty[56] is 'the lack of economic goods necessary for a human life worthy of the name. In this sense poverty is considered degrading and is rejected by the conscience of contemporary man'.[57]

'Concretely, to be poor means to die of hunger, to be illiterate, to be exploited by others, not to know that you are being exploited, not to know that you are a person'.[58]

Poverty is not just material: it is how others treat you in the whole of your existence, and it means how you value yourself, how you view the world and human existence.

This Christian insight of 'wholeness' reminds us of Karl Marx. He proclaimed the unity of theory and practice, just as Latin American 'liberation theologies' speak of theology as 'critical reflection on Christian praxis'[59] and also on current social and political structures. Marx regarded the belief in the autonomy of theoretical discourse as illusory and the sin of 'bourgeois idealism'. This and more we can learn from him, without regarding his view of society as 'scientific'. We cannot truly have theological and ethical reflection without morality and Christian practice. The gospel must not be reduced to 'right praxis', but a theology which makes no

[55] 'Ethical Standards in World Religions, (X) Christianity' in *Expository Times*, vol. 85, no. 11, 1974, p. 327.
[56] Poverty is an ambiguous term as Gutiérrez points out.
[57] G. Gutiérrez, *op. cit.*, p. 288.
[58] *Ibid.*, p. 289.
[59] *Ibid.*, p. 13.

difference to practice distorts the Christian message. Nor can we have theological and ethical reflection in a vacuum: it has to be on some current issue. This involves discovering the facts, seeking the views of experts in the field or fields and deciding which are the significant facts: hence the selection and valuation which Christian social ethics must bring to the empirical situation in the light of the Christian message.

Many theologians were aware of this even before liberation theology came on the scene. It has come to be generally accepted for some time in the West, among both Protestant and Roman Catholic scholars, that Christian faith necessarily finds expression in political activity, as it finds expression in moral action. But this has not been self-evident in all ages. It is far from being self-evident today to Eastern Orthodoxy[60] and it is contested even in some Protestant circles. Nor was it self-evident in the first centuries of Christianity. It had to await certain political developments.

'In order for the ethical interest of politics and the responsibility that each of us assumes in politics to appear in clearer fashion, political power had to become more extended, and instead of concerning itself only with the general order of society and with juridical relations, it had to penetrate to the very heart of individual and familial existence'.[61]

The view that Christian faith necessarily finds expression in political activity also only became reasonable when humanity was able to assume responsibility for the control of its own destiny, i.e., with the emergence of a democratised political world, and that means only relatively recently. Where there are oppressive centralist regimes, this will involve today the conscious struggle for democratic control. Where democracy has been established, there will be constant vigilance to maintain and enhance the degree of accountability to the people.

But we can learn much both from the Marxist critique of religion and from liberation theology, without going overboard for either. They make us aware that too often the Church has identified itself with the status quo—even when it did so unconsciously and unintentionally, but no less effectively. In the West, for example, there has been a tacit defence of the status quo in the name of being non-political, while all the time an ideology was being transmitted. We are more aware today of the socio-economic determinants of our ideologies.[62] There have been many ways in which a

---

[60] Of course, in certain contexts—e.g., in some totalitarian states—it may be extremely difficult to give overt political expression to Christian faith: but there are many forms of resistance to such states, and the way of active overt resistance is not the only option.

[61] Roger Mehl, *The Sociology of Protestantism*, 1970, p. 267.

[62] The term ideology has had a long and varied history and is used in a number of different senses. Our use is derived from Marx for whom the term was a co-relative to 'alienation' and meant 'a deceptive attempt to rationalise, justify, and alleviate the basic estrangement of man' (Patrick Masterson, *Atheism and Alienation*, 1971, p. 86). In our use, the most important distinguishing marks of an ideology are (1) the presence in it of deception, illusion and dogmatism because history and experience are not properly and critically observed and evaluated, but must conform to the ideology; (2) the attempt to justify, and, therefore, to

theology has been a support for the *status quo*. For example, pietistic presentations of the Christian message have isolated our relation to God and almost completely severed it from our relation to our neighbour— except in one-to-one relations of kindness, mercy and charity. Again, some Christians have understood Providence as some Muslims appear to understand 'the will of Allah'. Whatever happens—e.g., illness and recovery, or illness and consequent death—is the will of God. Even events within human power to change, or those immediately due to human incompetence, misjudgement, imprudence or pride are treated as part of God's plan. In the same way, the social system has been sacralised, and, therefore, is to be endured.

Christians should never give complete commitment to the *status quo* for two reasons. First, there is strictly no such thing as the *status quo*, for the conditions of human life are constantly changing. Secondly, the Christian message is always in search of social and political expression, but can never settle happily in any. The Kingdom of God can never be equated with any arrangement of human affairs. By the same token, the Church has to respond to social change, but not to accept it uncritically. Christian ethics is always a quest, and never a solution, nor is it a complete resolution of conflicting views, though these can have positive value in motivating critical reflection. One of the tasks of Christian ethics is to disturb us, for 'here we have no lasting city, but we seek the city which is to come'.[63] As we have already indicated,[64] Christian social ethics must nowadays be immensely interested in how changes in the form of human existence-in-the-world can illuminate the human moral situation today. New dimensions—for good and ill—are introduced in human relations by technological advance, and we know not what new dimensions may come forth in the future. Christian social ethics will continue to be a quest.

The relational model in the past has so often suffered from internal incoherence when the law-model has been introduced to provide norms for social morality. It has been our endeavour to demonstrate that the personal model can be made consistent enough to embrace social morality with its general norms. They are justified on the ground that they provide the minimum conditions for the emergence and growth of persons. Without freedom, justice and peace, there can be no such growth. Though these are political goals, the Christian sees them governed by the eschatological perspective of the new humanity. But they are too abstract and vague for

---

(footnote 62 continued)
preserve the established order; and (3) the giving of stereotypes of people, policies and others' points of view, the oversimplifying of social and political conditions, and the communicating of tendentious and partisan accounts of all of these with the air of authority but in fact of dogmatism. None of this need be done consciously or deliberately: those who communicate an ideology may be unaware of the nature of an ideology or of how they have come to hold it. An ideology can be absorbed from the 'mental' environment without the use of critical reason.
[63] *Hebrews* 13:14 (RSV).
[64] Above, pp. 229f.

Christian social ethics, which must always be endeavouring to frame 'middle axioms' for its own society, axioms that mediate between the Christian message and particular actions and social policies.

The personal model has some advantages over a law-model, as it puts law, rules and prohibitions in their proper perspective. It reminds us of the goal law is meant to achieve: law is never just law for law's sake. It reminds us that not all laws are justifiable, and that laws have to be constantly revised and reframed to meet a greater approximation to justice in changed conditions and to prevent in those circumstances the inhibiting of personal growth and flourishing. A personal model reminds us that Christian and general morality is never merely a matter of toeing the line given by externally imposed rules. Moral judgement is a matter of discernment and insight, and more akin to an art. But this art is always practised as we look at and evaluate the historical, empirical situation. The Christian never says, 'Forget the facts and remember God'. God does not give us such an easy option. As his historical creatures, he does not free us from our responsibility to make decisions in the light of our faith.

BIBLIOGRAPHY

Acton, H. B. *Kant's Moral Philosophy*, London, 1970

Alexander, A. B. D. *Christianity and Ethics*, London, 1914

Altizer, T. J. J. (ed.) *Toward a New Christianity: Readings in the Death of God Theology*, New York, 1967

Anderson, J. N. D. *Islamic Law in the Modern World*, London, 1959; *Law Reform in the Muslim World*, London, 1976

Anscombe, G. E. M. *Intention*, Oxford, 1969

Arnold, M. *Literature and Dogma*, London, 1888

Audet, J-P. *La Didaché: instructions des apôtres*, Paris, 1958

Baillie, J. *Our Knowledge of God*, London, 1939, (6) 1952

Barth G. *see* Bornkamm G

Barth, K. *The Word of God and the Word of Man*, Eng. tr., London, 1928; *Church Dogmatics* I–IV, Eng. tr., Edinburgh, 1936–69; *Against the Steam, Shorter Post-War Writings, 1948–51*, London, 1954; *The Humanity of God*, Eng. tr., London, 1961; *The Epistle to the Romans*, Eng. tr., London, 1968 (1933); *How I Changed My Mind*, Edinburgh, 1969; *Ethics* (ed. Braun), Edinburgh, 1981

Bartsch, H. W. (ed.) *Kerygma and Myth*, I and II, Eng. tr., London, 1954, 1955

Beach, W. and Niebuhr, H. R. (edd.) *Christian Ethics, Sources of the Living Tradition*, New York, 1955

Bennett, J. C. *Christian Ethics and Social Policy*, New York, 1946

Bennett, J. C. *et al.*, *Storm over Ethics*, St Louis, Mo., 1967

Bentley, J. *Between Marx and Christ*, London, 1982

Berger, P. *A Rumour of Angels; modern society and the rediscovery of the supernatural*, London, 1970

Blumhardt, C. *Gottes Reich kommt!* Zurich, 1932

Böckle, F. *Fundamental Moral Theology*, Dublin, 1980; *Law and Conscience*, New York, 1966

Boesak, A. A. *Black Theology, Black Power*, London, 1978

Bonhoeffer, D. *Ethics*, Eng. tr., London, 1955, (4) 1983; *Letters and Papers from Prison* (enlarged edition, ed. E. Bethge), London, 1971, (4) 1979

Bornkamm, G. (with Barth, G. and Held, H. J.), *Tradition and Interpretation in Matthew*, Eng. tr., London, 1963

Bowden, J. *Karl Barth*, London, 1971

Bowden, J. (ed.) *see* Richmond, J

Braun, H. 'The Problem of a New Testament Theology', *Journal for Theology and Church 1*, 1965, pp. 169–83.

Brightman, E. S. *Personality and Religion*, New York, 1934

Brody, B. A. (ed.), *Moral Rules and Particular Circumstances*, Englewood Cliffs, N.J., 1970

Brunner, E. *Das Gebot und die Ordnungen; Entwurf einer protestantisch–theologischen Ethik*, Tübingen, 1932; *The Divine Imperative*, Eng. tr., London, 1937, (8) 1964; *Justice in the Social Order*, Eng. tr., London, 1945, (2) 1948; *The Church in the New Social Order*, London, 1952

Bultmann, R. *Jesus and the Word*, Eng. tr., London, 1935, 1958; *Theology of the New Testament*, Eng. tr., I, II, London, 1952, 1955; *Glauben und Verstehen: Gesammelte Aufsätze*, (4 vols.), Tübingen, 1952–67; *Essays Philosophical and Theological*, Eng. tr., London, 1955; *Existence and Faith*, Eng. tr., London, 1964

Campbell, C. A. *In Defence of Free Will*, London, 1967.

Carmignac, J. 'Les dangers de l'eschatologie', *New Testament Studies 17*, 1970–71, pp. 365–90

Chomsky, N. *Reflections on Language*, London, 1976; *Language and Mind*, New York, 1968

Cohen, A. *Everyman's Talmud*, London, New York, 1932

Cone, J. H. *Black Theology and Black Power*, New York, 1969

Cone, J. H. (ed.) *see* Wilmore, G. S.

Cooley, C. S. *Social Organization*, New York, 1909

Cox, H. (ed.) *The Situation Ethics Debate*, Philadelphia, 1968

Crouch, J. E. *The Origin and Intention of the Colossian Haustafeln*, Göttingen, 1972

Cunningham, R. L. (ed.) *Situationism and the New Morality*, New York, 1970

Curran, C. E. *A New Look at Christian Morality*, London, (1969) 1976; *Contemporary Problems in Moral Theology*, Notre Dame, 1970; *Catholic Moral Theology in Dialogue*, Notre Dame, 1972; *Politics, Medicine and Christian Ethics, A Dialogue with Paul Ramsey*, Philadelphia, 1973

D'Arcy, M. C. *Thomas Aquinas*, London, 1930

Davies, W. D. *Sermon on the Mount*, Cambridge, (1966) 1980

Diamond, C. and Teichman, J. (edd.) *Intention and Intentionality* (Essays in Honour of G. E. M. Anscombe), Brighton, 1979

Dodd, C. H. *The Parables of the Kingdom*, London, 1935, rev. 1961; *Gospel and Law*, London, 1951

Dominian, J. *Proposals for a New Sexual Ethic*, London, 1977

Dunn, J. D. G. 'Prophetic "I"-Sayings and the Jesus Tradition: the Importance of Testing Prophetic Utterances within Early Christianity', *New Testament Studies 24*, 1978, pp. 175–98

Dunstan, G. R. *Duty and Discernment*, London, 1975

Emmet, D. M. *Rules, Roles and Relations*, London, 1966

Ewing, A. C. 'The Autonomy of Ethics' in Ramsey, I. T. (ed.) *Prospect for Metaphysics*, q.v.

Fairweather, I. C. M. *see* Scotland, J.

Farmer, W. R. (with Moule, C. F. D. and Niebuhr, R. R. edd.) *Christian History and Interpretation*, Cambridge, 1967

Feinberg, J. (ed.) *Moral Concepts*, London, 1969

Fierro, A. *The Militant Gospel: an analysis of contemporary political theologies*, Eng. tr., London, 1977

Fletcher, J. *Situation Ethics: the new morality*, London, 1966 (cited as S.E.) *Moral Responsibility: situation ethics at work*, London, 1967 (M.R.)

Foot, Philippa (ed.) *Theories of Ethics*, London, 1967

Forell, G. W. *Christian Social Teachings, A Reader*, Minneapolis, (1966) 1971

Frankena, W. K. *Ethics*, Englewood Cliffs, N.J., 1963, (2) 1973

Freire, P. *Pedagogy of the Oppressed*, Eng. tr., Harmondsworth, (1972) 1975

Fuchs, J. *Human Values and Christian Morality*, Eng. tr., Dublin, (1970) 1973

Fuller, R. H. *The Mission and Achievement of Jesus*, London, 1954

Furnish, V. P. *The Love Command in the New Testament*, London, 1972

Galloway, A. D. (ed.) *Basic Readings in Theology*, London, 1964; 'Fact and Value in Theological Ethics', in *Religious Studies* 5, 1969

Geach, P. *God and the Soul*, London, 1969

Gerhardsson, B. *Memory and Manuscript*, Lund, 1961

Gill, R. *Theology and Social Structure*, London, 1977

Gilson, E. *The Elements of Christian Philosophy*. New York, (1960) 1963

Gustafson, D. F. (ed.) *Essays in Philosophical Psychology*, London, (1967) 1970

Gustafson, J. M. 'Context Versus Principles: A Misplaced Debate in Christian Ethics', *The New Theology* 3, ed. Marty (q.v.) and Peerman, 1966, pp. 69–102; *Protestant and Roman Catholic Ethics, Prospects for Rapprochement*, London, 1979; *Theology and Ethics*, Oxford, 1981

Gutiérrez, G. *A Theology of Liberation: history, politics and salvation*, London, (5) 1981; *The Power of the Poor in History: Selected Writings*, Eng. tr., London, 1983

Hare, R. H. *Freedom and Reason*, London, 1963; *The Language of Morals*, Oxford, (1952) 1964

Hargreaves, D. H. *Interpersonal Relations and Education*, London, (1972) 1975

Häring, B. *The Law of Christ* (3 vols.), Ramsey, N.J., 1961; *Morality is for Persons*, London, 1972; *Faith and Morality in a Secular Age*, Slough, 1973; *Free and Faithful in Christ, moral theology for priests and laity*, (3 vols.) Slough, 1978–81

Hart, H. L. A. *The Concept of Law*, Oxford, 1961

Held, H. J. *see* Bornkamm, G.

Henry, C. F. H. *Christian Personal Ethics*, Grand Rapids, 1957

Heron, A. I. C. *A Century of Protestant Theology*, Guildford, 1980

Hill, D. 'On the Evidence for the Creative Role of Christian Prophets', *New Testament Studies* 20, 1973–74, pp. 262–70

Hirst, P. H. *Knowledge and the Curriculum*, London, 1974

Hirst, P. H. and Peters, R. S. *The Logic of Education*, London, 1970

Hodgson, L. *For Faith and Freedom*, (2 vols.), Oxford, 1956

Hospers, J. *Human Conduct, An introduction to the problem of ethics*, London, 1963, (2) 1970

Jeffreys, M. V. C. *Glaucon: an inquiry into the aims of education*, London, (1950) 1963

Jenkins, D. E. *The Glory of Man*, London, 1967

Jeremias, J. *The Parables of Jesus*, Eng. tr., London, 1954, rev. 1963

Johnson, F. E. (ed.) *Patterns of Ethics in America Today*, New York, 1960

Kähler, M. *Der sogenannte historische Jesus und der geschichtliche biblische Christus*, Leipzig, 1892: Eng. tr., Philadelphia, 1964

Käsemann, E. *New Testament Questions of Today*, Eng. tr., London, 1969

Kee, A. *Seeds of Liberation: spiritual dimensions to political struggle*, London, 1973

Kee, A. (ed.) *The Scope of Political Theology*, London, 1978

Kegley, C. W. (ed.) *The Theology of Rudolf Bultmann*, London, 1966

Kenny, A. *Action, Emotion and Will*, London, 1963

King, M. L. *Stride Toward Freedom: the Montgomery story*, New York, 1958; *Strength to Love*, New York, 1963; *Why We Can't Wait*, New York, 1964; *Where Do We Go From Here: Chaos or Community?* New York, 1967; *A Comparison of the Conceptions of God in the Thinking of Paul Tillich and Henry Nelson Wieman*, Ann Arbor, Mich., 1981 (Ph.D. thesis, University of Boston, 1955); *see also* Lewis, D. L.

Kirk, K. E. *The Vision of God*, London, 1931

Knight, M. *Morals without Religion*, London, 1960

Knox, J. *Chapters in a Life of Paul*, New York, (1950) 1954; *The Ethic of Jesus in the Teaching of the Church*, London, 1962

Knudson, A. C. *The Principles of Christian Ethics*, New York, 1943

Kockelmans, J. J. (ed.) *Contemporary European Ethics: Selected Readings*, New York, 1972

Kosnik, A. (*et al.* edd.) *Human Sexuality: New Directions in Catholic Thought* (A study commissioned by the Catholic Theological Society of America), London, 1977

Lawrence, R. *Motive and Intention*, Evanston, 1972

Lehmann, P. L. *Ethics in a Christian Context*, London, 1963; *The Transfiguration of Politics*, London, 1975

Lewis, C. I. *Values and Imperatives* (ed. Longe, J.), Stanford, 1969

Lewis, D. L. *Martin Luther King: A Critical Biography*, New York and London, 1970

Lewis, H. D. *Morals and the New Theology*, London, 1947; *Our Experience of God*, London, (1959) 1970; *Philosophy and Religion*, London, 1965 (3) 1972

Little, D. and Twiss, S. B. *Comparative Religious Ethics, A New Method*, New York, 1978

Long, E. LeRoy Jr. *A Survey of Christian Ethics*, New York, 1967; *A Survey of Recent Christian Ethics*, Oxford, 1983

Lundström, G. *The Kingdom of God in the Teaching of Jesus*, Eng. tr., Edinburgh, 1963

McArthur, H. K. *Understanding the Sermon on the Mount*, New York, 1961

McDonagh, E. *Invitation and Response; an essay in Christian moral theology*, Dublin, 1972; *Gift and Call; towards a Christian theology of morality*, Dublin, 1975

McDonald, J. I. H. *Kerygma and Didache*, Cambridge, 1980; 'The Concept of Reward in the Teaching of Jesus', *Expository Times*, 89, 9, 1978, pp. 266–73

MacIntyre, A. *A Short History of Ethics*, London, (2) 1968

Mackey, J. P. (ed.) *Morals, Law and Authority*, Dublin, 1969

McKinney, R. W. A. (ed.) *Creation, Christ and Culture, Studies in Honour of T. F. Torrance*, Edinburgh, 1976

Maclagan, W. G. *The Theological Frontier of Ethics*, London, 1961

Macmurray, J. *Persons in Relation*, London, 1961

McPhail, P. *et al. Moral Education in the Secondary School*, London, 1972

Macquarrie, J. *Principles of Christian Theology*. London, (1966) 1967; (ed.) *A Dictionary of Christian Ethics*, London, 1967; 'Ethical Standards in World Religions, (X) Christianity', *Expository Times* 85, 11, 1974.

Mabbott, J. D., 'Moral Rules', *Proc. of the British Academy*, vol. 39, 1953, pp. 97–118

Mace, C. A. (ed.), *British Philosophy in the Mid-Century: A Cambridge Symposium*, London, 1957

Malvern Conference (Church of England), *The Life of the Church and the Order of Society*, London, 1941

Mandela, N. *No Easy Walk to Freedom; articles, speeches and trial addresses*, London, (1973) 1980

Manson, T. W. *The Sayings of Jesus*, London, 1949; *On Paul and John*, London, 1963

Marquardt, F.-W. *Theologie und Socialismus. Das Beispiel Karl Barths*, (2) Munich, 1972

Marshall, I. H. 'Slippery Words (I) Eschatology', *Expository Times* 89, 9, 1978, pp. 264–69

Marty, M. E. and Peerman, D. G. (edd.), *The New Theology 3*, New York, 1966

Mascall, E. L. *The Openness of Being, Natural Theology Today*, London, 1971

Maslow, A. *The Farthest Reaches of Human Nature*, Harmondsworth, 1973

Masterson, P. *Atheism and Alienation; a study of the philosophical sources of contemporary atheism*, Dublin, 1971

Matheson, P. C. *Profile of Love*, Belfast, 1979; (ed.) *The Third Reich and the Christian Churches*, Edinburgh, 1981

Mehl, R. *The Sociology of Protestantism*, Eng. tr., London, 1970

Metz, J. B. *Theology of the World*, Eng. tr., London, 1969; (ed.) *Christianity and the Bourgeoisie* (Concilium), Edinburgh, 1979

Míguez Bonino, J. *Christians and Marxists, the mutual challenge to revolution*, London, 1976

Minear, P. S. *Commands of Christ*, Edinburgh, 1972

Miller, A. *The Renewal of Man*, London, 1956

Mitchell, B. *Law, Morality and Religion in a Secular Society*, London, 1967

Mohrlang, R. *Matthew and Paul*, Cambridge, 1983

Moltmann, J. *The Crucified God*, Eng. tr., London, 1974; *The Church in the Power of the Spirit*, Eng. tr., London, 1977; *The Trinity and the Kingdom of God*, Eng. tr., London, 1981

Moore, G. E. *Principia Ethica*, Cambridge, (1903) 1922

Moore, G. F. *Judaism* I, II, Cambridge, Mass., 1927, (7) 1954

Moule, C. F. D. *see* Farmer, W. R.

Muilenburg, J. *The Way of Israel: Biblical Faith and Ethics*, London, 1962

Murdoch, Iris *The Sovereignty of Good*, London, 1970.

Naudé, B. *The Trial of Beyers Naudé: Christian Witness and the Rule of Law* (ed. the International Commission of Jurists, Geneva), London, 1975

Niebuhr, H. R. *Christ and Culture*, London, 1952; *The Meaning of Revelation*, New York, (1941) 1960; *The Responsible Self*, New York, 1963

Niebuhr, R. *Moral Man and Immoral Society*, New York, 1932; *An Interpretation of Christian Ethics*, New York, (1935) 1963; *The Nature and Destiny of Man; a Christian interpretation* (2 vols.), London, 1941–43

Nowell-Smith, P. H. *Ethics*, Harmondsworth, 1954

Nygren, A. *Agape and Eros*, Eng. tr., London, 1953

O'Connell, T. E. *Principles for a Catholic Morality*, New York, (1976) 1978

O'Connor, D. J. *Aquinas and Natural Law*, London, 1967

Oldham, J. H. *see* Visser't Hooft, W. A.

Otto, R. *The Idea of the Holy*, Oxford, 1923 (*Das Heilige*, 1917)

Outka, G. H. and Ramsey, P. *Norm and Context in Christian Ethics*, London, 1969

Paton, H. J. *The Good Will*, London, 1927; *The Moral Law, or Kant's groundwork of the metaphysic of morals*, London, (1955) 1969

Peacocke, A. R. *Science and the Christian Experiment*, Oxford, 1971; *Creation and the World of Science*, Oxford, 1979; 'The Nature and Purpose of Man in Science and Christian Theology', *Zygon* 8, 3–4

Peerman, D. G. *see* Marty, M. E.

Pelikan, J. (ed.) *Luther's Works*, St. Louis, 1959

Peters, R. S. *The Concept of Motivation*, London, 1958; *see also* Hirst, P. H.

Phenix, P. H. *Realms of Meaning, A Philosophy of the Curriculum for General Education*, New York, 1964

Plantinga, A. (ed.) *Faith and Philosophy*, Grand Rapids, 1964

Preston, R. H. *Explorations in Theology 9*, London, 1981

Quinton, A. *Utilitarian Ethics*, London, 1973

Rahner, K. *Theological Investigations*, (vols. 1–17, 20) Eng. tr., London, 1961–83; *Nature and Grace and other essays*, London, 1963; *The Shape of the Church to Come*, London, 1974

Ramsey, I. T. *Religious Language*, London, (1957) 1963; *Christian Discourse*, London, 1965; (ed.) *Christian Ethics and Contemporary Philosophy*, London, 1966 (sometimes cited as C.E.C.P.); (ed.) *Prospect for Metaphysics*, London, 1961

Ramsey, P. *Basic Christian Ethics*, London, 1953; *Deeds and Rules in Christian Ethics*, Edinburgh and London, (1965) 1967; *see* Outka, G. H.

Rauschenbusch, W. *Christianity and the Social Crisis*, New York, (1907) 1913; *A Theology for the Social Gospel*, New York, 1922

Rawls, J. *A Theory of Justice*, Oxford, 1972

Reicke Bo 'The New Testament Conception of Reward', *Aux sources de la tradition chrétienne* (Mélanges M. Goguel), Neuchâtel, 1950

Richmond, J. *Faith and Philosophy*, London, 1966

Richmond, J. and Bowden, J. (edd.) *A Reader in Contemporary Theology*, London, 1967

Robinson, J. A. T. *Honest to God*, London, 1963; *Exploration into God*, London, 1967

Robinson, N. H. G. *The Groundwork of Christian Ethics*, London, 1971

Ross, W. D. *The Right and the Good*, Oxford, 1930; *The Foundations of Ethics*, Oxford, (1939) 1960

Ryle, G. *The Concept of Mind*, London, (1949) 1969

Sanders, J. T. *Ethics in the New Testament: change and development*, London, 1975

Schilling, S. P. *Contemporary Continental Theologians*, London, 1966

Schmithals, W. *An Introduction to the Theology of Rudolf Bultmann*, Eng. tr., London, 1968

Schnackenburg, R. *The Moral Teaching of the New Testament*, Eng. tr.,· Freiburg, 1965

Schrey, H.-H. *see* Thielicke, H.

Schweitzer, A. *Von Reimarus zu Wrede*, Tübingen, 1906; *The Quest of the Historical Jesus*, Eng. tr., London, 1910, (3) 1954

Scotland, J. and Fairweather, I. C. M. (edd.) *A Good Education*, (Church of Scotland), Edinburgh, 1981

Scott, E. F. *The Ethical Teaching of Jesus*, New York, (1924) 1925

Sellars, W. and Hospers, J. (edd.) *Readings in Ethical Theory*, New York, 1970

Sen, A. and Williams, B. (edd.) *Utilitarianism and Beyond*, Cambridge, 1982

Singer, M. G. *Generalisation in Ethics, an essay in the logic of ethics*, London, 1963

Sittler, J. *The Structure of Christian Ethics*, Baton Rouge, 1958

Slack, K. *Martin Luther King*, London, 1970

Smart, J. J. C. and Williams, B. *Utilitarianism For and Against*, Cambridge, 1973

Smith, E. *The Ethics of Martin Luther King Jr.*, New York, 1981

Smith, K. L. with Zepp, I. G. Jr. *Search for the Beloved Community*, Valley Forge, Pa., 1974

Smith, M. *Tannaitic Parallels to the Gospels*, Philadelphia, 1951

Smith, R. Gregor *The New Man*, London, 1956; *Secular Christianity*, London, 1966; *The Doctrine of God*, London, 1970

Smurl, J. F. *Religious Ethics; A Systems Approach*, Englewood Cliffs, N.J., 1972

Sölle, D. *Political Theology*, Eng. tr., Philadelphia, 1974

Southern, R. W. *Medieval Humanism and other Studies*, Oxford, 1970

Sprott, W. J. M. *Human Groups*, Harmondsworth, 1958

Stendahl, K. 'Commentary on Matthew' in Peake, *One Volume Commentary on the Bible*, London, 1962

Strawson, W. 'Social Morality and Individual Ideal', *Philosophy*, 1961

Teichman, J. *see* Diamond, C.

Thielicke, H. *Theological Ethics*, I, II, Eng. tr., London, 1968

Thielicke, H. and Schrey, H.-H. (edd.) *Faith and Action; basic problems in Christian ethics*, Eng. tr., Edinburgh, 1970

Tillich, P. *Systematic Theology* (3 vols.), London, 1953–64; *Love, Power and Justice*, London, 1954; *Morality and Beyond*, London, (1964) 1969; *Political Expectation* (ed. Adams, J. L.), New York, 1971

Toulmin, S. E. *An Examination of the Place of Reason in Ethics*, Cambridge, 1950

United Reformed Church (Commission on Non-violent Action), *Non-Violent Action: A Christian Appraisal*, London, 1973

Vatican documents: *Declaration on Certain Questions Concerning Sexual Ethics*, Sacred Congregation For the Doctrine of the Faith, Roma, 1975; *Humanae Vitae*, Papal Encyclical, 1968

Visser't Hooft, W. A. and Oldham, J. H. (edd.), *The Chruch and its Function in Society*, London, 1937

Warnock, M. *Existentialist Ethics*, London, 1967

Weiss, J. *Jesus' Proclamation of the Kingdom of God*, Eng. tr., London, 1971; (German, 1872).

West, C. *Communism and the Theologians: Study of an Encounter*, London, 1958

Welty, E. *A Handbook of Christian Social Ethics* (2 vols.), Freiburg, 1960–63

Whaling, F. 'Christianity as a World Religion', *Education in Religion*, Journal of the Scottish Working Party on Religions of the World in Education, I. 2, 1977

Williams, B. *see* Sen, A.

Willis, R. E. *The Ethics of Karl Barth*, Leiden, 1971

Wilmore, G. S. and Cone, J. H. (edd.) *Black Theology: A Documentary History, 1966–1979*, Maryknoll, N.Y., (1979) 1980

Winter, G. (ed.) *Social Ethics*, London, 1968

Wittgenstein, L. *Philosophical Investigations*, Eng. tr., Oxford, (1953) 1958

Woods, G. F. *A Defence of Theological Ethics*, Cambridge, 1966

Zahrnt, H. *The Question of God*, Eng. tr., London, 1963

Zepp, I. G. Jr. *see* Smith, K. L.

INDEX OF AUTHORS AND PERSONS

INDEX OF SUBJECTS